FEAR ITSELF
WOLVERINE

WRITER
SETH PECK

ARTIST
ROLAND BOSCHI
WITH ROBBI RODRIGUEZ (ISSUE #2)
AND JOHN LUCAS (INKS, ISSUE #3)

COLOR ARTIST
DAN BROWN
WITH RACHELLE ROSENBERG & CHRIS SOTOMAYOR (ISSUE #3)

LETTERER
VC'S JOE SABINO

COVER ARTISTS
DANIEL ACUÑA (ISSUE #1)
& JORGE MOLINA (ISSUES #2-3)

DESIGNER
JARED K. FLETCHER

ASSISTANT EDITOR
JODY LeHEUP

EDITOR
JEANINE SCHAEFER

GROUP EDITOR
NICK LOWE

FEAR ITSELF: WOLVERINE/NEW MUTANTS. Contains material originally published in magazine form as FEAR ITSELF: WOLVERINE #1-3 and NEW MUTANTS #29-32. First printing 2012. ISBN# 978-0-7851-5743-4. Published by MARVEL WORLDWIDE, INC., a subsidiary of MARVEL ENTERTAINMENT, LLC. OFFICE OF PUBLICATION: 135 West 50th Street, New York, NY 10020. Copyright © 2011 and 2012 Marvel Characters, Inc. All rights reserved. $19.99 per copy in the U.S. and $21.99 in Canada (GST #R127032852); Canadian Agreement #40668537. All characters featured in this issue and the distinctive names and likenesses thereof, and all related indicia are trademarks of Marvel Characters, Inc. No similarity between any of the names, characters, persons, and/or institutions in this magazine with those of any living or dead person or institution is intended, and any such similarity which may exist is purely coincidental. **Printed in the U.S.A.** ALAN FINE, EVP - Office of the President, Marvel Worldwide, Inc. and EVP & CMO Marvel Characters B.V.; DAN BUCKLEY, Publisher & President - Print, Animation & Digital Divisions; JOE QUESADA, Chief Creative Officer; TOM BREVOORT, SVP of Publishing; DAVID BOGART, SVP of Operations & Procurement, Publishing; RUWAN JAYATILLEKE, SVP & Associate Publisher, Publishing; C.B. CEBULSKI, SVP of Creator & Content Development; DAVID GABRIEL, SVP of Publishing Sales & Circulation; MICHAEL PASCIULLO, SVP of Brand Planning & Communications; JIM O'KEEFE, VP of Operations & Logistics; DAN CARR, Executive Director of Publishing Technology; SUSAN CRESPI, Editorial Operations Manager; ALEX MORALES, Publishing Operations Manager; STAN LEE, Chairman Emeritus. For information regarding advertising in Marvel Comics or on Marvel.com, please contact Niza Disla, Director of Marvel Partnerships, at ndisla@marvel.com. For Marvel subscription inquiries, please call 800-217-9158. **Manufactured between 9/19/2012 and 10/22/2012 by R.R. DONNELLEY, INC., SALEM, VA, USA.**

10 9 8 7 6 5 4 3 2 1

FEAR ITSELF
NEW MUTANTS

WRITERS
DAN ABNETT & ANDY LANNING

ARTIST
DAVID LAFUENTE
WITH ROBBI RODRIGUEZ (ISSUE #32)

COLOR ARTIST
VAL STAPLES
WITH CHRIS SOTOMAYOR (ISSUES #30 & #32)

LETTERER
VC'S JOE CARAMAGNA

COVER ARTISTS
DAVID LAFUENTE
WITH VAL STAPLES (ISSUES #29 & #31)
AND JASON PEARSON (ISSUES #30 & #32)

ASSISTANT EDITOR
SEBASTIAN GIRNER

SENIOR EDITOR
NICK LOWE

COLLECTION EDITOR: CORY LEVINE
ASSISTANT EDITORS: ALEX STARBUCK & NELSON RIBEIRO
EDITORS, SPECIAL PROJECTS: JENNIFER GRÜNWALD & MARK D. BEAZLEY
SENIOR EDITOR, SPECIAL PROJECTS: JEFF YOUNGQUIST
SENIOR VICE PRESIDENT OF SALES: DAVID GABRIEL
SVP OF BRAND PLANNING & COMMUNICATIONS: MICHAEL PASCIULLO
BOOK DESIGN: JEFF POWELL

EDITOR IN CHIEF: AXEL ALONSO
CHIEF CREATIVE OFFICER: JOE QUESADA
PUBLISHER: DAN BUCKLEY
EXECUTIVE PRODUCER: ALAN FINE

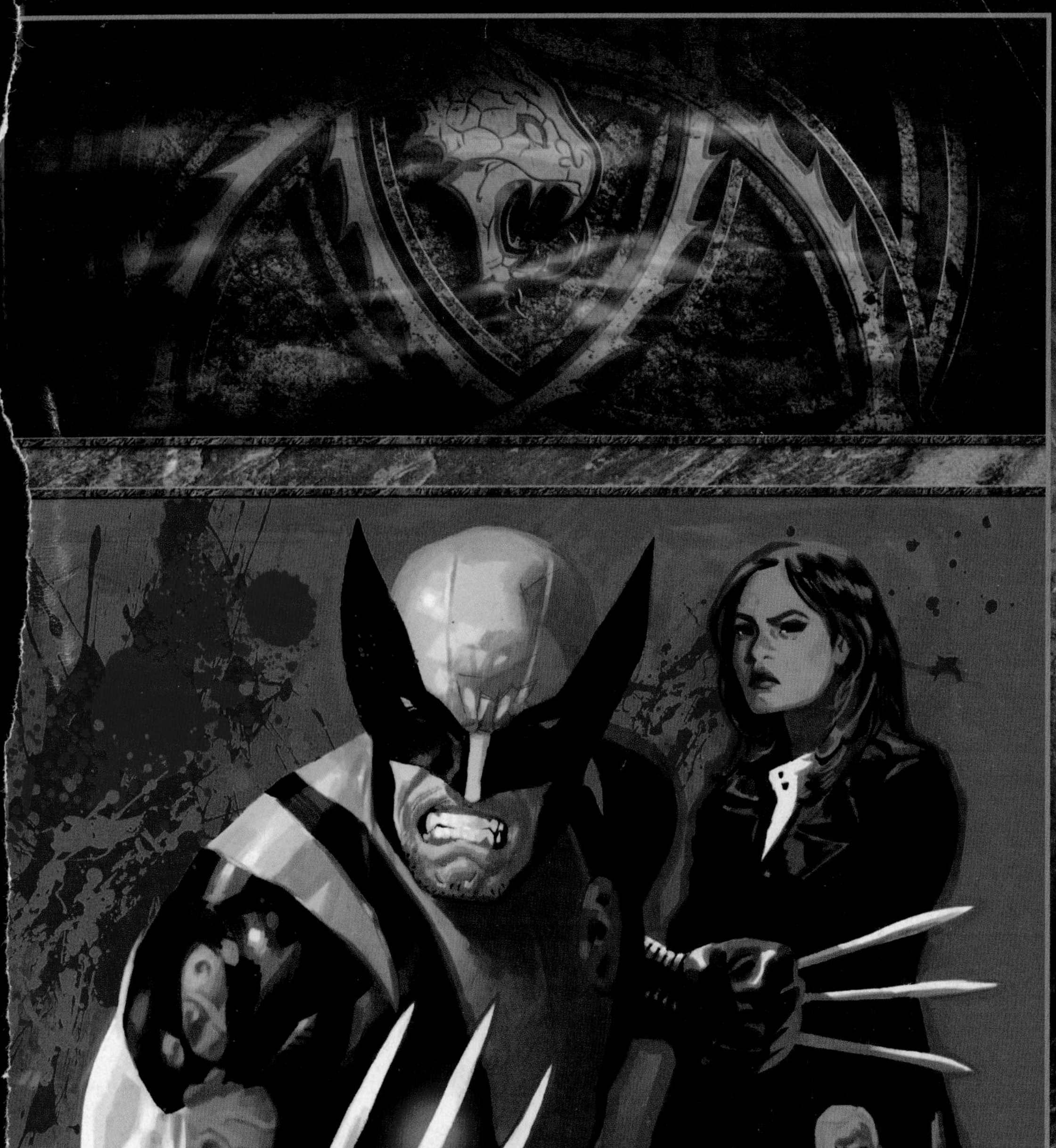

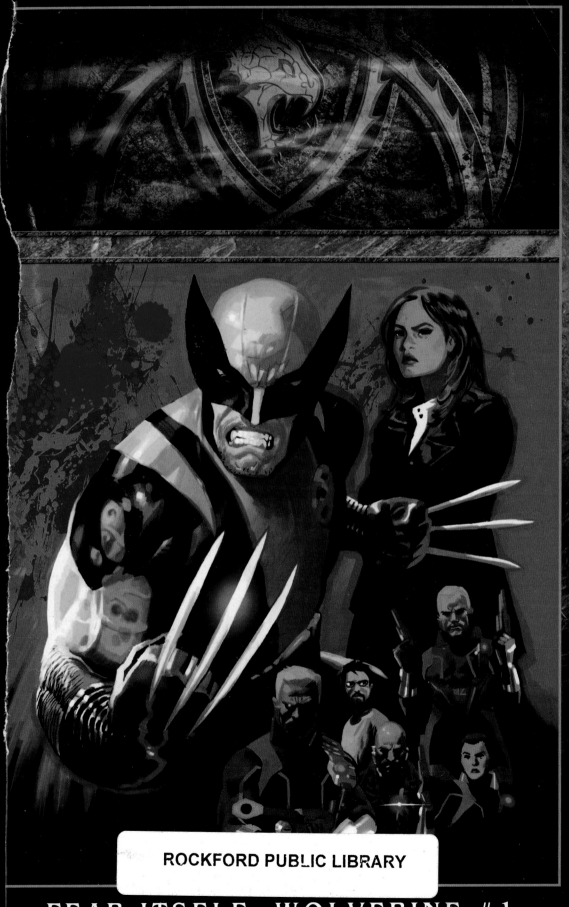

FEAR ITSELF: WOLVERINE #1

*Many years ago, a secret government organization abducted the man called Logan, a mutant possessing razor-sharp ba
claws and the ability to heal from any wound. In their attempt to create the perfect living weapon, the organization bonde
the unbreakable metal Adamantium to his skeleton. The process was excruciating and by the end, there was little left of
the man known as Logan. He had become...*

WOLVERINE

PREVIOUSLY...

Sin, the daughter of the now-deceased Red Skull, has released the Asgardian Serpent God of Fear from his long imprisonment. Now, tremendous fear and chaos have been unleashed upon the world, as seven hammers of immense power have been claimed by the Worthy—individuals chosen specifically as vessels for the Serpent's dark energies. These avatars have set out on a path of total annihilation, destroying anything and everything that stands in their path...

Unfortunately, that means life for Logan and his steady girlfriend, Melita Garner, just got a hell of a lot harder.

FEAR ITSELF: WOLVERINE

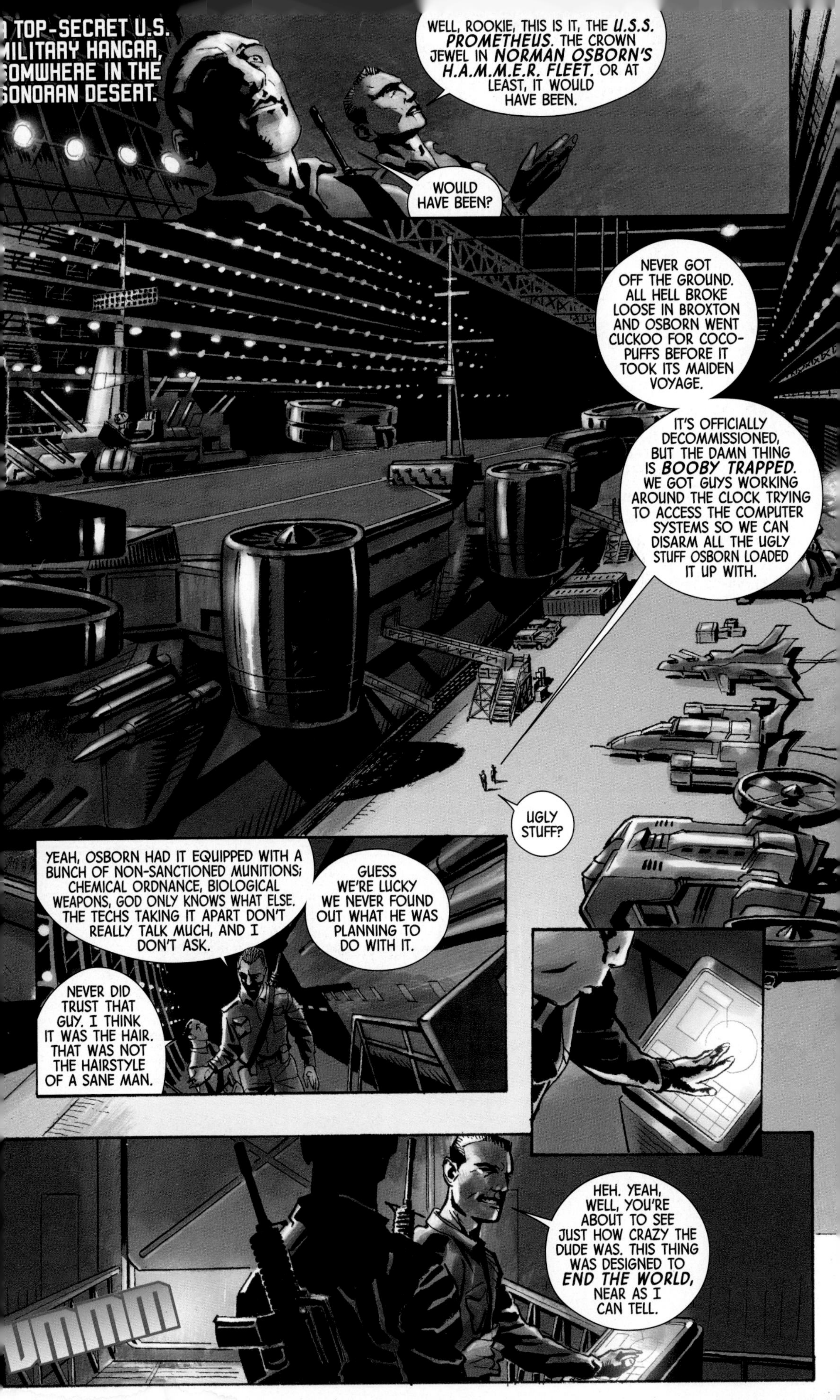

A TOP-SECRET U.S. MILITARY HANGAR, SOMWHERE IN THE SONORAN DESERT.
WELL, ROOKIE, THIS IS IT, THE U.S.S. PROMETHEUS. THE CROWN JEWEL IN NORMAN OSBORN'S H.A.M.M.E.R. FLEET. OR AT LEAST, IT WOULD HAVE BEEN.
WOULD HAVE BEEN?
NEVER GOT OFF THE GROUND. ALL HELL BROKE LOOSE IN BROXTON AND OSBORN WENT CUCKOO FOR COCO-PUFFS BEFORE IT TOOK ITS MAIDEN VOYAGE.
IT'S OFFICIALLY DECOMMISSIONED, BUT THE DAMN THING IS BOOBY TRAPPED. WE GOT GUYS WORKING AROUND THE CLOCK TRYING TO ACCESS THE COMPUTER SYSTEMS SO WE CAN DISARM ALL THE UGLY STUFF OSBORN LOADED IT UP WITH.
UGLY STUFF?
YEAH, OSBORN HAD IT EQUIPPED WITH A BUNCH OF NON-SANCTIONED MUNITIONS; CHEMICAL ORDNANCE, BIOLOGICAL WEAPONS, GOD ONLY KNOWS WHAT ELSE. THE TECHS TAKING IT APART DON'T REALLY TALK MUCH, AND I DON'T ASK.
GUESS WE'RE LUCKY WE NEVER FOUND OUT WHAT HE WAS PLANNING TO DO WITH IT.
NEVER DID TRUST THAT GUY. I THINK IT WAS THE HAIR. THAT WAS NOT THE HAIRSTYLE OF A SANE MAN.
HEH. YEAH, WELL, YOU'RE ABOUT TO SEE JUST HOW CRAZY THE DUDE WAS. THIS THING WAS DESIGNED TO END THE WORLD, NEAR AS I CAN TELL.
UMMM

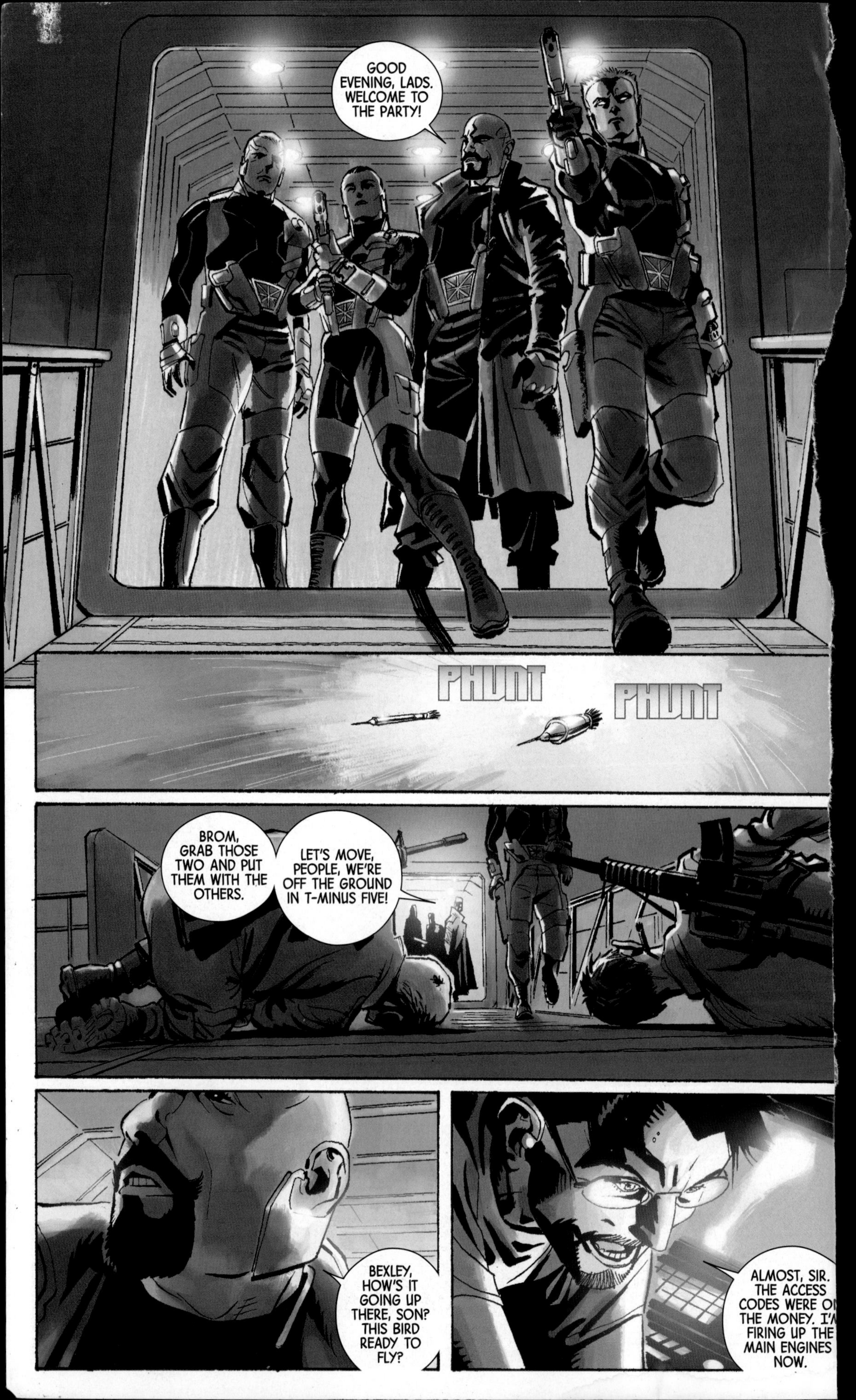
GOOD EVENING, LADS. WELCOME TO THE PARTY!
PHUNT
PHUNT
BROM, GRAB THOSE TWO AND PUT THEM WITH THE OTHERS.
LET'S MOVE, PEOPLE, WE'RE OFF THE GROUND IN T-MINUS FIVE!
BEXLEY, HOW'S IT GOING UP THERE, SON? THIS BIRD READY TO FLY?
ALMOST, SIR. THE ACCESS CODES WERE ON THE MONEY. I'M FIRING UP THE MAIN ENGINES NOW.

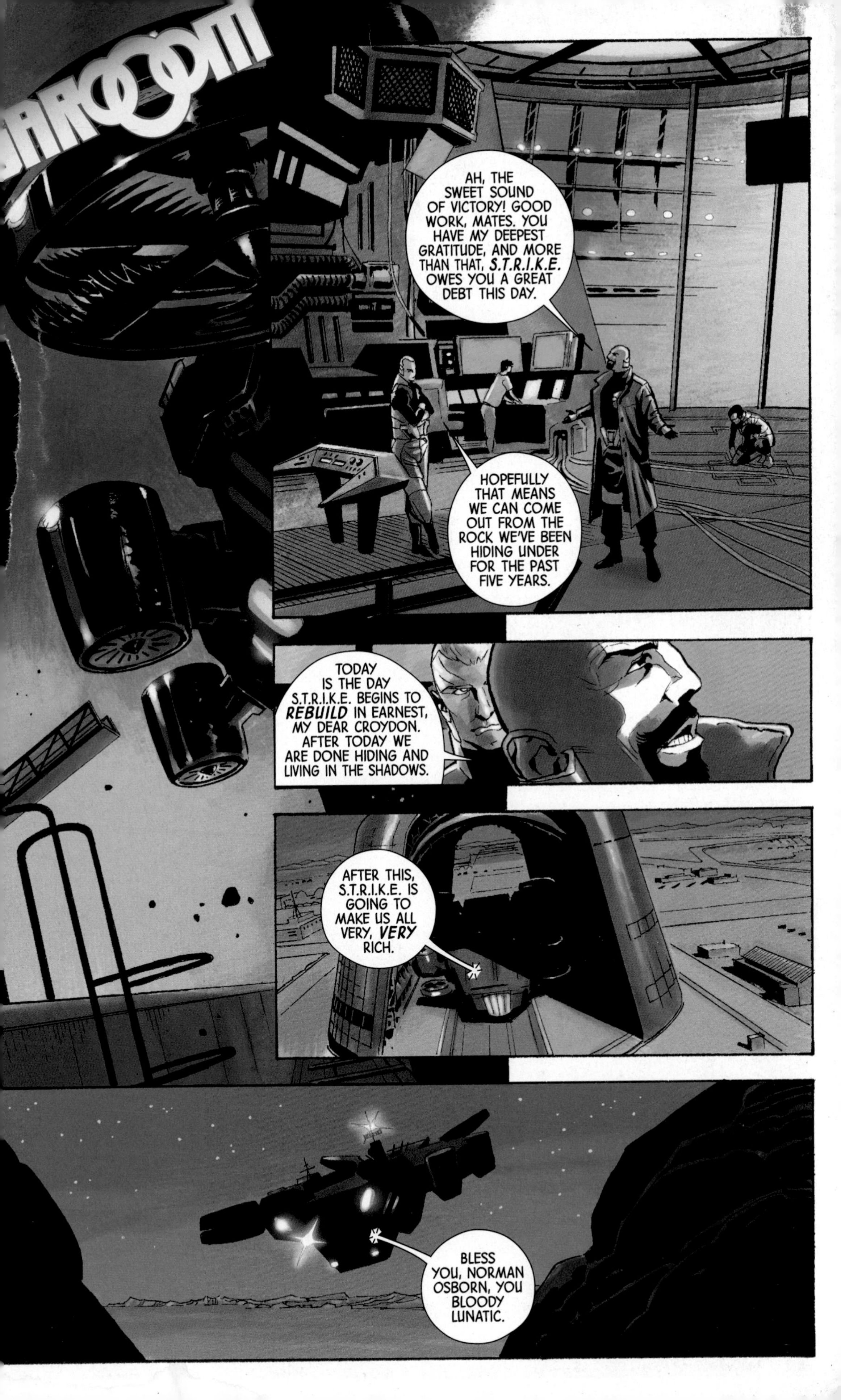
SHROOOM
AH, THE SWEET SOUND OF VICTORY! GOOD WORK, MATES. YOU HAVE MY DEEPEST GRATITUDE, AND MORE THAN THAT, S.T.R.I.K.E. OWES YOU A GREAT DEBT THIS DAY.
HOPEFULLY THAT MEANS WE CAN COME OUT FROM THE ROCK WE'VE BEEN HIDING UNDER FOR THE PAST FIVE YEARS.
TODAY IS THE DAY S.T.R.I.K.E. BEGINS TO REBUILD IN EARNEST, MY DEAR CROYDON. AFTER TODAY WE ARE DONE HIDING AND LIVING IN THE SHADOWS.
AFTER THIS, S.T.R.I.K.E. IS GOING TO MAKE US ALL VERY, VERY RICH.
BLESS YOU, NORMAN OSBORN, YOU BLOODY LUNATIC.

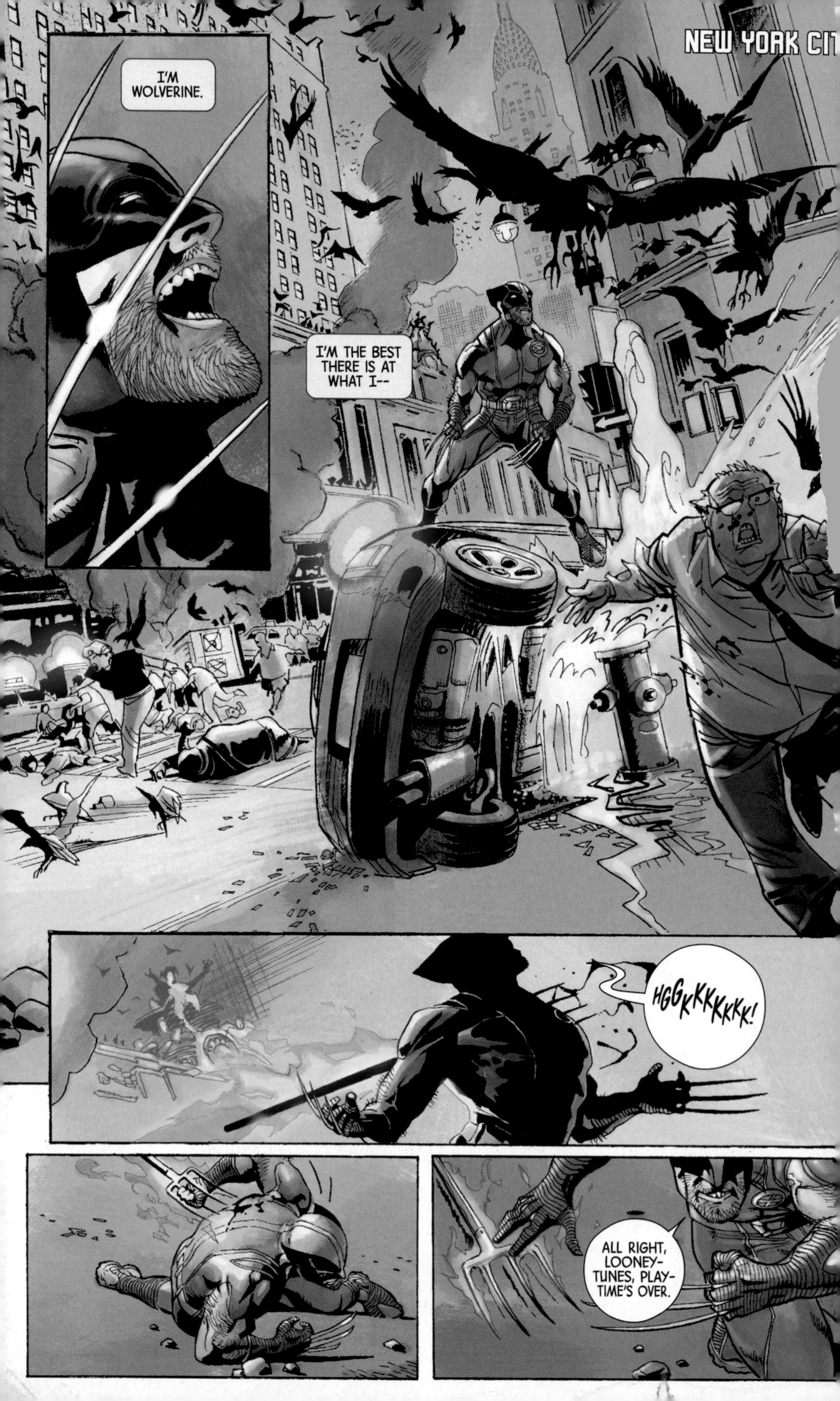
NEW YORK CIT
I'M WOLVERINE.
I'M THE BEST THERE IS AT WHAT I--
HGGKKKKKKK!
ALL RIGHT, LOONEY-TUNES, PLAY-TIME'S OVER.

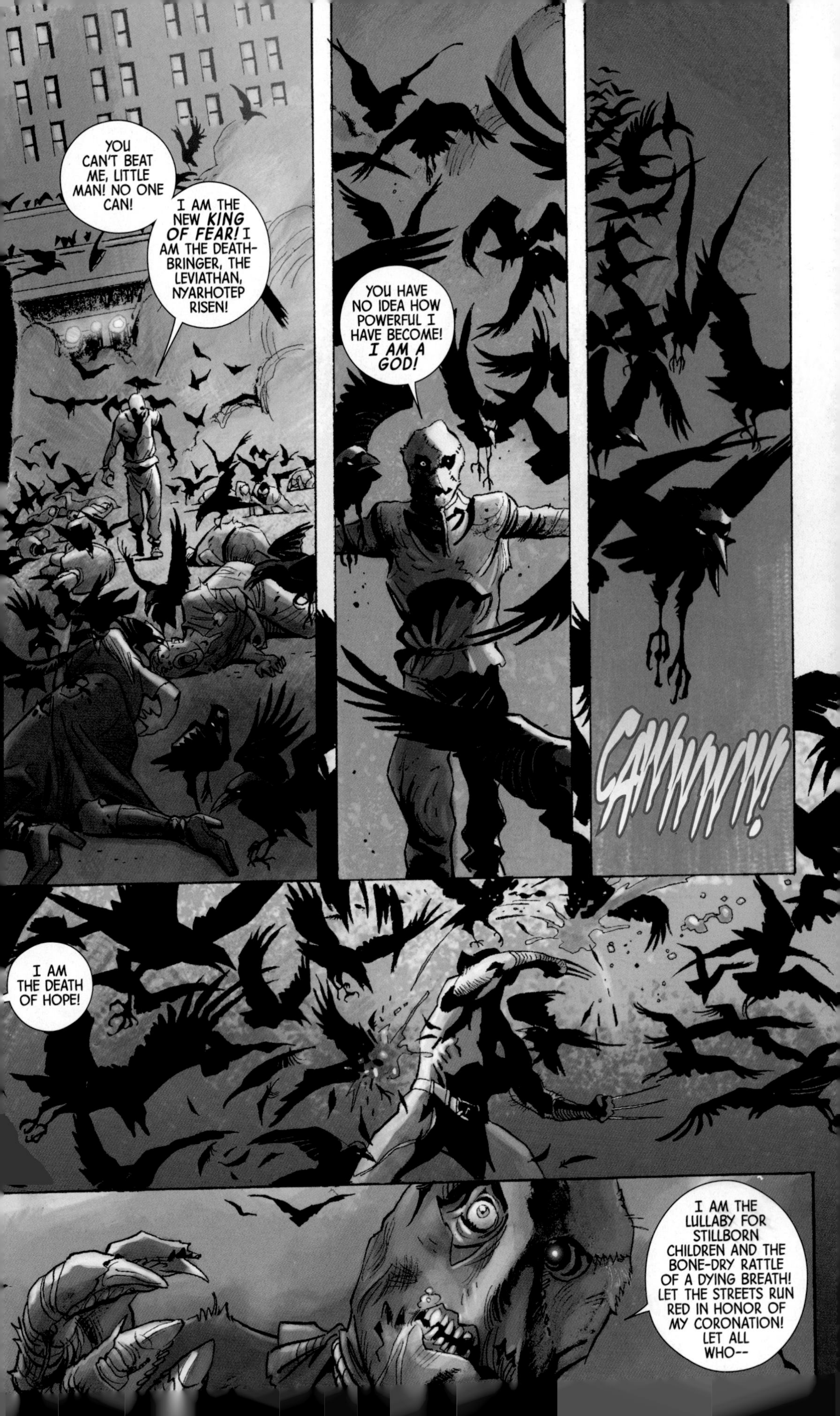
YOU CAN'T BEAT ME, LITTLE MAN! NO ONE CAN!
I AM THE NEW *KING OF FEAR!* I AM THE DEATH-BRINGER, THE LEVIATHAN, NYARHOTEP RISEN!
YOU HAVE NO IDEA HOW POWERFUL I HAVE BECOME! *I AM A GOD!*
CAWWWW!!
I AM THE DEATH OF HOPE!
I AM THE LULLABY FOR STILLBORN CHILDREN AND THE BONE-DRY RATTLE OF A DYING BREATH! LET THE STREETS RUN RED IN HONOR OF MY CORONATION! LET ALL WHO--

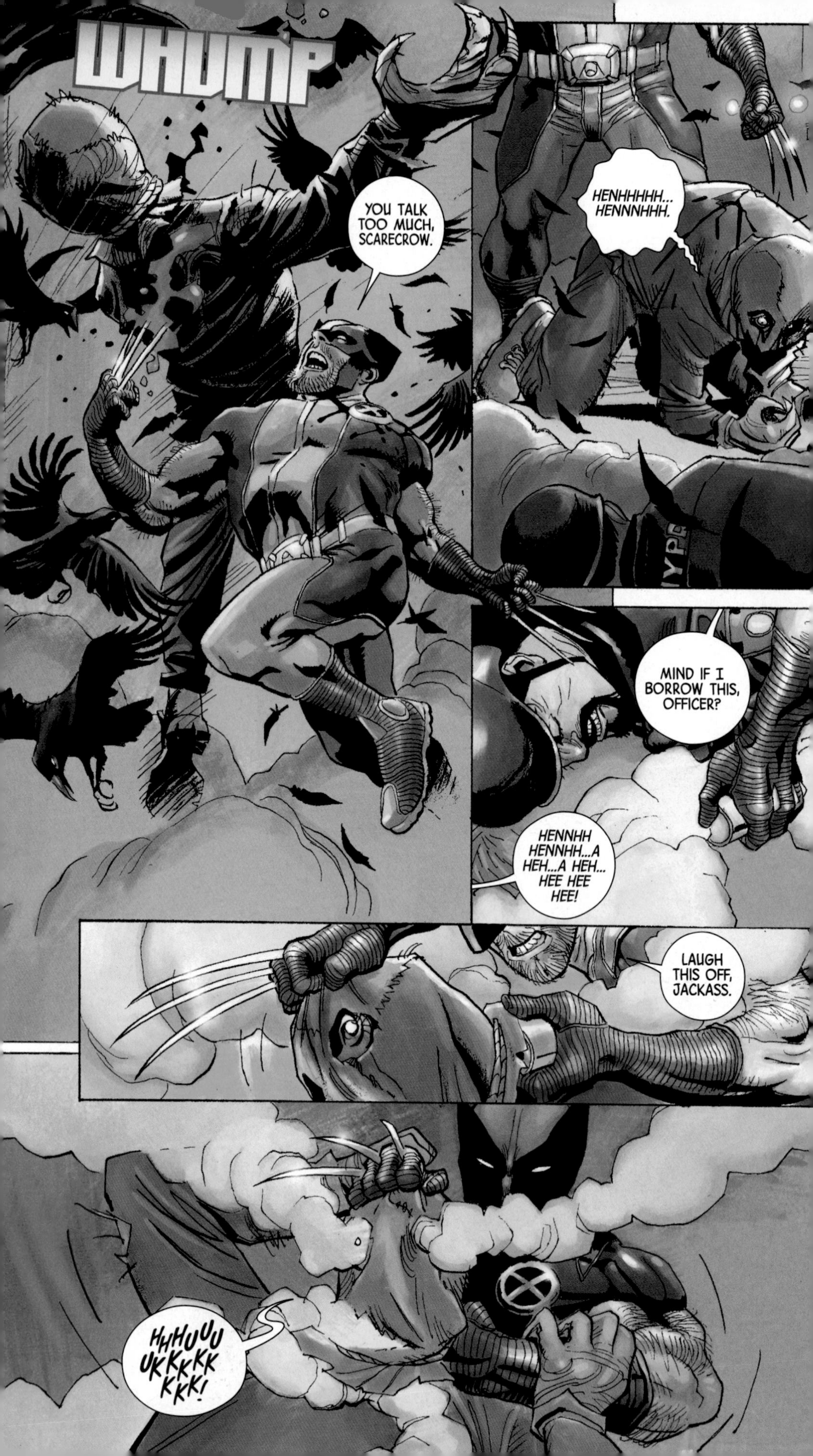
WHUMP
YOU TALK TOO MUCH, SCARECROW.
HENHHHHH... HENNNHHH.
MIND IF I BORROW THIS, OFFICER?
HENNHH HENNHH...A HEH...A HEH... HEE HEE HEE!
LAUGH THIS OFF, JACKASS.
HHHUUU UKKKKK KKK!

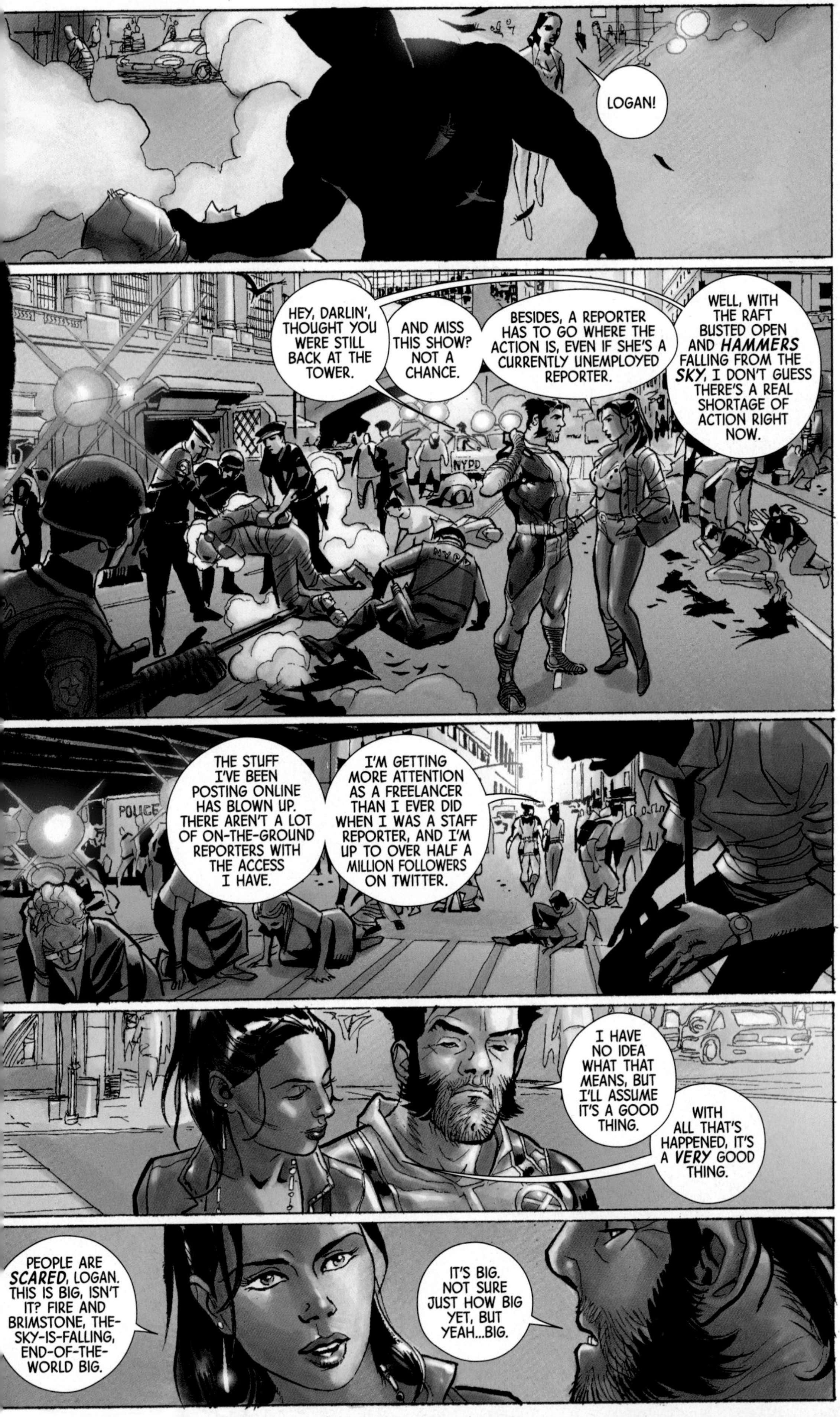
LOGAN!
HEY, DARLIN', THOUGHT YOU WERE STILL BACK AT THE TOWER.
AND MISS THIS SHOW? NOT A CHANCE.
BESIDES, A REPORTER HAS TO GO WHERE THE ACTION IS, EVEN IF SHE'S A CURRENTLY UNEMPLOYED REPORTER.
WELL, WITH THE RAFT BUSTED OPEN AND **HAMMERS** FALLING FROM THE **SKY**, I DON'T GUESS THERE'S A REAL SHORTAGE OF ACTION RIGHT NOW.
NYPD
POLICE
THE STUFF I'VE BEEN POSTING ONLINE HAS BLOWN UP. THERE AREN'T A LOT OF ON-THE-GROUND REPORTERS WITH THE ACCESS I HAVE.
I'M GETTING MORE ATTENTION AS A FREELANCER THAN I EVER DID WHEN I WAS A STAFF REPORTER, AND I'M UP TO OVER HALF A MILLION FOLLOWERS ON TWITTER.
I HAVE NO IDEA WHAT THAT MEANS, BUT I'LL ASSUME IT'S A GOOD THING.
WITH ALL THAT'S HAPPENED, IT'S A **VERY** GOOD THING.
PEOPLE ARE **SCARED**, LOGAN. THIS IS BIG, ISN'T IT? FIRE AND BRIMSTONE, THE-SKY-IS-FALLING, END-OF-THE-WORLD BIG.
IT'S BIG. NOT SURE JUST HOW BIG YET, BUT YEAH...BIG.

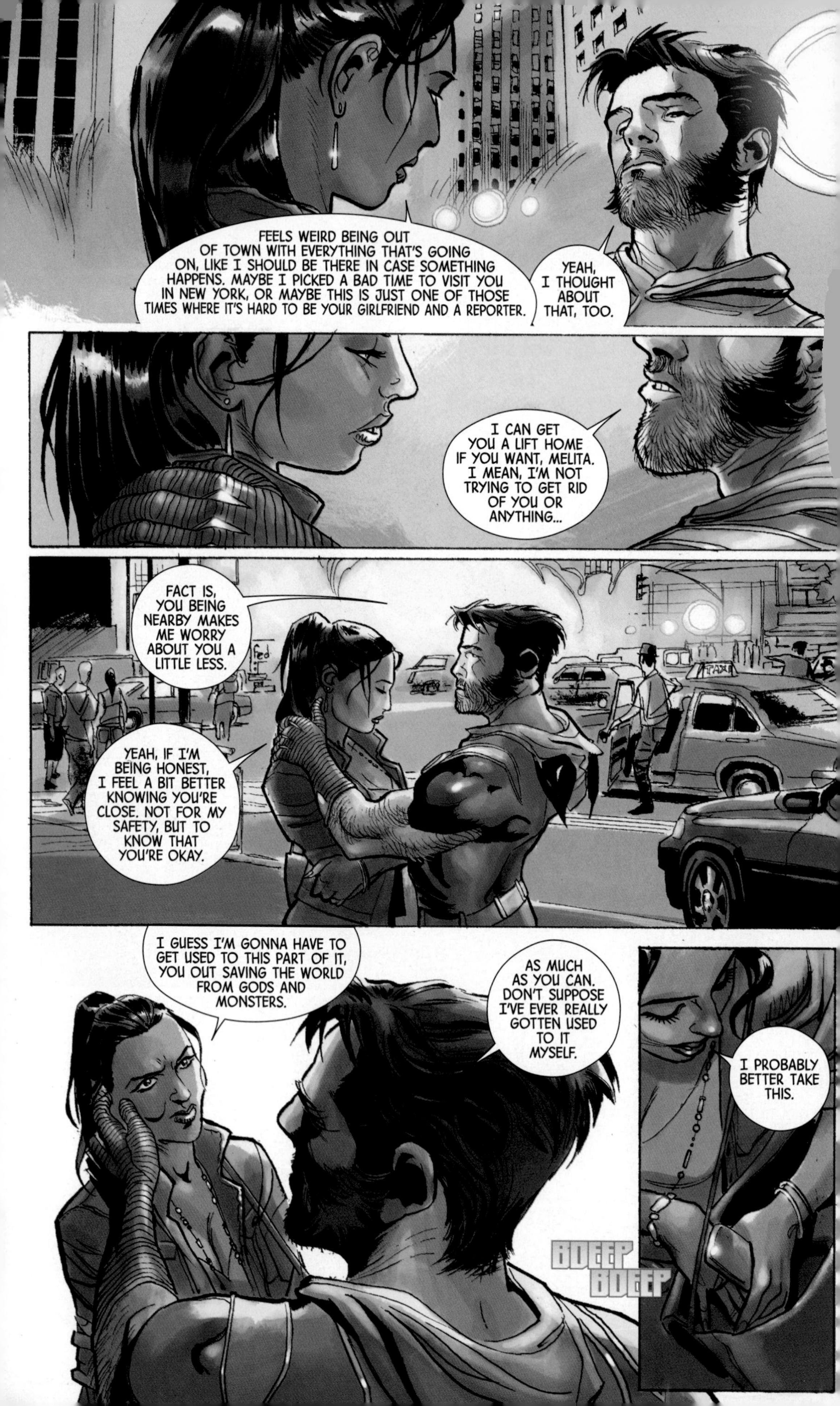
FEELS WEIRD BEING OUT OF TOWN WITH EVERYTHING THAT'S GOING ON, LIKE I SHOULD BE THERE IN CASE SOMETHING HAPPENS. MAYBE I PICKED A BAD TIME TO VISIT YOU IN NEW YORK, OR MAYBE THIS IS JUST ONE OF THOSE TIMES WHERE IT'S HARD TO BE YOUR GIRLFRIEND AND A REPORTER.
YEAH, I THOUGHT ABOUT THAT, TOO.
I CAN GET YOU A LIFT HOME IF YOU WANT, MELITA. I MEAN, I'M NOT TRYING TO GET RID OF YOU OR ANYTHING...
FACT IS, YOU BEING NEARBY MAKES ME WORRY ABOUT YOU A LITTLE LESS.
YEAH, IF I'M BEING HONEST, I FEEL A BIT BETTER KNOWING YOU'RE CLOSE. NOT FOR MY SAFETY, BUT TO KNOW THAT YOU'RE OKAY.
I GUESS I'M GONNA HAVE TO GET USED TO THIS PART OF IT, YOU OUT SAVING THE WORLD FROM GODS AND MONSTERS.
AS MUCH AS YOU CAN. DON'T SUPPOSE I'VE EVER REALLY GOTTEN USED TO IT MYSELF.
BDEEP BDEEP
I PROBABLY BETTER TAKE THIS.

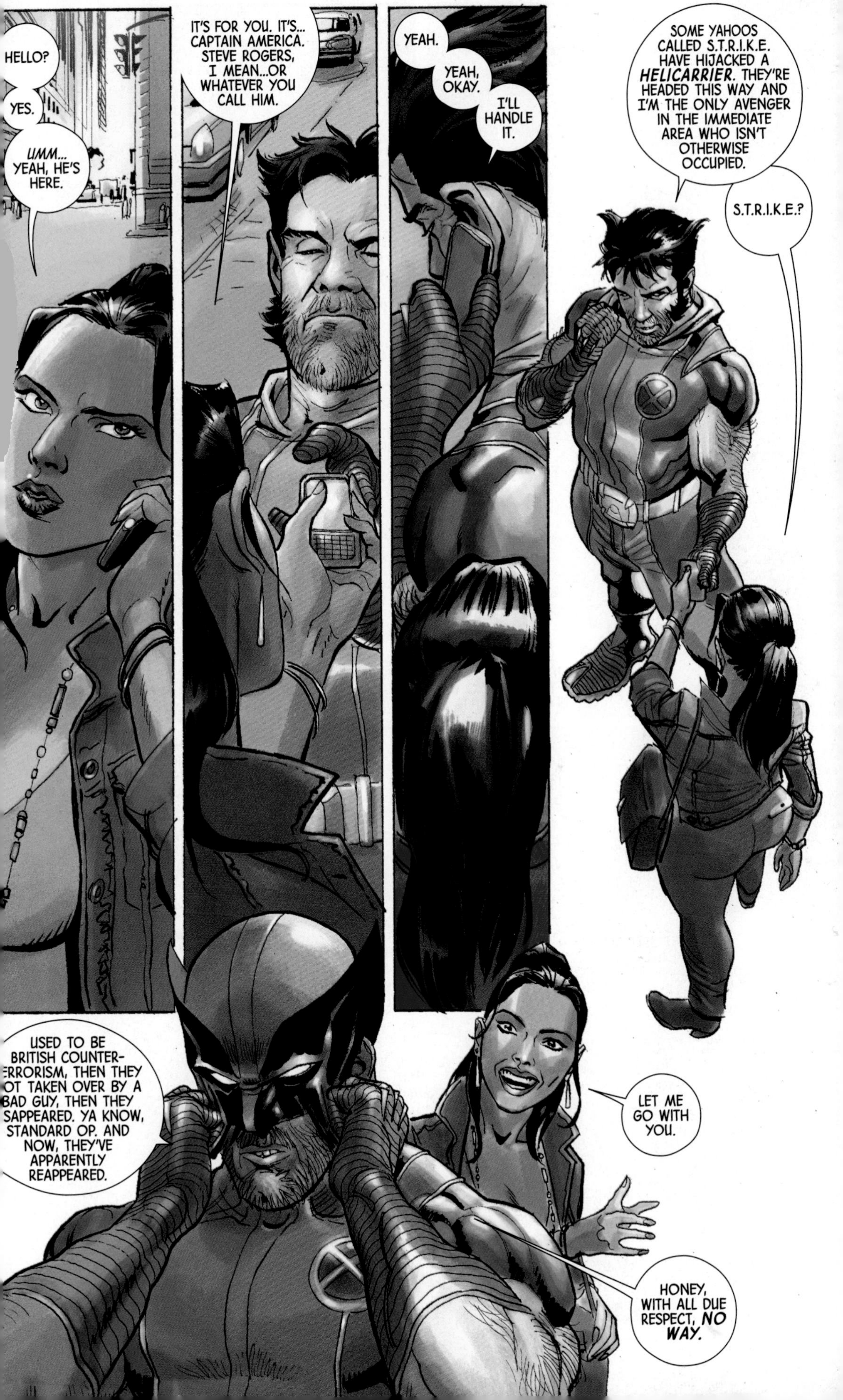
HELLO?
YES.
UMM... YEAH, HE'S HERE.
IT'S FOR YOU. IT'S... CAPTAIN AMERICA. STEVE ROGERS, I MEAN...OR WHATEVER YOU CALL HIM.
YEAH.
YEAH, OKAY.
I'LL HANDLE IT.
SOME YAHOOS CALLED S.T.R.I.K.E. HAVE HIJACKED A HELICARRIER. THEY'RE HEADED THIS WAY AND I'M THE ONLY AVENGER IN THE IMMEDIATE AREA WHO ISN'T OTHERWISE OCCUPIED.
S.T.R.I.K.E.?
USED TO BE BRITISH COUNTER-ERRORISM, THEN THEY OT TAKEN OVER BY A BAD GUY, THEN THEY SAPPEARED. YA KNOW, STANDARD OP. AND NOW, THEY'VE APPARENTLY REAPPEARED.
LET ME GO WITH YOU.
HONEY, WITH ALL DUE RESPECT, NO WAY.

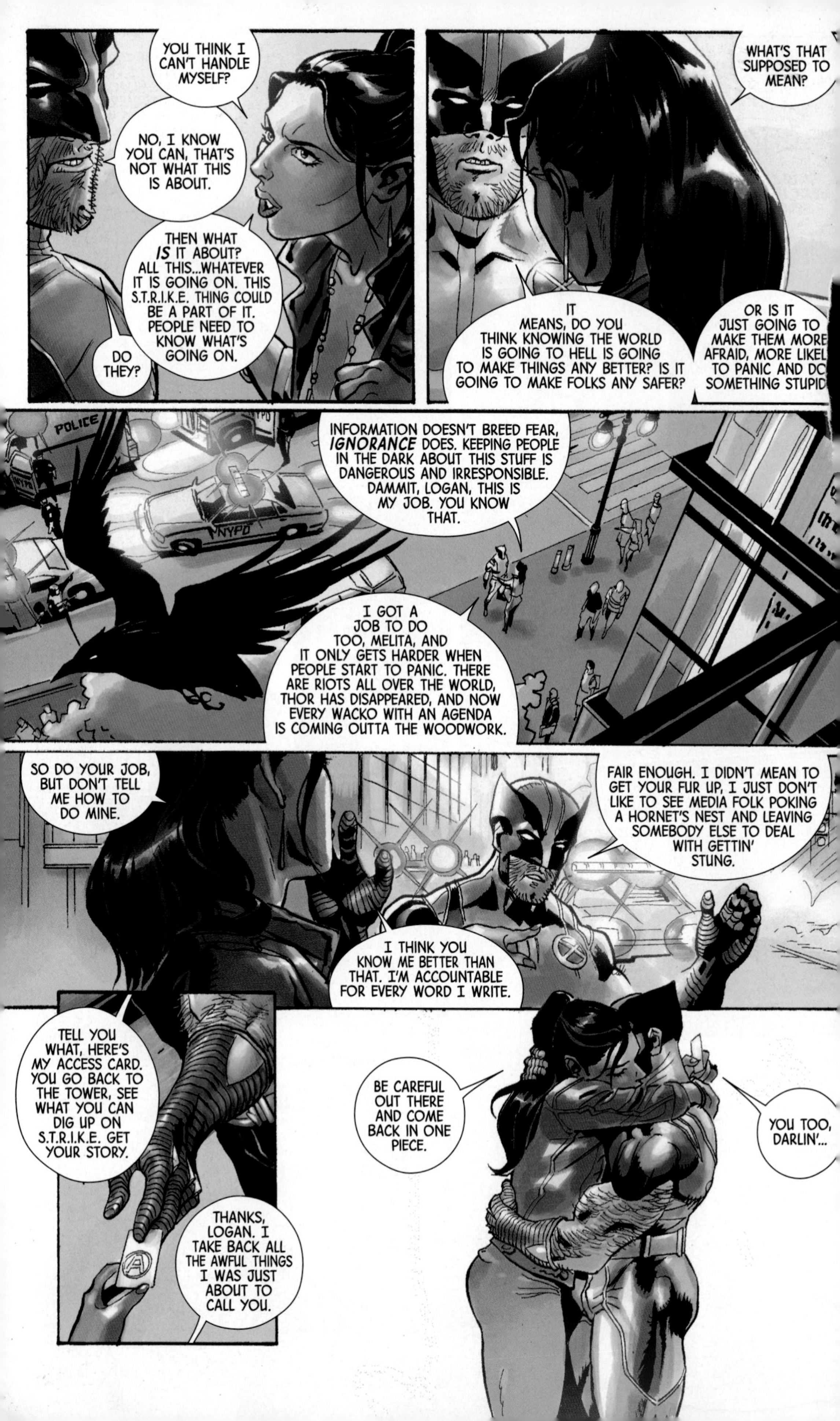

YOU THINK I CAN'T HANDLE MYSELF?
NO, I KNOW YOU CAN, THAT'S NOT WHAT THIS IS ABOUT.
THEN WHAT IS IT ABOUT? ALL THIS...WHATEVER IT IS GOING ON. THIS S.T.R.I.K.E. THING COULD BE A PART OF IT. PEOPLE NEED TO KNOW WHAT'S GOING ON.
DO THEY?
WHAT'S THAT SUPPOSED TO MEAN?
IT MEANS, DO YOU THINK KNOWING THE WORLD IS GOING TO HELL IS GOING TO MAKE THINGS ANY BETTER? IS IT GOING TO MAKE FOLKS ANY SAFER?
OR IS IT JUST GOING TO MAKE THEM MORE AFRAID, MORE LIKEL TO PANIC AND DO SOMETHING STUPID
INFORMATION DOESN'T BREED FEAR, IGNORANCE DOES. KEEPING PEOPLE IN THE DARK ABOUT THIS STUFF IS DANGEROUS AND IRRESPONSIBLE. DAMMIT, LOGAN, THIS IS MY JOB. YOU KNOW THAT.
I GOT A JOB TO DO TOO, MELITA, AND IT ONLY GETS HARDER WHEN PEOPLE START TO PANIC. THERE ARE RIOTS ALL OVER THE WORLD, THOR HAS DISAPPEARED, AND NOW EVERY WACKO WITH AN AGENDA IS COMING OUTTA THE WOODWORK.
SO DO YOUR JOB, BUT DON'T TELL ME HOW TO DO MINE.
FAIR ENOUGH. I DIDN'T MEAN TO GET YOUR FUR UP, I JUST DON'T LIKE TO SEE MEDIA FOLK POKING A HORNET'S NEST AND LEAVING SOMEBODY ELSE TO DEAL WITH GETTIN' STUNG.
I THINK YOU KNOW ME BETTER THAN THAT. I'M ACCOUNTABLE FOR EVERY WORD I WRITE.
TELL YOU WHAT, HERE'S MY ACCESS CARD. YOU GO BACK TO THE TOWER, SEE WHAT YOU CAN DIG UP ON S.T.R.I.K.E. GET YOUR STORY.
THANKS, LOGAN. I TAKE BACK ALL THE AWFUL THINGS I WAS JUST ABOUT TO CALL YOU.
BE CAREFUL OUT THERE AND COME BACK IN ONE PIECE.
YOU TOO, DARLIN'...

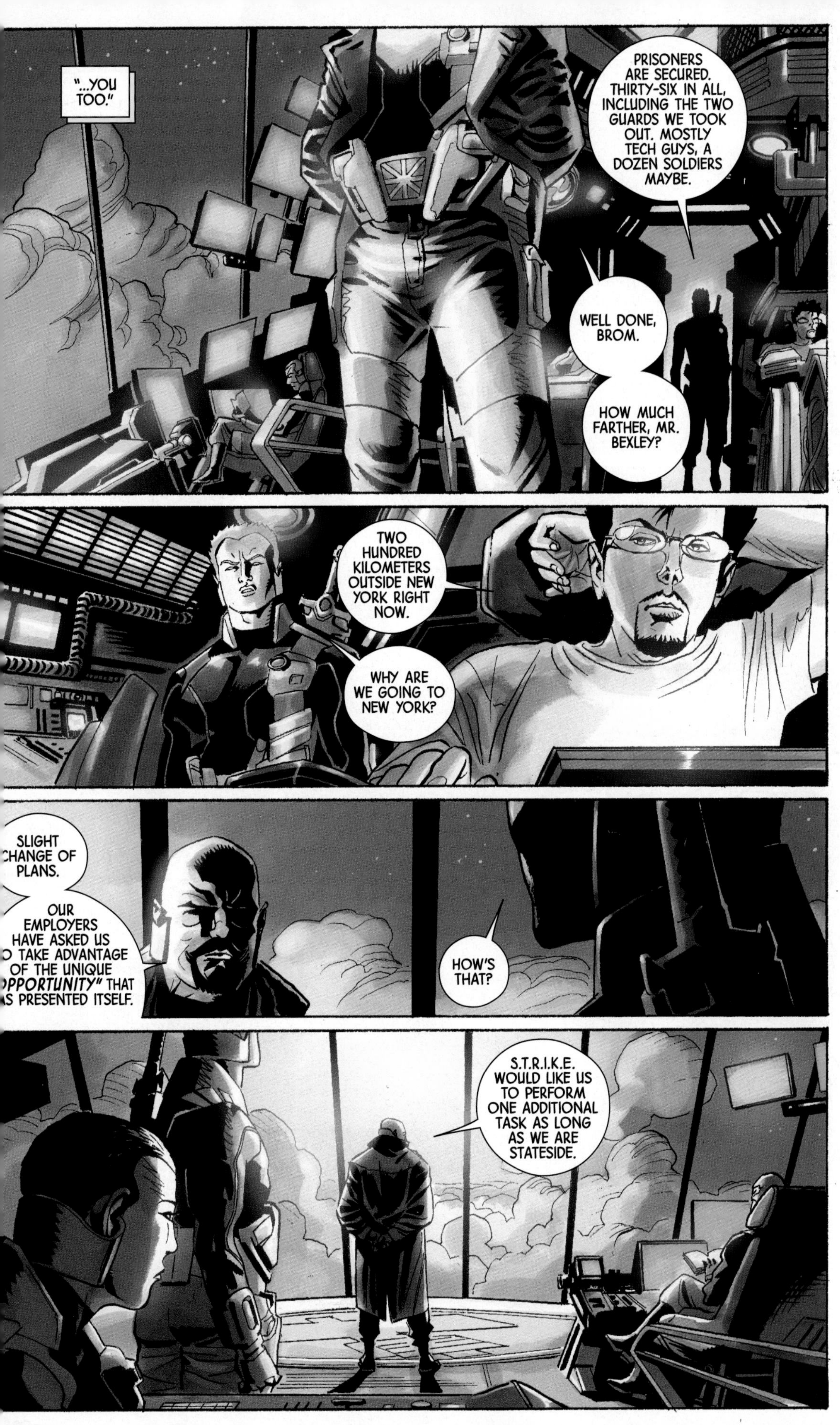
"...YOU TOO."
PRISONERS ARE SECURED. THIRTY-SIX IN ALL, INCLUDING THE TWO GUARDS WE TOOK OUT. MOSTLY TECH GUYS, A DOZEN SOLDIERS MAYBE.
WELL DONE, BROM.
HOW MUCH FARTHER, MR. BEXLEY?
TWO HUNDRED KILOMETERS OUTSIDE NEW YORK RIGHT NOW.
WHY ARE WE GOING TO NEW YORK?
SLIGHT CHANGE OF PLANS.
OUR EMPLOYERS HAVE ASKED US TO TAKE ADVANTAGE OF THE UNIQUE "OPPORTUNITY" THAT HAS PRESENTED ITSELF.
HOW'S THAT?
S.T.R.I.K.E. WOULD LIKE US TO PERFORM ONE ADDITIONAL TASK AS LONG AS WE ARE STATESIDE.

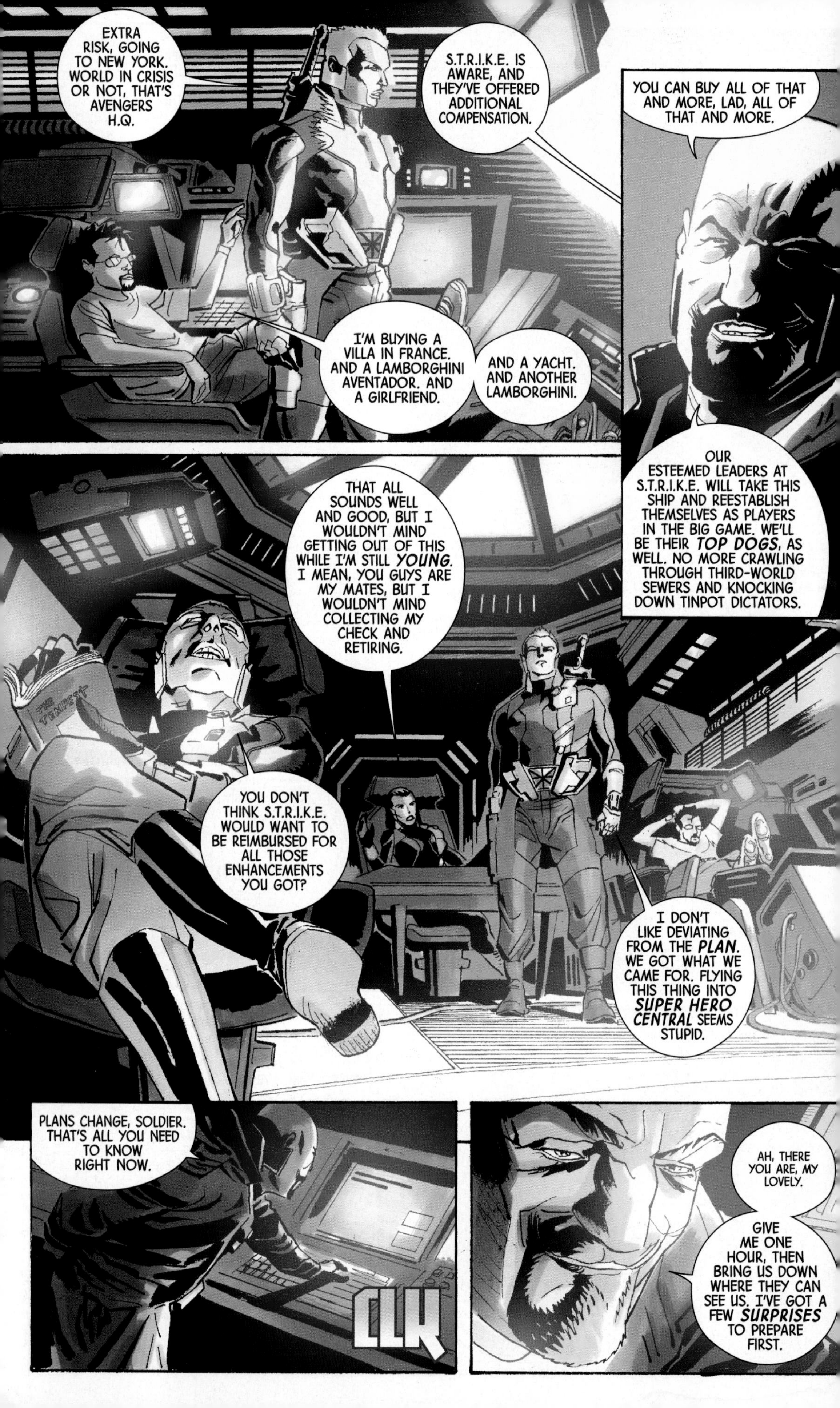

EXTRA RISK, GOING TO NEW YORK. WORLD IN CRISIS OR NOT, THAT'S AVENGERS H.Q.
S.T.R.I.K.E. IS AWARE, AND THEY'VE OFFERED ADDITIONAL COMPENSATION.
I'M BUYING A VILLA IN FRANCE. AND A LAMBORGHINI AVENTADOR. AND A GIRLFRIEND.
AND A YACHT. AND ANOTHER LAMBORGHINI.
YOU CAN BUY ALL OF THAT AND MORE, LAD, ALL OF THAT AND MORE.
OUR ESTEEMED LEADERS AT S.T.R.I.K.E. WILL TAKE THIS SHIP AND REESTABLISH THEMSELVES AS PLAYERS IN THE BIG GAME. WE'LL BE THEIR TOP DOGS, AS WELL. NO MORE CRAWLING THROUGH THIRD-WORLD SEWERS AND KNOCKING DOWN TINPOT DICTATORS.
THAT ALL SOUNDS WELL AND GOOD, BUT I WOULDN'T MIND GETTING OUT OF THIS WHILE I'M STILL YOUNG. I MEAN, YOU GUYS ARE MY MATES, BUT I WOULDN'T MIND COLLECTING MY CHECK AND RETIRING.
THE TEMPEST
YOU DON'T THINK S.T.R.I.K.E. WOULD WANT TO BE REIMBURSED FOR ALL THOSE ENHANCEMENTS YOU GOT?
I DON'T LIKE DEVIATING FROM THE PLAN. WE GOT WHAT WE CAME FOR. FLYING THIS THING INTO SUPER HERO CENTRAL SEEMS STUPID.
PLANS CHANGE, SOLDIER. THAT'S ALL YOU NEED TO KNOW RIGHT NOW.
CLK
AH, THERE YOU ARE, MY LOVELY.
GIVE ME ONE HOUR, THEN BRING US DOWN WHERE THEY CAN SEE US. I'VE GOT A FEW SURPRISES TO PREPARE FIRST.

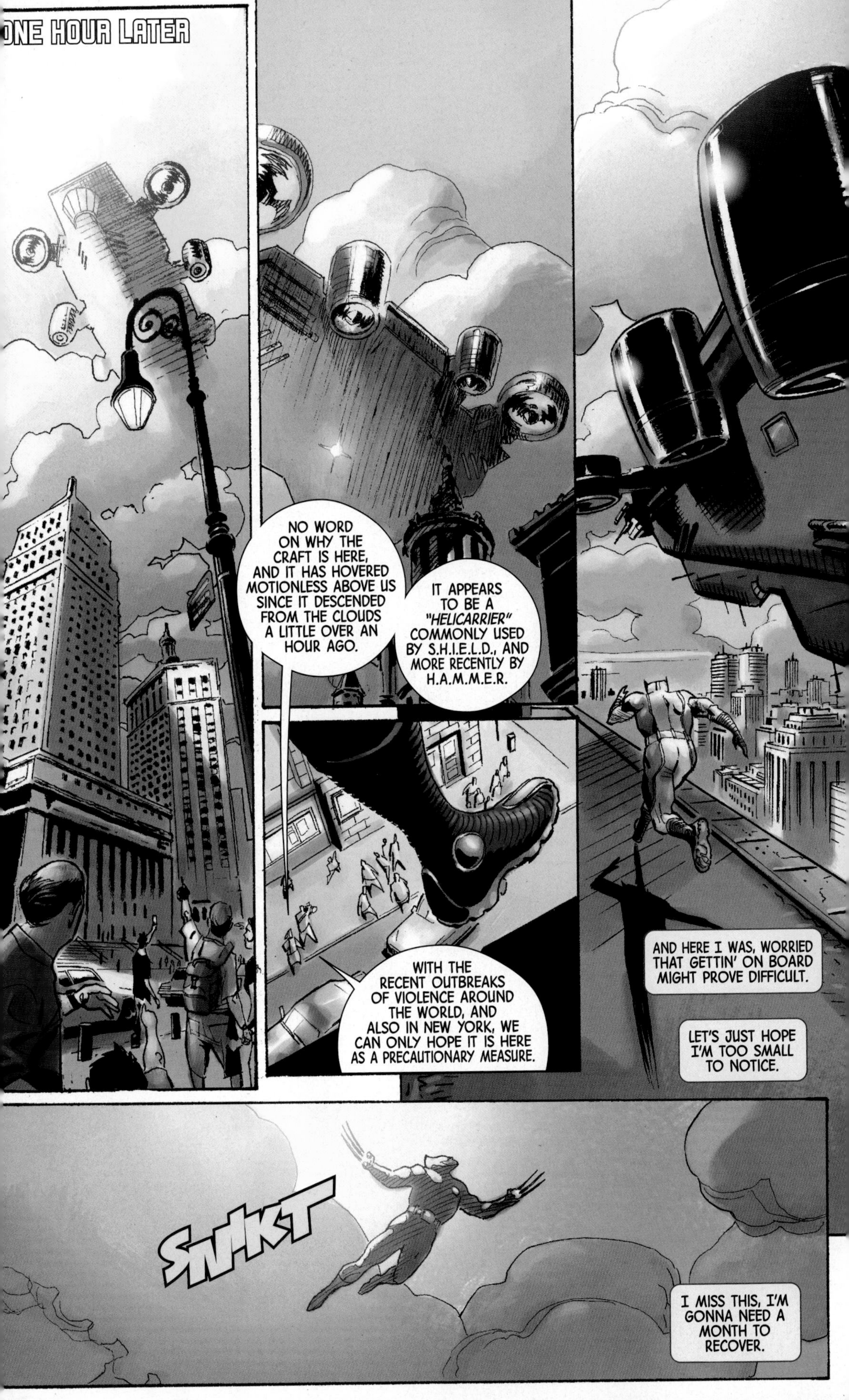
ONE HOUR LATER
NO WORD ON WHY THE CRAFT IS HERE, AND IT HAS HOVERED MOTIONLESS ABOVE US SINCE IT DESCENDED FROM THE CLOUDS A LITTLE OVER AN HOUR AGO.
IT APPEARS TO BE A "HELICARRIER" COMMONLY USED BY S.H.I.E.L.D., AND MORE RECENTLY BY H.A.M.M.E.R.
WITH THE RECENT OUTBREAKS OF VIOLENCE AROUND THE WORLD, AND ALSO IN NEW YORK, WE CAN ONLY HOPE IT IS HERE AS A PRECAUTIONARY MEASURE.
AND HERE I WAS, WORRIED THAT GETTIN' ON BOARD MIGHT PROVE DIFFICULT.
LET'S JUST HOPE I'M TOO SMALL TO NOTICE.
SNIKT
I MISS THIS, I'M GONNA NEED A MONTH TO RECOVER.

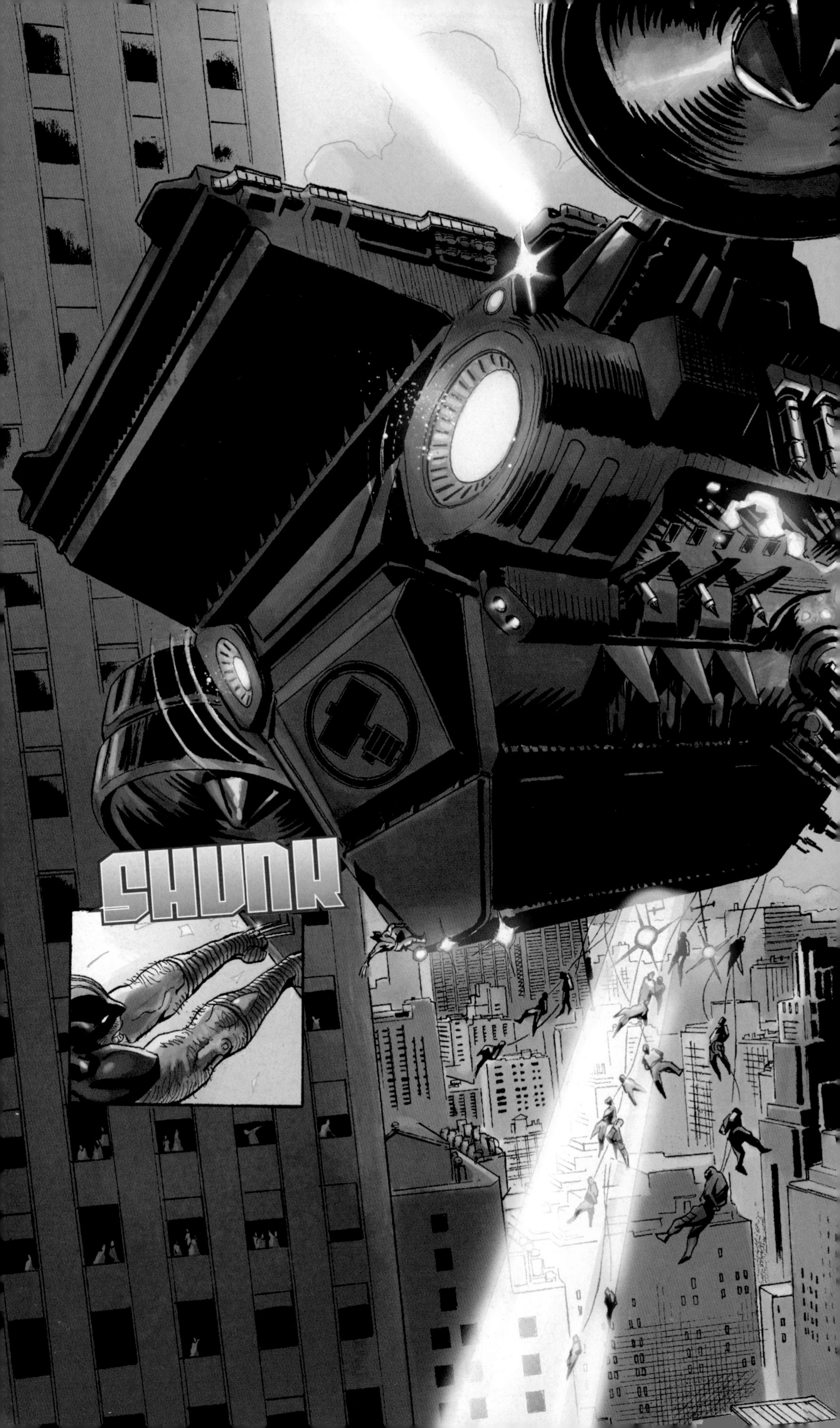
SHUNK

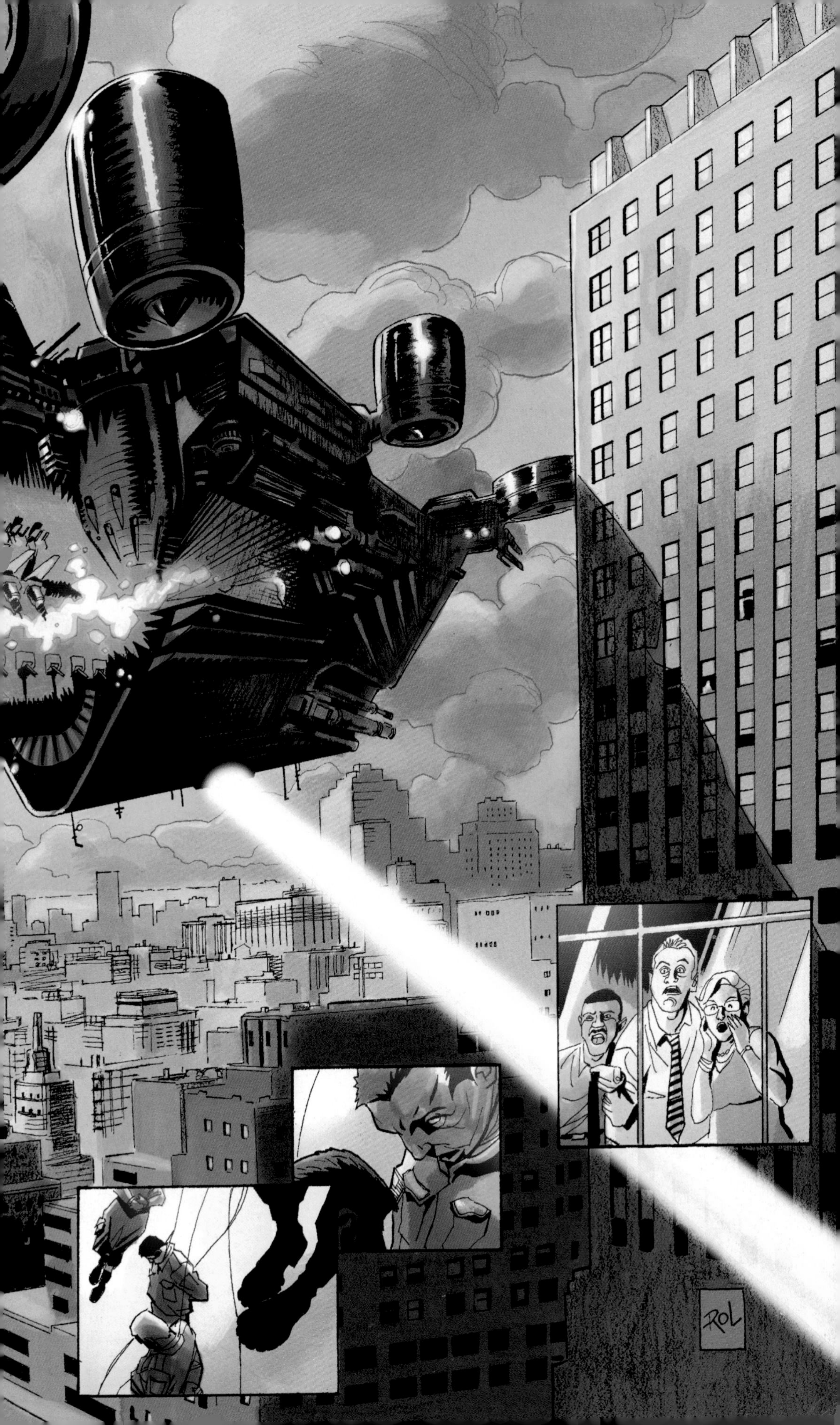
ROL

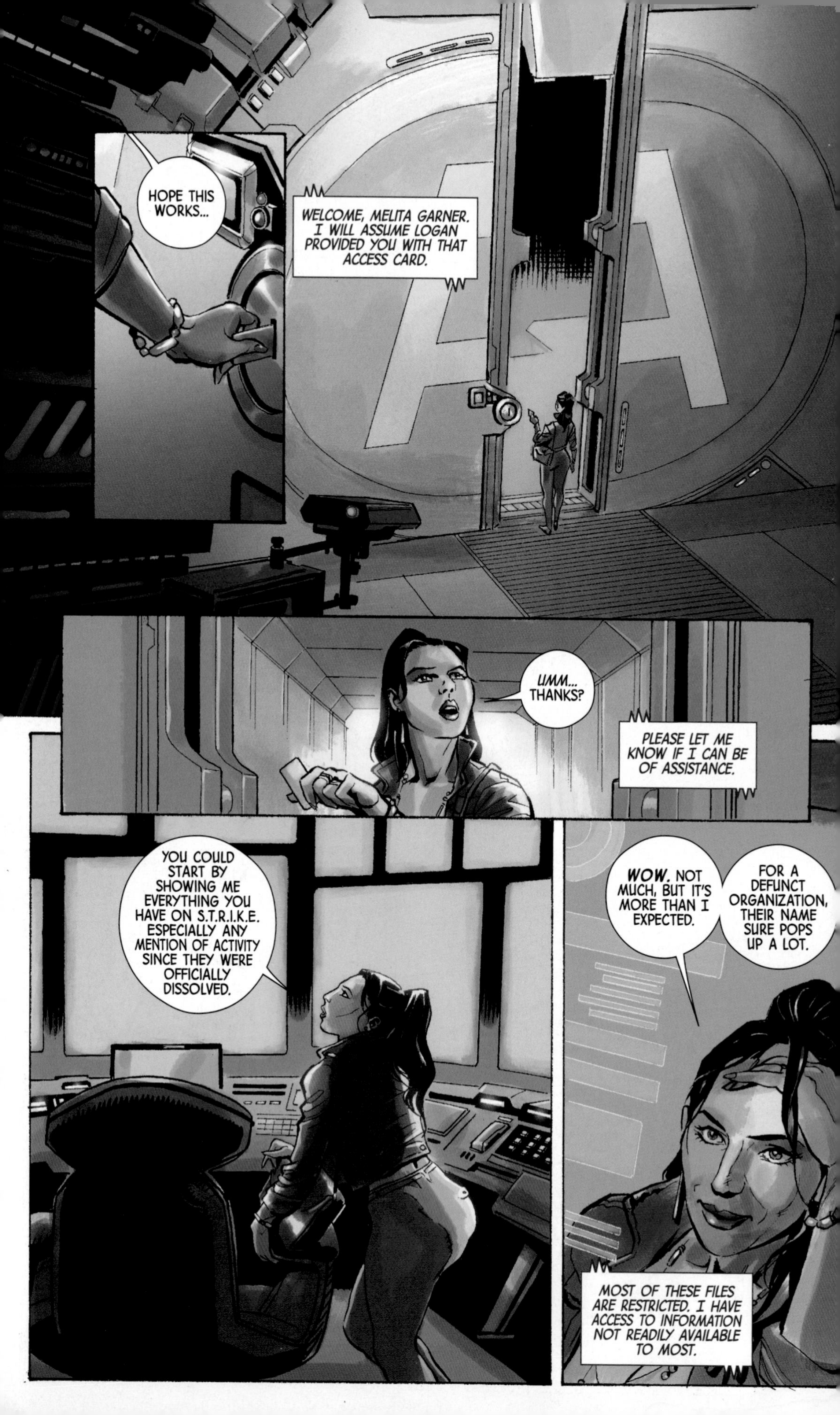
HOPE THIS WORKS...
WELCOME, MELITA GARNER. I WILL ASSUME LOGAN PROVIDED YOU WITH THAT ACCESS CARD.
UMM... THANKS?
PLEASE LET ME KNOW IF I CAN BE OF ASSISTANCE.
YOU COULD START BY SHOWING ME EVERYTHING YOU HAVE ON S.T.R.I.K.E. ESPECIALLY ANY MENTION OF ACTIVITY SINCE THEY WERE OFFICIALLY DISSOLVED.
WOW. NOT MUCH, BUT IT'S MORE THAN I EXPECTED.
FOR A DEFUNCT ORGANIZATION, THEIR NAME SURE POPS UP A LOT.
MOST OF THESE FILES ARE RESTRICTED. I HAVE ACCESS TO INFORMATION NOT READILY AVAILABLE TO MOST.

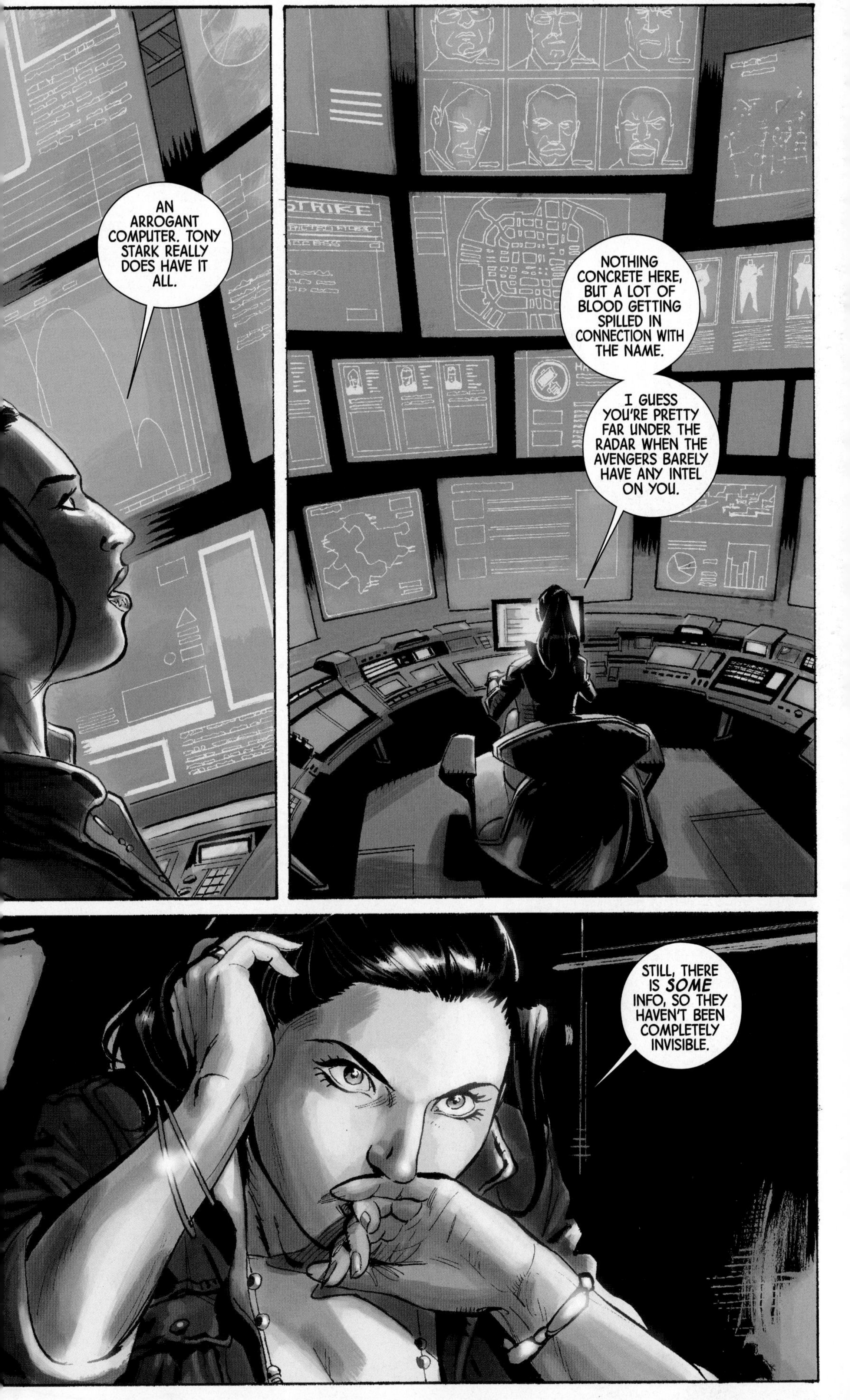
AN ARROGANT COMPUTER. TONY STARK REALLY DOES HAVE IT ALL.
STRIKE
NOTHING CONCRETE HERE, BUT A LOT OF BLOOD GETTING SPILLED IN CONNECTION WITH THE NAME.
I GUESS YOU'RE PRETTY FAR UNDER THE RADAR WHEN THE AVENGERS BARELY HAVE ANY INTEL ON YOU.
STILL, THERE IS *SOME* INFO, SO THEY HAVEN'T BEEN COMPLETELY INVISIBLE.

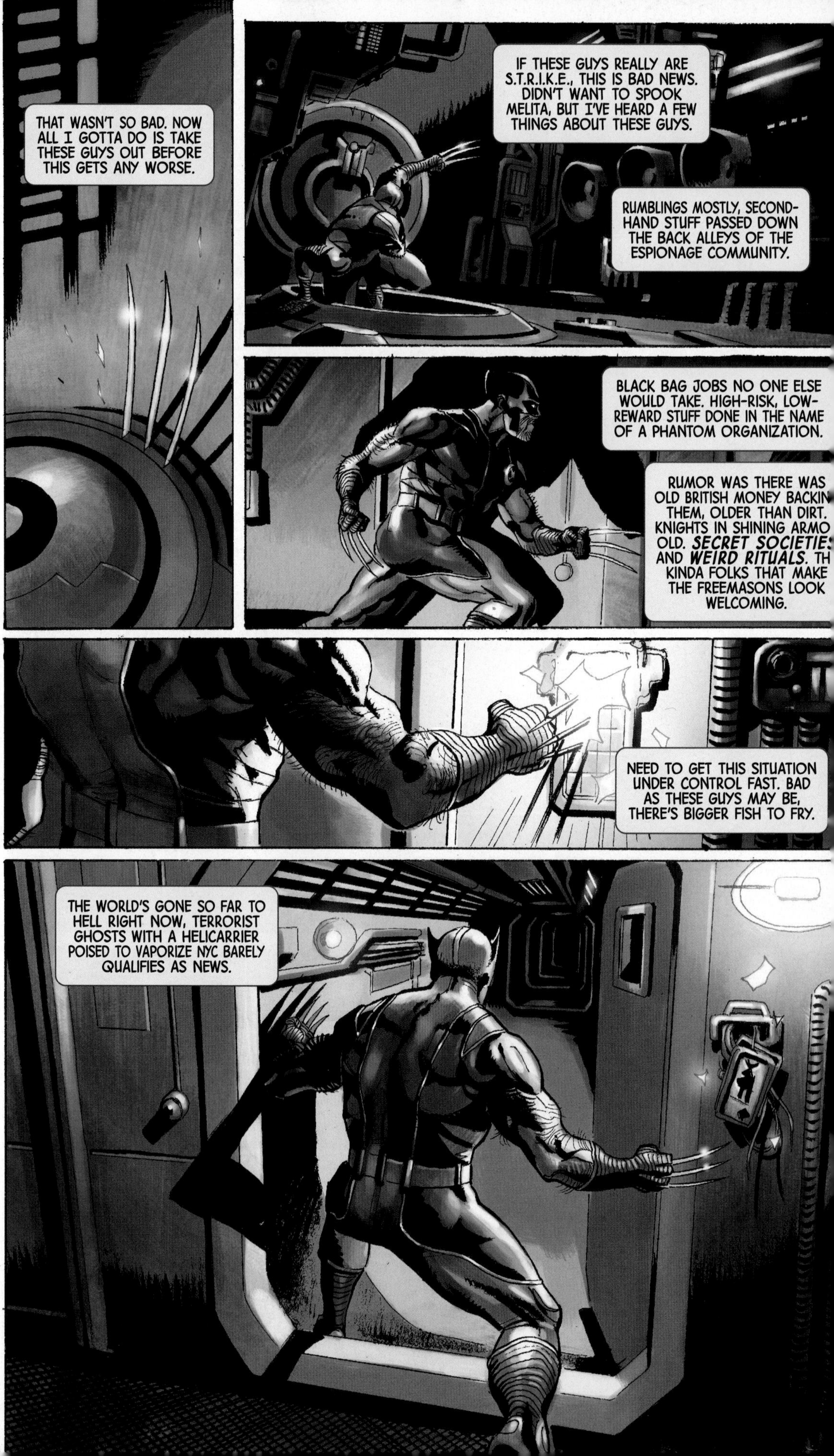

THAT WASN'T SO BAD. NOW ALL I GOTTA DO IS TAKE THESE GUYS OUT BEFORE THIS GETS ANY WORSE.
IF THESE GUYS REALLY ARE S.T.R.I.K.E., THIS IS BAD NEWS. DIDN'T WANT TO SPOOK MELITA, BUT I'VE HEARD A FEW THINGS ABOUT THESE GUYS.
RUMBLINGS MOSTLY, SECOND-HAND STUFF PASSED DOWN THE BACK ALLEYS OF THE ESPIONAGE COMMUNITY.
BLACK BAG JOBS NO ONE ELSE WOULD TAKE. HIGH-RISK, LOW-REWARD STUFF DONE IN THE NAME OF A PHANTOM ORGANIZATION.
RUMOR WAS THERE WAS OLD BRITISH MONEY BACKIN THEM, OLDER THAN DIRT. KNIGHTS IN SHINING ARMO OLD. SECRET SOCIETIE AND WEIRD RITUALS. TH KINDA FOLKS THAT MAKE THE FREEMASONS LOOK WELCOMING.
NEED TO GET THIS SITUATION UNDER CONTROL FAST. BAD AS THESE GUYS MAY BE, THERE'S BIGGER FISH TO FRY.
THE WORLD'S GONE SO FAR TO HELL RIGHT NOW, TERRORIST GHOSTS WITH A HELICARRIER POISED TO VAPORIZE NYC BARELY QUALIFIES AS NEWS.

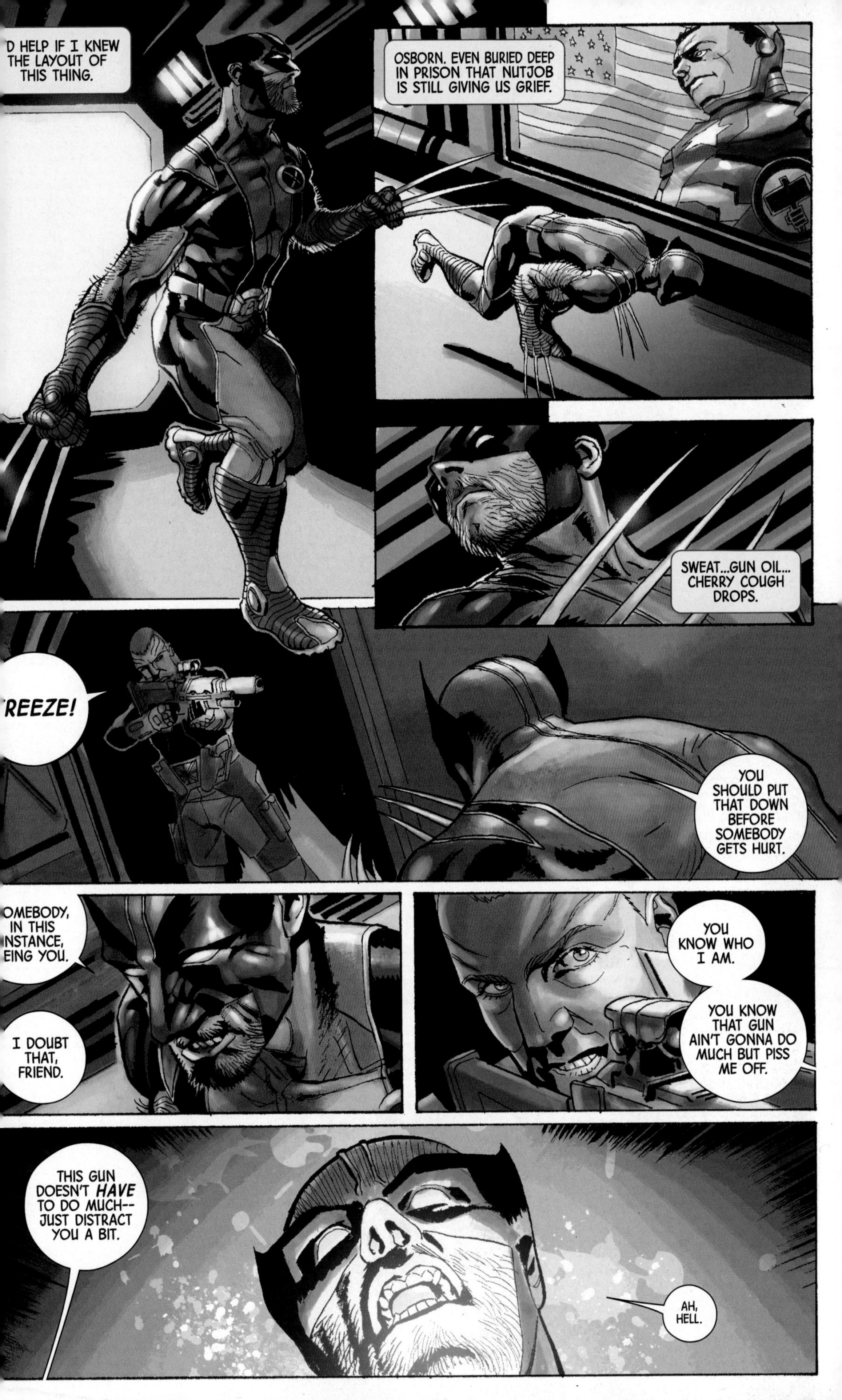
'D HELP IF I KNEW THE LAYOUT OF THIS THING.
OSBORN. EVEN BURIED DEEP IN PRISON THAT NUTJOB IS STILL GIVING US GRIEF.
SWEAT...GUN OIL... CHERRY COUGH DROPS.
'REEZE!
YOU SHOULD PUT THAT DOWN BEFORE SOMEBODY GETS HURT.
OMEBODY, IN THIS NSTANCE, EING YOU.
I DOUBT THAT, FRIEND.
YOU KNOW WHO I AM.
YOU KNOW THAT GUN AIN'T GONNA DO MUCH BUT PISS ME OFF.
THIS GUN DOESN'T *HAVE* TO DO MUCH-- JUST DISTRACT YOU A BIT.
AH, HELL.

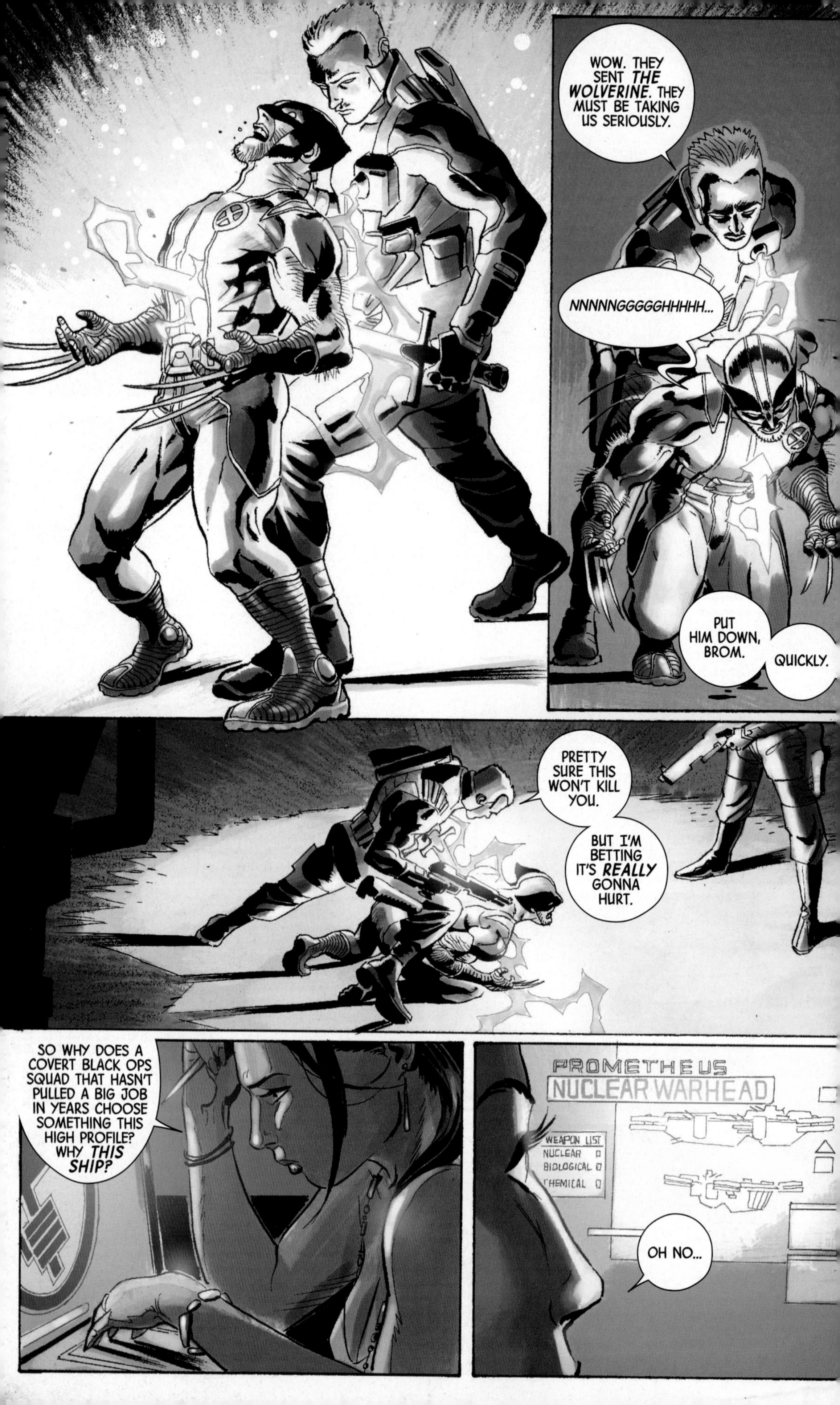
WOW. THEY SENT THE WOLVERINE. THEY MUST BE TAKING US SERIOUSLY.
NNNNNGGGGGHHHHH...
PUT HIM DOWN, BROM.
QUICKLY.
PRETTY SURE THIS WON'T KILL YOU.
BUT I'M BETTING IT'S REALLY GONNA HURT.
SO WHY DOES A COVERT BLACK OPS SQUAD THAT HASN'T PULLED A BIG JOB IN YEARS CHOOSE SOMETHING THIS HIGH PROFILE? WHY THIS SHIP?
PROMETHEUS
NUCLEAR WARHEAD
WEAPON LIST
NUCLEAR
BIOLOGICAL
CHEMICAL
OH NO...

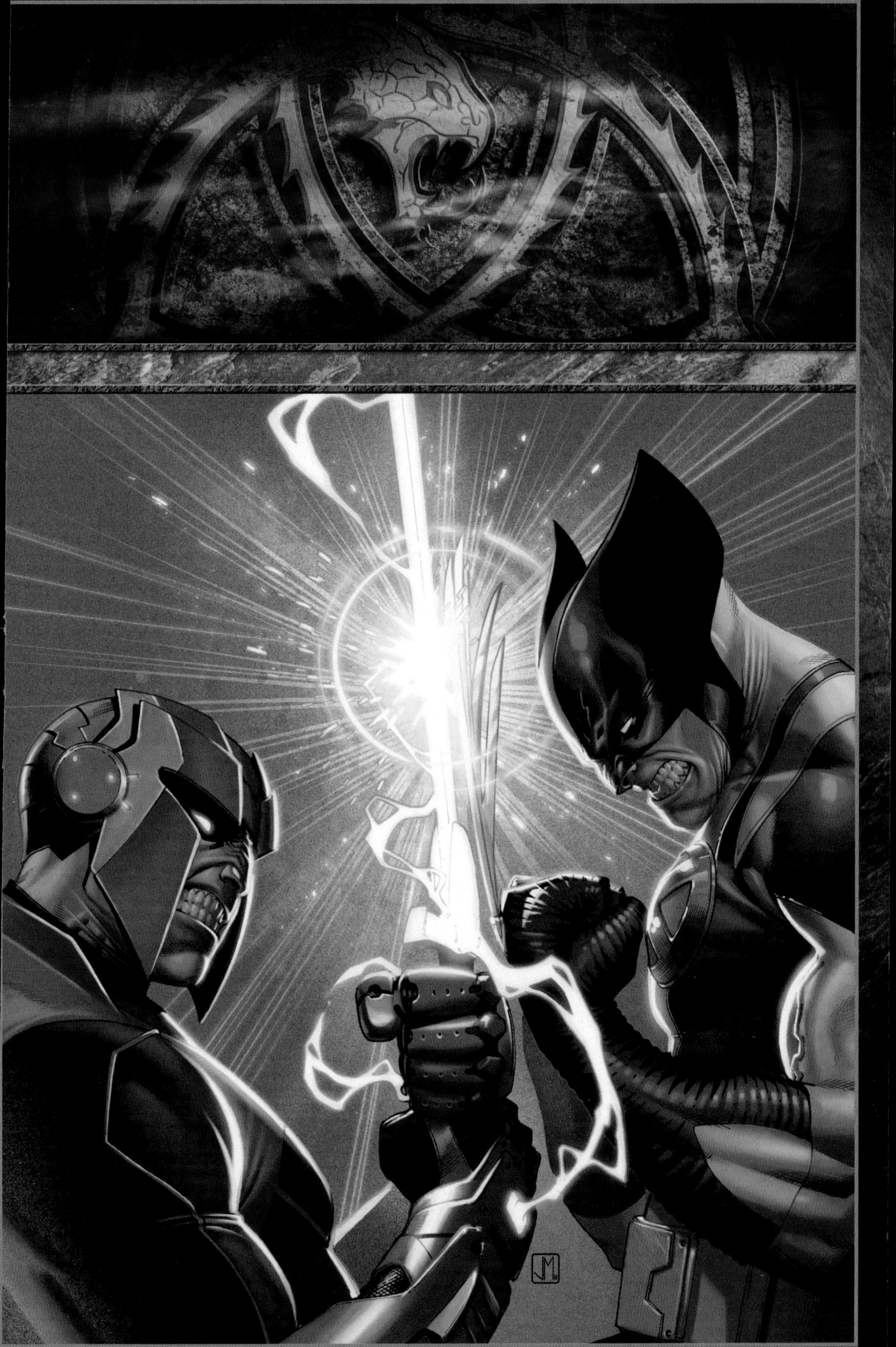

FEAR ITSELF: WOLVERINE #2

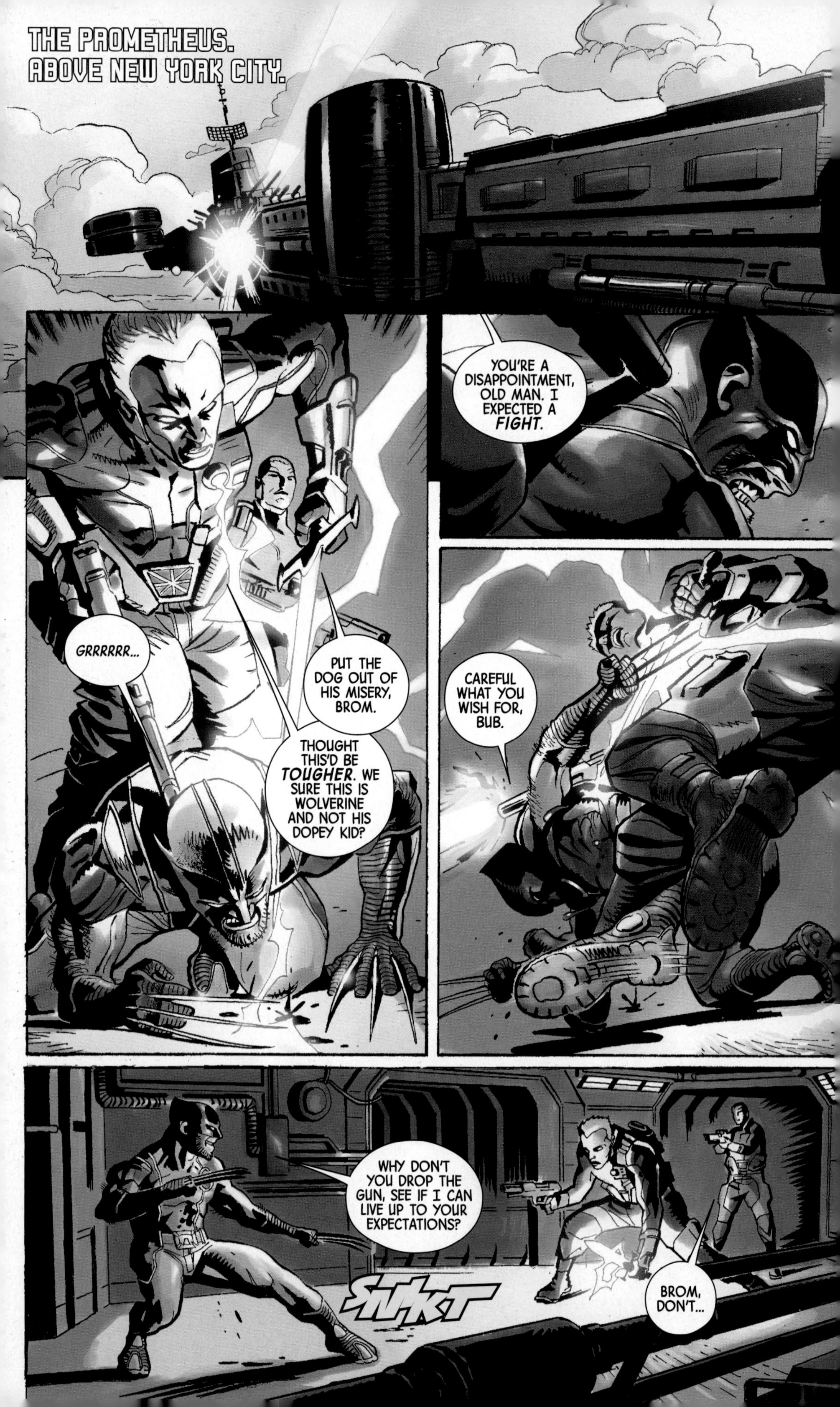

THE PROMETHEUS.
ABOVE NEW YORK CITY.
YOU'RE A DISAPPOINTMENT, OLD MAN. I EXPECTED A FIGHT.
GRRRRRR...
PUT THE DOG OUT OF HIS MISERY, BROM.
THOUGHT THIS'D BE TOUGHER. WE SURE THIS IS WOLVERINE AND NOT HIS DOPEY KID?
CAREFUL WHAT YOU WISH FOR, BUB.
WHY DON'T YOU DROP THE GUN, SEE IF I CAN LIVE UP TO YOUR EXPECTATIONS?
SNIKT
BROM, DON'T...

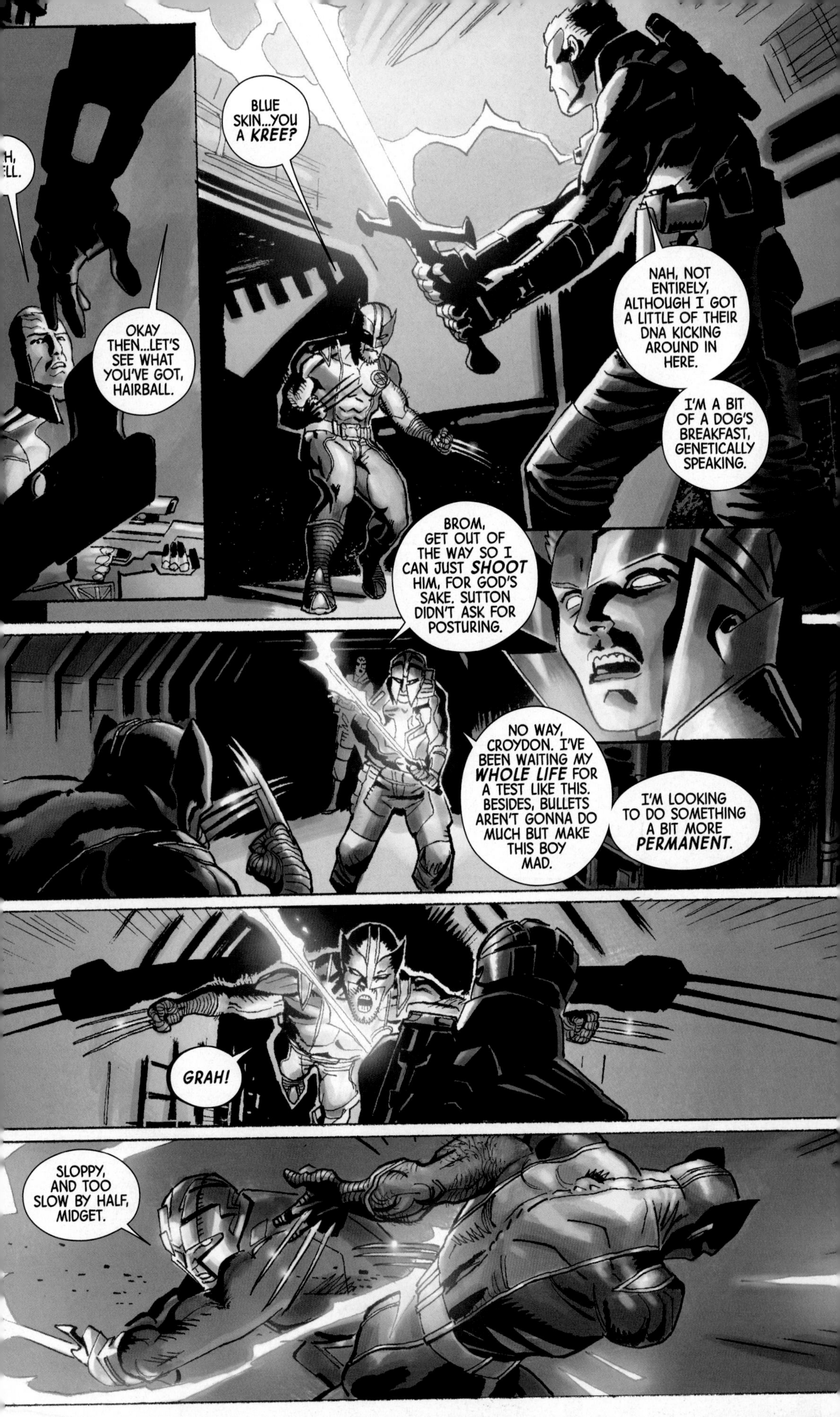
H,
ELL.
BLUE SKIN...YOU A KREE?
OKAY THEN...LET'S SEE WHAT YOU'VE GOT, HAIRBALL.
NAH, NOT ENTIRELY, ALTHOUGH I GOT A LITTLE OF THEIR DNA KICKING AROUND IN HERE.
I'M A BIT OF A DOG'S BREAKFAST, GENETICALLY SPEAKING.
BROM, GET OUT OF THE WAY SO I CAN JUST SHOOT HIM, FOR GOD'S SAKE. SUTTON DIDN'T ASK FOR POSTURING.
NO WAY, CROYDON. I'VE BEEN WAITING MY WHOLE LIFE FOR A TEST LIKE THIS. BESIDES, BULLETS AREN'T GONNA DO MUCH BUT MAKE THIS BOY MAD.
I'M LOOKING TO DO SOMETHING A BIT MORE PERMANENT.
GRAH!
SLOPPY, AND TOO SLOW BY HALF, MIDGET.

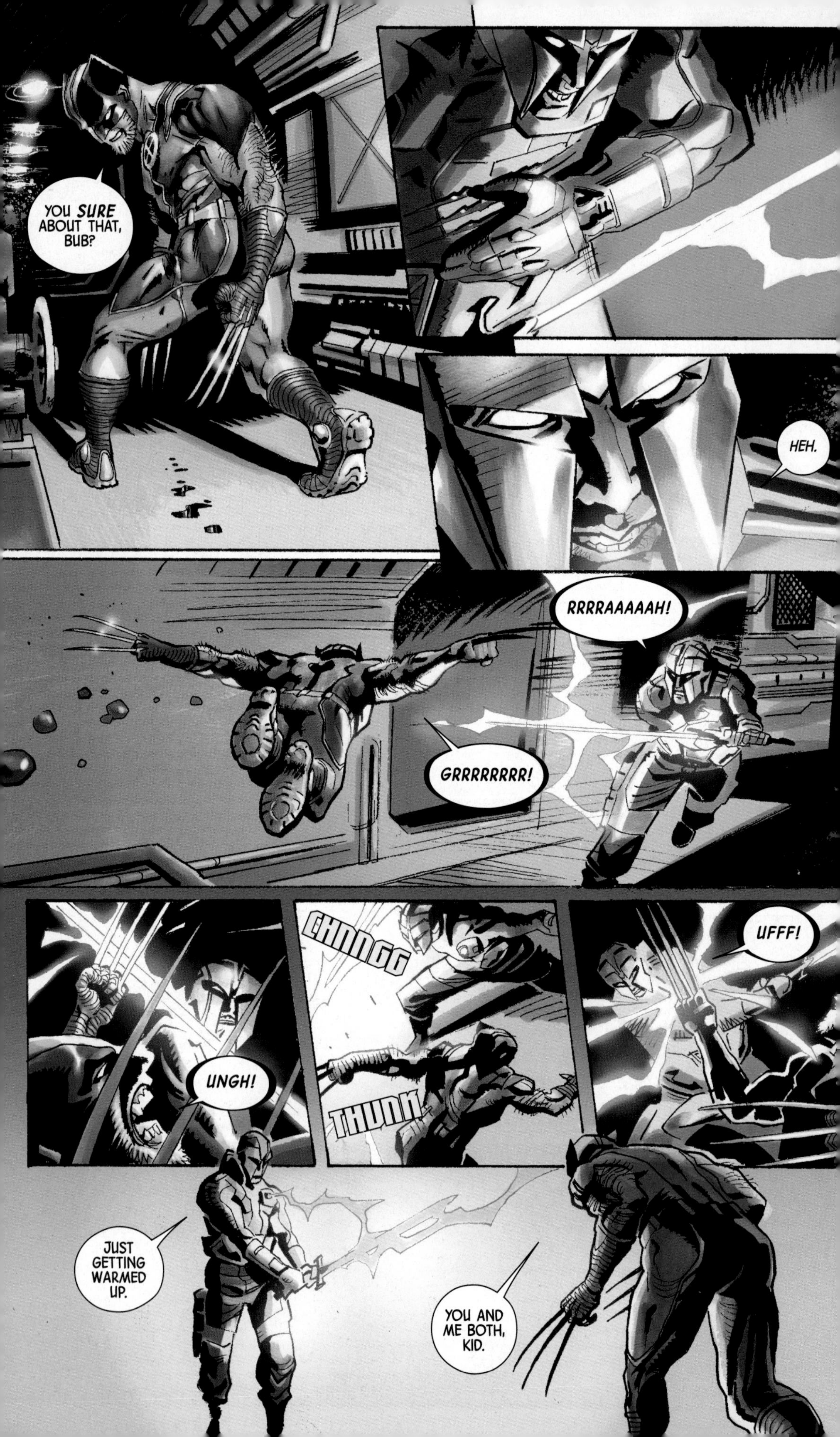
YOU SURE ABOUT THAT, BUB?
HEH.
RRRRAAAAAH!
GRRRRRRRR!
UNGH!
CHNNGG
THUNK
UFFF!
JUST GETTING WARMED UP.
YOU AND ME BOTH, KID.

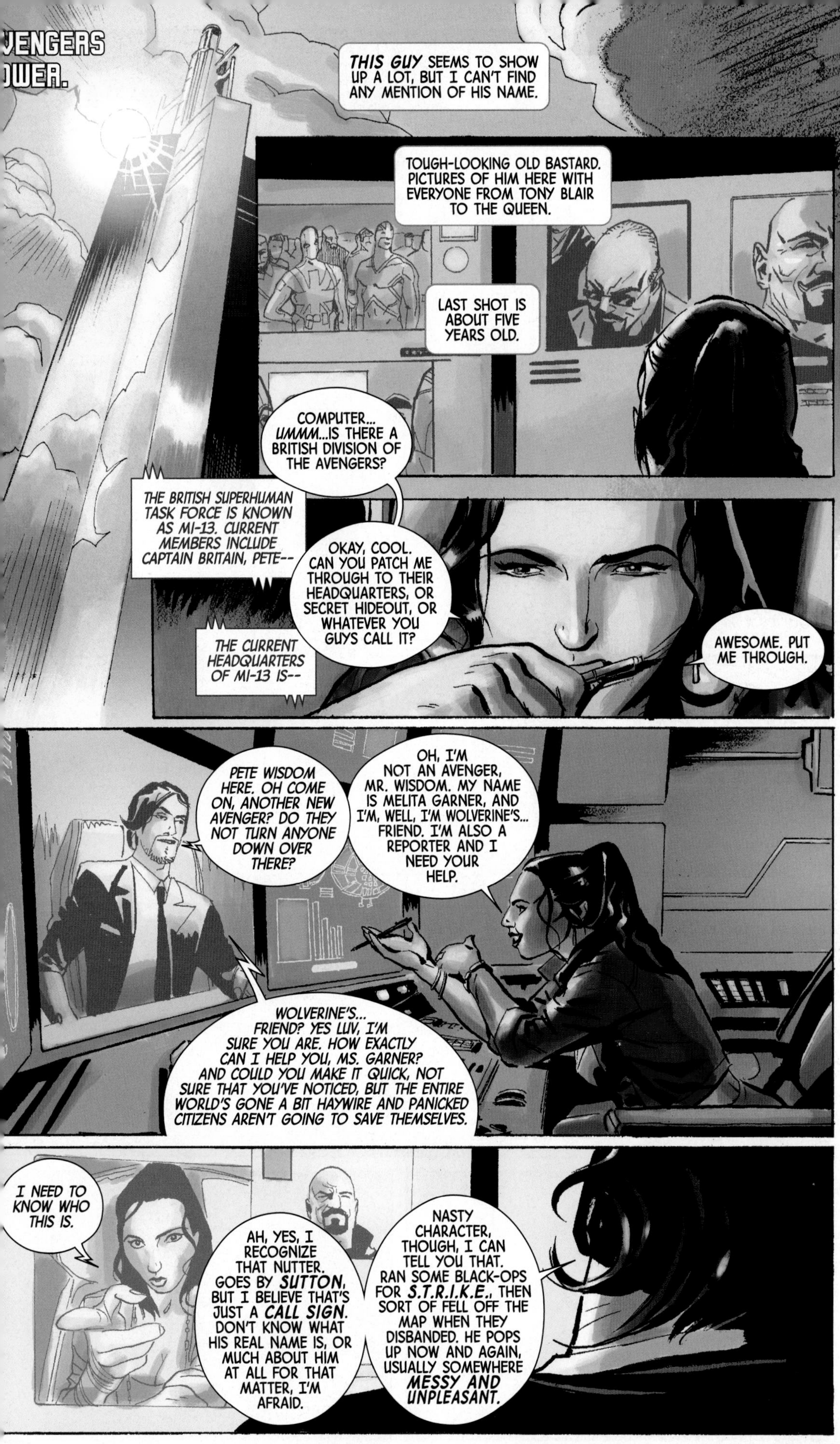
VENGERS
OWER.
THIS GUY SEEMS TO SHOW UP A LOT, BUT I CAN'T FIND ANY MENTION OF HIS NAME.
TOUGH-LOOKING OLD BASTARD. PICTURES OF HIM HERE WITH EVERYONE FROM TONY BLAIR TO THE QUEEN.
LAST SHOT IS ABOUT FIVE YEARS OLD.
COMPUTER... UMMM...IS THERE A BRITISH DIVISION OF THE AVENGERS?
THE BRITISH SUPERHUMAN TASK FORCE IS KNOWN AS MI-13. CURRENT MEMBERS INCLUDE CAPTAIN BRITAIN, PETE--
OKAY, COOL. CAN YOU PATCH ME THROUGH TO THEIR HEADQUARTERS, OR SECRET HIDEOUT, OR WHATEVER YOU GUYS CALL IT?
THE CURRENT HEADQUARTERS OF MI-13 IS--
AWESOME. PUT ME THROUGH.
PETE WISDOM HERE. OH COME ON, ANOTHER NEW AVENGER? DO THEY NOT TURN ANYONE DOWN OVER THERE?
OH, I'M NOT AN AVENGER, MR. WISDOM. MY NAME IS MELITA GARNER, AND I'M, WELL, I'M WOLVERINE'S... FRIEND. I'M ALSO A REPORTER AND I NEED YOUR HELP.
WOLVERINE'S... FRIEND? YES LUV, I'M SURE YOU ARE. HOW EXACTLY CAN I HELP YOU, MS. GARNER? AND COULD YOU MAKE IT QUICK, NOT SURE THAT YOU'VE NOTICED, BUT THE ENTIRE WORLD'S GONE A BIT HAYWIRE AND PANICKED CITIZENS AREN'T GOING TO SAVE THEMSELVES.
I NEED TO KNOW WHO THIS IS.
AH, YES, I RECOGNIZE THAT NUTTER. GOES BY SUTTON, BUT I BELIEVE THAT'S JUST A CALL SIGN. DON'T KNOW WHAT HIS REAL NAME IS, OR MUCH ABOUT HIM AT ALL FOR THAT MATTER, I'M AFRAID.
NASTY CHARACTER, THOUGH, I CAN TELL YOU THAT. RAN SOME BLACK-OPS FOR S.T.R.I.K.E., THEN SORT OF FELL OFF THE MAP WHEN THEY DISBANDED. HE POPS UP NOW AND AGAIN, USUALLY SOMEWHERE MESSY AND UNPLEASANT.

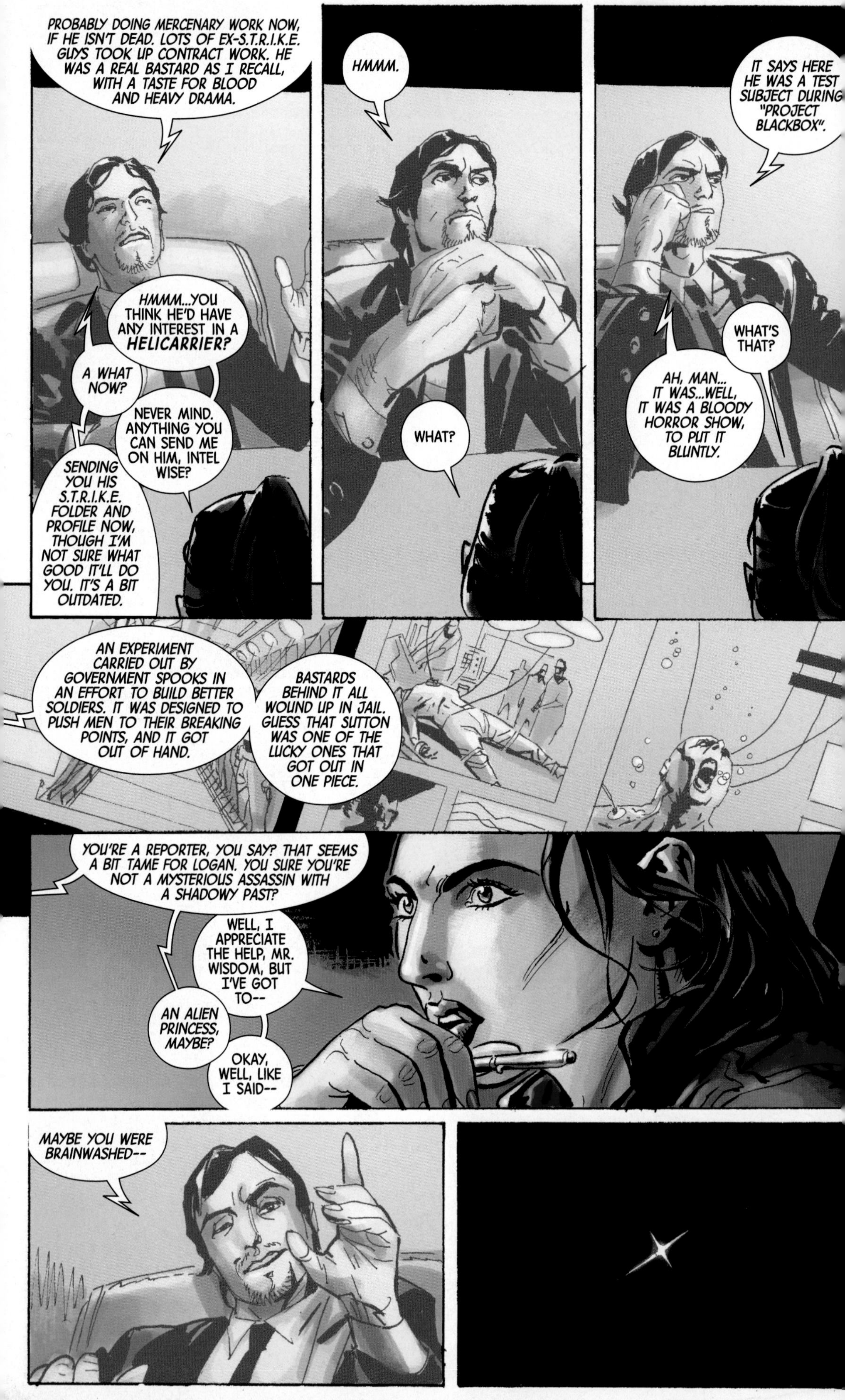
PROBABLY DOING MERCENARY WORK NOW, IF HE ISN'T DEAD. LOTS OF EX-S.T.R.I.K.E. GUYS TOOK UP CONTRACT WORK. HE WAS A REAL BASTARD AS I RECALL, WITH A TASTE FOR BLOOD AND HEAVY DRAMA.
HMMM...YOU THINK HE'D HAVE ANY INTEREST IN A HELICARRIER?
A WHAT NOW?
NEVER MIND. ANYTHING YOU CAN SEND ME ON HIM, INTEL WISE?
SENDING YOU HIS S.T.R.I.K.E. FOLDER AND PROFILE NOW, THOUGH I'M NOT SURE WHAT GOOD IT'LL DO YOU. IT'S A BIT OUTDATED.
HMMM.
WHAT?
IT SAYS HERE HE WAS A TEST SUBJECT DURING "PROJECT BLACKBOX".
WHAT'S THAT?
AH, MAN... IT WAS...WELL, IT WAS A BLOODY HORROR SHOW, TO PUT IT BLUNTLY.
AN EXPERIMENT CARRIED OUT BY GOVERNMENT SPOOKS IN AN EFFORT TO BUILD BETTER SOLDIERS. IT WAS DESIGNED TO PUSH MEN TO THEIR BREAKING POINTS, AND IT GOT OUT OF HAND.
BASTARDS BEHIND IT ALL WOUND UP IN JAIL. GUESS THAT SUTTON WAS ONE OF THE LUCKY ONES THAT GOT OUT IN ONE PIECE.
YOU'RE A REPORTER, YOU SAY? THAT SEEMS A BIT TAME FOR LOGAN. YOU SURE YOU'RE NOT A MYSTERIOUS ASSASSIN WITH A SHADOWY PAST?
WELL, I APPRECIATE THE HELP, MR. WISDOM, BUT I'VE GOT TO--
AN ALIEN PRINCESS, MAYBE?
OKAY, WELL, LIKE I SAID--
MAYBE YOU WERE BRAINWASHED--

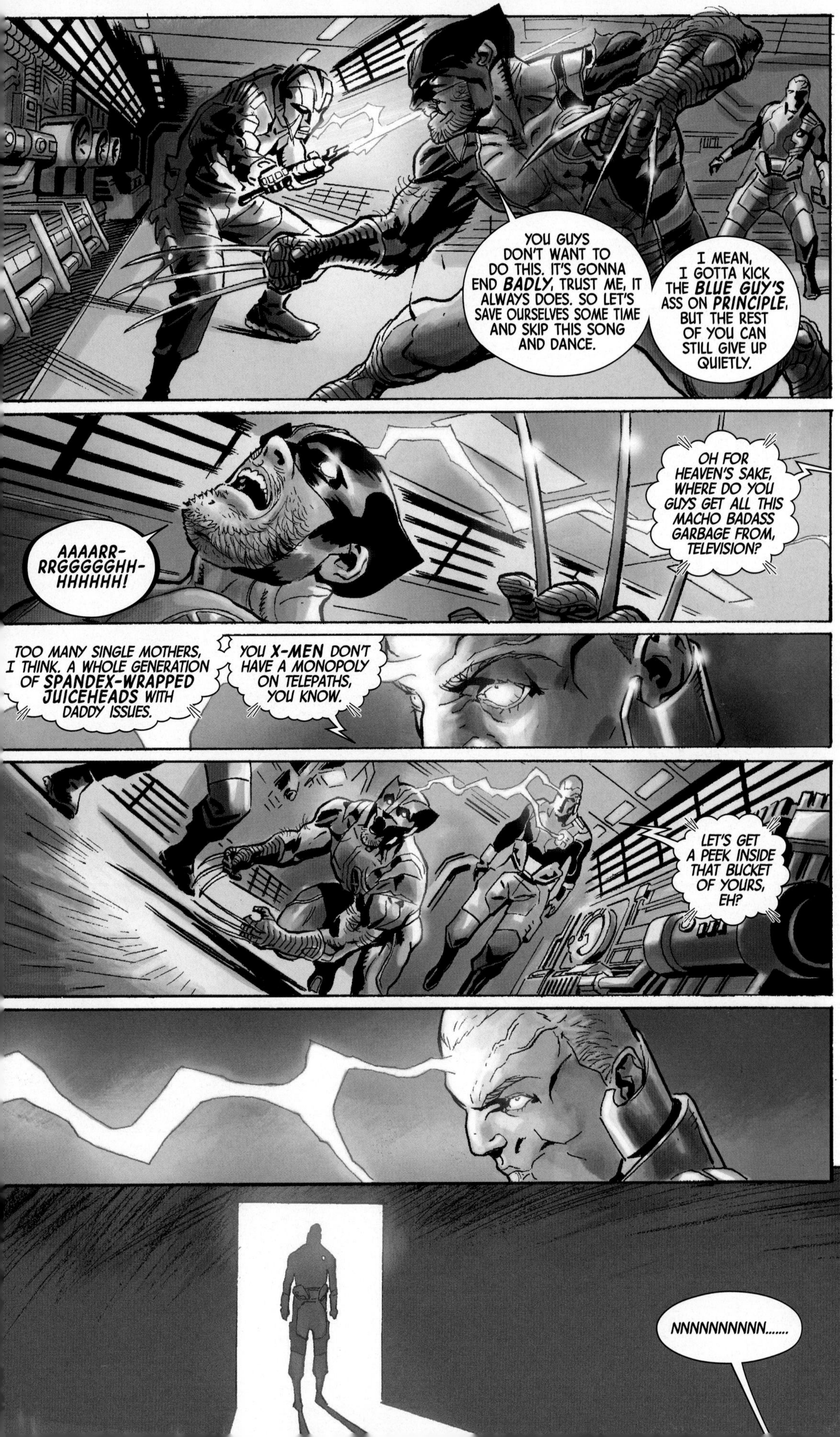
YOU GUYS DON'T WANT TO DO THIS. IT'S GONNA END BADLY, TRUST ME, IT ALWAYS DOES. SO LET'S SAVE OURSELVES SOME TIME AND SKIP THIS SONG AND DANCE.
I MEAN, I GOTTA KICK THE BLUE GUY'S ASS ON PRINCIPLE, BUT THE REST OF YOU CAN STILL GIVE UP QUIETLY.
AAAARR-RRGGGGGHH-HHHHHH!
OH FOR HEAVEN'S SAKE, WHERE DO YOU GUYS GET ALL THIS MACHO BADASS GARBAGE FROM, TELEVISION?
TOO MANY SINGLE MOTHERS, I THINK. A WHOLE GENERATION OF SPANDEX-WRAPPED JUICEHEADS WITH DADDY ISSUES.
YOU X-MEN DON'T HAVE A MONOPOLY ON TELEPATHS, YOU KNOW.
LET'S GET A PEEK INSIDE THAT BUCKET OF YOURS, EH?
NNNNNNNNN.......

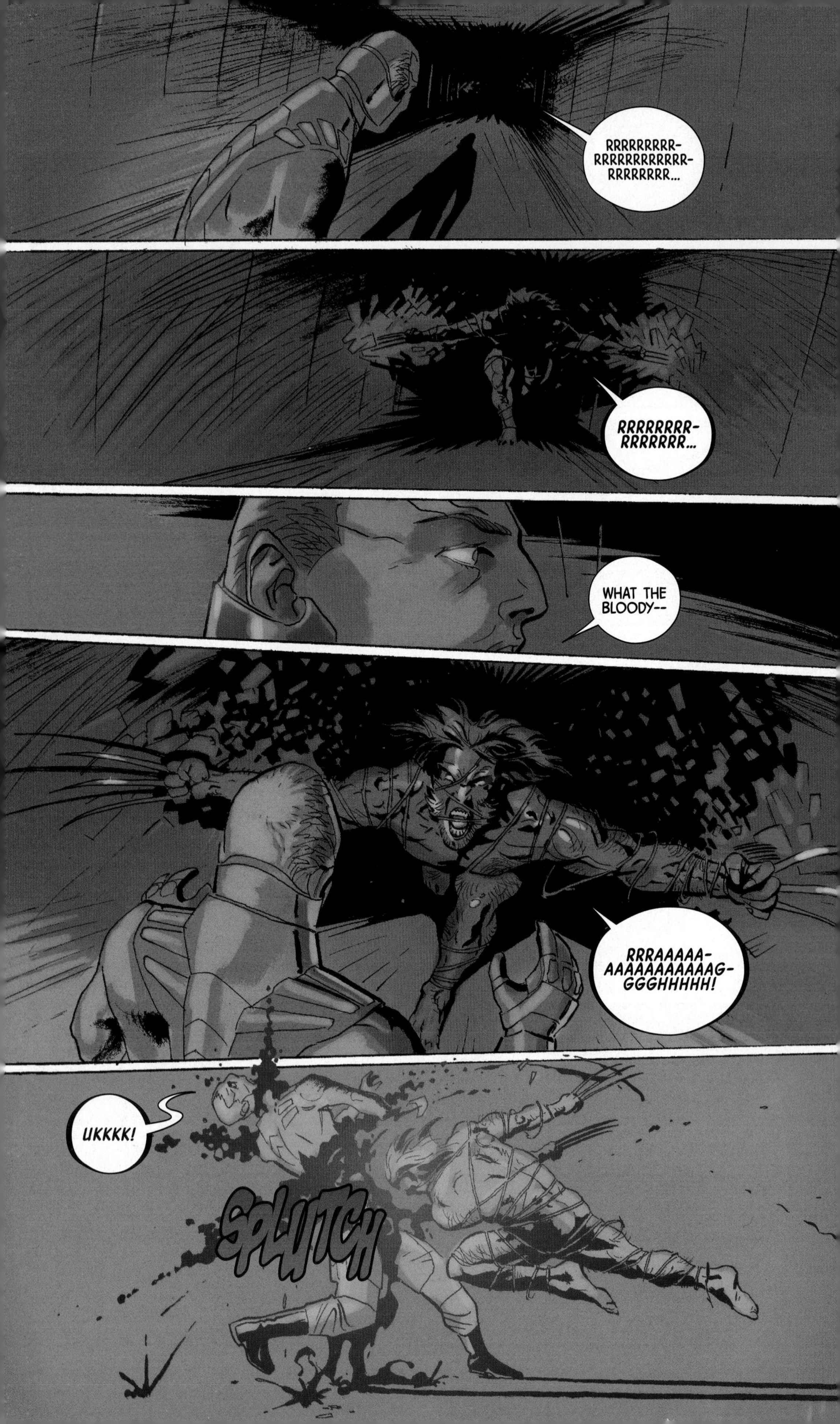
RRRRRRRRR-
RRRRRRRRRRRR-
RRRRRRRR...
RRRRRRRR-
RRRRRRR...
WHAT THE
BLOODY--
RRRAAAAA-
AAAAAAAAAAAG-
GGGHHHHH!
UKKKK!
SPLUTCH

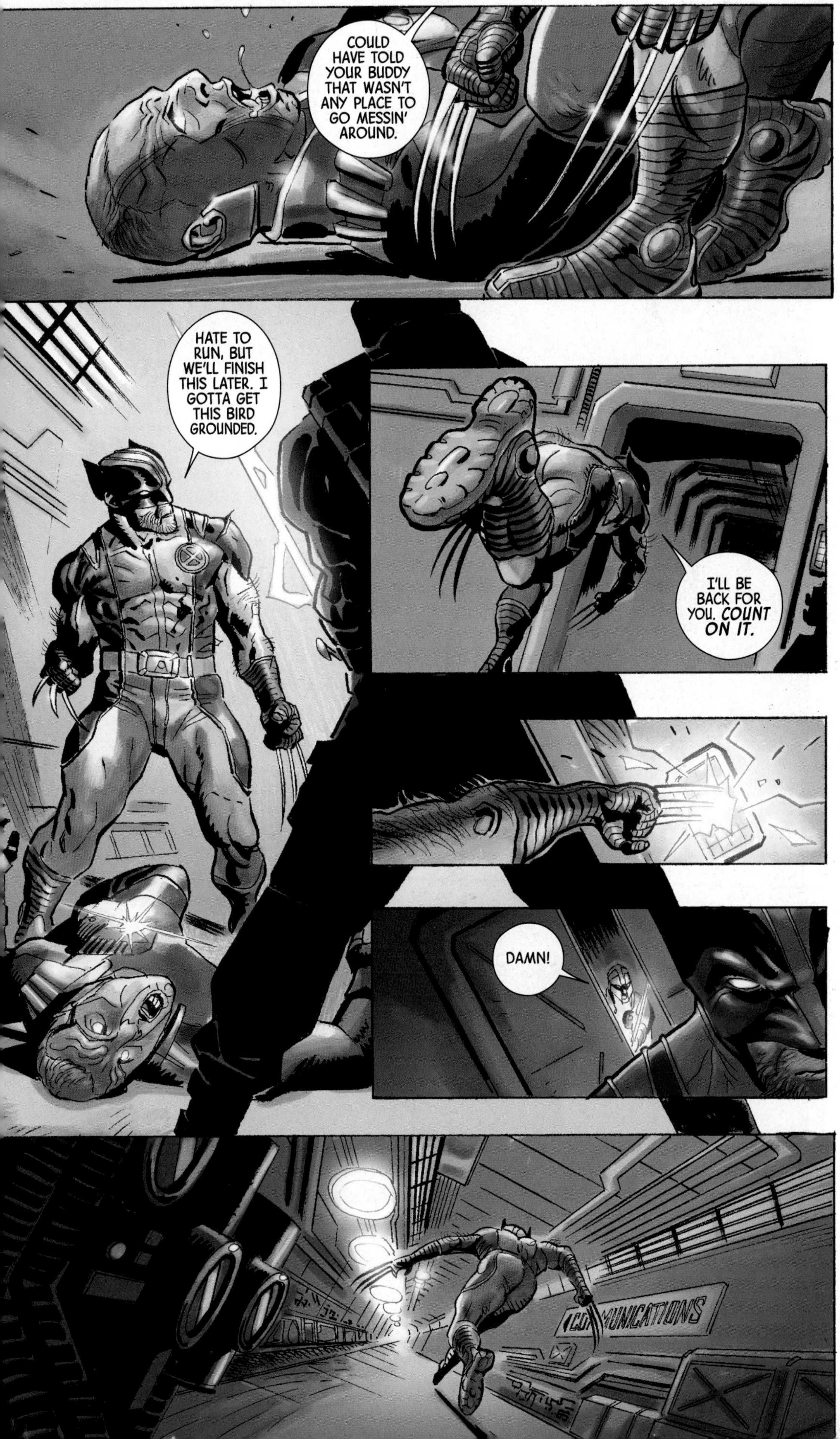
COULD HAVE TOLD YOUR BUDDY THAT WASN'T ANY PLACE TO GO MESSIN' AROUND.
HATE TO RUN, BUT WE'LL FINISH THIS LATER. I GOTTA GET THIS BIRD GROUNDED.
I'LL BE BACK FOR YOU. COUNT ON IT.
DAMN!
COMMUNICATIONS

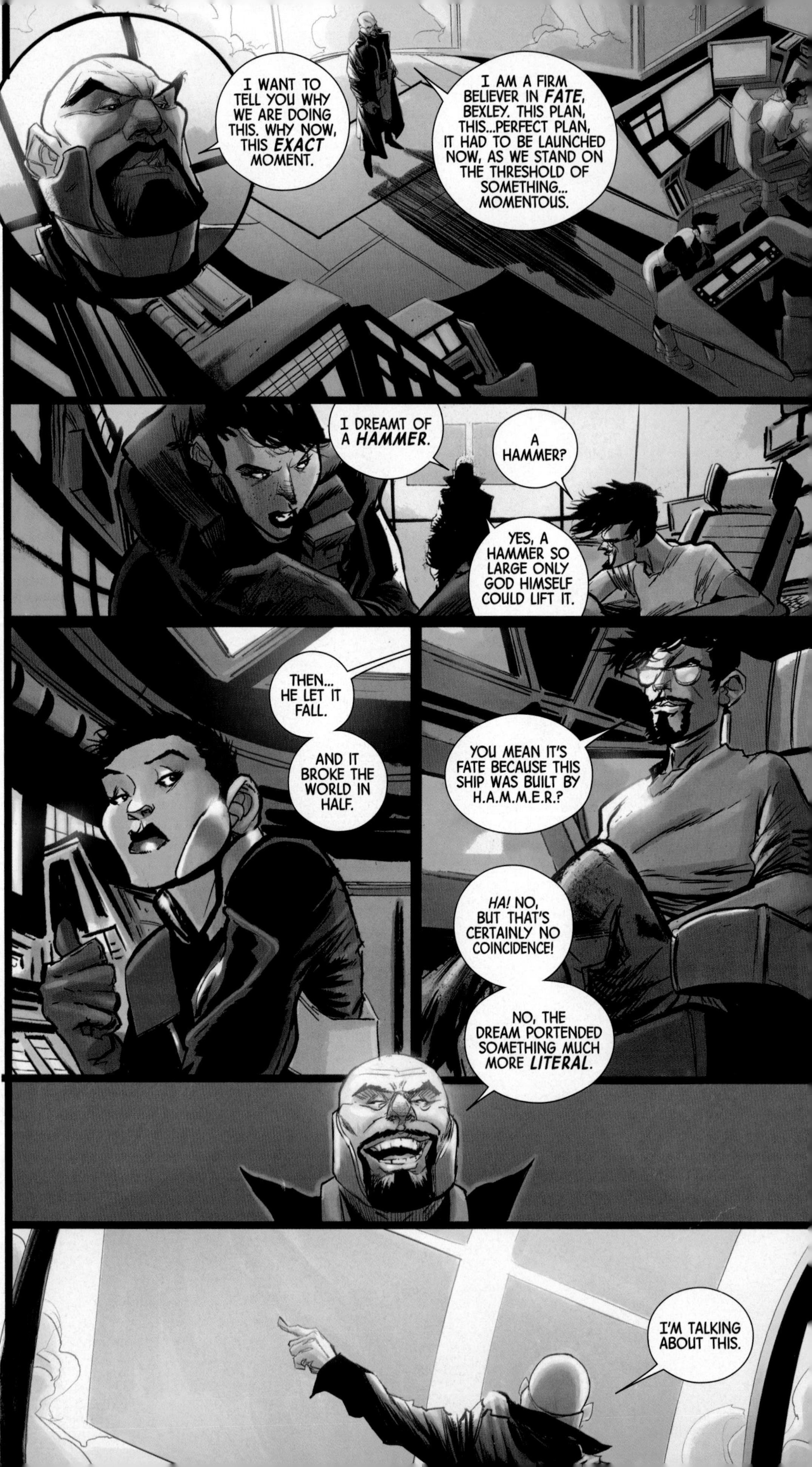
I WANT TO TELL YOU WHY WE ARE DOING THIS. WHY NOW, THIS *EXACT* MOMENT.
I AM A FIRM BELIEVER IN *FATE*, BEXLEY. THIS PLAN, THIS...PERFECT PLAN, IT HAD TO BE LAUNCHED NOW, AS WE STAND ON THE THRESHOLD OF SOMETHING... MOMENTOUS.
I DREAMT OF A *HAMMER*.
A HAMMER?
YES, A HAMMER SO LARGE ONLY GOD HIMSELF COULD LIFT IT.
THEN... HE LET IT FALL.
AND IT BROKE THE WORLD IN HALF.
YOU MEAN IT'S FATE BECAUSE THIS SHIP WAS BUILT BY H.A.M.M.E.R.?
HA! NO, BUT THAT'S CERTAINLY NO COINCIDENCE!
NO, THE DREAM PORTENDED SOMETHING MUCH MORE *LITERAL*.
I'M TALKING ABOUT THIS.

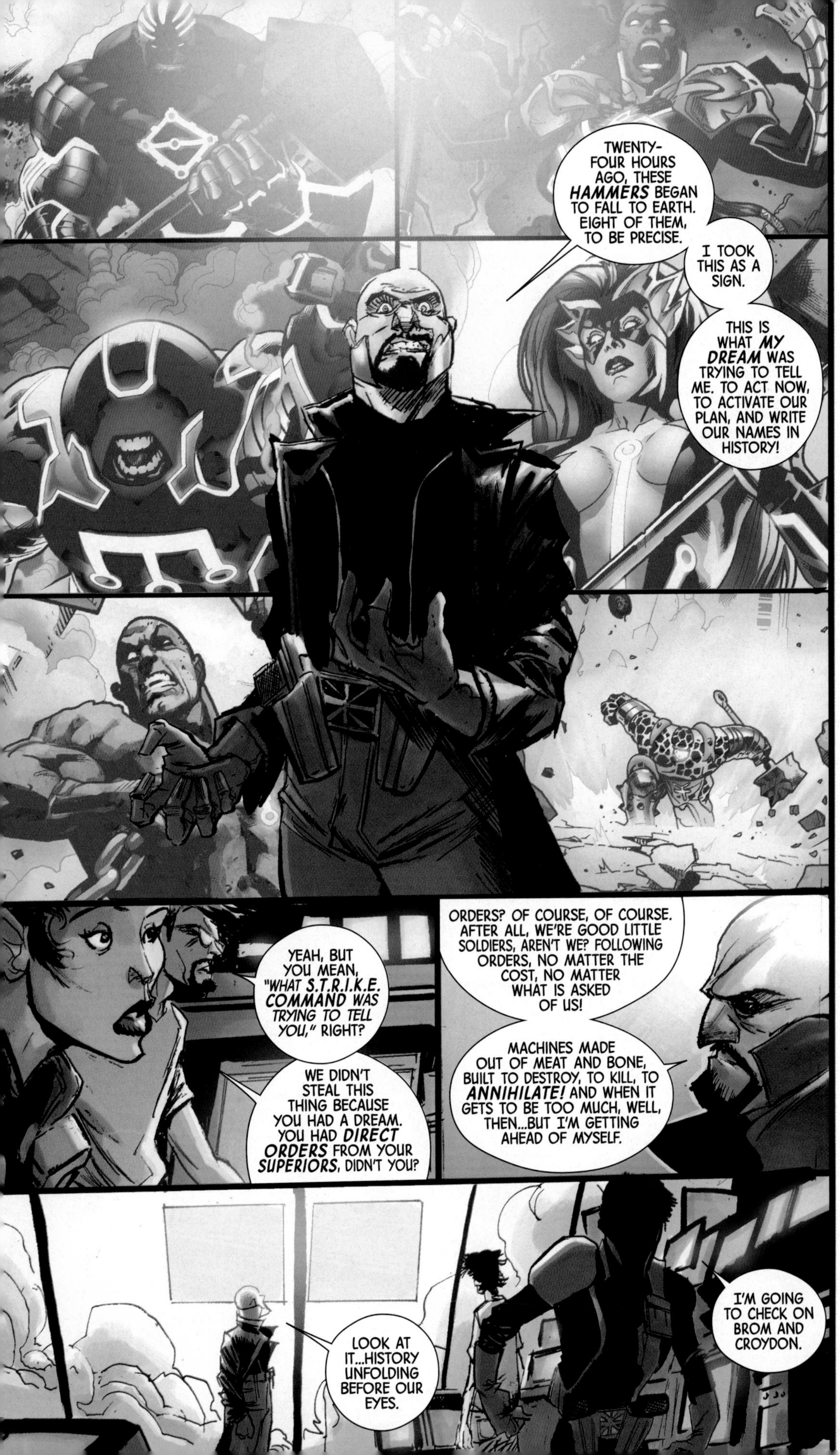

TWENTY-FOUR HOURS AGO, THESE HAMMERS BEGAN TO FALL TO EARTH. EIGHT OF THEM, TO BE PRECISE.
I TOOK THIS AS A SIGN.
THIS IS WHAT MY DREAM WAS TRYING TO TELL ME. TO ACT NOW, TO ACTIVATE OUR PLAN, AND WRITE OUR NAMES IN HISTORY!
YEAH, BUT YOU MEAN, "WHAT S.T.R.I.K.E. COMMAND WAS TRYING TO TELL YOU," RIGHT?
WE DIDN'T STEAL THIS THING BECAUSE YOU HAD A DREAM. YOU HAD DIRECT ORDERS FROM YOUR SUPERIORS, DIDN'T YOU?
ORDERS? OF COURSE, OF COURSE. AFTER ALL, WE'RE GOOD LITTLE SOLDIERS, AREN'T WE? FOLLOWING ORDERS, NO MATTER THE COST, NO MATTER WHAT IS ASKED OF US!
MACHINES MADE OUT OF MEAT AND BONE, BUILT TO DESTROY, TO KILL, TO ANNIHILATE! AND WHEN IT GETS TO BE TOO MUCH, WELL, THEN...BUT I'M GETTING AHEAD OF MYSELF.
LOOK AT IT...HISTORY UNFOLDING BEFORE OUR EYES.
I'M GOING TO CHECK ON BROM AND CROYDON.

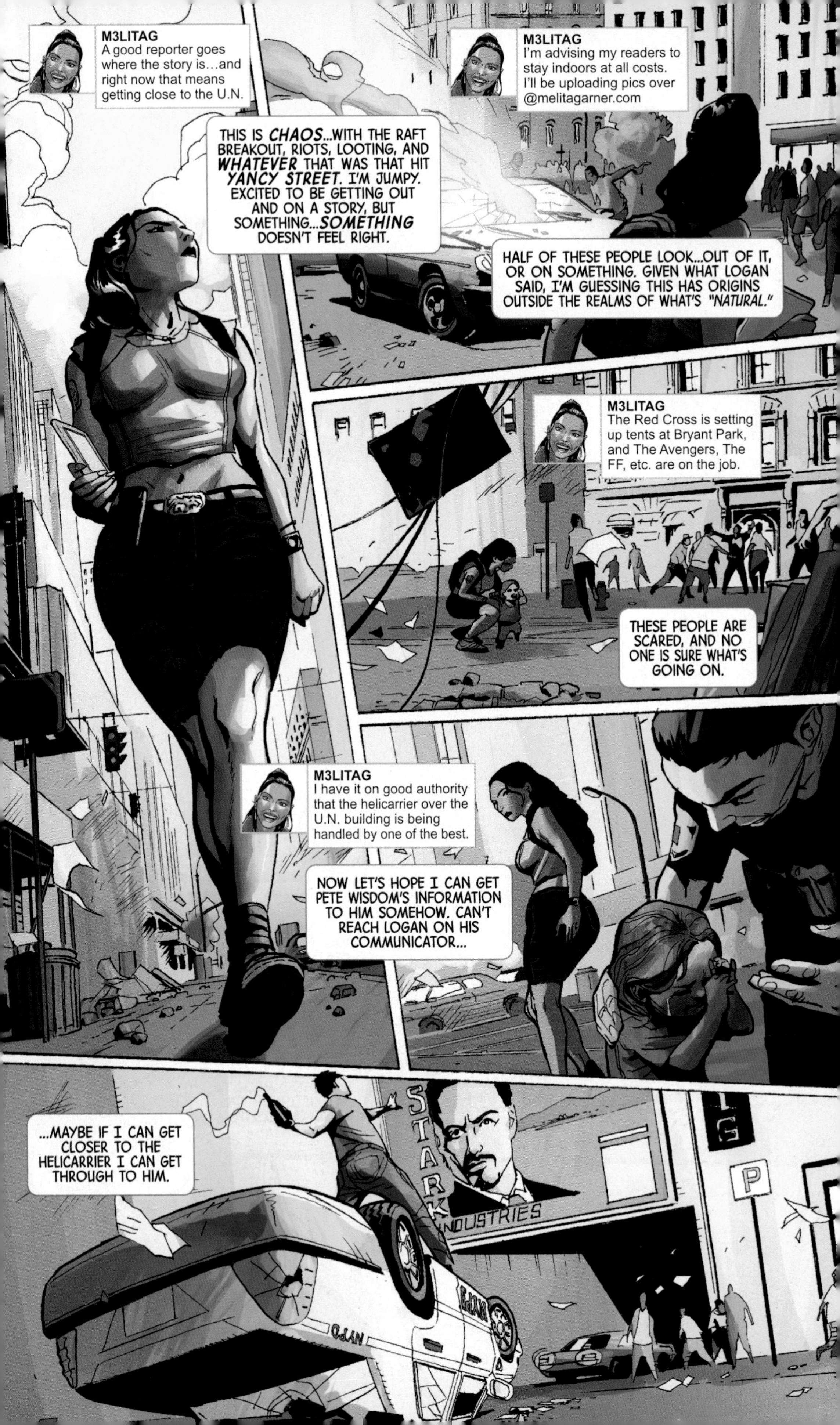
M3LITAG
A good reporter goes where the story is…and right now that means getting close to the U.N.
THIS IS CHAOS...WITH THE RAFT BREAKOUT, RIOTS, LOOTING, AND WHATEVER THAT WAS THAT HIT YANCY STREET. I'M JUMPY. EXCITED TO BE GETTING OUT AND ON A STORY, BUT SOMETHING...SOMETHING DOESN'T FEEL RIGHT.
M3LITAG
I'm advising my readers to stay indoors at all costs. I'll be uploading pics over @melitagarner.com
HALF OF THESE PEOPLE LOOK...OUT OF IT, OR ON SOMETHING. GIVEN WHAT LOGAN SAID, I'M GUESSING THIS HAS ORIGINS OUTSIDE THE REALMS OF WHAT'S "NATURAL."
M3LITAG
The Red Cross is setting up tents at Bryant Park, and The Avengers, The FF, etc. are on the job.
THESE PEOPLE ARE SCARED, AND NO ONE IS SURE WHAT'S GOING ON.
M3LITAG
I have it on good authority that the helicarrier over the U.N. building is being handled by one of the best.
NOW LET'S HOPE I CAN GET PETE WISDOM'S INFORMATION TO HIM SOMEHOW. CAN'T REACH LOGAN ON HIS COMMUNICATOR...
...MAYBE IF I CAN GET CLOSER TO THE HELICARRIER I CAN GET THROUGH TO HIM.
STARK
INDUSTRIES
P
NYPD

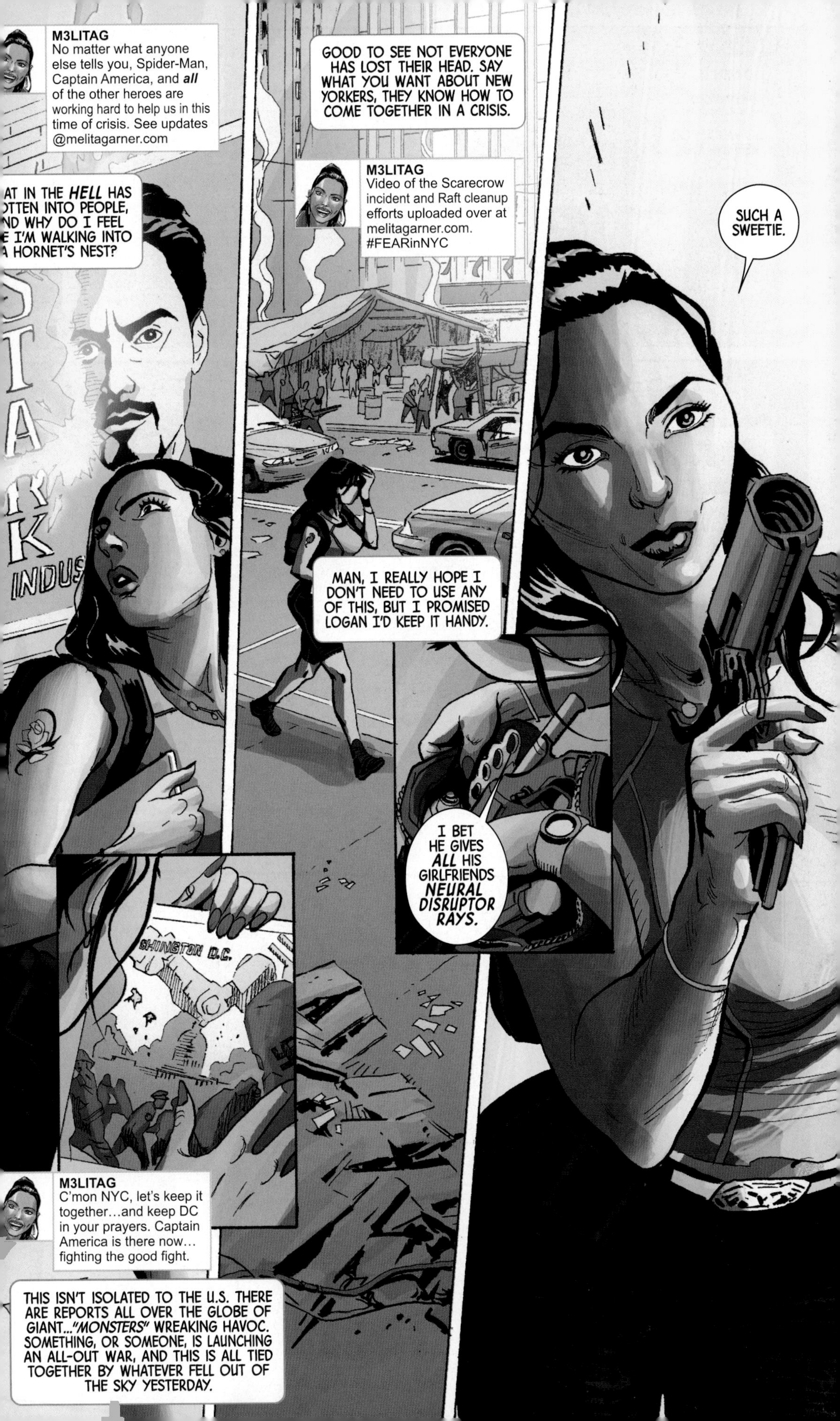

M3LITAG
No matter what anyone else tells you, Spider-Man, Captain America, and *all* of the other heroes are working hard to help us in this time of crisis. See updates @melitagarner.com
AT IN THE *HELL* HAS
OTTEN INTO PEOPLE,
ND WHY DO I FEEL
E I'M WALKING INTO
A HORNET'S NEST?
INDUS
SHINGTON D.C.
GOOD TO SEE NOT EVERYONE HAS LOST THEIR HEAD. SAY WHAT YOU WANT ABOUT NEW YORKERS, THEY KNOW HOW TO COME TOGETHER IN A CRISIS.
M3LITAG
Video of the Scarecrow incident and Raft cleanup efforts uploaded over at melitagarner.com. #FEARinNYC
MAN, I REALLY HOPE I DON'T NEED TO USE ANY OF THIS, BUT I PROMISED LOGAN I'D KEEP IT HANDY.
I BET HE GIVES *ALL* HIS GIRLFRIENDS *NEURAL DISRUPTOR RAYS.*
SUCH A SWEETIE.
M3LITAG
C'mon NYC, let's keep it together...and keep DC in your prayers. Captain America is there now... fighting the good fight.
THIS ISN'T ISOLATED TO THE U.S. THERE ARE REPORTS ALL OVER THE GLOBE OF GIANT..."*MONSTERS*" WREAKING HAVOC. SOMETHING, OR SOMEONE, IS LAUNCHING AN ALL-OUT WAR, AND THIS IS ALL TIED TOGETHER BY WHATEVER FELL OUT OF THE SKY YESTERDAY.

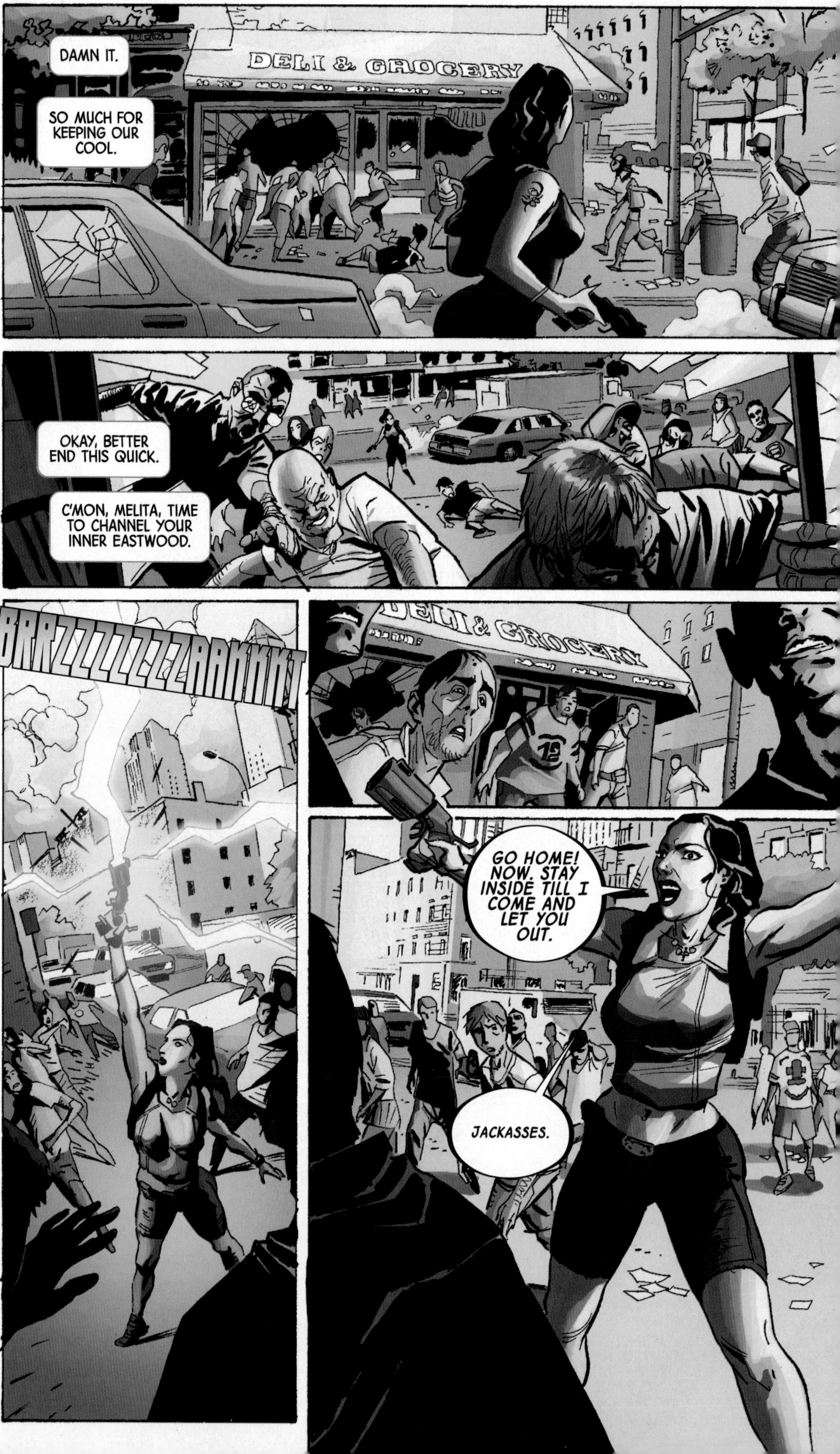
DELI & GROCERY
DAMN IT.
SO MUCH FOR KEEPING OUR COOL.
OKAY, BETTER END THIS QUICK.
C'MON, MELITA, TIME TO CHANNEL YOUR INNER EASTWOOD.
BRRZZZZZZZZAAKKKT
DELI & GROCERY
GO HOME! NOW. STAY INSIDE TILL I COME AND LET YOU OUT.
JACKASSES.

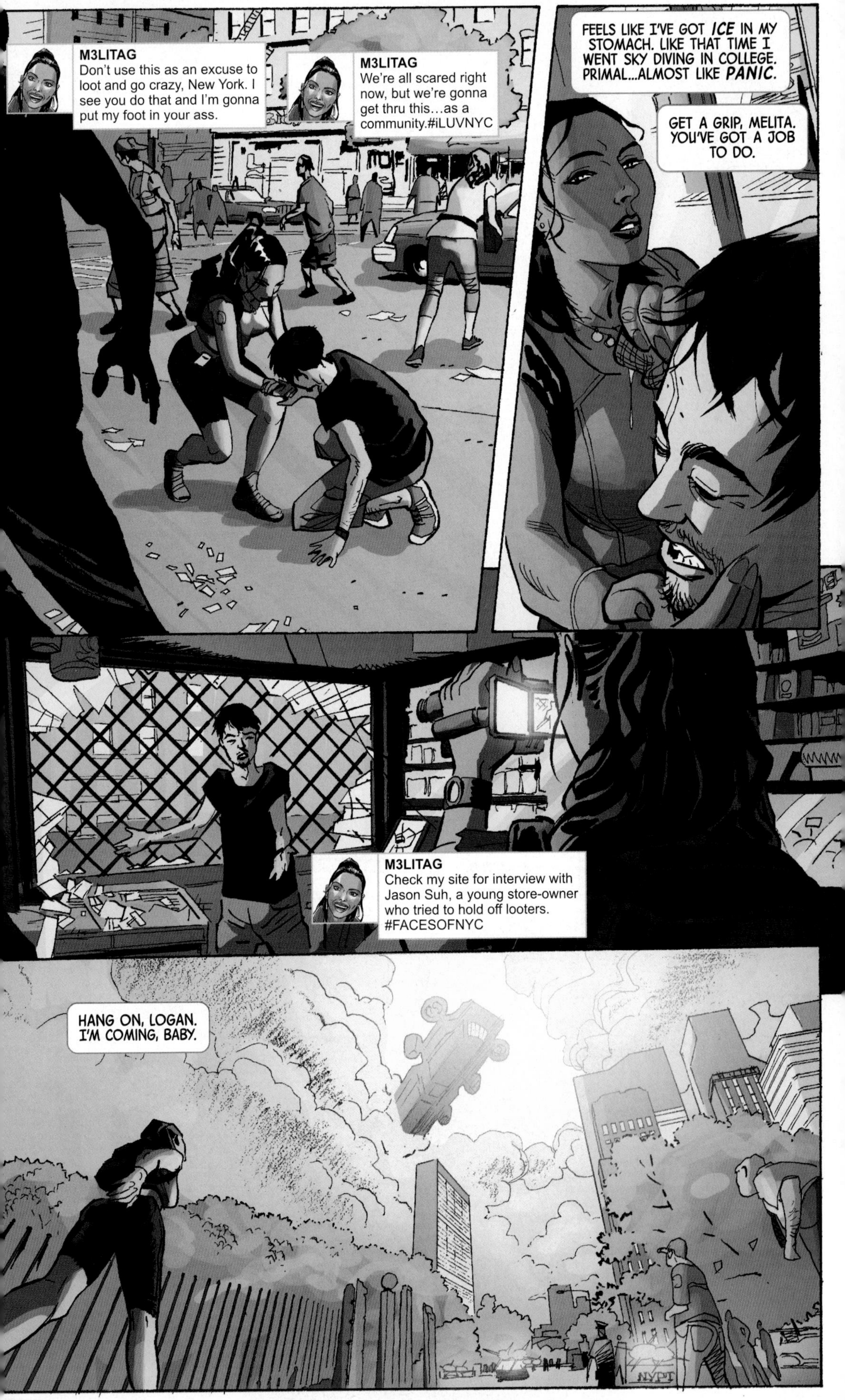
M3LITAG
Don't use this as an excuse to loot and go crazy, New York. I see you do that and I'm gonna put my foot in your ass.
M3LITAG
We're all scared right now, but we're gonna get thru this…as a community.#iLUVNYC
FEELS LIKE I'VE GOT ICE IN MY STOMACH. LIKE THAT TIME I WENT SKY DIVING IN COLLEGE. PRIMAL...ALMOST LIKE PANIC.
GET A GRIP, MELITA. YOU'VE GOT A JOB TO DO.
M3LITAG
Check my site for interview with Jason Suh, a young store-owner who tried to hold off looters. #FACESOFNYC
HANG ON, LOGAN. I'M COMING, BABY.
NYPD

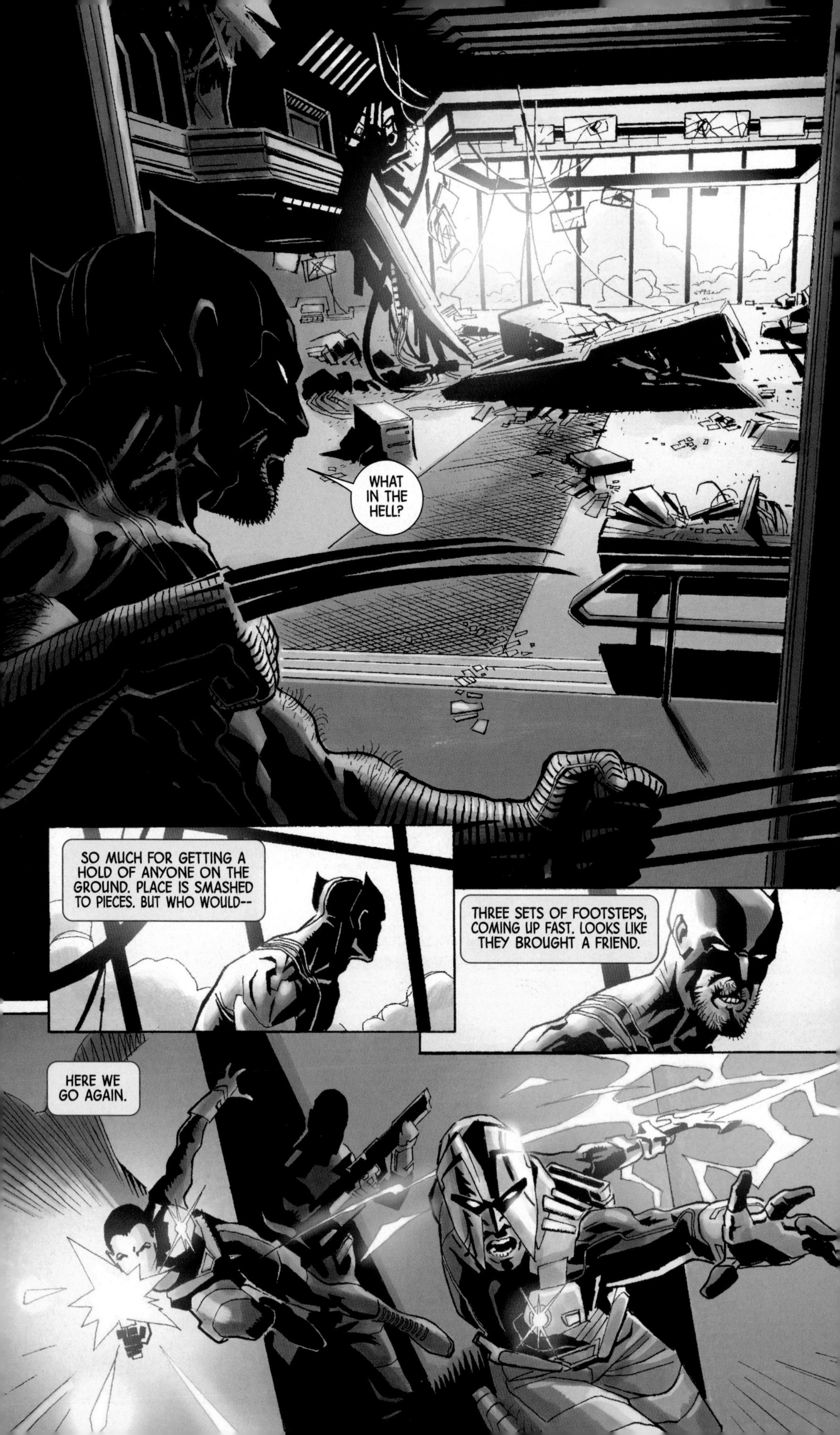
WHAT IN THE HELL?
SO MUCH FOR GETTING A HOLD OF ANYONE ON THE GROUND. PLACE IS SMASHED TO PIECES. BUT WHO WOULD--
THREE SETS OF FOOTSTEPS, COMING UP FAST. LOOKS LIKE THEY BROUGHT A FRIEND.
HERE WE GO AGAIN.

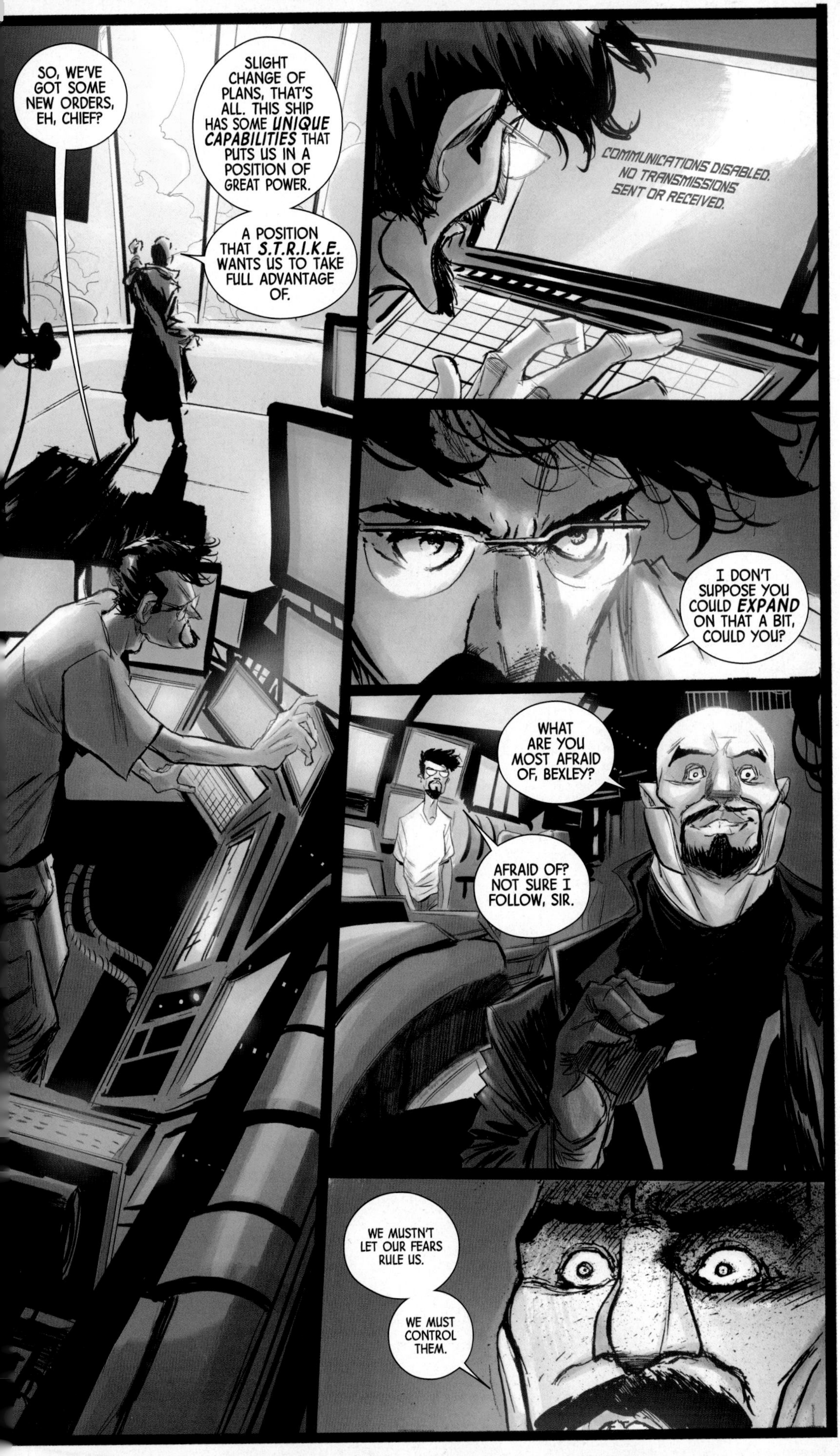
SO, WE'VE GOT SOME NEW ORDERS, EH, CHIEF?
SLIGHT CHANGE OF PLANS, THAT'S ALL. THIS SHIP HAS SOME UNIQUE CAPABILITIES THAT PUTS US IN A POSITION OF GREAT POWER.
A POSITION THAT S.T.R.I.K.E. WANTS US TO TAKE FULL ADVANTAGE OF.
COMMUNICATIONS DISABLED. NO TRANSMISSIONS SENT OR RECEIVED.
I DON'T SUPPOSE YOU COULD EXPAND ON THAT A BIT, COULD YOU?
WHAT ARE YOU MOST AFRAID OF, BEXLEY?
AFRAID OF? NOT SURE I FOLLOW, SIR.
WE MUSTN'T LET OUR FEARS RULE US.
WE MUST CONTROL THEM.

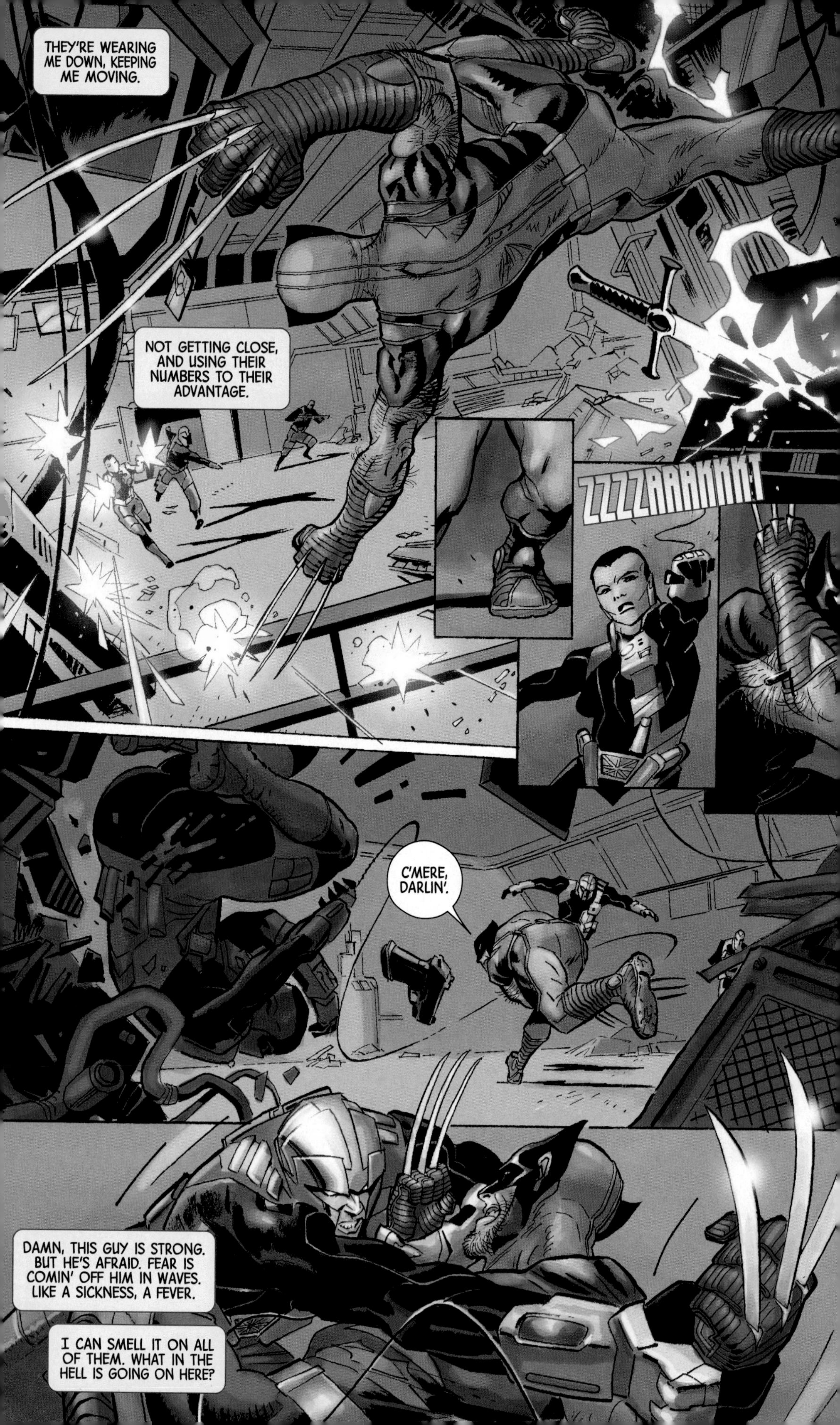

THEY'RE WEARING ME DOWN, KEEPING ME MOVING.
NOT GETTING CLOSE, AND USING THEIR NUMBERS TO THEIR ADVANTAGE.
ZZZZAAAAKKKT
C'MERE, DARLIN'.
DAMN, THIS GUY IS STRONG. BUT HE'S AFRAID. FEAR IS COMIN' OFF HIM IN WAVES. LIKE A SICKNESS, A FEVER.
I CAN SMELL IT ON ALL OF THEM. WHAT IN THE HELL IS GOING ON HERE?

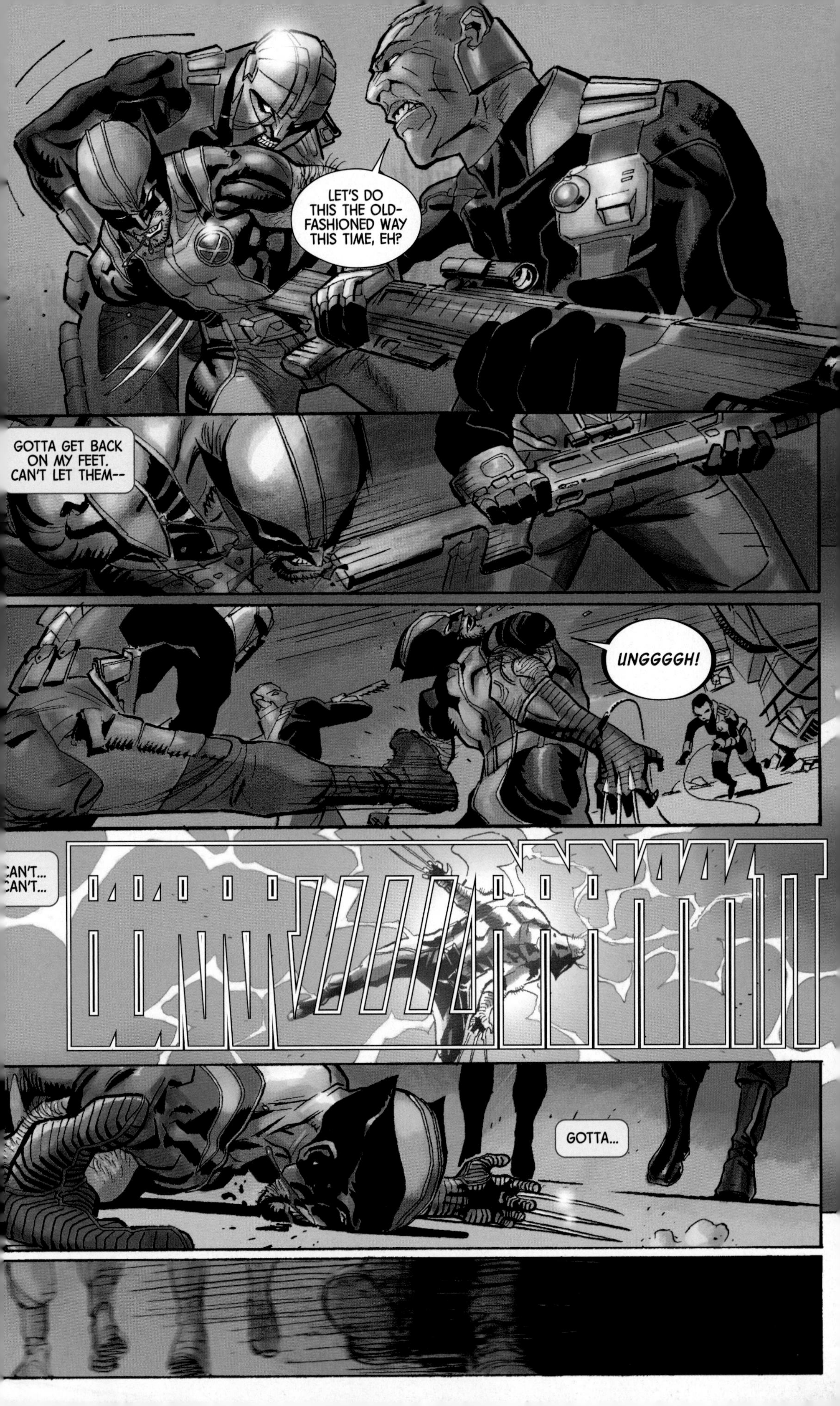

LET'S DO THIS THE OLD-FASHIONED WAY THIS TIME, EH?
GOTTA GET BACK ON MY FEET. CAN'T LET THEM--
UNGGGGH!
CAN'T... CAN'T...
GOTTA...

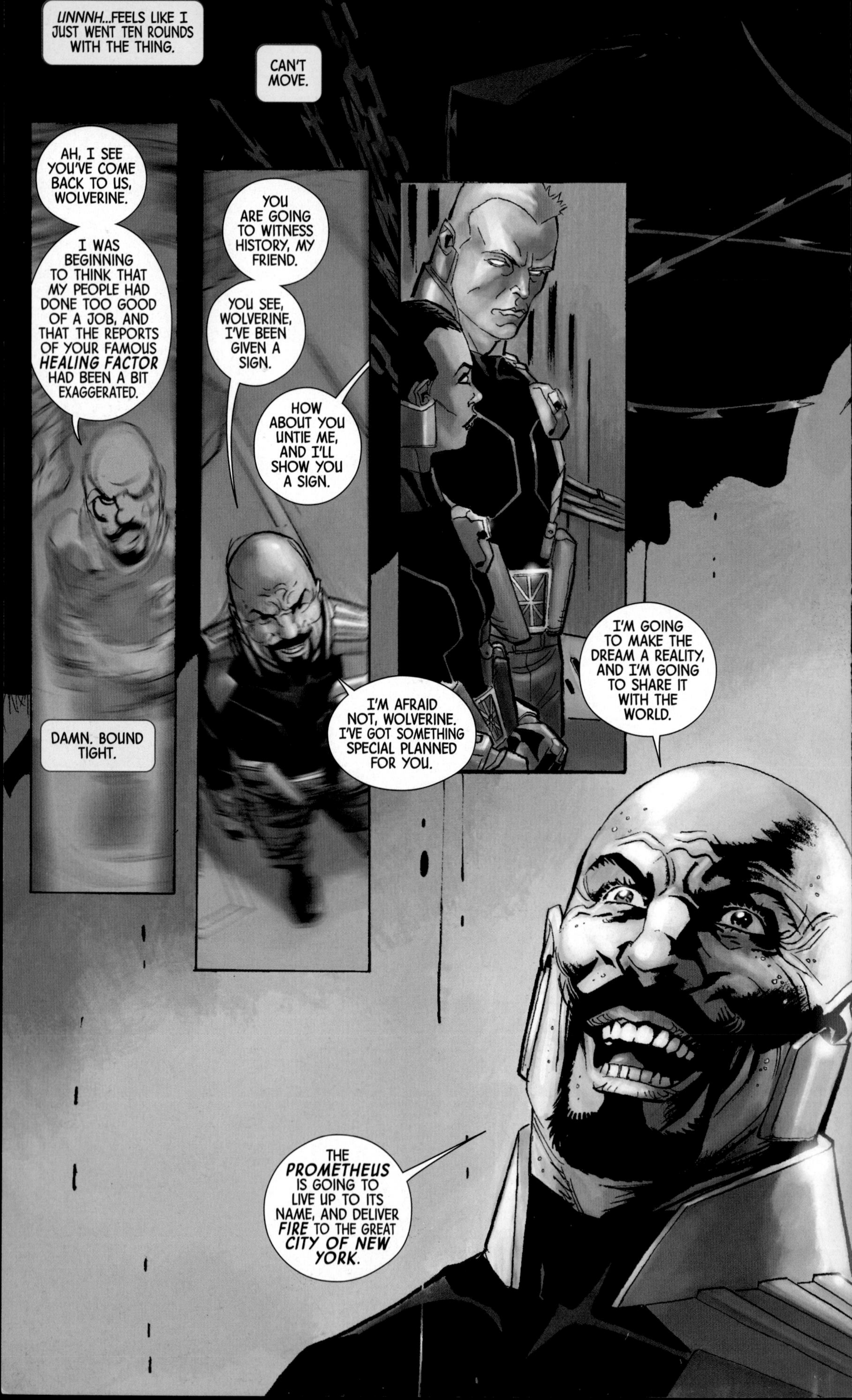

UNNNH...FEELS LIKE I JUST WENT TEN ROUNDS WITH THE THING.
CAN'T MOVE.
AH, I SEE YOU'VE COME BACK TO US, WOLVERINE.
I WAS BEGINNING TO THINK THAT MY PEOPLE HAD DONE TOO GOOD OF A JOB, AND THAT THE REPORTS OF YOUR FAMOUS ***HEALING FACTOR*** HAD BEEN A BIT EXAGGERATED.
DAMN. BOUND TIGHT.
YOU ARE GOING TO WITNESS HISTORY, MY FRIEND.
YOU SEE, WOLVERINE, I'VE BEEN GIVEN A SIGN.
HOW ABOUT YOU UNTIE ME, AND I'LL SHOW YOU A SIGN.
I'M AFRAID NOT, WOLVERINE. I'VE GOT SOMETHING SPECIAL PLANNED FOR YOU.
I'M GOING TO MAKE THE DREAM A REALITY, AND I'M GOING TO SHARE IT WITH THE WORLD.
THE ***PROMETHEUS*** IS GOING TO LIVE UP TO ITS NAME, AND DELIVER ***FIRE*** TO THE GREAT ***CITY OF NEW YORK***.

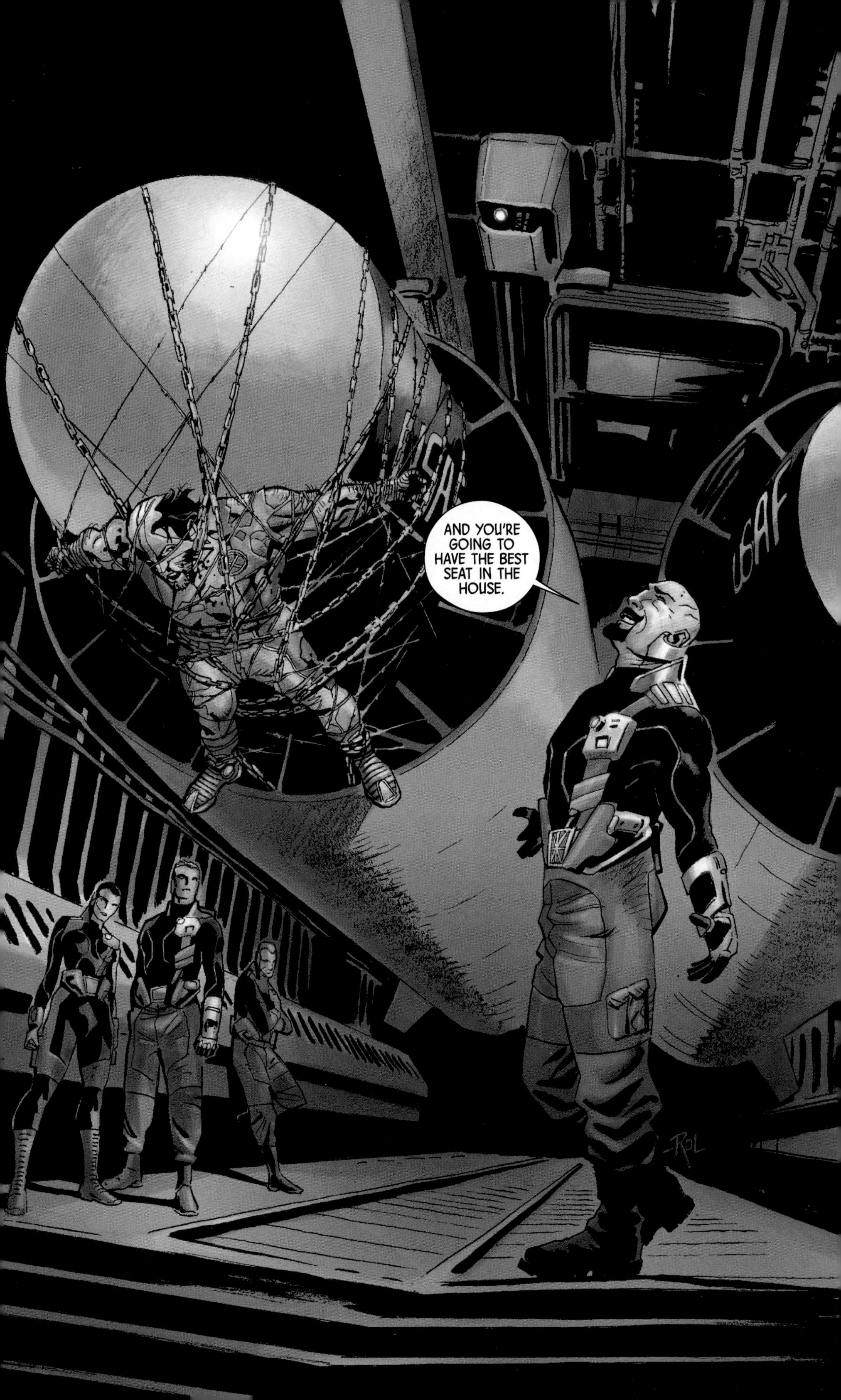
AND YOU'RE GOING TO HAVE THE BEST SEAT IN THE HOUSE.
USAF
USAF
ROL

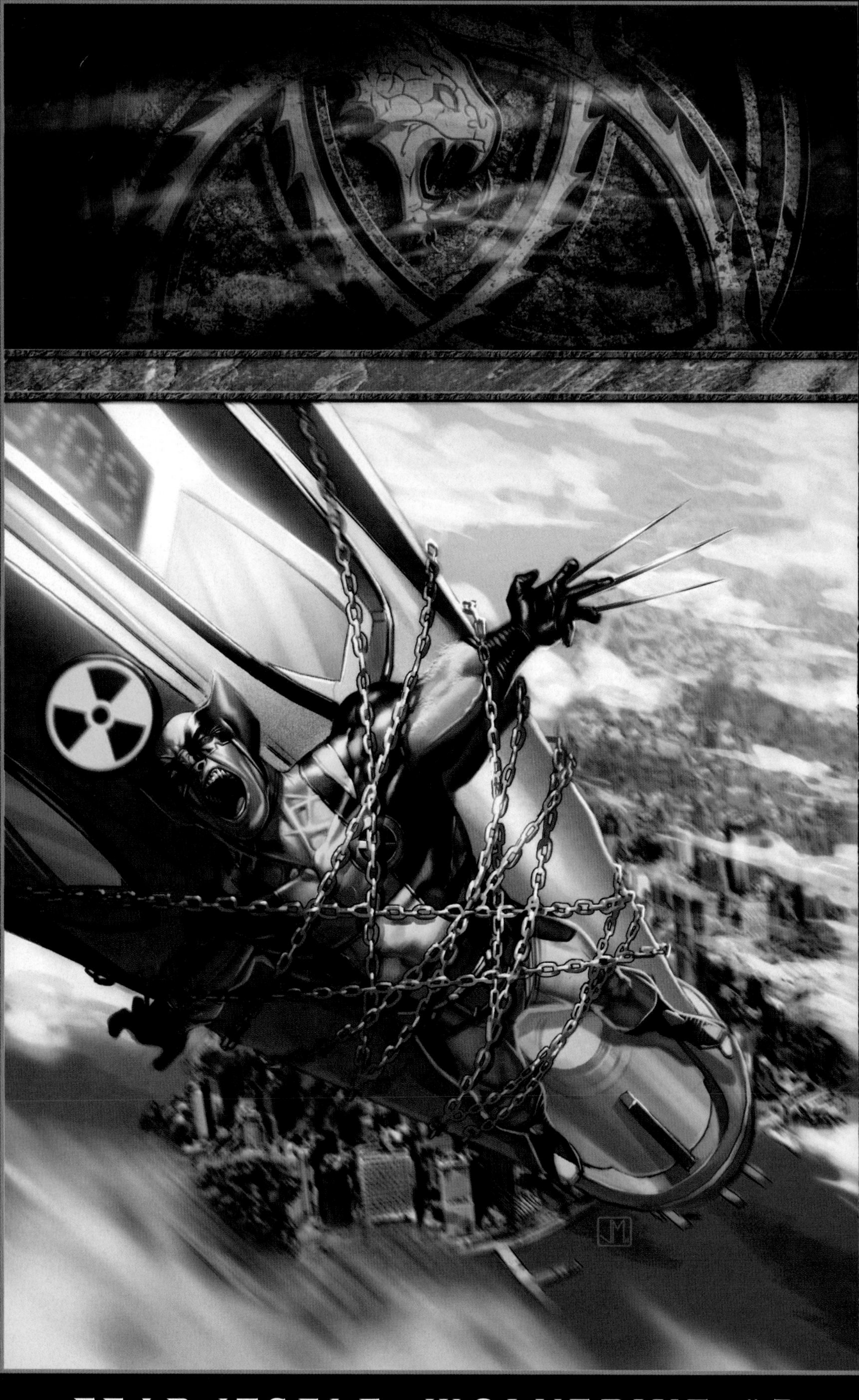

FEAR ITSELF: WOLVERINE #3

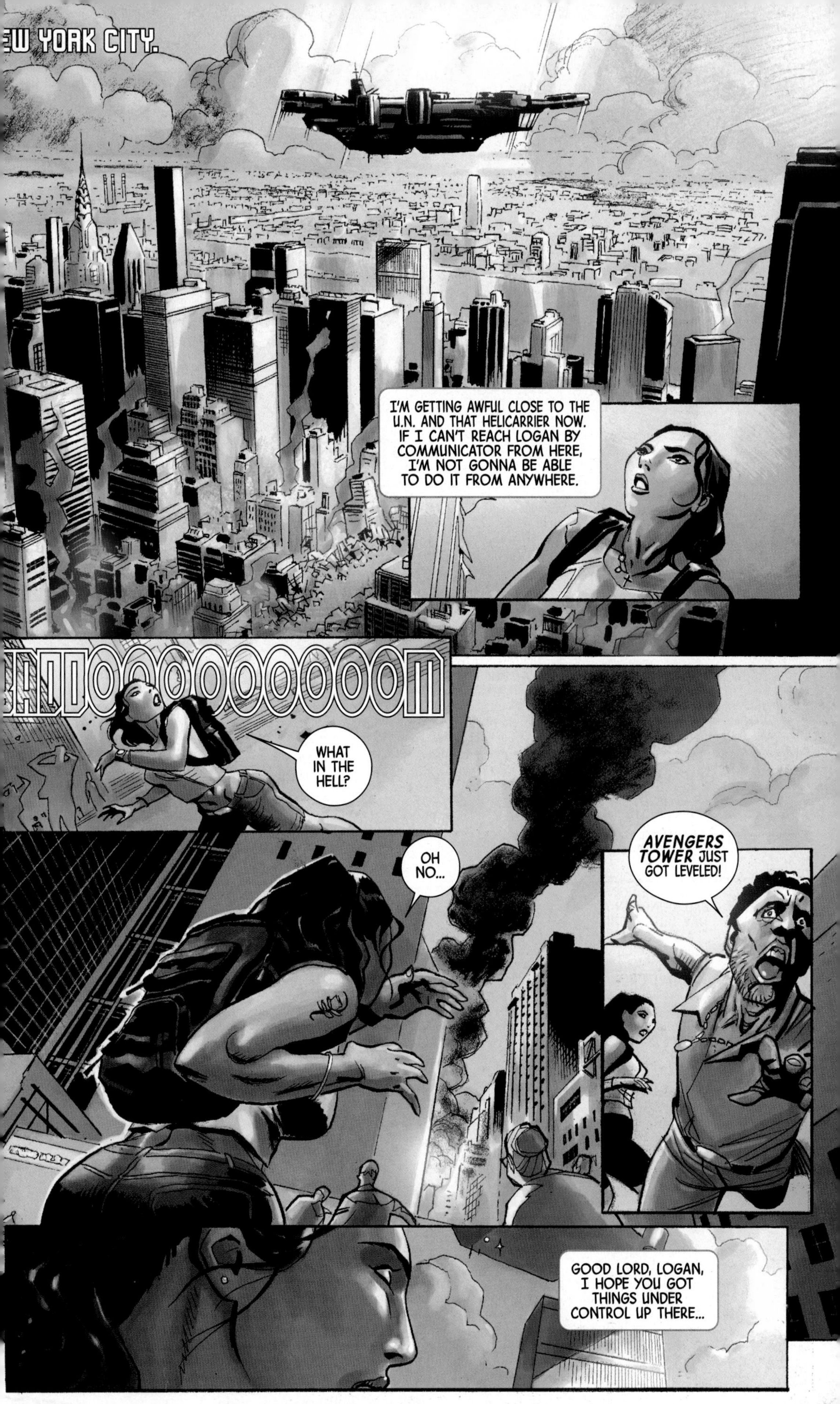

EW YORK CITY.
I'M GETTING AWFUL CLOSE TO THE U.N. AND THAT HELICARRIER NOW. IF I CAN'T REACH LOGAN BY COMMUNICATOR FROM HERE, I'M NOT GONNA BE ABLE TO DO IT FROM ANYWHERE.
BADOOOOOOOOOOOM
WHAT IN THE HELL?
OH NO...
AVENGERS TOWER JUST GOT LEVELED!
GOOD LORD, LOGAN, I HOPE YOU GOT THINGS UNDER CONTROL UP THERE...

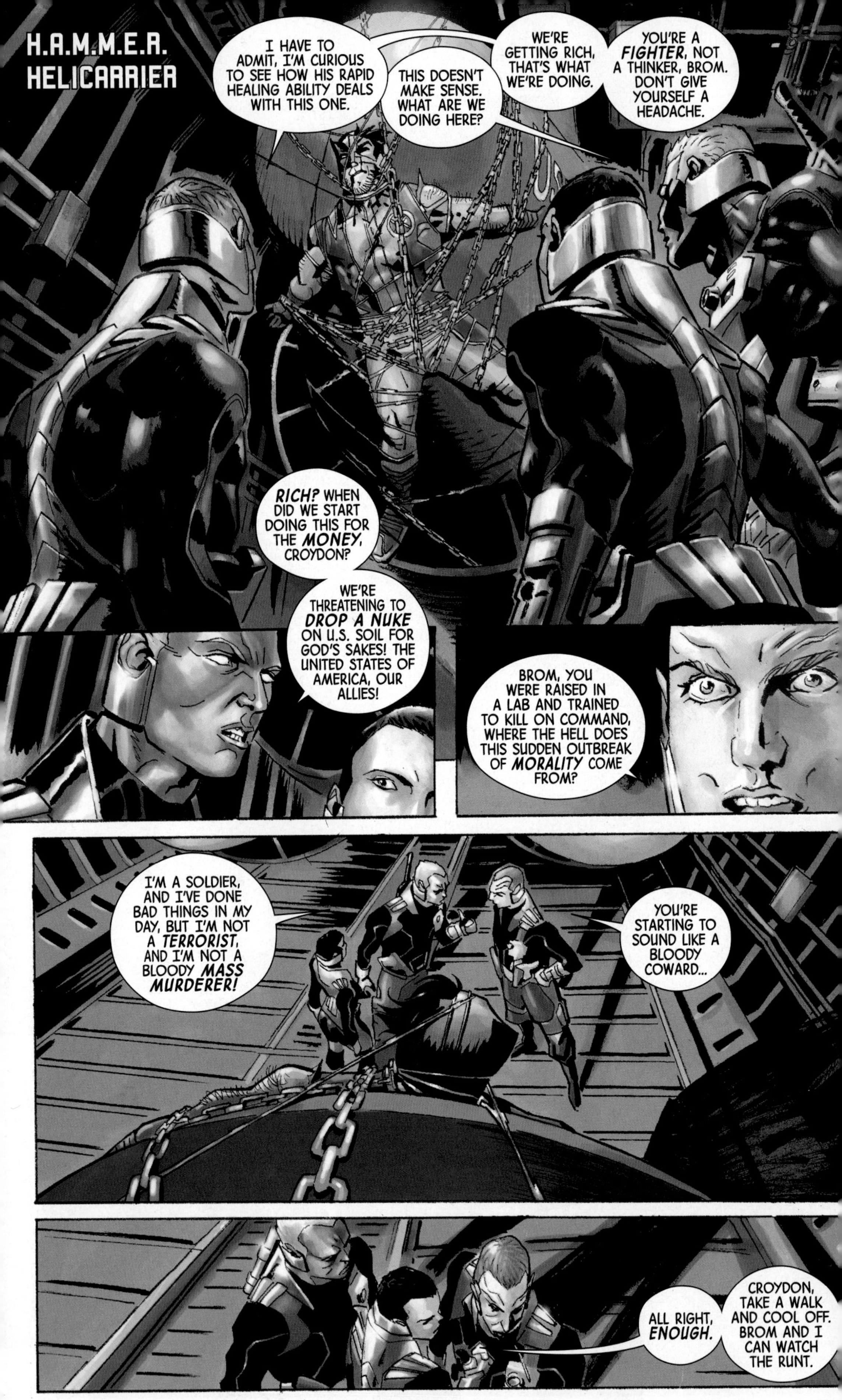
H.A.M.M.E.R. HELICARRIER
I HAVE TO ADMIT, I'M CURIOUS TO SEE HOW HIS RAPID HEALING ABILITY DEALS WITH THIS ONE.
THIS DOESN'T MAKE SENSE. WHAT ARE WE DOING HERE?
WE'RE GETTING RICH, THAT'S WHAT WE'RE DOING.
YOU'RE A FIGHTER, NOT A THINKER, BROM. DON'T GIVE YOURSELF A HEADACHE.
RICH? WHEN DID WE START DOING THIS FOR THE MONEY, CROYDON?
WE'RE THREATENING TO DROP A NUKE ON U.S. SOIL FOR GOD'S SAKES! THE UNITED STATES OF AMERICA, OUR ALLIES!
BROM, YOU WERE RAISED IN A LAB AND TRAINED TO KILL ON COMMAND, WHERE THE HELL DOES THIS SUDDEN OUTBREAK OF MORALITY COME FROM?
I'M A SOLDIER, AND I'VE DONE BAD THINGS IN MY DAY, BUT I'M NOT A TERRORIST, AND I'M NOT A BLOODY MASS MURDERER!
YOU'RE STARTING TO SOUND LIKE A BLOODY COWARD...
ALL RIGHT, ENOUGH.
CROYDON, TAKE A WALK AND COOL OFF. BROM AND I CAN WATCH THE RUNT.

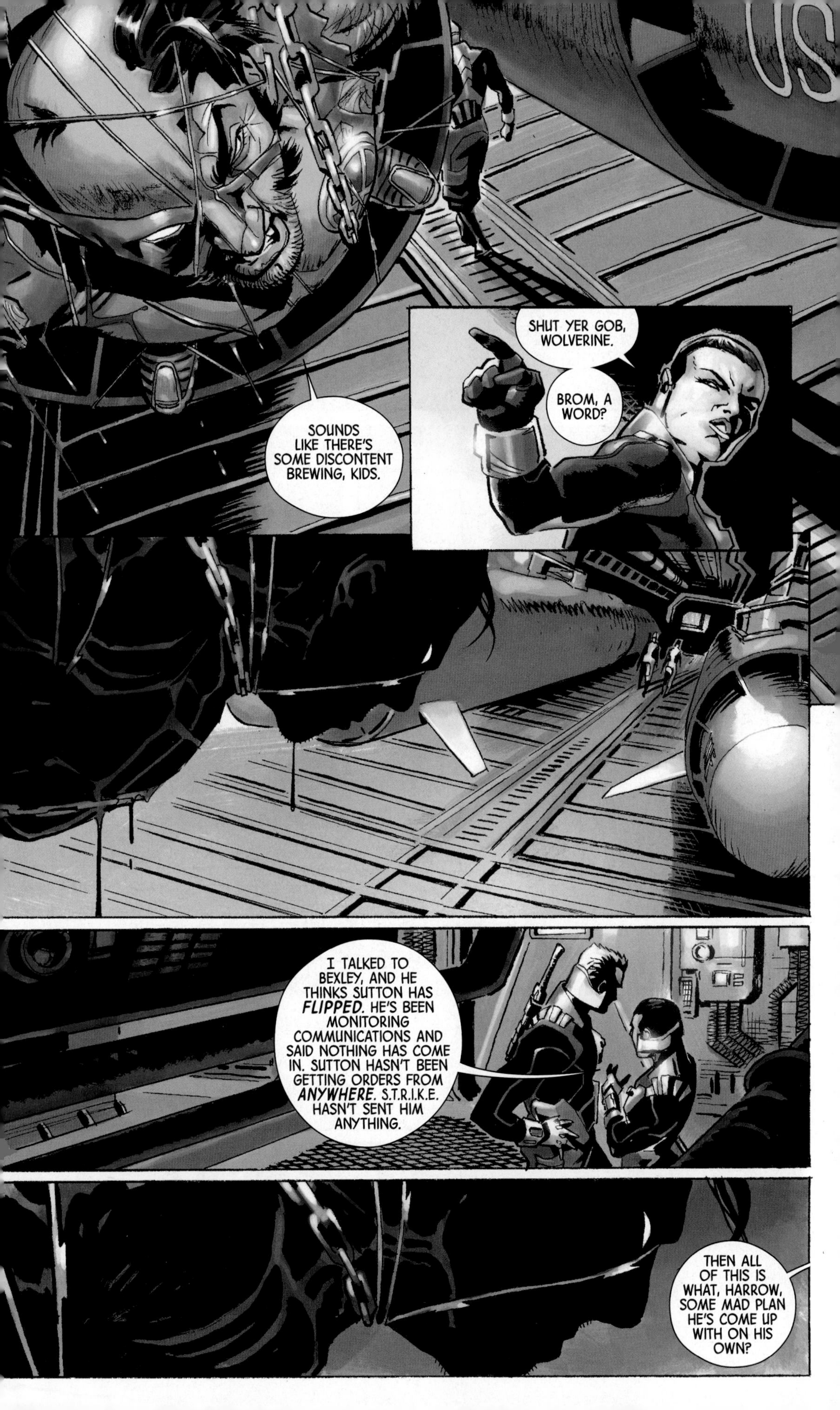
SOUNDS LIKE THERE'S SOME DISCONTENT BREWING, KIDS.
SHUT YER GOB, WOLVERINE.
BROM, A WORD?
I TALKED TO BEXLEY, AND HE THINKS SUTTON HAS *FLIPPED*. HE'S BEEN MONITORING COMMUNICATIONS AND SAID NOTHING HAS COME IN. SUTTON HASN'T BEEN GETTING ORDERS FROM *ANYWHERE*. S.T.R.I.K.E. HASN'T SENT HIM ANYTHING.
THEN ALL OF THIS IS WHAT, HARROW, SOME MAD PLAN HE'S COME UP WITH ON HIS OWN?

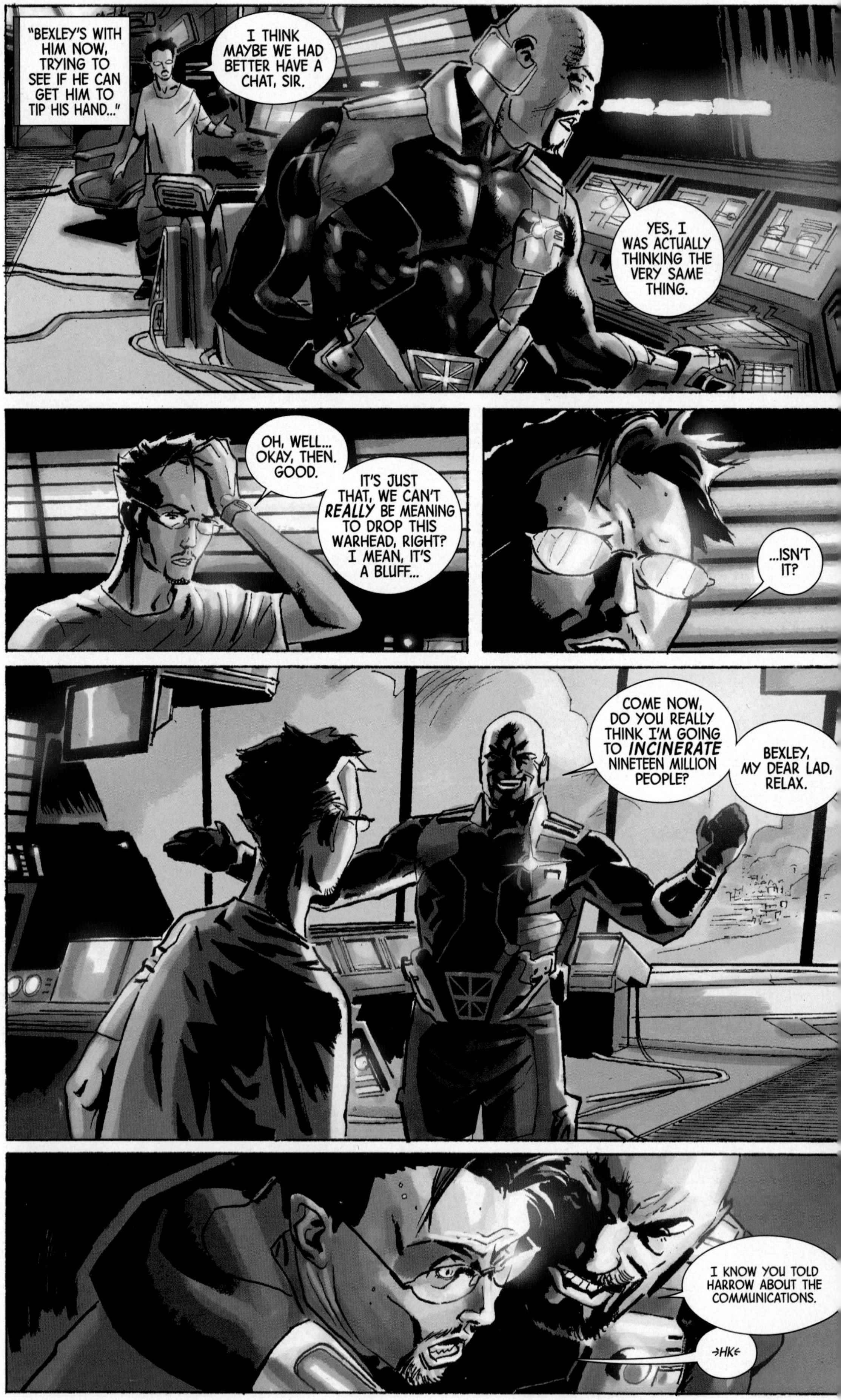
"BEXLEY'S WITH HIM NOW, TRYING TO SEE IF HE CAN GET HIM TO TIP HIS HAND..."
I THINK MAYBE WE HAD BETTER HAVE A CHAT, SIR.
YES, I WAS ACTUALLY THINKING THE VERY SAME THING.
OH, WELL... OKAY, THEN. GOOD.
IT'S JUST THAT, WE CAN'T REALLY BE MEANING TO DROP THIS WARHEAD, RIGHT? I MEAN, IT'S A BLUFF...
...ISN'T IT?
COME NOW, DO YOU REALLY THINK I'M GOING TO INCINERATE NINETEEN MILLION PEOPLE?
BEXLEY, MY DEAR LAD, RELAX.
I KNOW YOU TOLD HARROW ABOUT THE COMMUNICATIONS.
HK

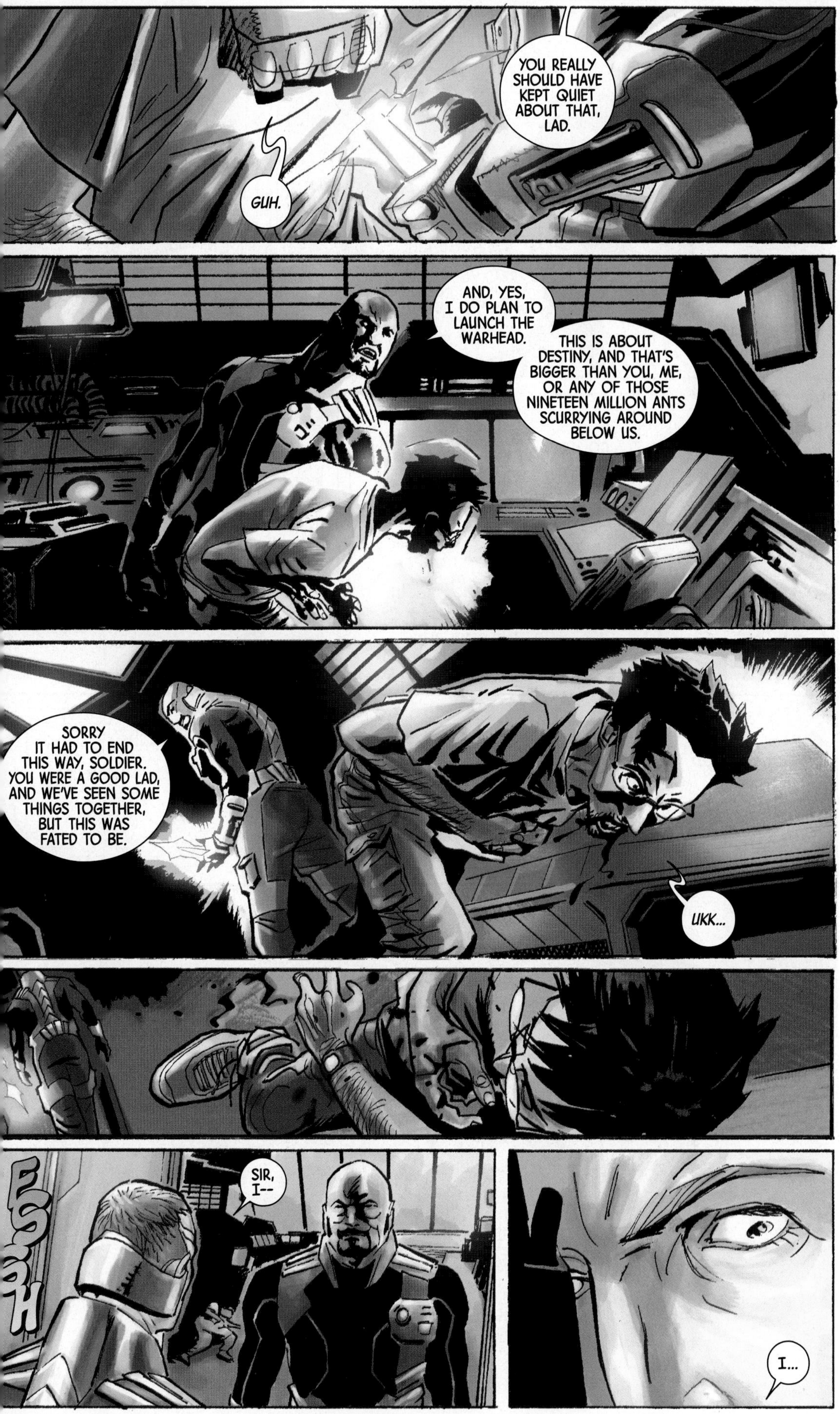
YOU REALLY SHOULD HAVE KEPT QUIET ABOUT THAT, LAD.
GUH.
AND, YES, I DO PLAN TO LAUNCH THE WARHEAD.
THIS IS ABOUT DESTINY, AND THAT'S BIGGER THAN YOU, ME, OR ANY OF THOSE NINETEEN MILLION ANTS SCURRYING AROUND BELOW US.
SORRY IT HAD TO END THIS WAY, SOLDIER. YOU WERE A GOOD LAD, AND WE'VE SEEN SOME THINGS TOGETHER, BUT THIS WAS FATED TO BE.
UKK...
SIR, I--
I...

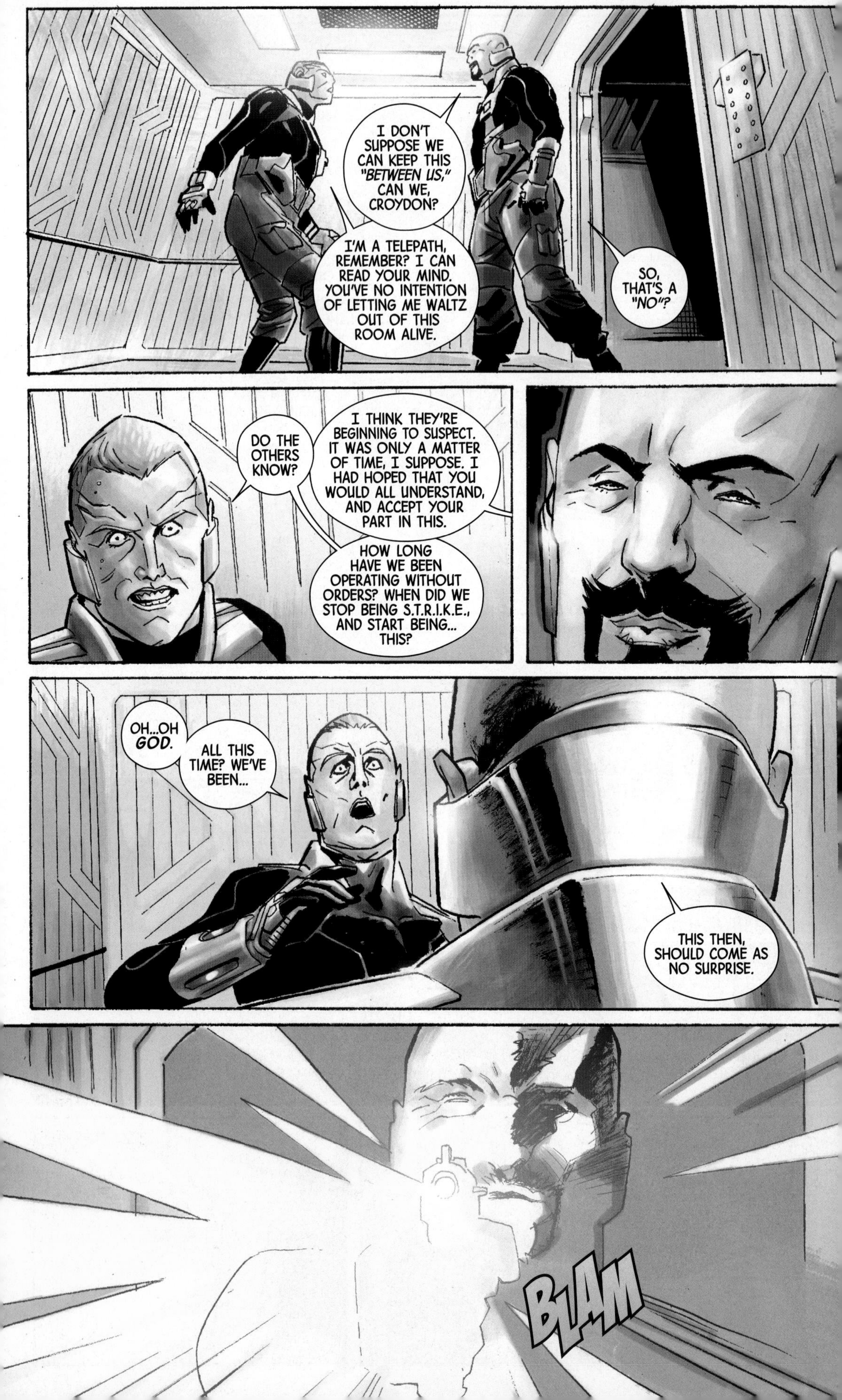
I DON'T SUPPOSE WE CAN KEEP THIS "BETWEEN US," CAN WE, CROYDON?
I'M A TELEPATH, REMEMBER? I CAN READ YOUR MIND. YOU'VE NO INTENTION OF LETTING ME WALTZ OUT OF THIS ROOM ALIVE.
SO, THAT'S A "NO"?
DO THE OTHERS KNOW?
I THINK THEY'RE BEGINNING TO SUSPECT. IT WAS ONLY A MATTER OF TIME, I SUPPOSE. I HAD HOPED THAT YOU WOULD ALL UNDERSTAND, AND ACCEPT YOUR PART IN THIS.
HOW LONG HAVE WE BEEN OPERATING WITHOUT ORDERS? WHEN DID WE STOP BEING S.T.R.I.K.E., AND START BEING... THIS?
OH...OH GOD.
ALL THIS TIME? WE'VE BEEN...
THIS THEN, SHOULD COME AS NO SURPRISE.
BLAM

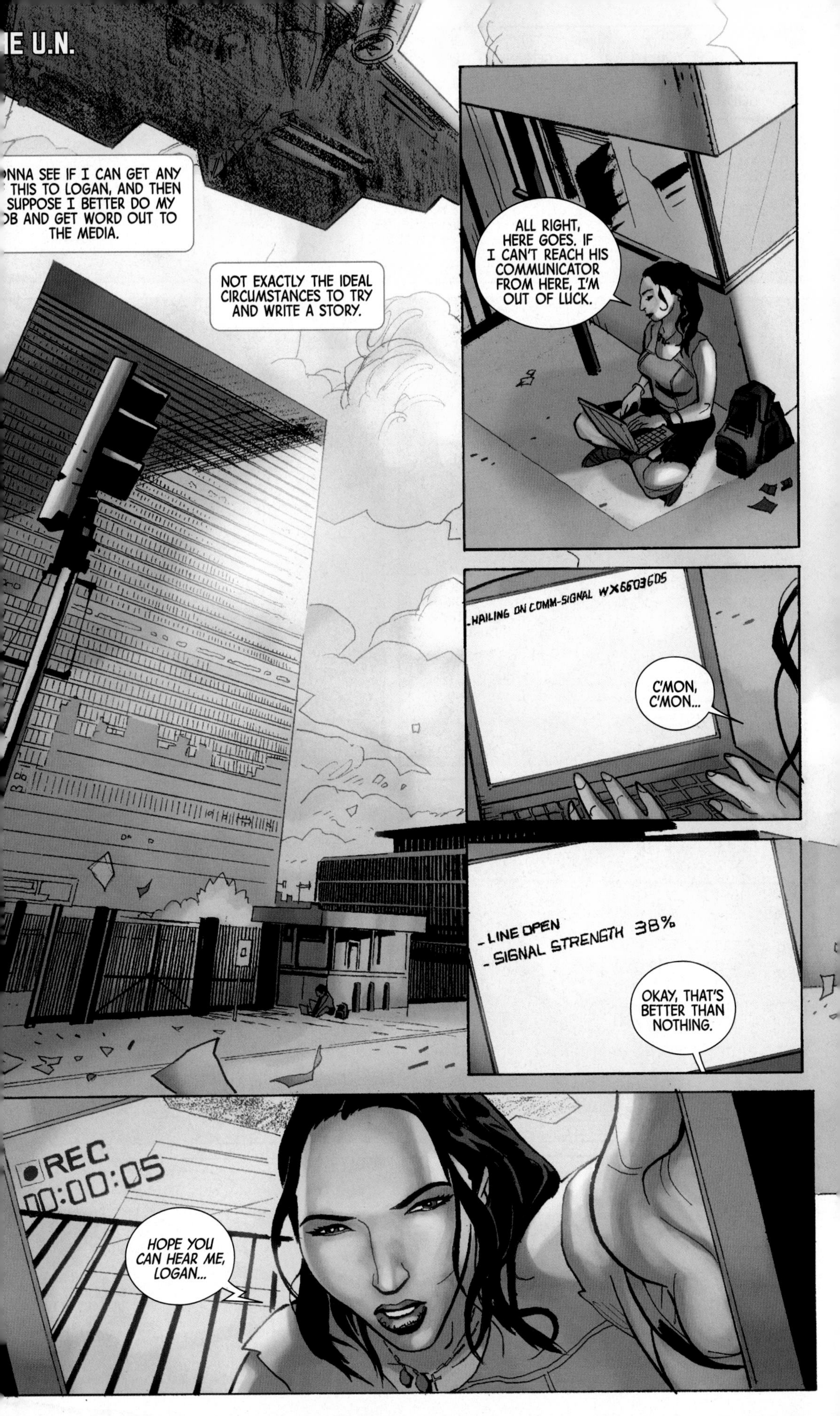
E U.N.
ONNA SEE IF I CAN GET ANY THIS TO LOGAN, AND THEN SUPPOSE I BETTER DO MY OB AND GET WORD OUT TO THE MEDIA.
NOT EXACTLY THE IDEAL CIRCUMSTANCES TO TRY AND WRITE A STORY.
ALL RIGHT, HERE GOES. IF I CAN'T REACH HIS COMMUNICATOR FROM HERE, I'M OUT OF LUCK.
_HAILING ON COMM-SIGNAL WX6603605
C'MON, C'MON...
- LINE OPEN
- SIGNAL STRENGTH 38%
OKAY, THAT'S BETTER THAN NOTHING.
REC
00:00:05
HOPE YOU CAN HEAR ME, LOGAN...

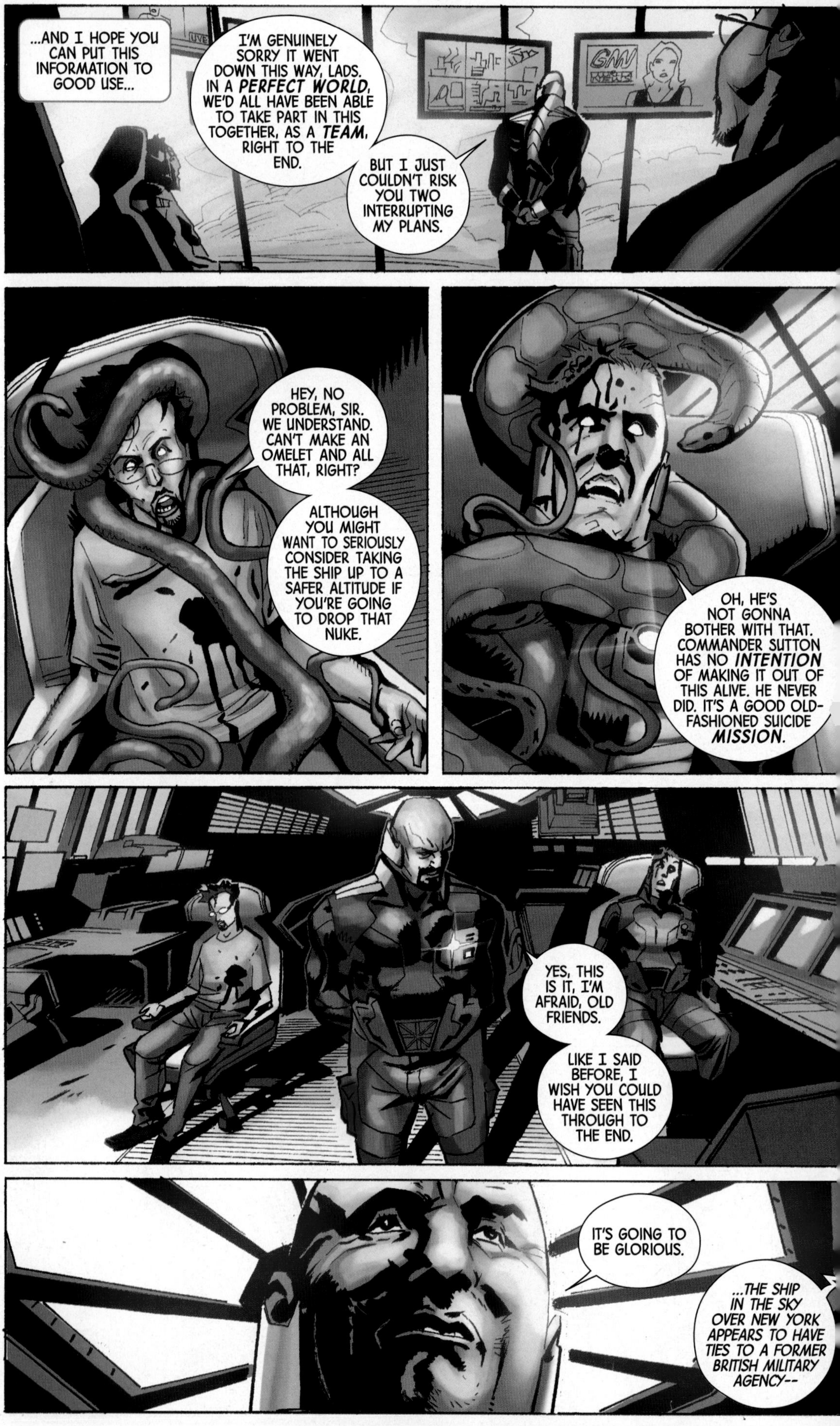

...AND I HOPE YOU CAN PUT THIS INFORMATION TO GOOD USE...
I'M GENUINELY SORRY IT WENT DOWN THIS WAY, LADS. IN A PERFECT WORLD, WE'D ALL HAVE BEEN ABLE TO TAKE PART IN THIS TOGETHER, AS A TEAM, RIGHT TO THE END.
BUT I JUST COULDN'T RISK YOU TWO INTERRUPTING MY PLANS.
HEY, NO PROBLEM, SIR. WE UNDERSTAND. CAN'T MAKE AN OMELET AND ALL THAT, RIGHT?
ALTHOUGH YOU MIGHT WANT TO SERIOUSLY CONSIDER TAKING THE SHIP UP TO A SAFER ALTITUDE IF YOU'RE GOING TO DROP THAT NUKE.
OH, HE'S NOT GONNA BOTHER WITH THAT. COMMANDER SUTTON HAS NO INTENTION OF MAKING IT OUT OF THIS ALIVE. HE NEVER DID. IT'S A GOOD OLD-FASHIONED SUICIDE MISSION.
YES, THIS IS IT, I'M AFRAID, OLD FRIENDS.
LIKE I SAID BEFORE, I WISH YOU COULD HAVE SEEN THIS THROUGH TO THE END.
IT'S GOING TO BE GLORIOUS.
...THE SHIP IN THE SKY OVER NEW YORK APPEARS TO HAVE TIES TO A FORMER BRITISH MILITARY AGENCY--

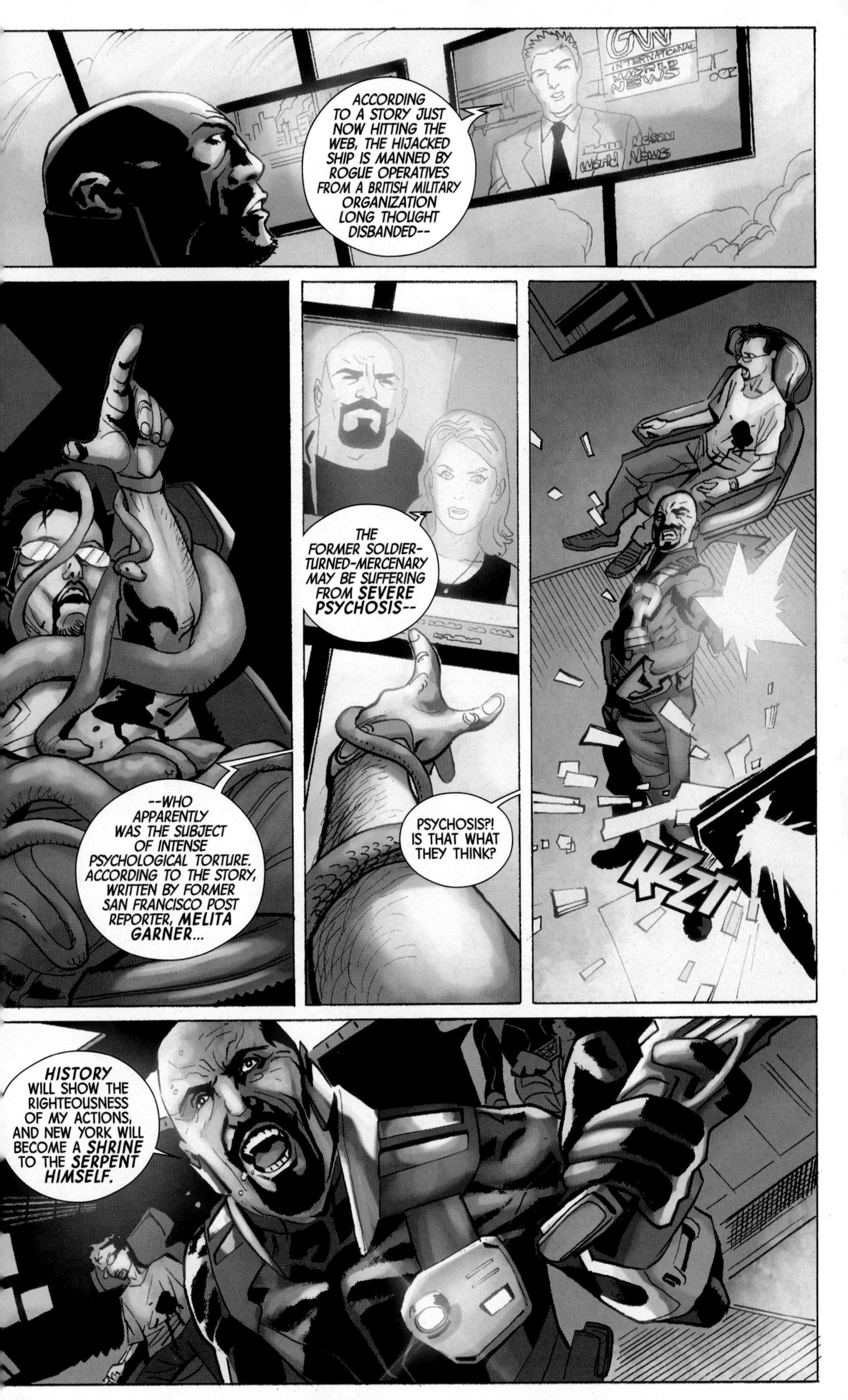

GNN INTERNATIONAL WORLD NEWS
ACCORDING TO A STORY JUST NOW HITTING THE WEB, THE HIJACKED SHIP IS MANNED BY ROGUE OPERATIVES FROM A BRITISH MILITARY ORGANIZATION LONG THOUGHT DISBANDED--
THE FORMER SOLDIER-TURNED-MERCENARY MAY BE SUFFERING FROM SEVERE PSYCHOSIS--
--WHO APPARENTLY WAS THE SUBJECT OF INTENSE PSYCHOLOGICAL TORTURE. ACCORDING TO THE STORY, WRITTEN BY FORMER SAN FRANCISCO POST REPORTER, MELITA GARNER...
PSYCHOSIS?! IS THAT WHAT THEY THINK?
KZZT
HISTORY WILL SHOW THE RIGHTEOUSNESS OF MY ACTIONS, AND NEW YORK WILL BECOME A SHRINE TO THE SERPENT HIMSELF.

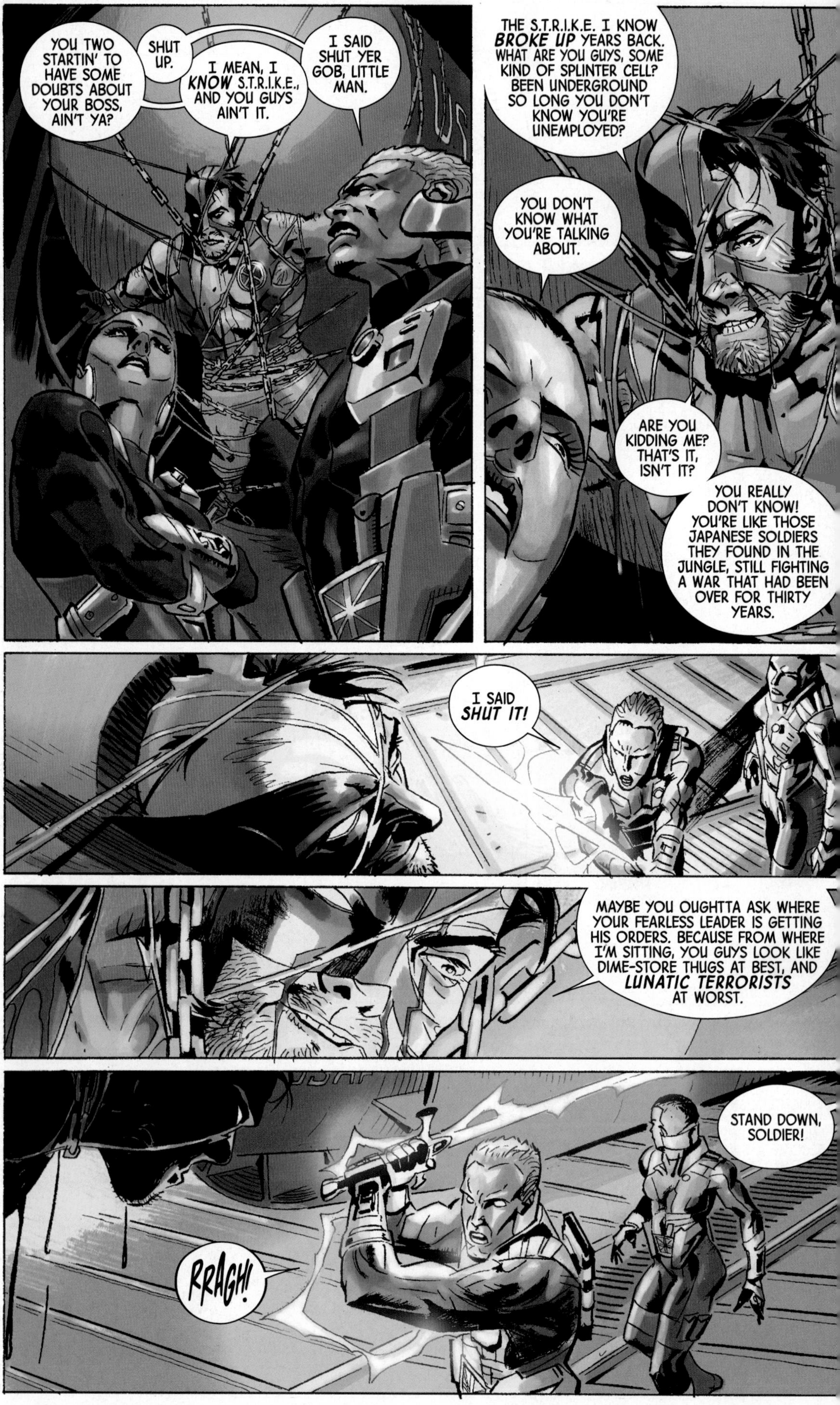

YOU TWO STARTIN' TO HAVE SOME DOUBTS ABOUT YOUR BOSS, AIN'T YA?
SHUT UP.
I MEAN, I KNOW S.T.R.I.K.E., AND YOU GUYS AIN'T IT.
I SAID SHUT YER GOB, LITTLE MAN.
THE S.T.R.I.K.E. I KNOW BROKE UP YEARS BACK. WHAT ARE YOU GUYS, SOME KIND OF SPLINTER CELL? BEEN UNDERGROUND SO LONG YOU DON'T KNOW YOU'RE UNEMPLOYED?
YOU DON'T KNOW WHAT YOU'RE TALKING ABOUT.
ARE YOU KIDDING ME? THAT'S IT, ISN'T IT?
YOU REALLY DON'T KNOW! YOU'RE LIKE THOSE JAPANESE SOLDIERS THEY FOUND IN THE JUNGLE, STILL FIGHTING A WAR THAT HAD BEEN OVER FOR THIRTY YEARS.
I SAID SHUT IT!
MAYBE YOU OUGHTTA ASK WHERE YOUR FEARLESS LEADER IS GETTING HIS ORDERS. BECAUSE FROM WHERE I'M SITTING, YOU GUYS LOOK LIKE DIME-STORE THUGS AT BEST, AND LUNATIC TERRORISTS AT WORST.
STAND DOWN, SOLDIER!
RRAGH!

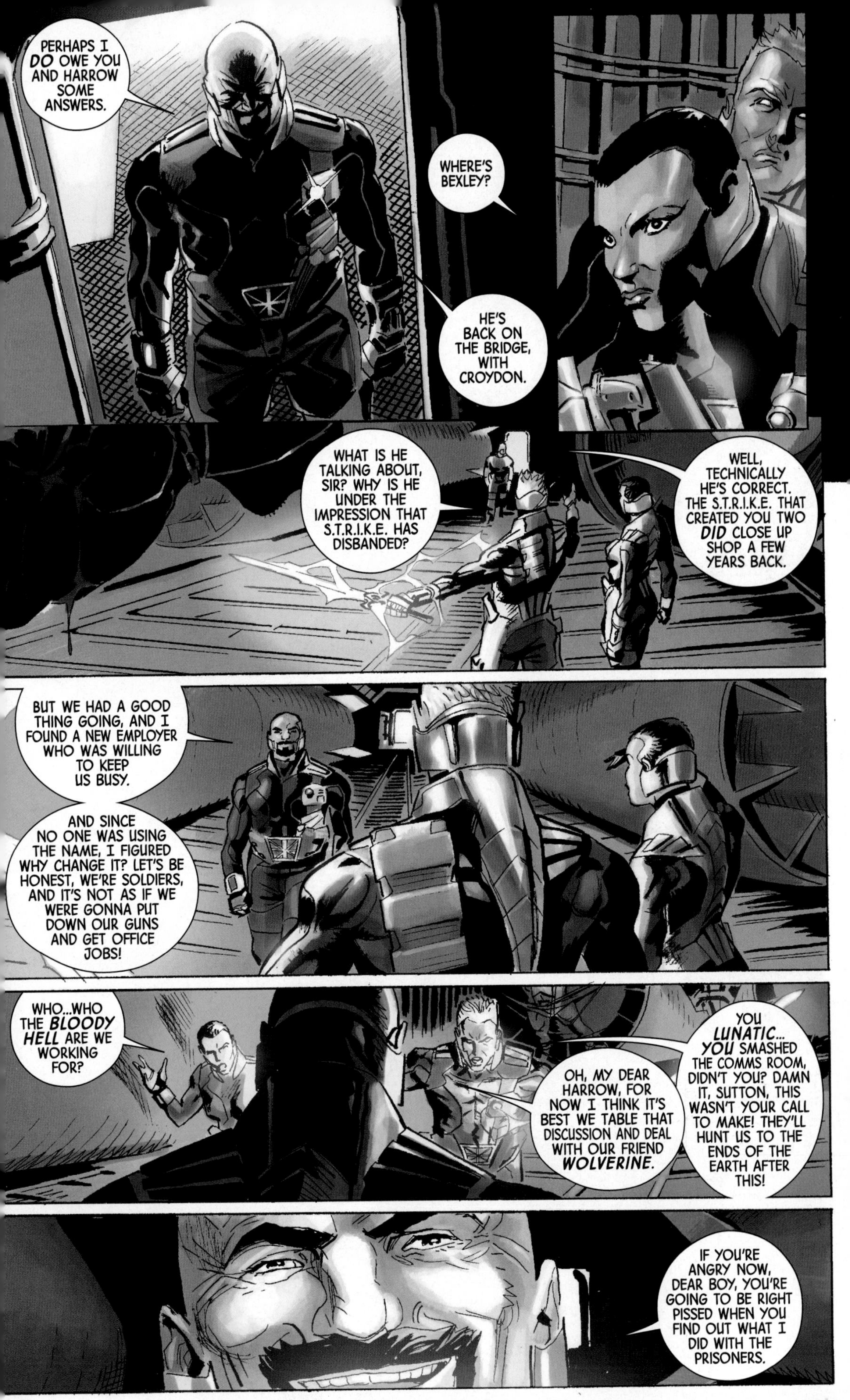
PERHAPS I DO OWE YOU AND HARROW SOME ANSWERS.
WHERE'S BEXLEY?
HE'S BACK ON THE BRIDGE, WITH CROYDON.
WHAT IS HE TALKING ABOUT, SIR? WHY IS HE UNDER THE IMPRESSION THAT S.T.R.I.K.E. HAS DISBANDED?
WELL, TECHNICALLY HE'S CORRECT. THE S.T.R.I.K.E. THAT CREATED YOU TWO DID CLOSE UP SHOP A FEW YEARS BACK.
BUT WE HAD A GOOD THING GOING, AND I FOUND A NEW EMPLOYER WHO WAS WILLING TO KEEP US BUSY.
AND SINCE NO ONE WAS USING THE NAME, I FIGURED WHY CHANGE IT? LET'S BE HONEST, WE'RE SOLDIERS, AND IT'S NOT AS IF WE WERE GONNA PUT DOWN OUR GUNS AND GET OFFICE JOBS!
WHO...WHO THE BLOODY HELL ARE WE WORKING FOR?
OH, MY DEAR HARROW, FOR NOW I THINK IT'S BEST WE TABLE THAT DISCUSSION AND DEAL WITH OUR FRIEND WOLVERINE.
YOU LUNATIC... YOU SMASHED THE COMMS ROOM, DIDN'T YOU? DAMN IT, SUTTON, THIS WASN'T YOUR CALL TO MAKE! THEY'LL HUNT US TO THE ENDS OF THE EARTH AFTER THIS!
IF YOU'RE ANGRY NOW, DEAR BOY, YOU'RE GOING TO BE RIGHT PISSED WHEN YOU FIND OUT WHAT I DID WITH THE PRISONERS.

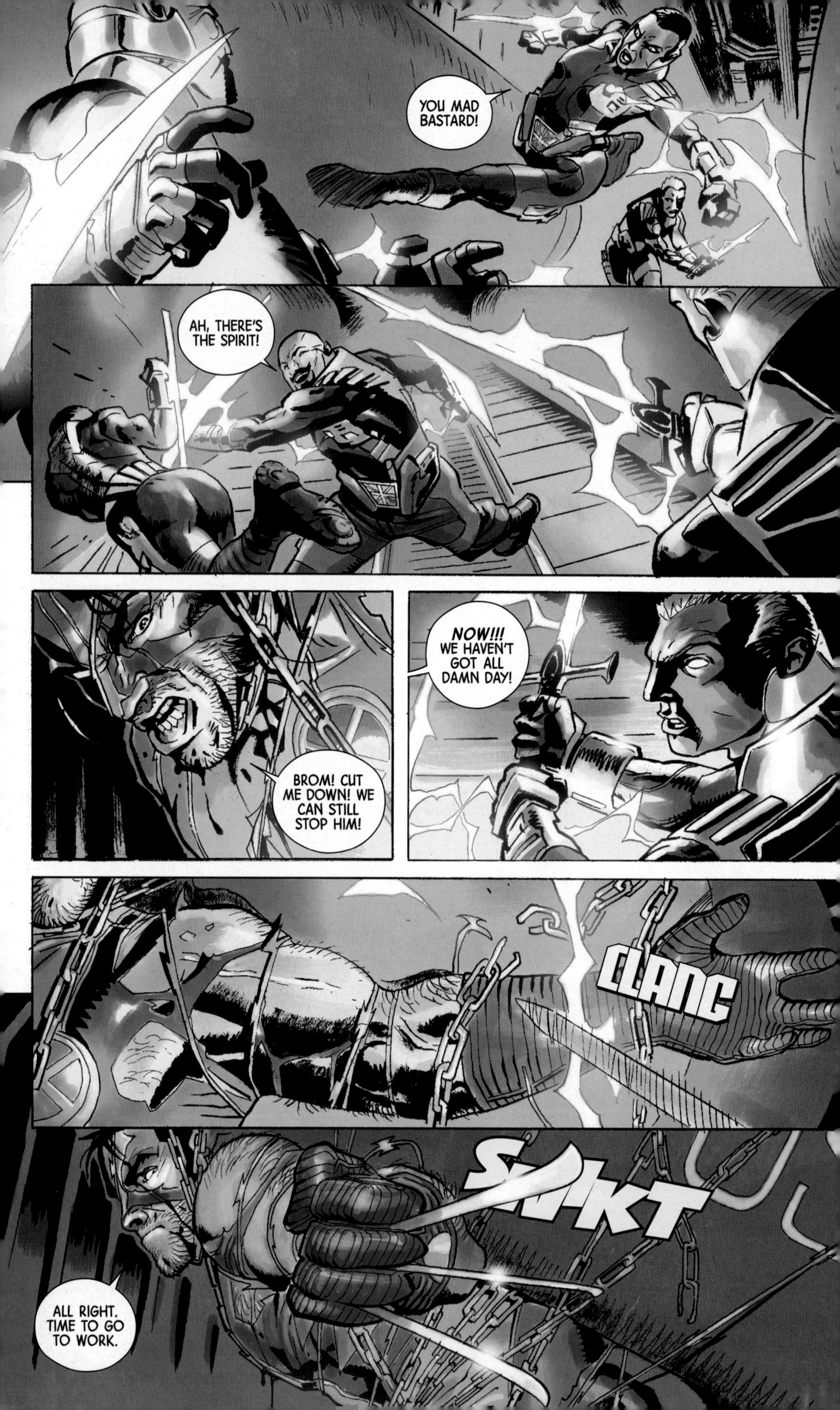
YOU MAD BASTARD!
AH, THERE'S THE SPIRIT!
BROM! CUT ME DOWN! WE CAN STILL STOP HIM!
NOW!!! WE HAVEN'T GOT ALL DAMN DAY!
CLANG
SNIKT
ALL RIGHT. TIME TO GO TO WORK.

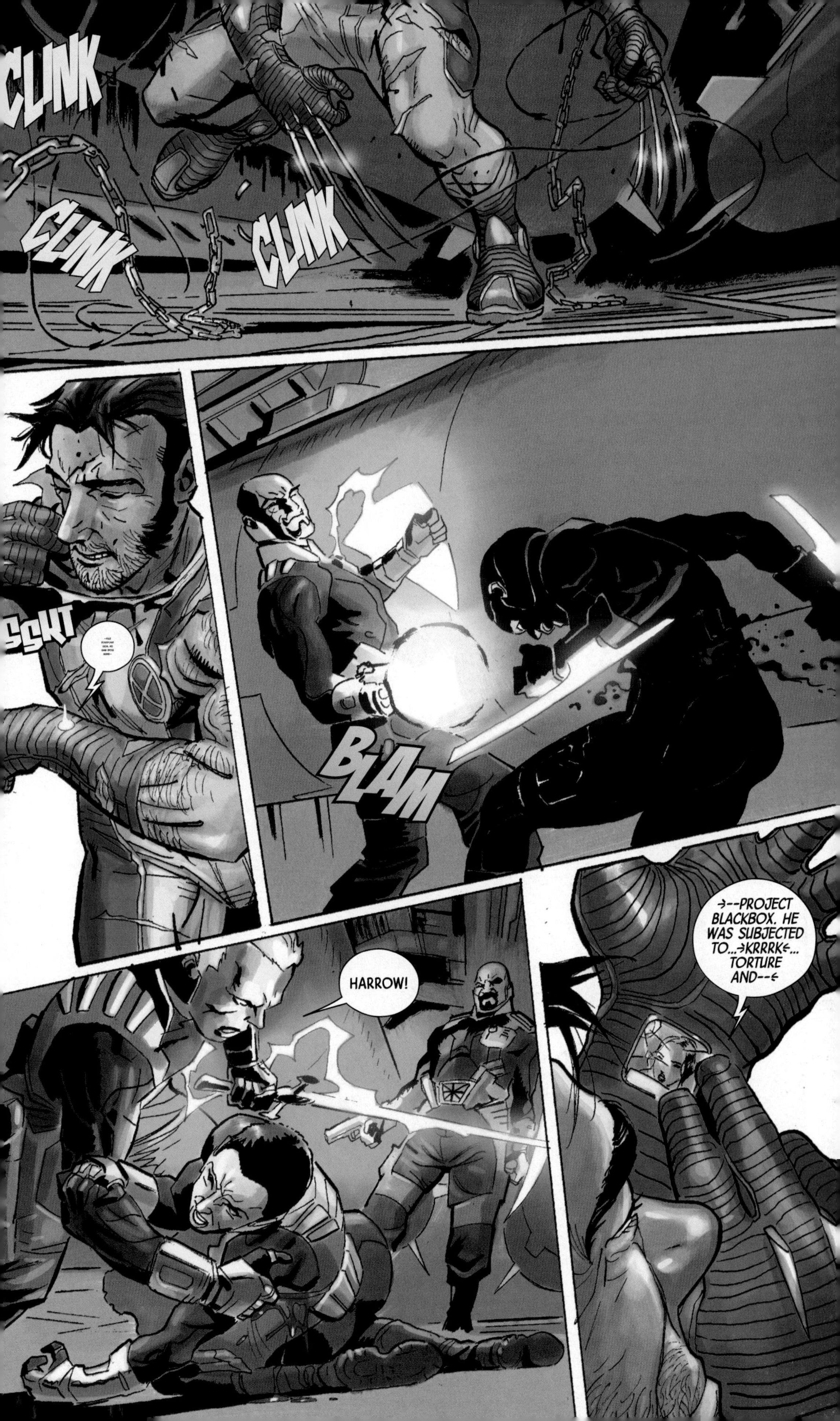
CLINK
CLINK
CLINK
SSKT
BLAM
HARROW!
→--PROJECT BLACKBOX. HE WAS SUBJECTED TO...→KRRRK←... TORTURE AND--←

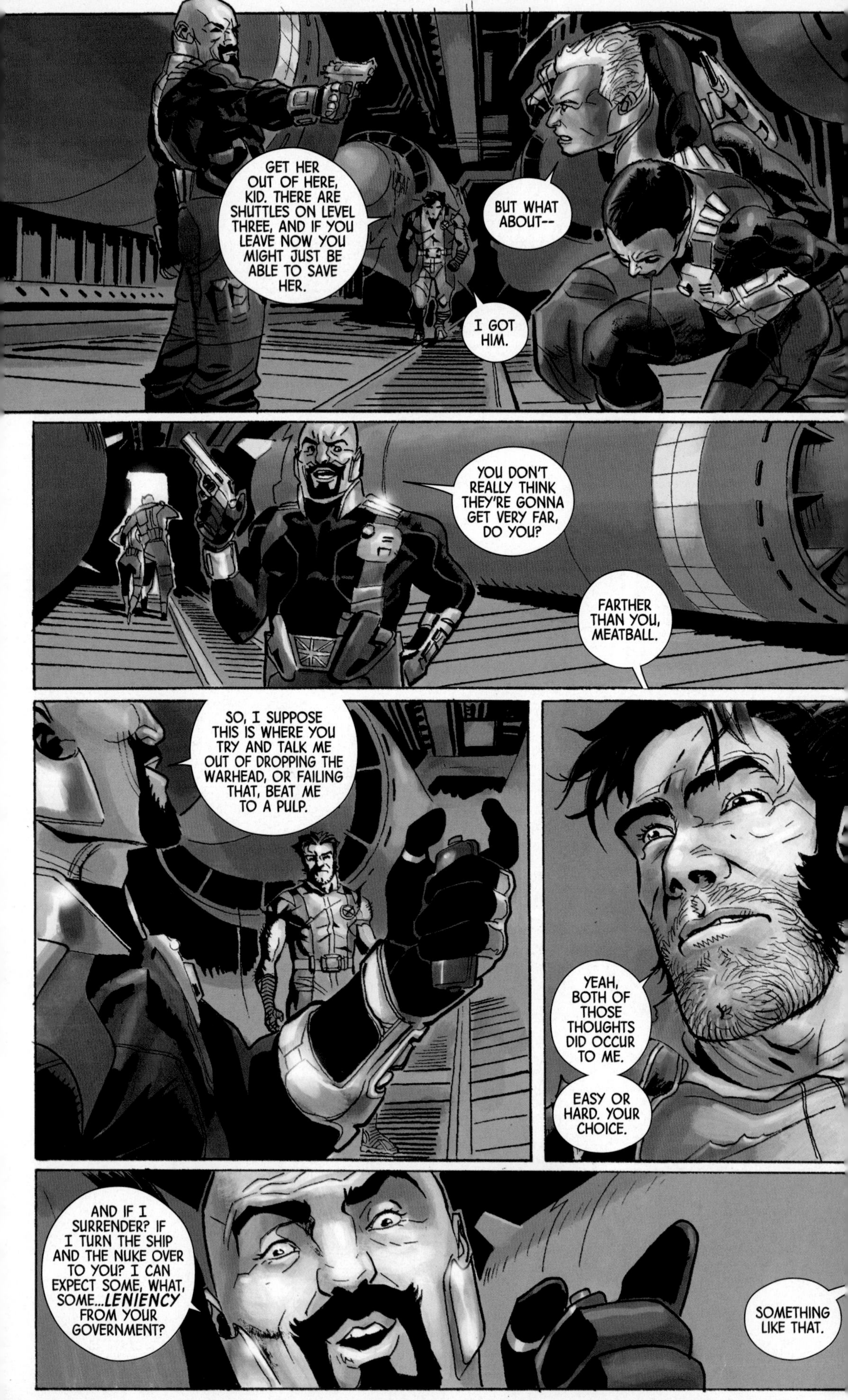
GET HER OUT OF HERE, KID. THERE ARE SHUTTLES ON LEVEL THREE, AND IF YOU LEAVE NOW YOU MIGHT JUST BE ABLE TO SAVE HER.
BUT WHAT ABOUT--
I GOT HIM.
YOU DON'T REALLY THINK THEY'RE GONNA GET VERY FAR, DO YOU?
FARTHER THAN YOU, MEATBALL.
SO, I SUPPOSE THIS IS WHERE YOU TRY AND TALK ME OUT OF DROPPING THE WARHEAD, OR FAILING THAT, BEAT ME TO A PULP.
YEAH, BOTH OF THOSE THOUGHTS DID OCCUR TO ME.
EASY OR HARD. YOUR CHOICE.
AND IF I SURRENDER? IF I TURN THE SHIP AND THE NUKE OVER TO YOU? I CAN EXPECT SOME, WHAT, SOME...*LENIENCY* FROM YOUR GOVERNMENT?
SOMETHING LIKE THAT.

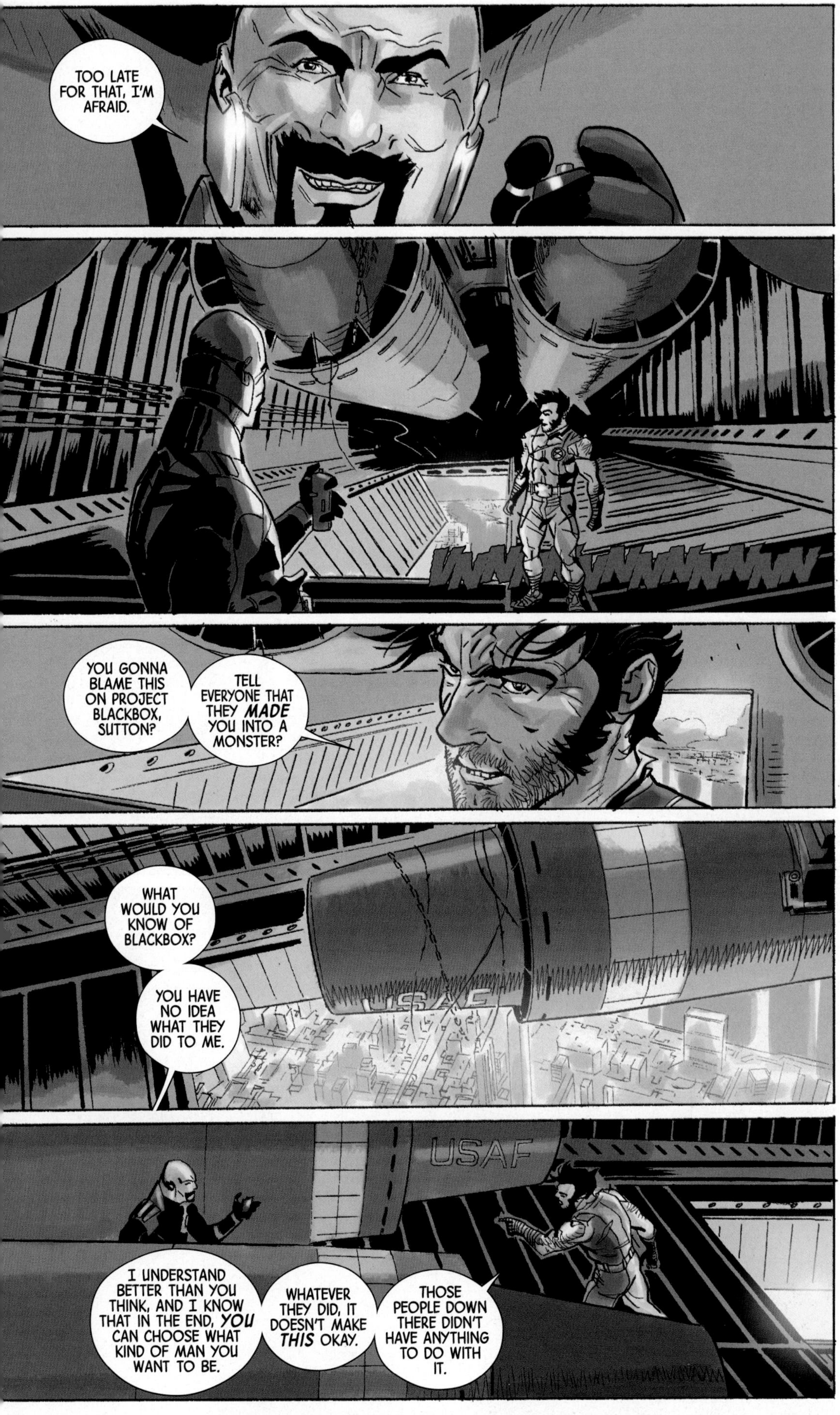

TOO LATE FOR THAT, I'M AFRAID.
VMMMMMMMMMMMMMN
YOU GONNA BLAME THIS ON PROJECT BLACKBOX, SUTTON?
TELL EVERYONE THAT THEY *MADE* YOU INTO A MONSTER?
WHAT WOULD YOU KNOW OF BLACKBOX?
YOU HAVE NO IDEA WHAT THEY DID TO ME.
USAF
I UNDERSTAND BETTER THAN YOU THINK, AND I KNOW THAT IN THE END, *YOU* CAN CHOOSE WHAT KIND OF MAN YOU WANT TO BE.
WHATEVER THEY DID, IT DOESN'T MAKE *THIS* OKAY.
THOSE PEOPLE DOWN THERE DIDN'T HAVE ANYTHING TO DO WITH IT.

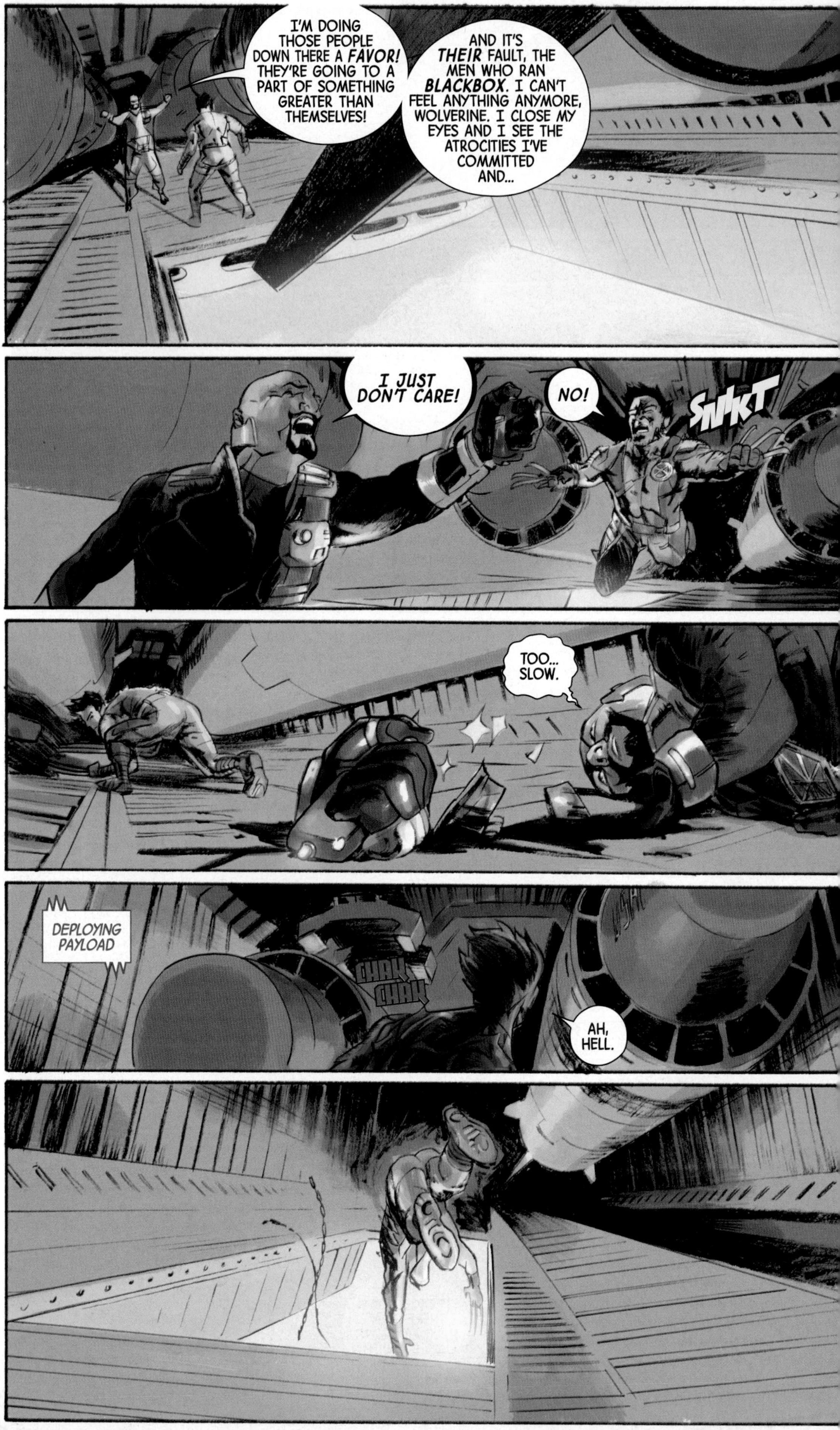

I'M DOING THOSE PEOPLE DOWN THERE A FAVOR! THEY'RE GOING TO A PART OF SOMETHING GREATER THAN THEMSELVES!
AND IT'S THEIR FAULT, THE MEN WHO RAN BLACKBOX. I CAN'T FEEL ANYTHING ANYMORE, WOLVERINE. I CLOSE MY EYES AND I SEE THE ATROCITIES I'VE COMMITTED AND...
I JUST DON'T CARE!
NO!
SNIKT
TOO... SLOW.
DEPLOYING PAYLOAD
CHAK CHAK
AH, HELL.

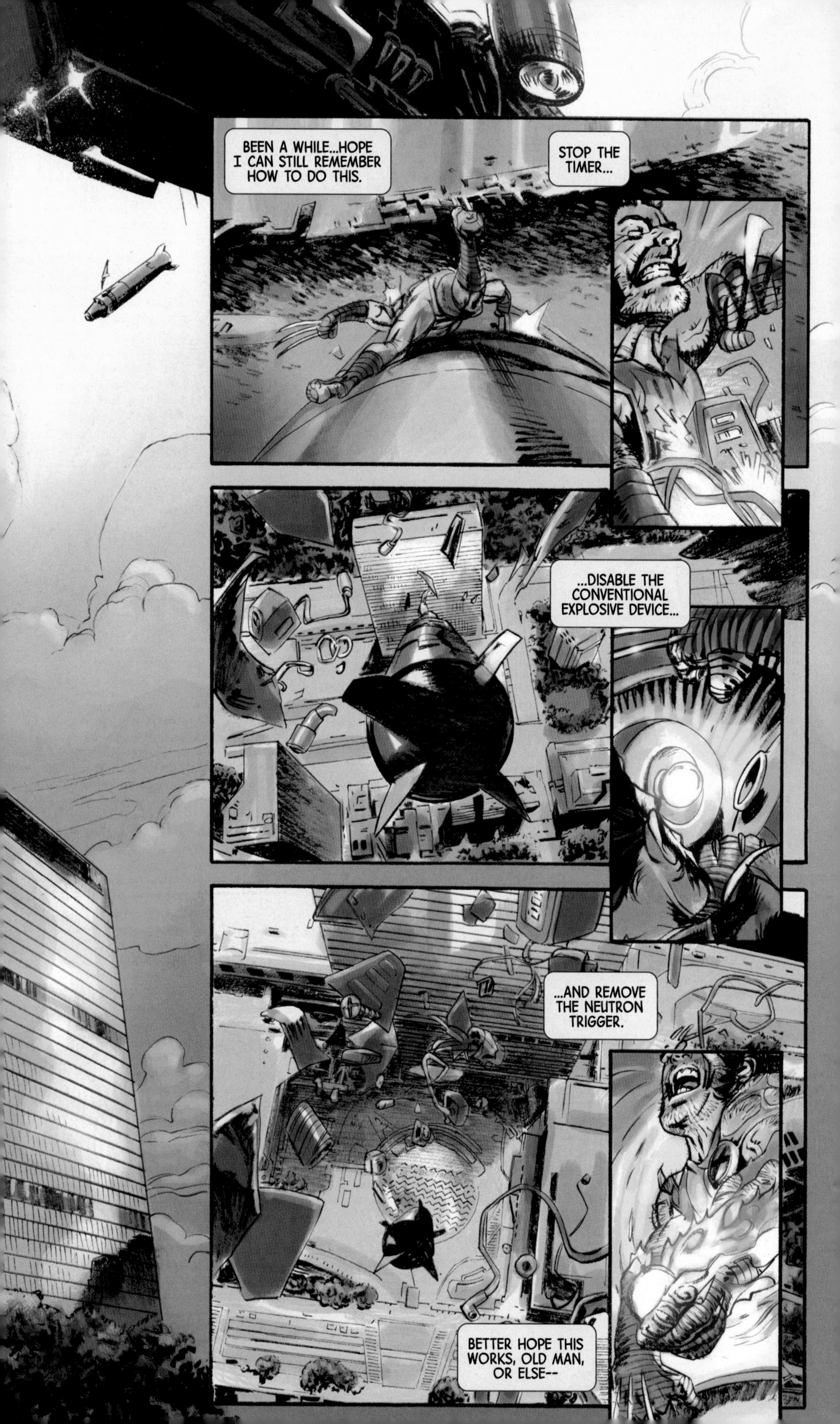
BEEN A WHILE...HOPE I CAN STILL REMEMBER HOW TO DO THIS.
STOP THE TIMER...
...DISABLE THE CONVENTIONAL EXPLOSIVE DEVICE...
...AND REMOVE THE NEUTRON TRIGGER.
BETTER HOPE THIS WORKS, OLD MAN, OR ELSE--

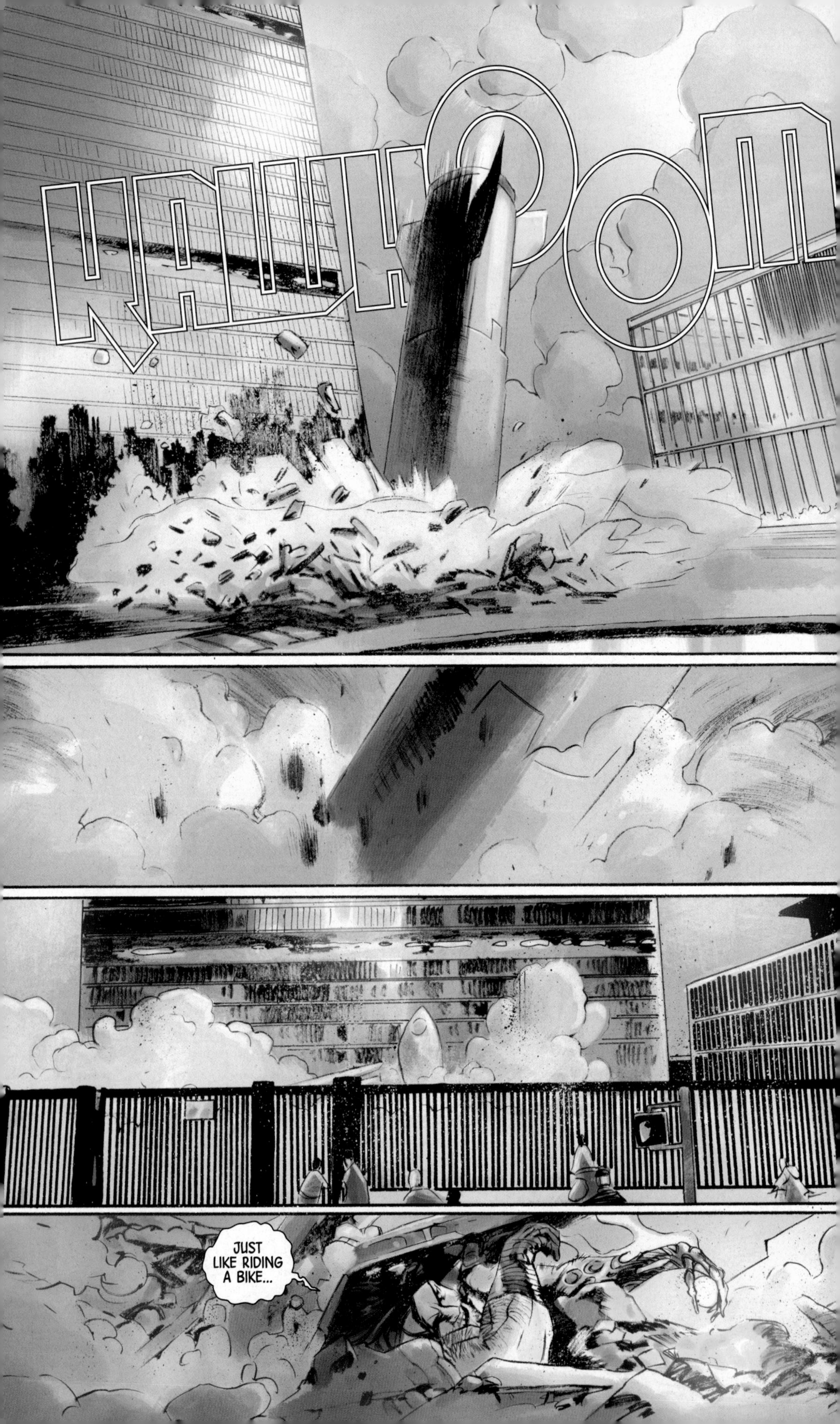
KRAKKOOM
JUST LIKE RIDING A BIKE...

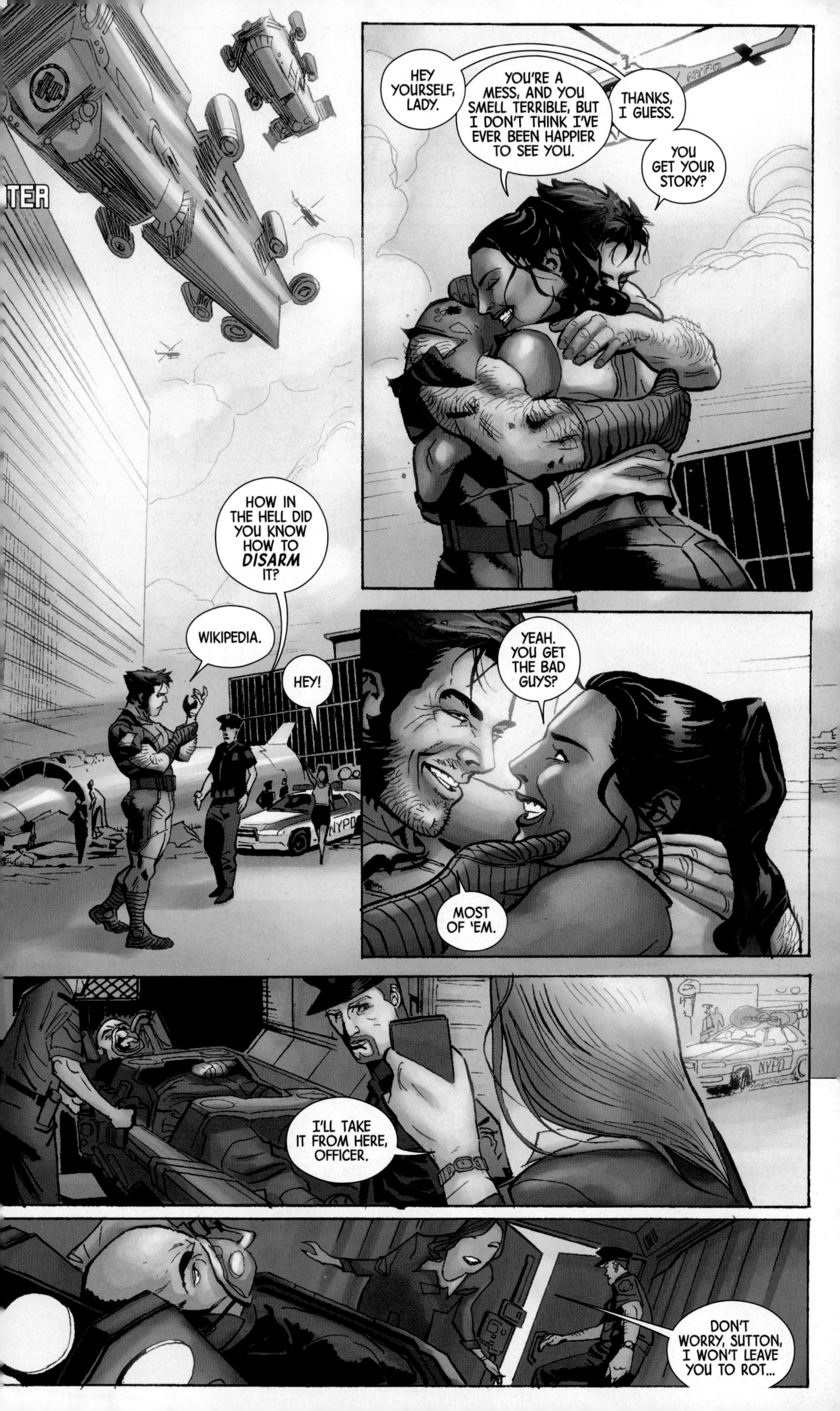
TER
HEY YOURSELF, LADY.
YOU'RE A MESS, AND YOU SMELL TERRIBLE, BUT I DON'T THINK I'VE EVER BEEN HAPPIER TO SEE YOU.
THANKS, I GUESS.
YOU GET YOUR STORY?
HOW IN THE HELL DID YOU KNOW HOW TO DISARM IT?
WIKIPEDIA.
HEY!
YEAH. YOU GET THE BAD GUYS?
MOST OF 'EM.
NYPD
I'LL TAKE IT FROM HERE, OFFICER.
DON'T WORRY, SUTTON, I WON'T LEAVE YOU TO ROT...

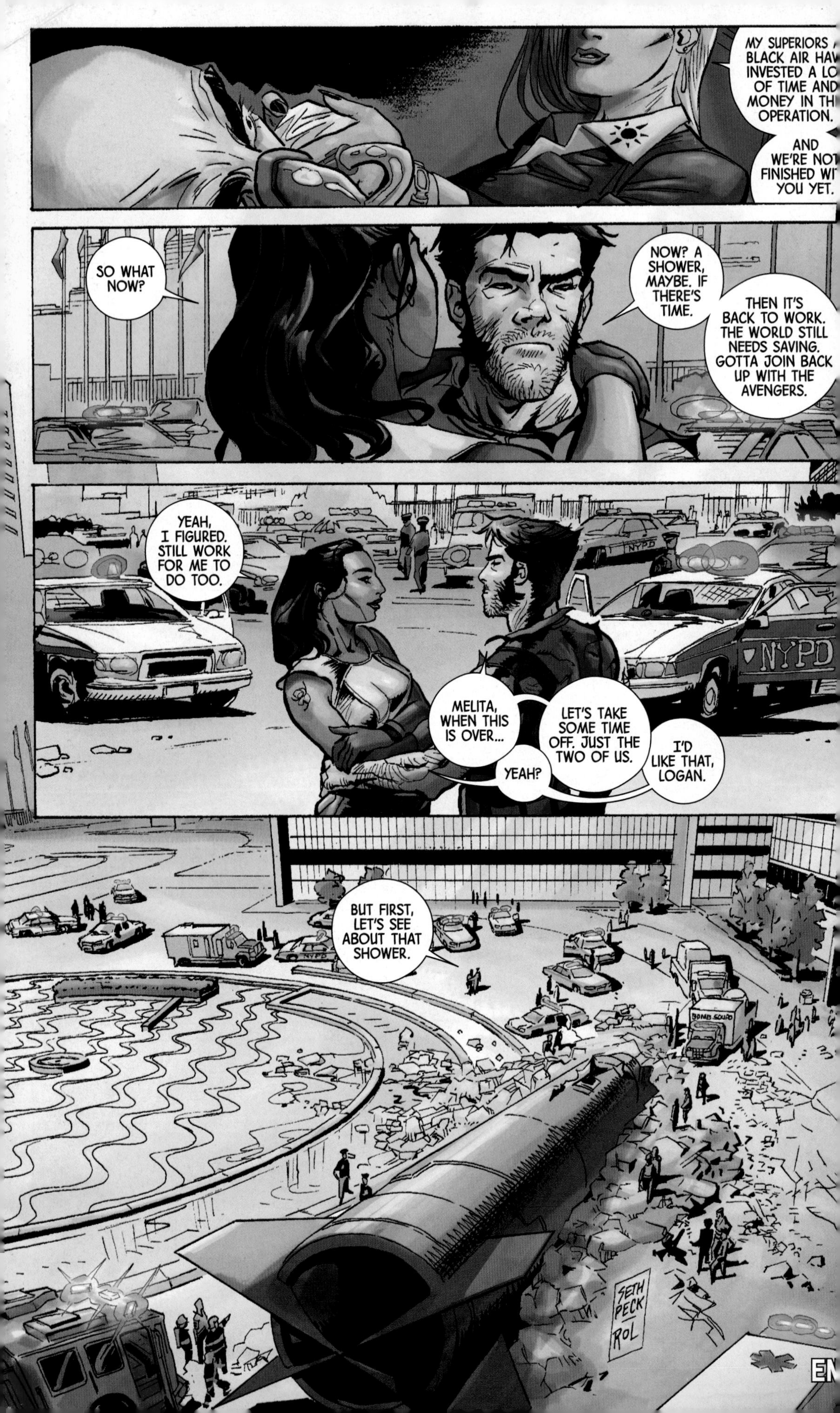
MY SUPERIORS AT BLACK AIR HAVE INVESTED A LOT OF TIME AND MONEY IN THIS OPERATION.
AND WE'RE NOT FINISHED WITH YOU YET.
SO WHAT NOW?
NOW? A SHOWER, MAYBE. IF THERE'S TIME.
THEN IT'S BACK TO WORK. THE WORLD STILL NEEDS SAVING. GOTTA JOIN BACK UP WITH THE AVENGERS.
YEAH, I FIGURED. STILL WORK FOR ME TO DO TOO.
NYPD
MELITA, WHEN THIS IS OVER...
YEAH?
LET'S TAKE SOME TIME OFF. JUST THE TWO OF US.
I'D LIKE THAT, LOGAN.
BUT FIRST, LET'S SEE ABOUT THAT SHOWER.
BOMB SQUAD
SETH PECK
ROL
END

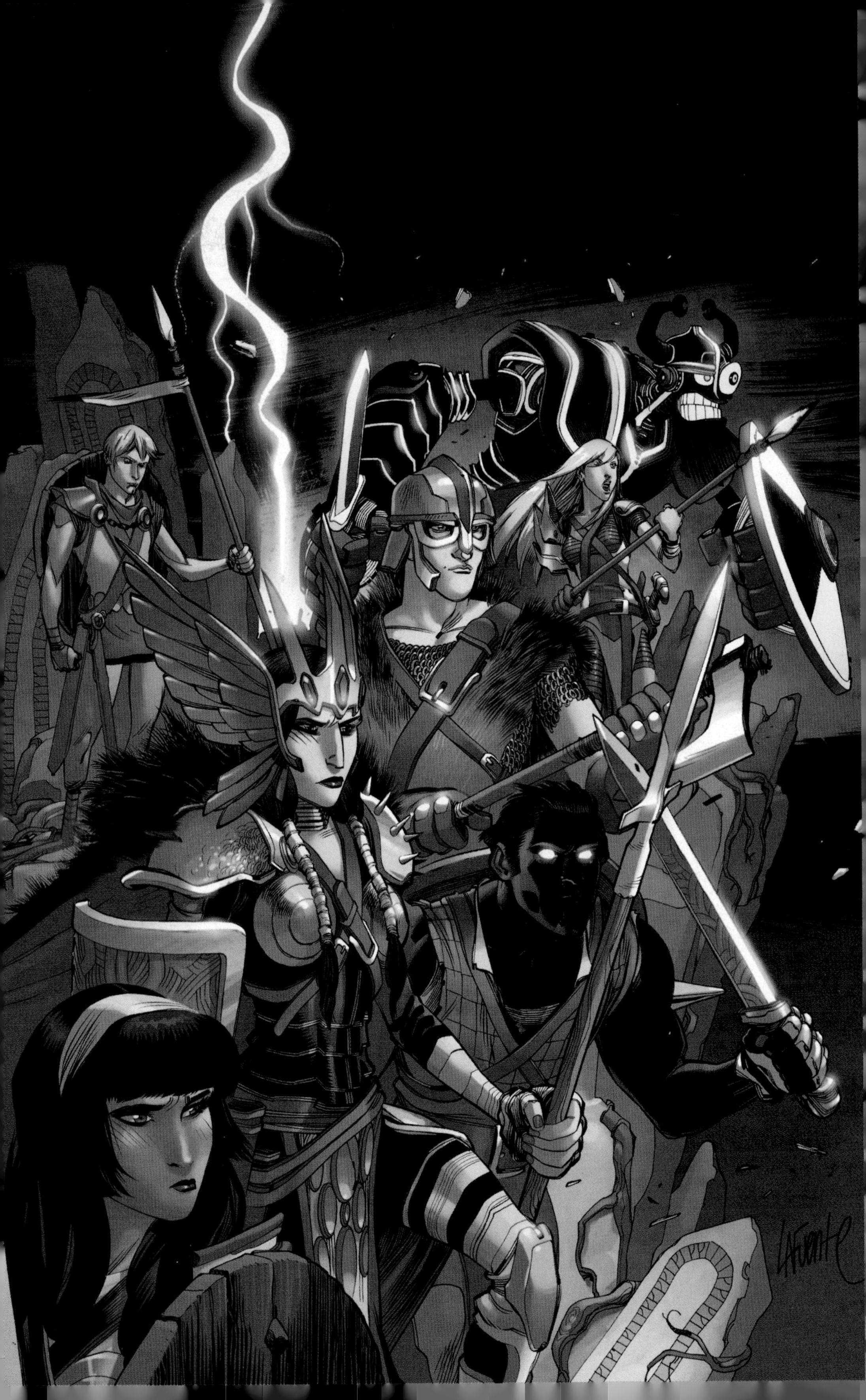

FEAR ITSELF

NEW MUTANTS

The world is in its death throes. The Asgardian God of Fear, the Serpent, has been unleashed and now chaos and panic are ripping the planet apart. The Serpent has bestowed seven hammers to the Worthy, making them his Avatars of destruction and annihilation on earth. Their purpose is to spread fear, upon which the Serpent thrives and grows ever stronger.

One of the Worthy is the Juggernaut, whose unstoppable rampage brings him ever closer to San Francisco, home to the X-Men and the New Mutants.

DANI MOONSTAR

SUNSPOT

KARMA

CYPHER

X-MAN

WARLOCK

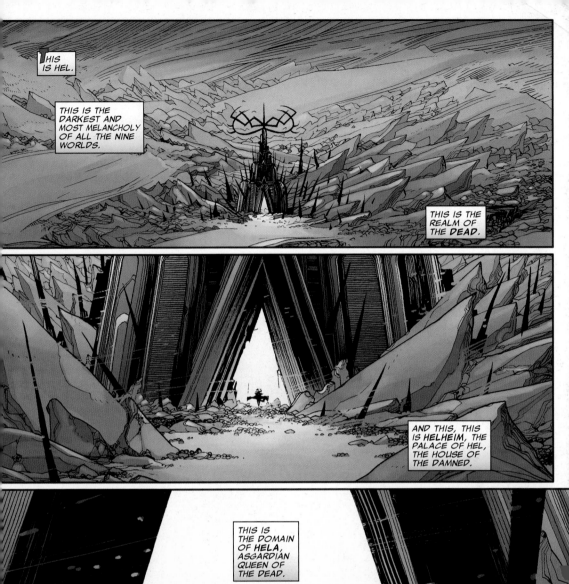

THIS IS HEL.

THIS IS THE DARKEST AND MOST MELANCHOLY OF ALL THE NINE WORLDS.

THIS IS THE REALM OF THE DEAD.

AND THIS, THIS IS HELHEIM, THE PALACE OF HEL, THE HOUSE OF THE DAMNED.

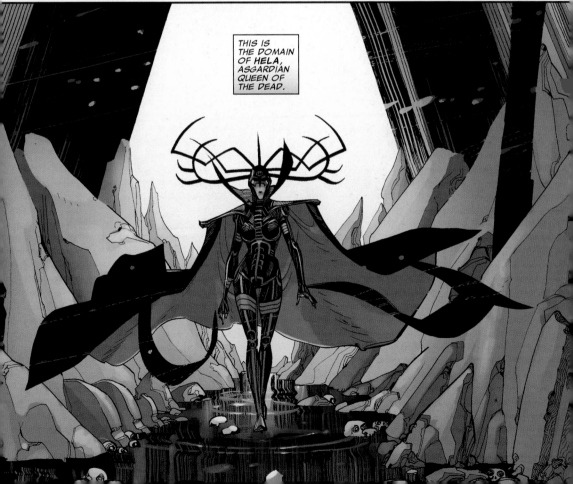

THIS IS THE DOMAIN OF HELA, ASGARDIAN QUEEN OF THE DEAD.

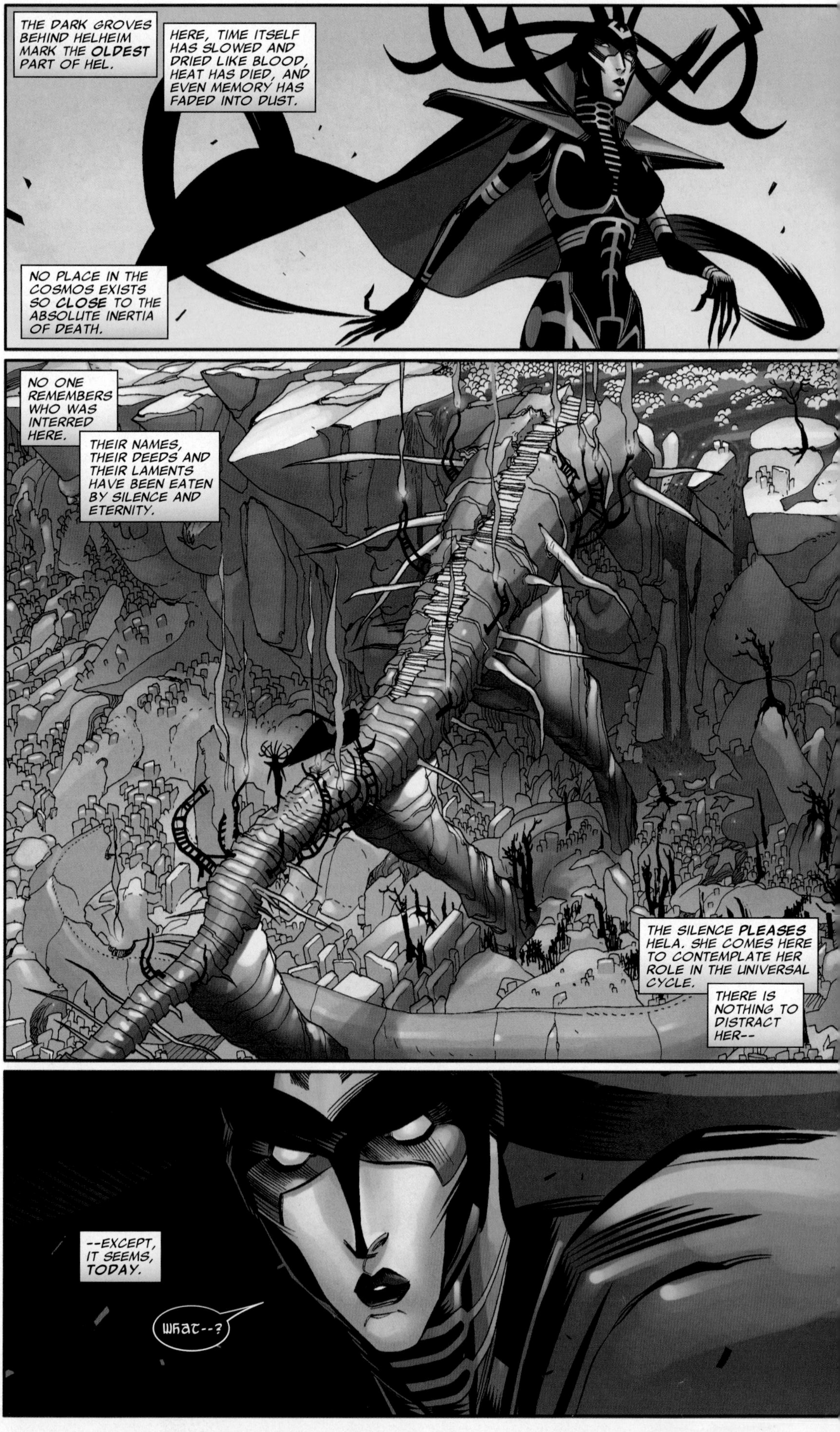
THE DARK GROVES BEHIND HELHEIM MARK THE OLDEST PART OF HEL.
HERE, TIME ITSELF HAS SLOWED AND DRIED LIKE BLOOD, HEAT HAS DIED, AND EVEN MEMORY HAS FADED INTO DUST.
NO PLACE IN THE COSMOS EXISTS SO CLOSE TO THE ABSOLUTE INERTIA OF DEATH.
NO ONE REMEMBERS WHO WAS INTERRED HERE.
THEIR NAMES, THEIR DEEDS AND THEIR LAMENTS HAVE BEEN EATEN BY SILENCE AND ETERNITY.
THE SILENCE PLEASES HELA. SHE COMES HERE TO CONTEMPLATE HER ROLE IN THE UNIVERSAL CYCLE.
THERE IS NOTHING TO DISTRACT HER--
--EXCEPT, IT SEEMS, TODAY.
WHAT--?

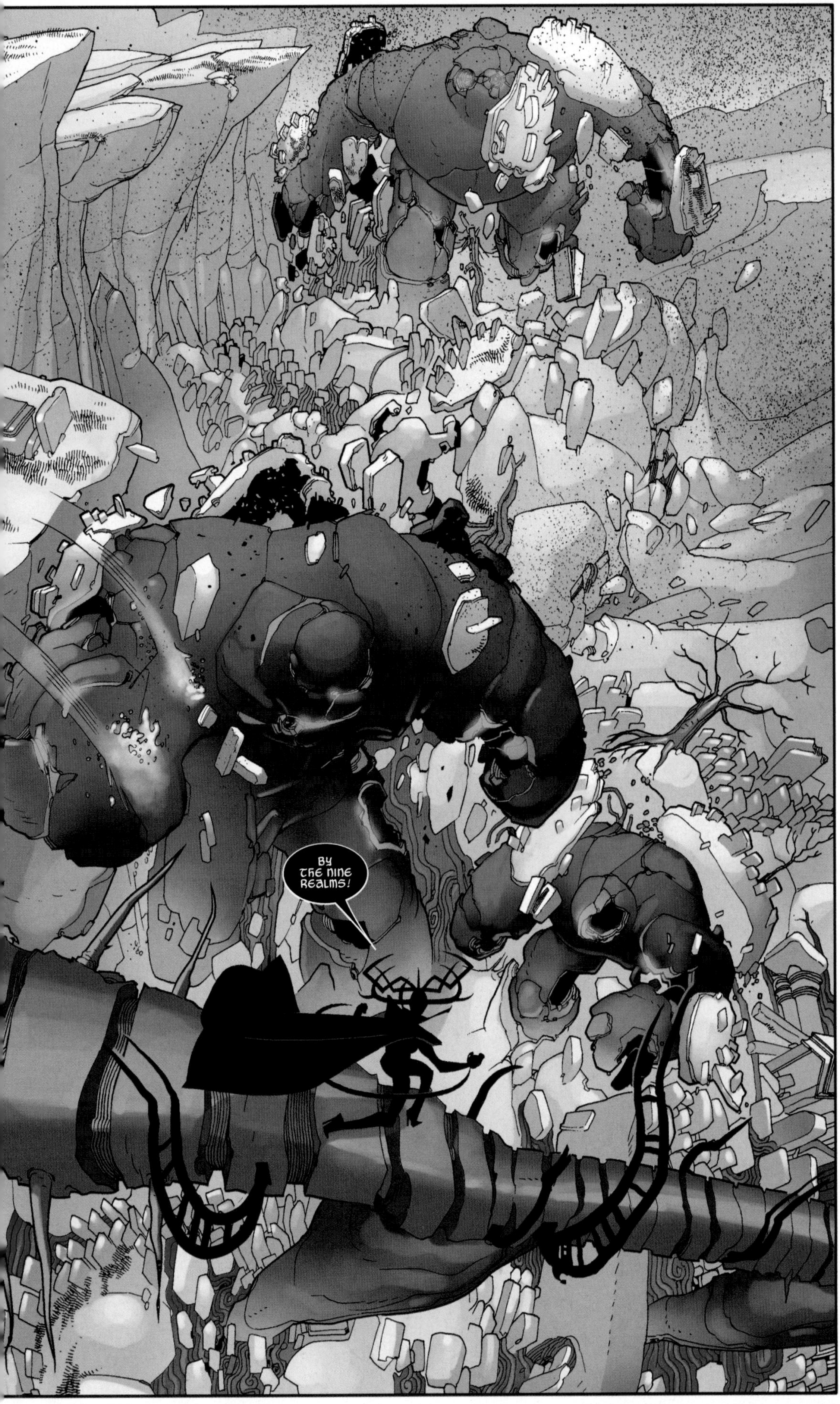
BY THE NINE REALMS!

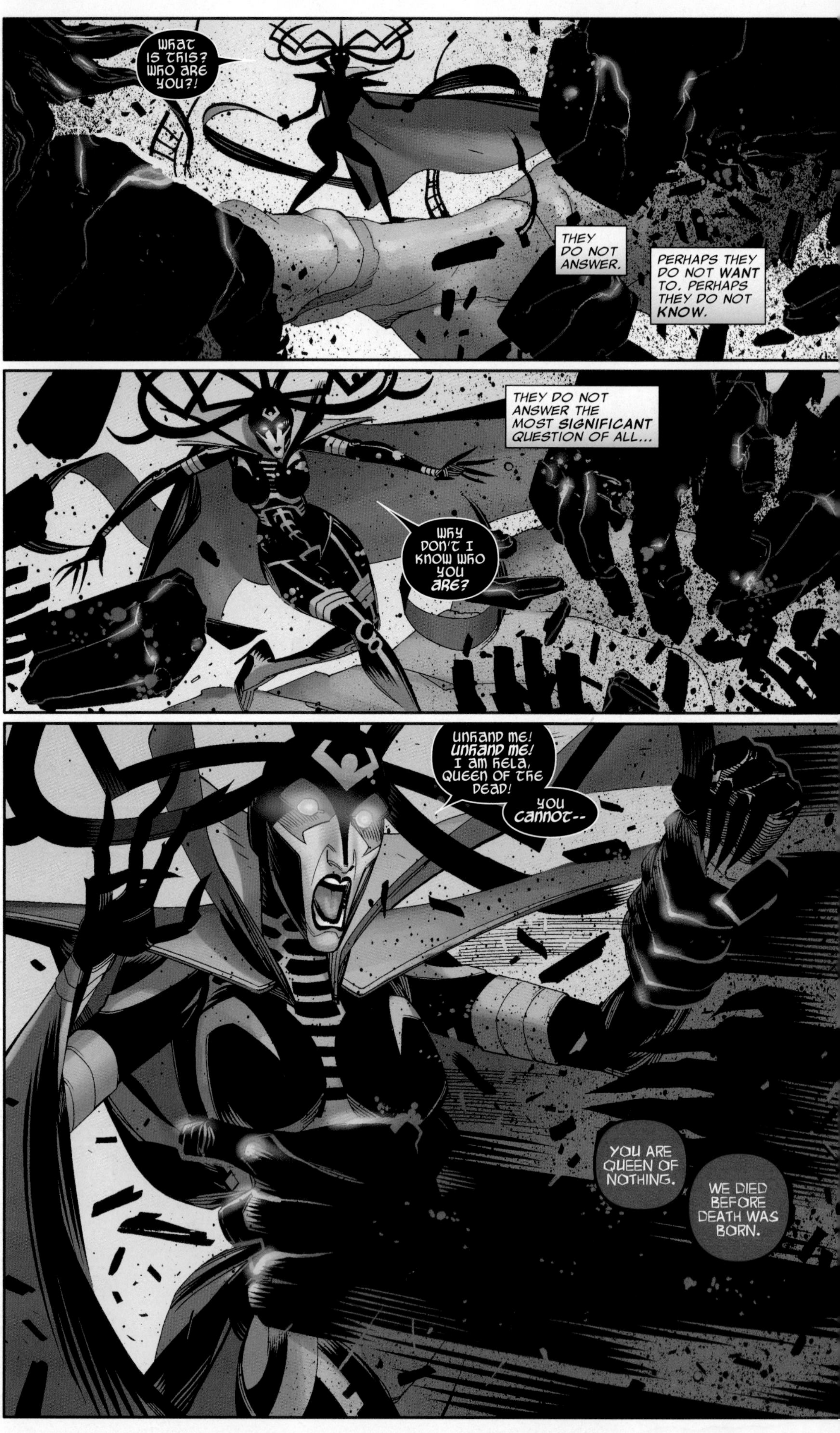
WHAT IS THIS? WHO ARE YOU?!
THEY DO NOT ANSWER.
PERHAPS THEY DO NOT WANT TO. PERHAPS THEY DO NOT KNOW.
THEY DO NOT ANSWER THE MOST SIGNIFICANT QUESTION OF ALL...
WHY DON'T I KNOW WHO YOU ARE?
UNHAND ME! UNHAND ME! I AM HELA, QUEEN OF THE DEAD!
YOU CANNOT--
YOU ARE QUEEN OF NOTHING.
WE DIED BEFORE DEATH WAS BORN.

NOO—!

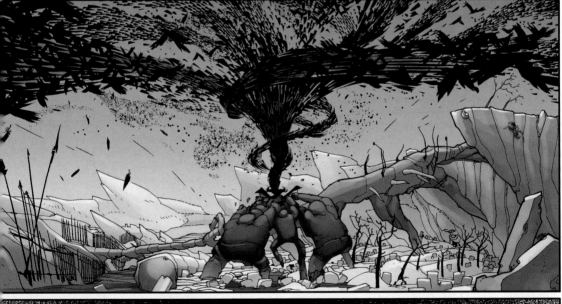

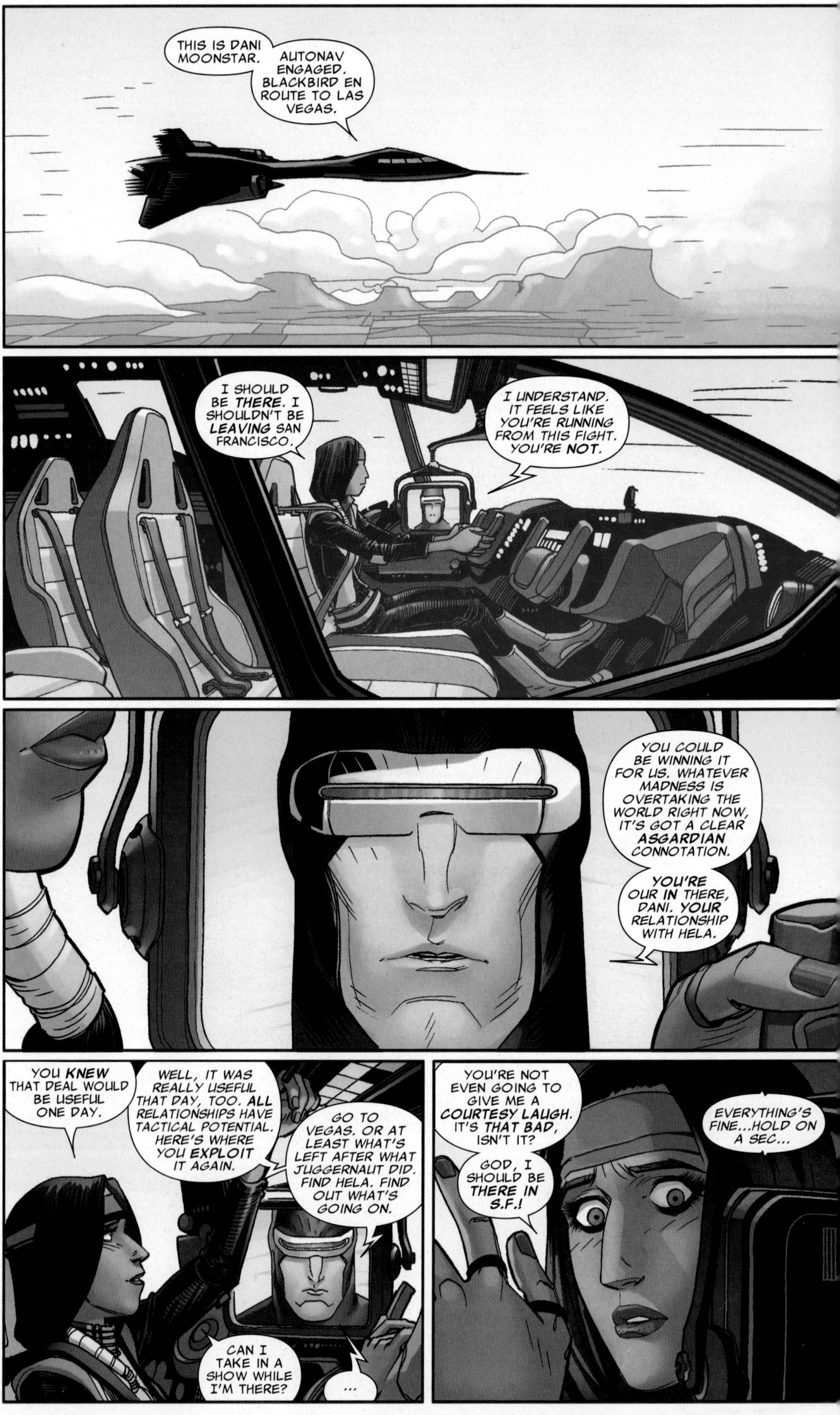
THIS IS DANI MOONSTAR.
AUTONAV ENGAGED. BLACKBIRD EN ROUTE TO LAS VEGAS.
I SHOULD BE THERE. I SHOULDN'T BE LEAVING SAN FRANCISCO.
I UNDERSTAND. IT FEELS LIKE YOU'RE RUNNING FROM THIS FIGHT. YOU'RE NOT.
YOU COULD BE WINNING IT FOR US. WHATEVER MADNESS IS OVERTAKING THE WORLD RIGHT NOW, IT'S GOT A CLEAR ASGARDIAN CONNOTATION.
YOU'RE OUR IN THERE, DANI. YOUR RELATIONSHIP WITH HELA.
YOU KNEW THAT DEAL WOULD BE USEFUL ONE DAY.
WELL, IT WAS REALLY USEFUL THAT DAY, TOO. ALL RELATIONSHIPS HAVE TACTICAL POTENTIAL. HERE'S WHERE YOU EXPLOIT IT AGAIN.
GO TO VEGAS. OR AT LEAST WHAT'S LEFT AFTER WHAT JUGGERNAUT DID. FIND HELA. FIND OUT WHAT'S GOING ON.
CAN I TAKE IN A SHOW WHILE I'M THERE?
...
YOU'RE NOT EVEN GOING TO GIVE ME A COURTESY LAUGH. IT'S THAT BAD, ISN'T IT?
GOD, I SHOULD BE THERE IN S.F.!
EVERYTHING'S FINE...HOLD ON A SEC...

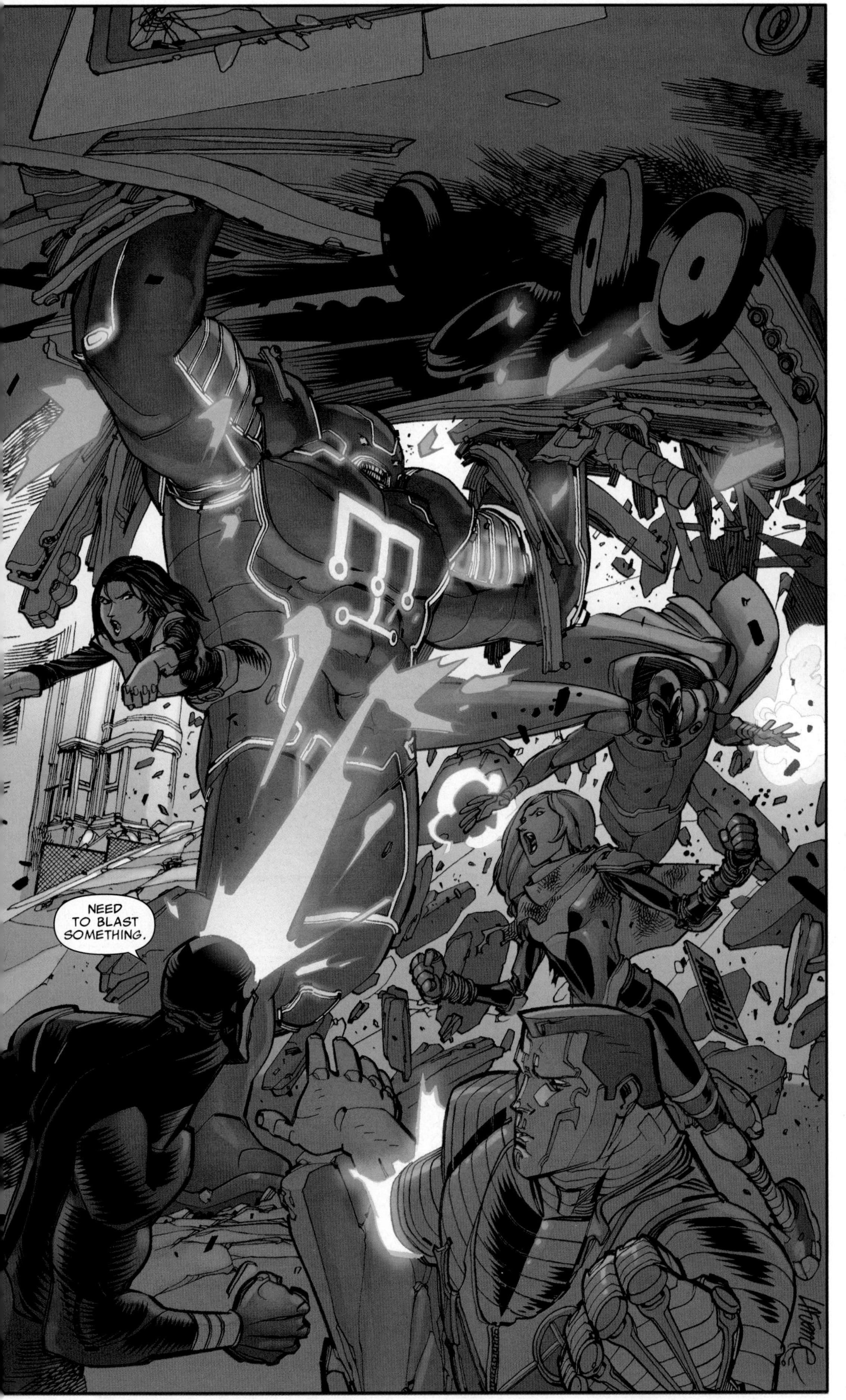
NEED TO BLAST SOMETHING.

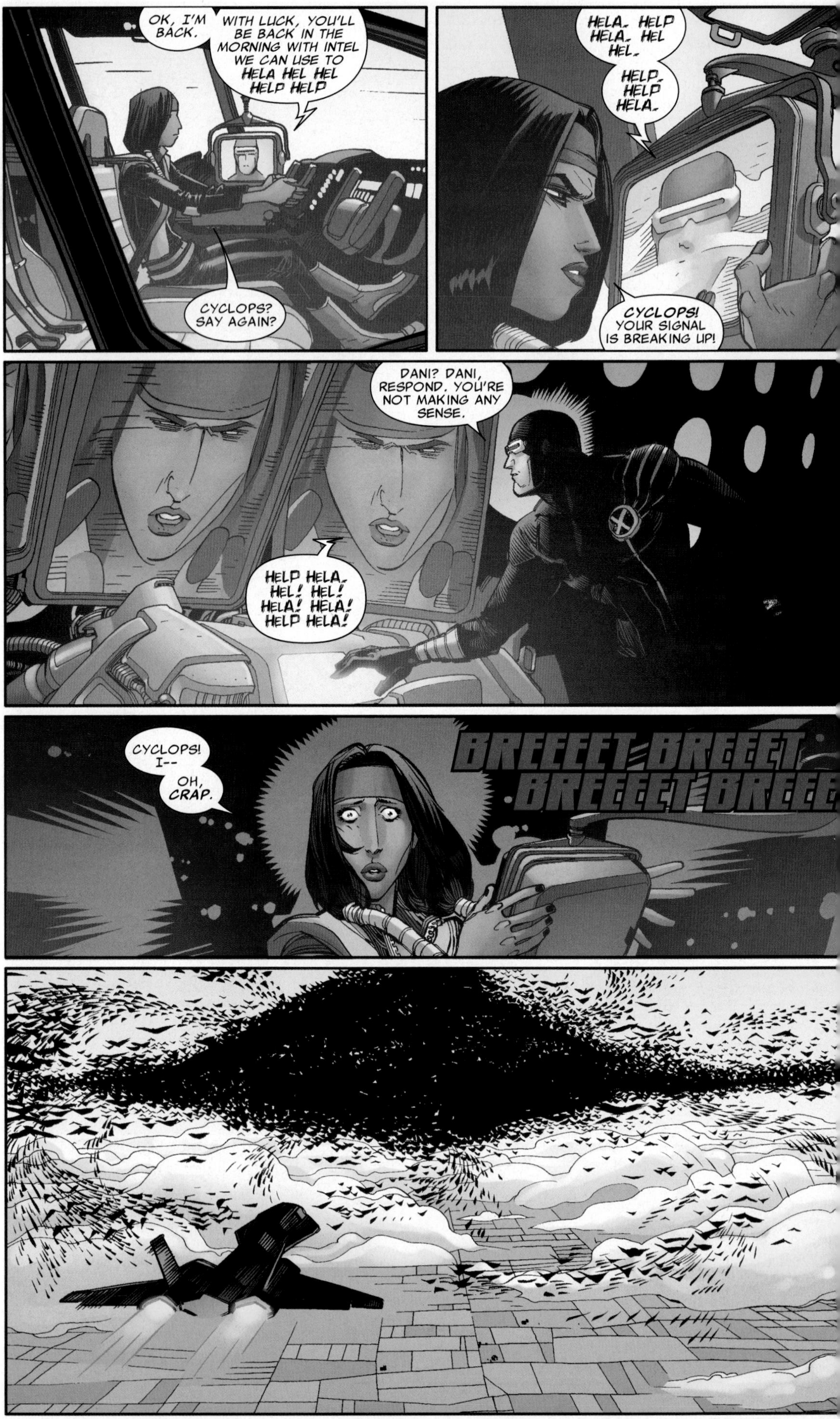
OK, I'M BACK.
WITH LUCK, YOU'LL BE BACK IN THE MORNING WITH INTEL WE CAN USE TO HELA HEL HEL HELP HELP
CYCLOPS? SAY AGAIN?
HELA. HELP HELA. HEL HEL.
HELP. HELP HELA.
CYCLOPS! YOUR SIGNAL IS BREAKING UP!
DANI? DANI, RESPOND. YOU'RE NOT MAKING ANY SENSE.
HELP HELA. HEL! HEL! HELA! HELA! HELP HELA!
CYCLOPS! I--
OH, CRAP.
BREEEET BREEET BREEEET

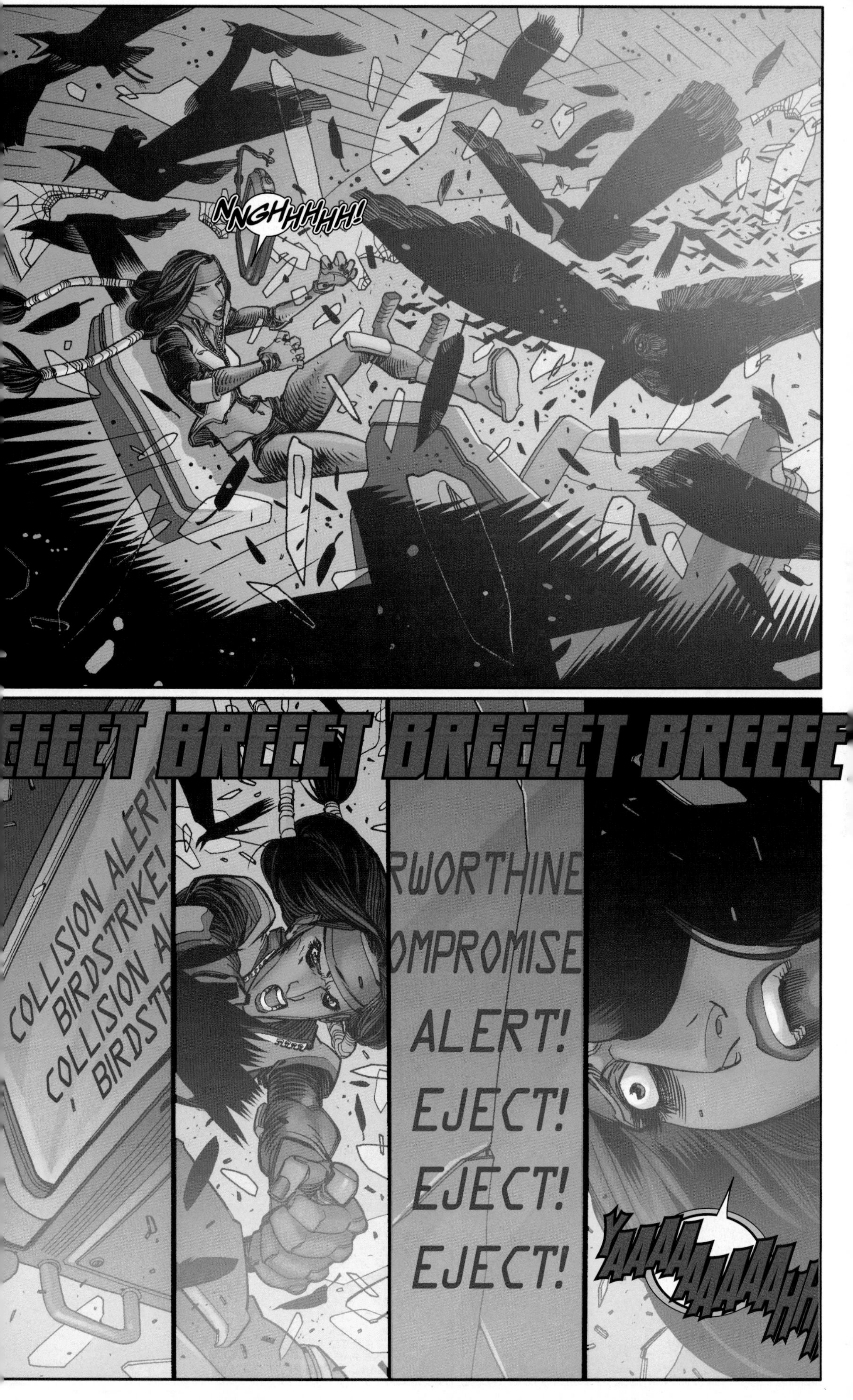
NNGHHHHH!
EEEET BREEET BREEEET BREEEE
COLLISION ALERT!
BIRDSTRIKE!
COLLISION AL
BIRDSTR
RWORTHINE
OMPROMISE
ALERT!
EJECT!
EJECT!
EJECT!
YAAAAAAAAAAHH

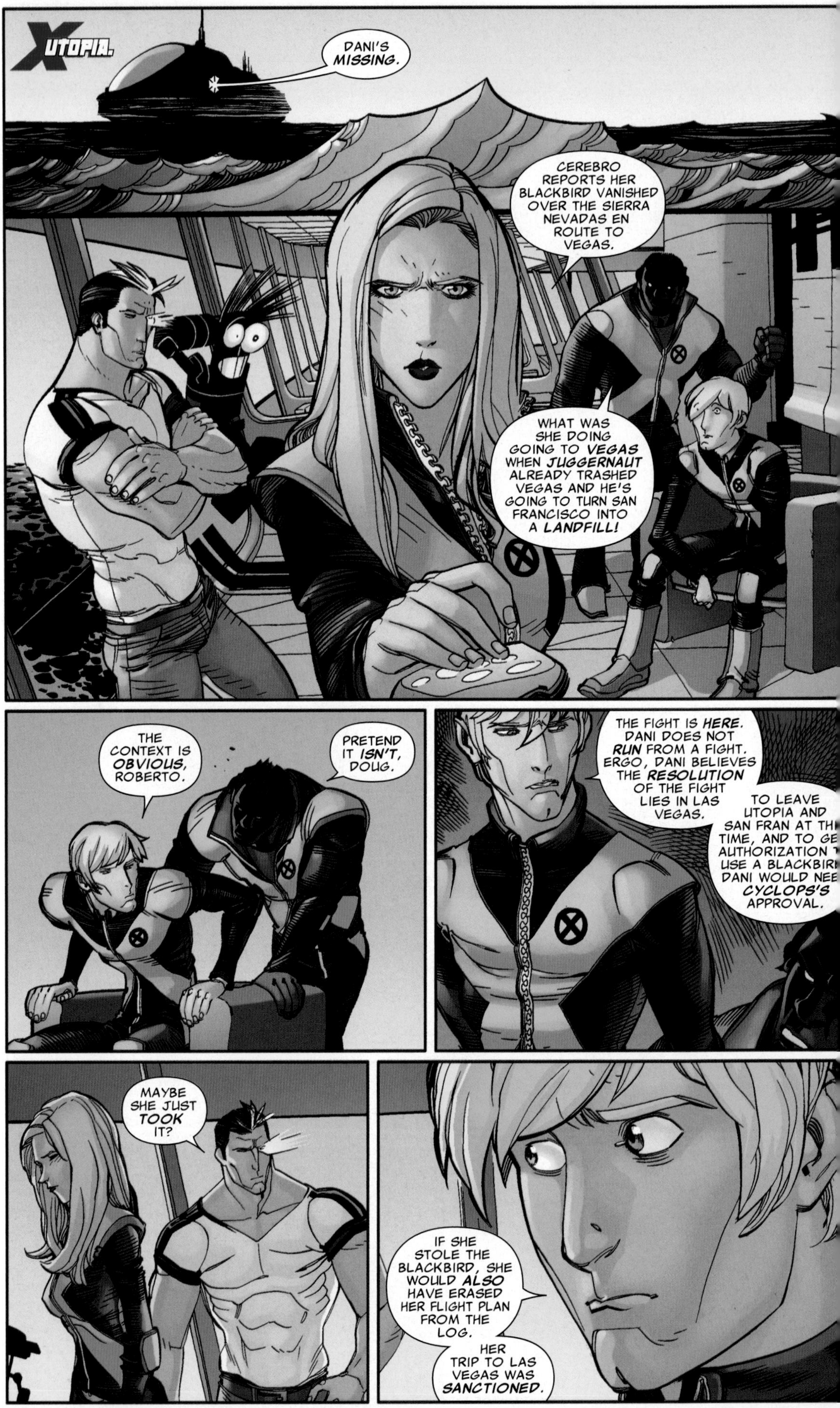
X UTOPIA.
DANI'S MISSING.
CEREBRO REPORTS HER BLACKBIRD VANISHED OVER THE SIERRA NEVADAS EN ROUTE TO VEGAS.
WHAT WAS SHE DOING GOING TO VEGAS WHEN JUGGERNAUT ALREADY TRASHED VEGAS AND HE'S GOING TO TURN SAN FRANCISCO INTO A LANDFILL!
THE CONTEXT IS OBVIOUS, ROBERTO.
PRETEND IT ISN'T, DOUG.
THE FIGHT IS HERE. DANI DOES NOT RUN FROM A FIGHT. ERGO, DANI BELIEVES THE RESOLUTION OF THE FIGHT LIES IN LAS VEGAS.
TO LEAVE UTOPIA AND SAN FRAN AT TH TIME, AND TO GE AUTHORIZATION T USE A BLACKBIRI DANI WOULD NEE CYCLOPS'S APPROVAL.
MAYBE SHE JUST TOOK IT?
IF SHE STOLE THE BLACKBIRD, SHE WOULD ALSO HAVE ERASED HER FLIGHT PLAN FROM THE LOG.
HER TRIP TO LAS VEGAS WAS SANCTIONED.

DANI'S **NORSE** CONNECTIONS ARE ESTABLISHED. AND THE LAST TIME WE WERE IN VEGAS SHE MUST HAVE HAD BUSINESS OF THAT SORT.

SHE IS MAKING AN **END-RUN** TO TRY AND **BREAK** THIS CRISIS.

SO WHAT DO **WE** DO ABOUT IT?

OH, I HAVE **NO** IDEA.

WE ASK CYCLOPS.

SELF/FRIEND CYCLOPS IS WITH THE **OTHER** X/FRIENDS, IN THE THICK OF THE FIGHTING.

WHICH IS WHERE **WE** SHOULD BE.

I'M NOT JUST GONNA JUST SIT HERE!

DANI'S IN **TROUBLE!**

NOT AS MUCH TROUBLE AS THIS **PLANET** RIGHT NOW.

SUNSPOT, YOU CAN'T JUST--

DID HE JUST WALK OUT ON ME?

SO DO WE STAY HERE AND **KEEP FIGHTING** THIS FIGHT, OR DO WE TRY TO FIND DANI IN THE HOPE THAT SHE CAN **WIN** IT?

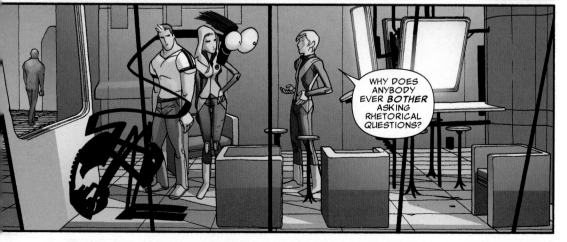

WHY DOES ANYBODY EVER **BOTHER** ASKING RHETORICAL QUESTIONS?

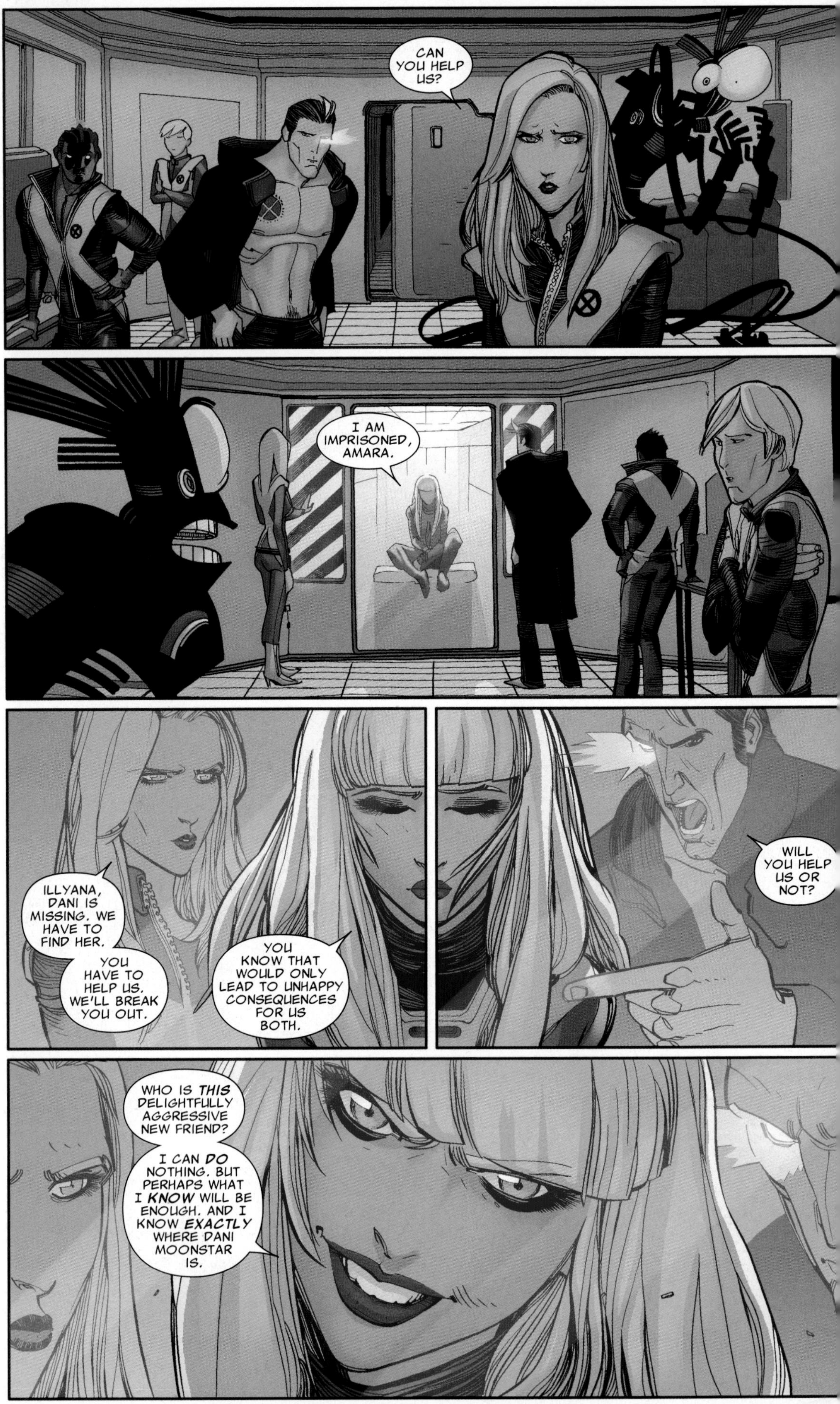
CAN YOU HELP US?
I AM IMPRISONED, AMARA.
ILLYANA, DANI IS MISSING. WE HAVE TO FIND HER.
YOU HAVE TO HELP US. WE'LL BREAK YOU OUT.
YOU KNOW THAT WOULD ONLY LEAD TO UNHAPPY CONSEQUENCES FOR US BOTH.
WILL YOU HELP US OR NOT?
WHO IS THIS DELIGHTFULLY AGGRESSIVE NEW FRIEND?
I CAN DO NOTHING. BUT PERHAPS WHAT I KNOW WILL BE ENOUGH. AND I KNOW EXACTLY WHERE DANI MOONSTAR IS.

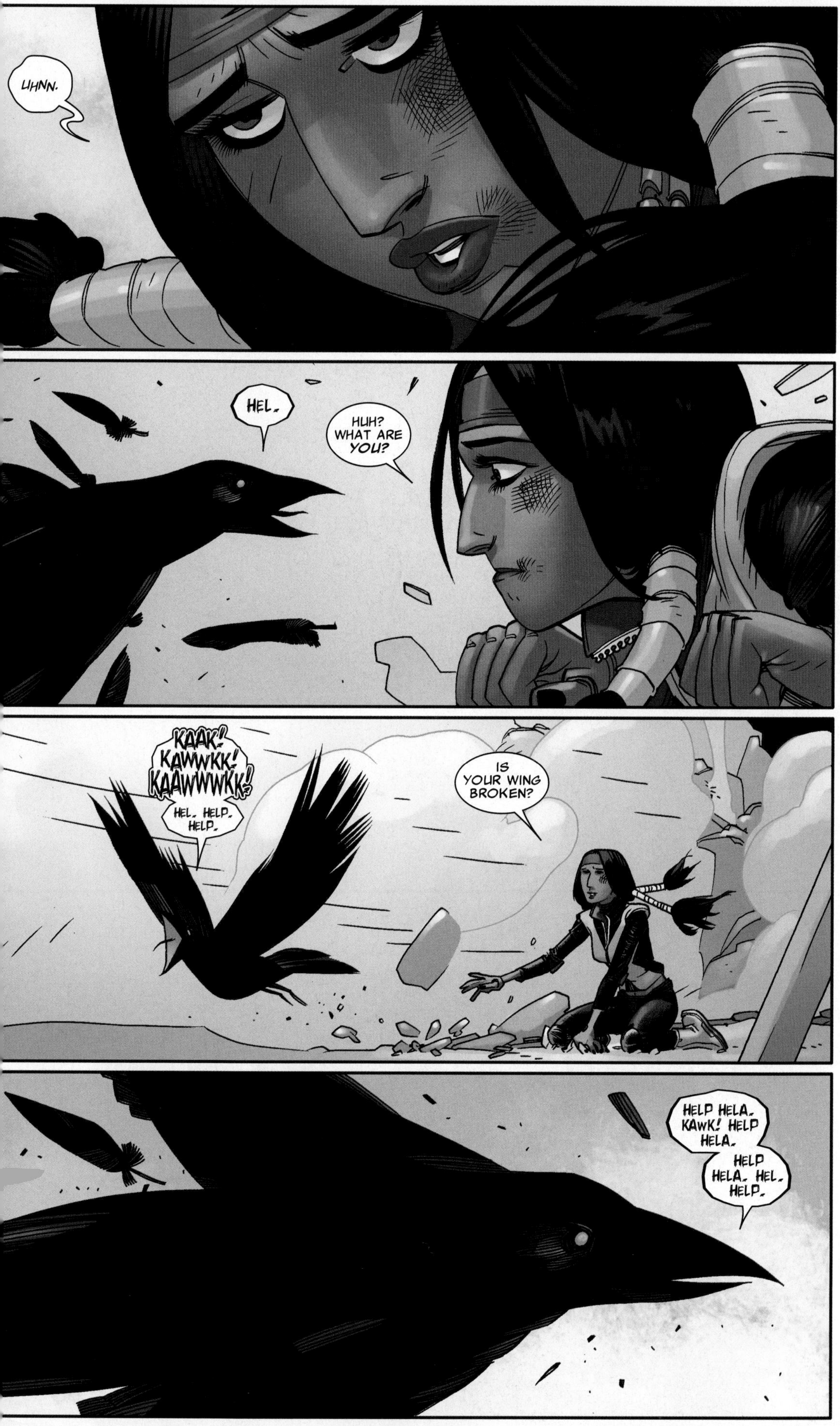
UHNN.
HEL.
HUH? WHAT ARE YOU?
KAAK! KAWWKK! KAAWWWKK!
HEL. HELP. HELP.
IS YOUR WING BROKEN?
HELP HELA. KAWK! HELP HELA.
HELP HELA. HEL. HELP.

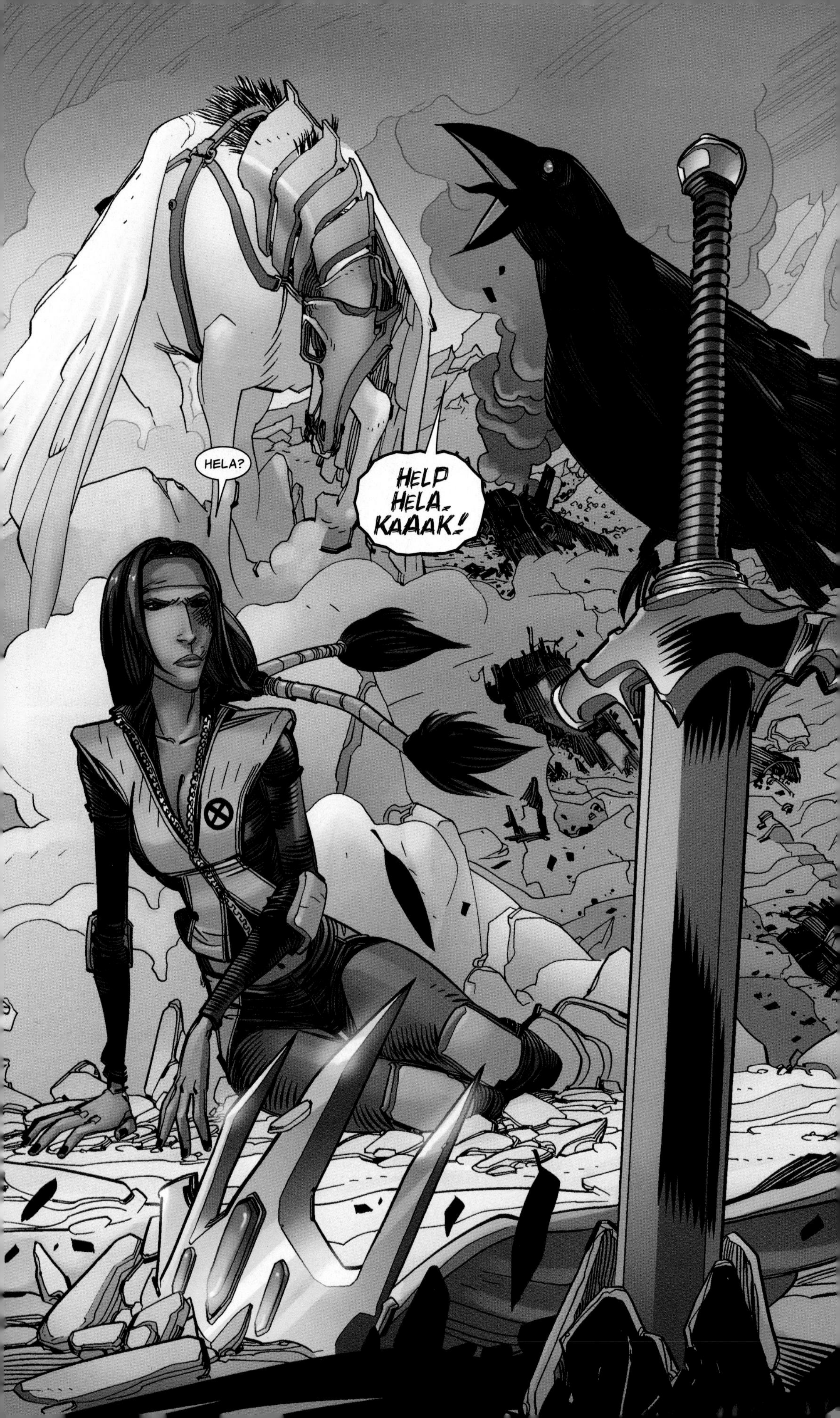
HELA?
HELP HELA. KAAAK!

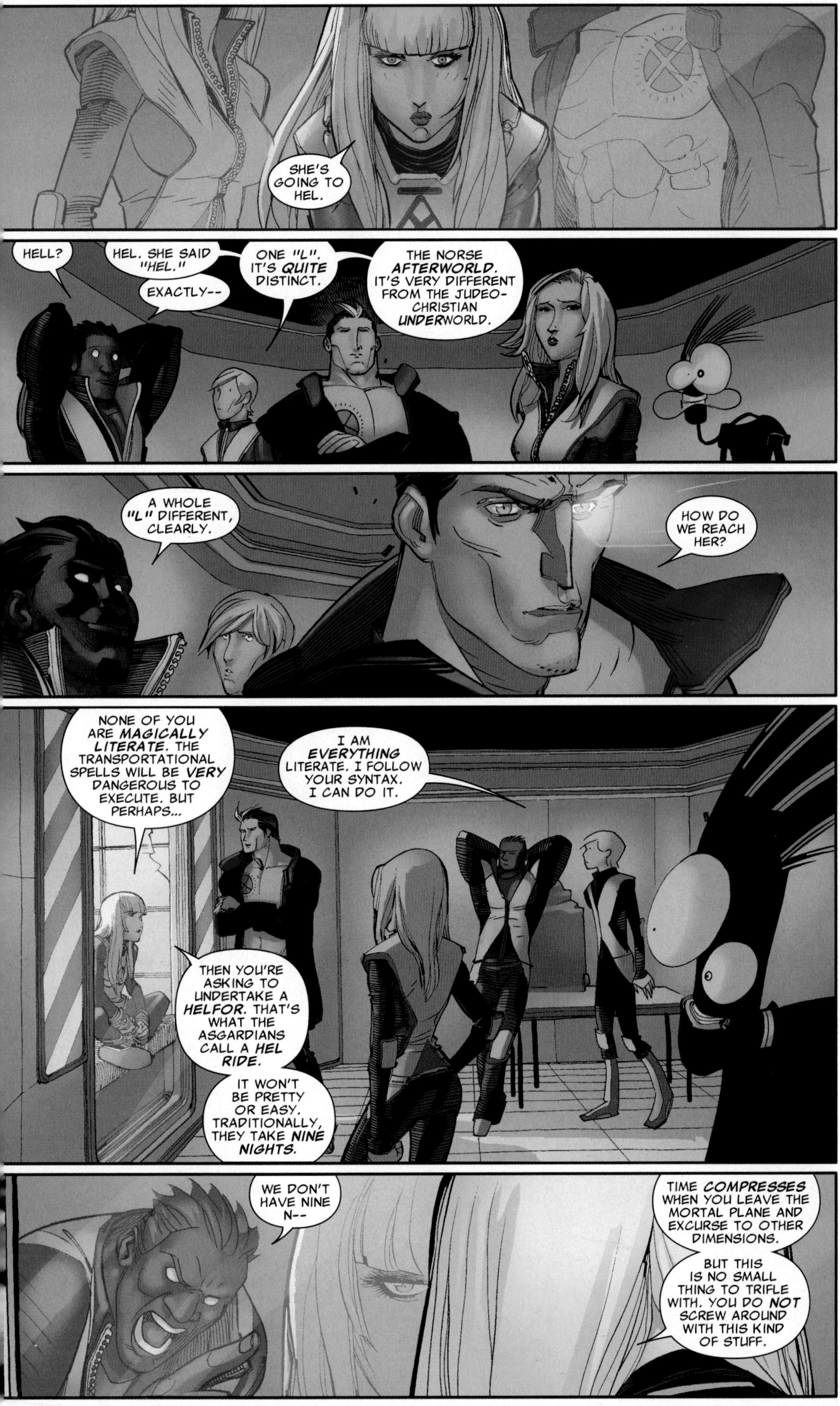

SHE'S GOING TO HEL.
HELL?
HEL. SHE SAID "HEL."
EXACTLY--
ONE "L". IT'S QUITE DISTINCT.
THE NORSE AFTERWORLD. IT'S VERY DIFFERENT FROM THE JUDEO-CHRISTIAN UNDERWORLD.
A WHOLE "L" DIFFERENT, CLEARLY.
HOW DO WE REACH HER?
NONE OF YOU ARE MAGICALLY LITERATE. THE TRANSPORTATIONAL SPELLS WILL BE VERY DANGEROUS TO EXECUTE. BUT PERHAPS...
I AM EVERYTHING LITERATE. I FOLLOW YOUR SYNTAX. I CAN DO IT.
THEN YOU'RE ASKING TO UNDERTAKE A HELFOR. THAT'S WHAT THE ASGARDIANS CALL A HEL RIDE.
IT WON'T BE PRETTY OR EASY. TRADITIONALLY, THEY TAKE NINE NIGHTS.
WE DON'T HAVE NINE N--
TIME COMPRESSES WHEN YOU LEAVE THE MORTAL PLANE AND EXCURSE TO OTHER DIMENSIONS.
BUT THIS IS NO SMALL THING TO TRIFLE WITH. YOU DO NOT SCREW AROUND WITH THIS KIND OF STUFF.

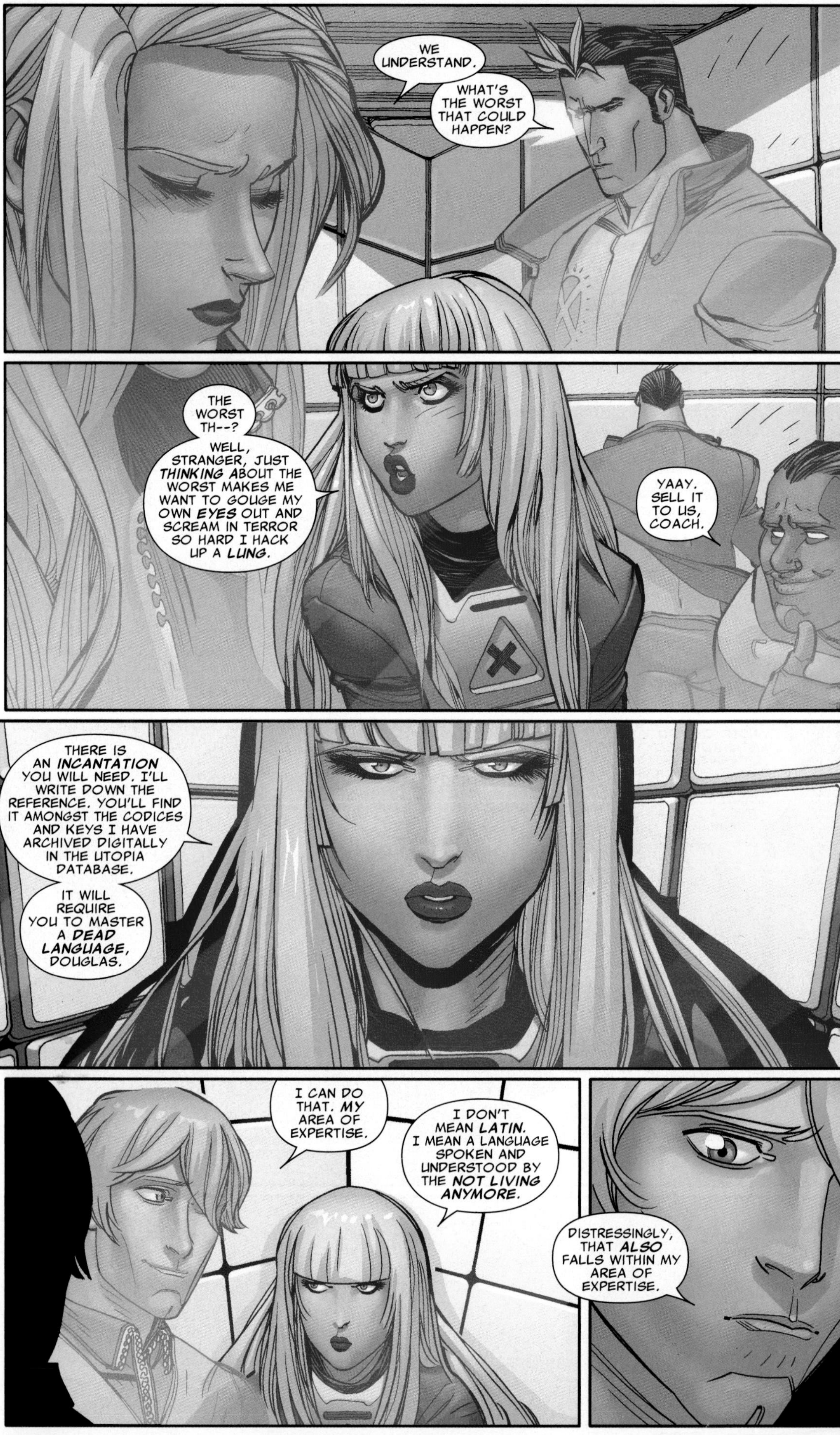
WE UNDERSTAND.
WHAT'S THE WORST THAT COULD HAPPEN?
THE WORST TH--?
WELL, STRANGER, JUST THINKING ABOUT THE WORST MAKES ME WANT TO GOUGE MY OWN EYES OUT AND SCREAM IN TERROR SO HARD I HACK UP A LUNG.
YAAY. SELL IT TO US, COACH.
THERE IS AN INCANTATION YOU WILL NEED. I'LL WRITE DOWN THE REFERENCE. YOU'LL FIND IT AMONGST THE CODICES AND KEYS I HAVE ARCHIVED DIGITALLY IN THE UTOPIA DATABASE.
IT WILL REQUIRE YOU TO MASTER A DEAD LANGUAGE, DOUGLAS.
I CAN DO THAT. MY AREA OF EXPERTISE.
I DON'T MEAN LATIN. I MEAN A LANGUAGE SPOKEN AND UNDERSTOOD BY THE NOT LIVING ANYMORE.
DISTRESSINGLY, THAT ALSO FALLS WITHIN MY AREA OF EXPERTISE.

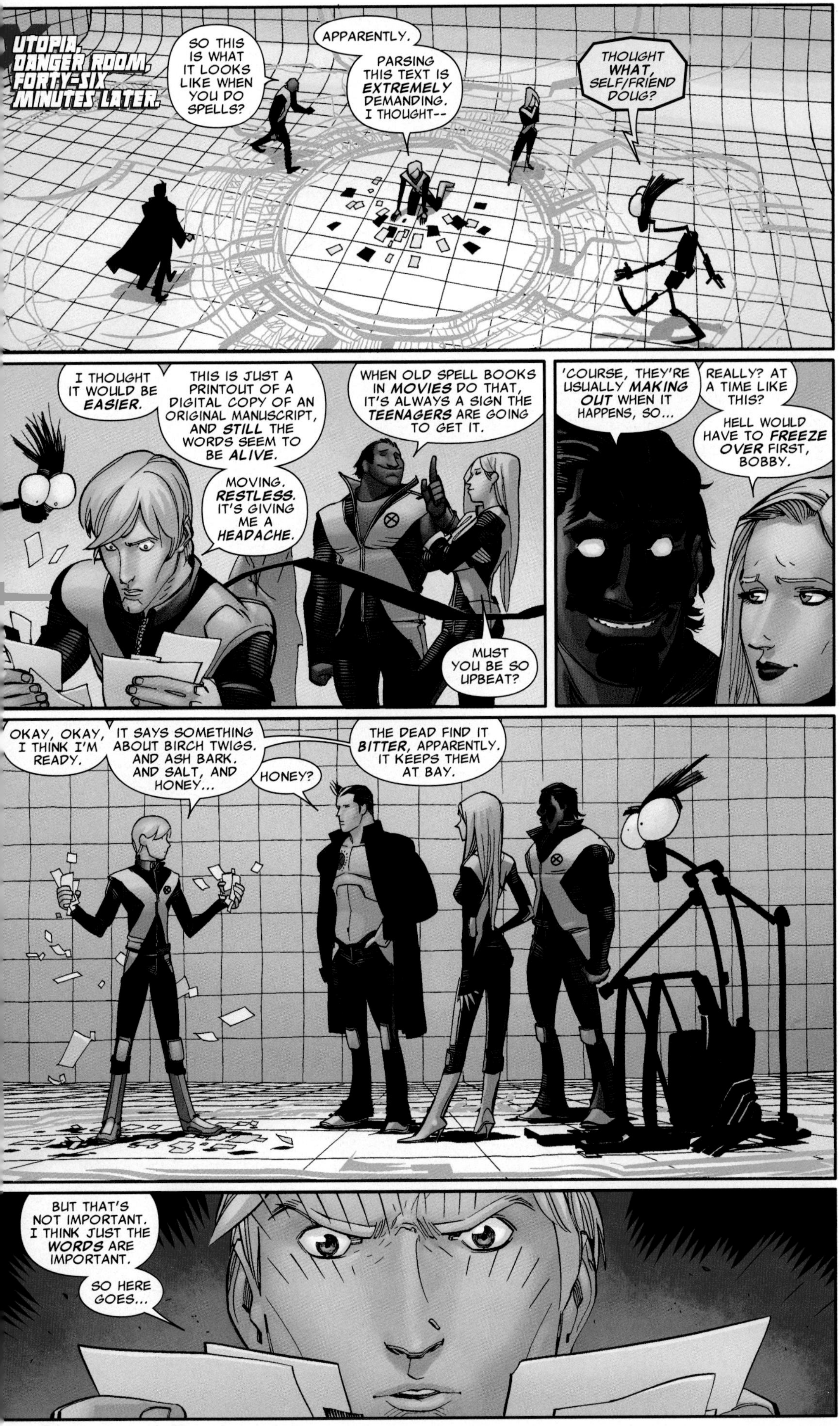
UTOPIA, DANGER ROOM, FORTY-SIX MINUTES LATER.
SO THIS IS WHAT IT LOOKS LIKE WHEN YOU DO SPELLS?
APPARENTLY.
PARSING THIS TEXT IS EXTREMELY DEMANDING. I THOUGHT--
THOUGHT WHAT, SELF/FRIEND DOUG?
I THOUGHT IT WOULD BE EASIER.
THIS IS JUST A PRINTOUT OF A DIGITAL COPY OF AN ORIGINAL MANUSCRIPT, AND STILL THE WORDS SEEM TO BE ALIVE.
MOVING. RESTLESS. IT'S GIVING ME A HEADACHE.
WHEN OLD SPELL BOOKS IN MOVIES DO THAT, IT'S ALWAYS A SIGN THE TEENAGERS ARE GOING TO GET IT.
MUST YOU BE SO UPBEAT?
'COURSE, THEY'RE USUALLY MAKING OUT WHEN IT HAPPENS, SO...
REALLY? AT A TIME LIKE THIS?
HELL WOULD HAVE TO FREEZE OVER FIRST, BOBBY.
OKAY, OKAY, I THINK I'M READY.
IT SAYS SOMETHING ABOUT BIRCH TWIGS. AND ASH BARK. AND SALT, AND HONEY...
HONEY?
THE DEAD FIND IT BITTER, APPARENTLY. IT KEEPS THEM AT BAY.
BUT THAT'S NOT IMPORTANT. I THINK JUST THE WORDS ARE IMPORTANT.
SO HERE GOES...

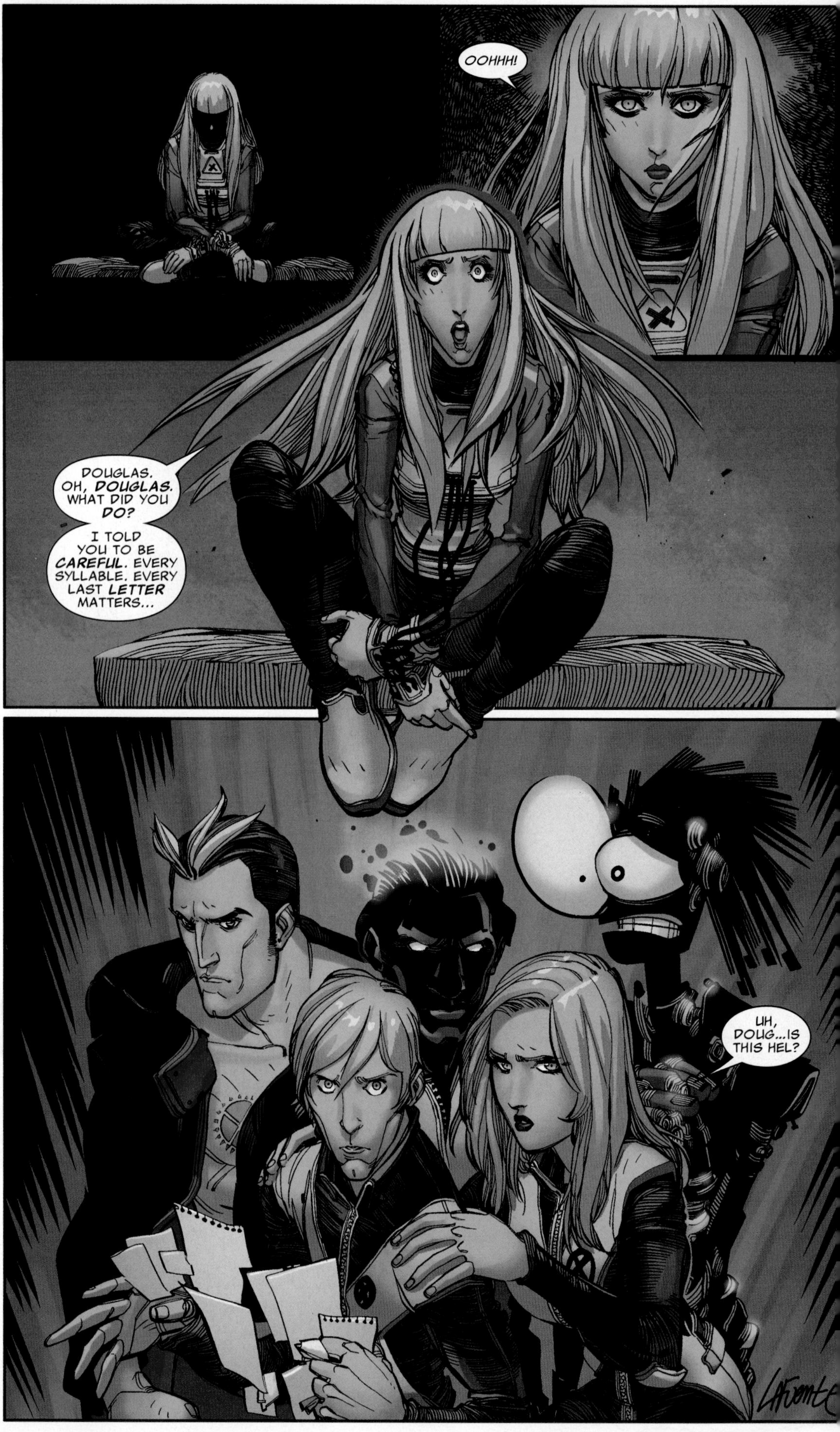
OOHHH!
DOUGLAS. OH, DOUGLAS. WHAT DID YOU DO?
I TOLD YOU TO BE CAREFUL. EVERY SYLLABLE. EVERY LAST LETTER MATTERS...
UH, DOUG...IS THIS HEL?
LAFUENTE

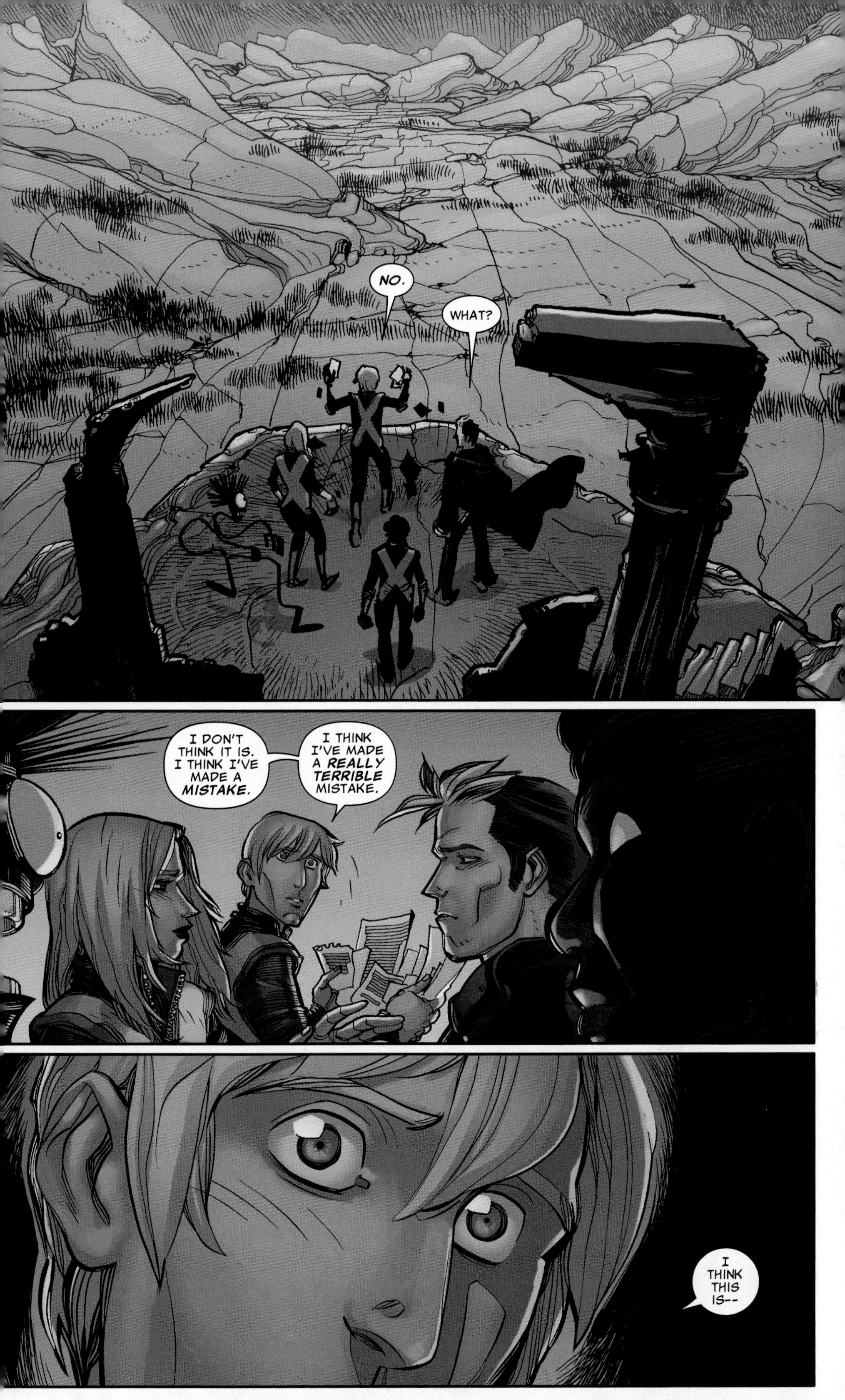
NO.
WHAT?
I DON'T THINK IT IS. I THINK I'VE MADE A MISTAKE.
I THINK I'VE MADE A REALLY TERRIBLE MISTAKE.
I THINK THIS IS--

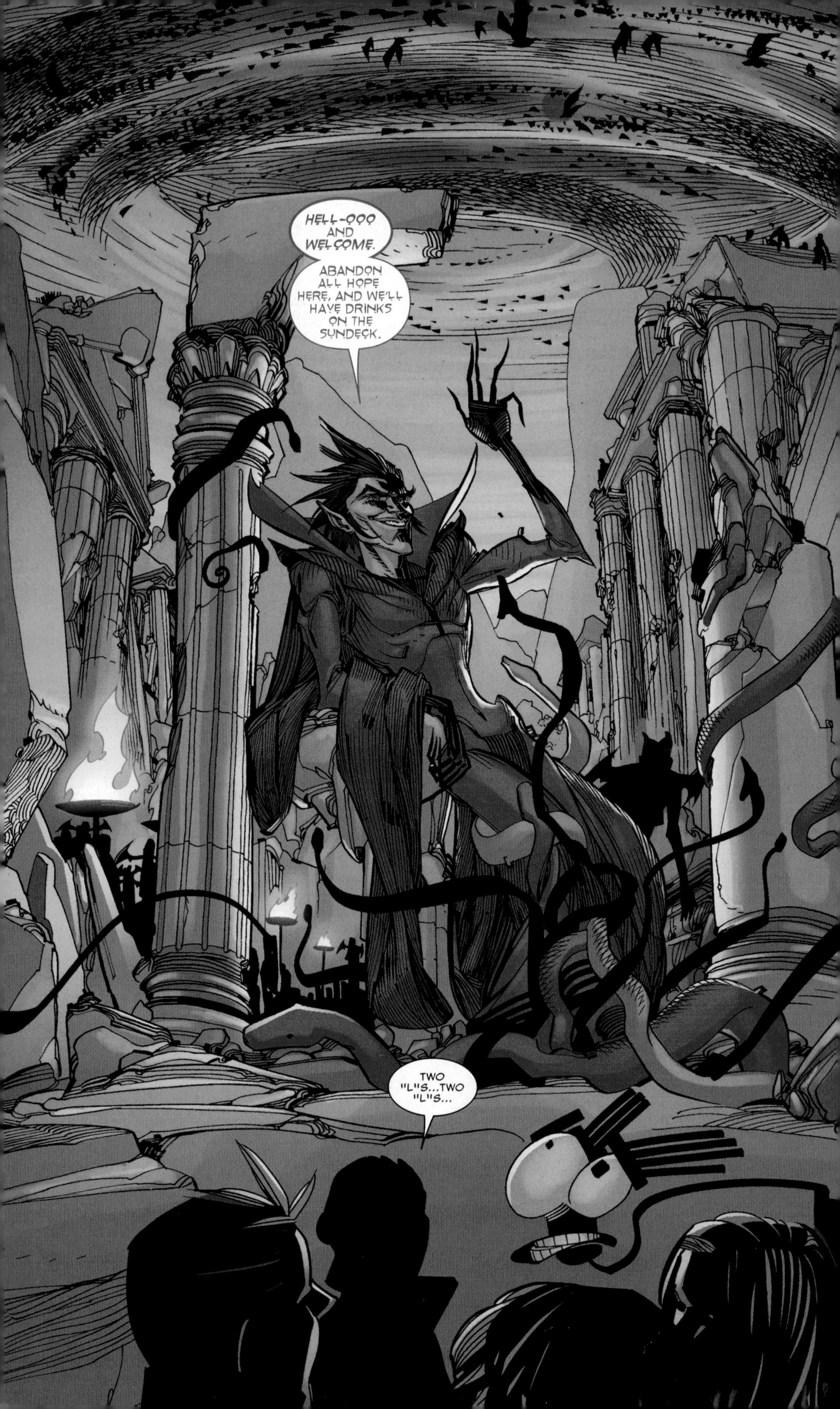
HELL-OOO AND WELCOME.
ABANDON ALL HOPE HERE, AND WE'LL HAVE DRINKS ON THE SUNDECK.
TWO "L"S...TWO "L"S...

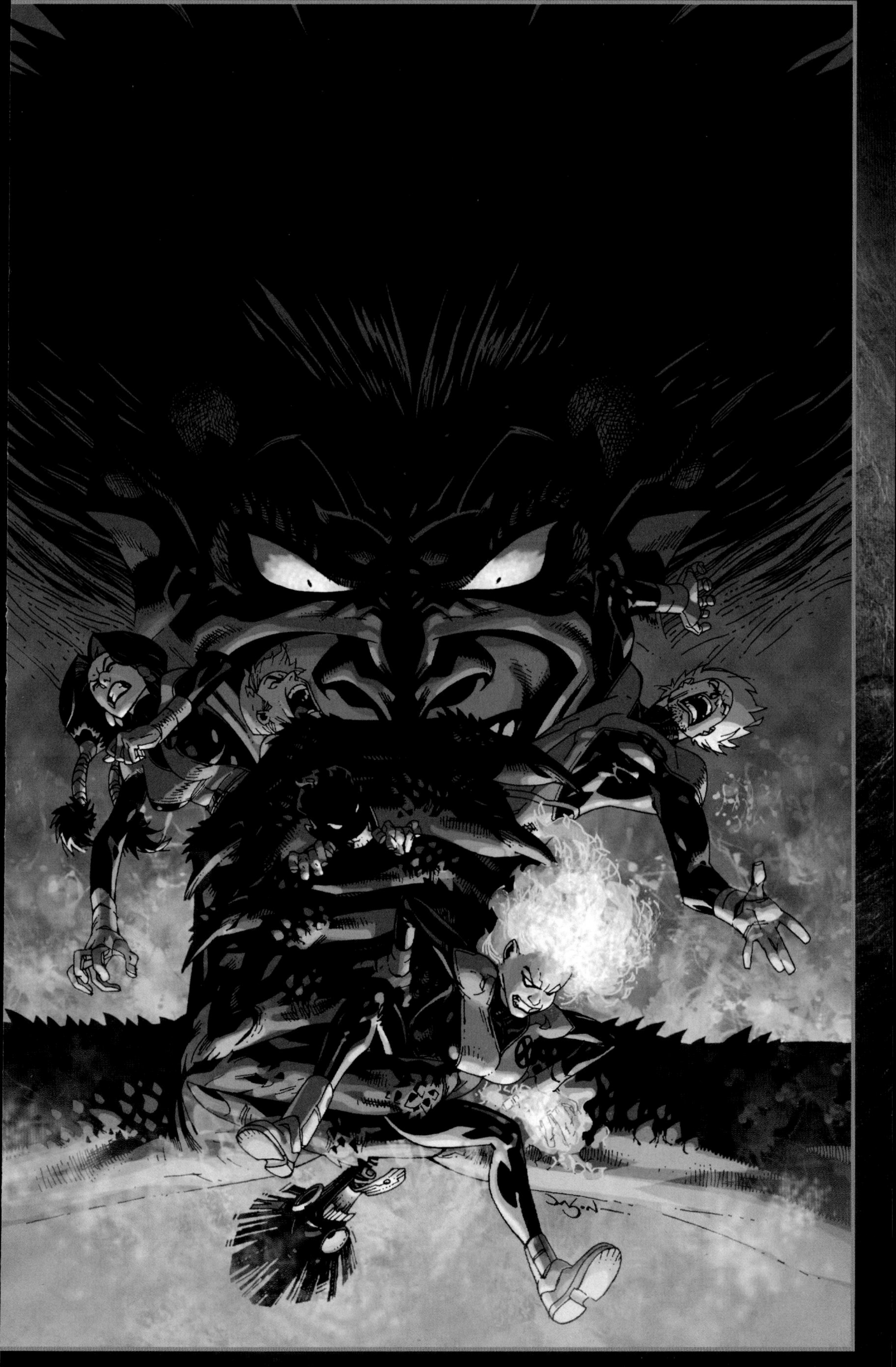

NEW MUTANTS #30

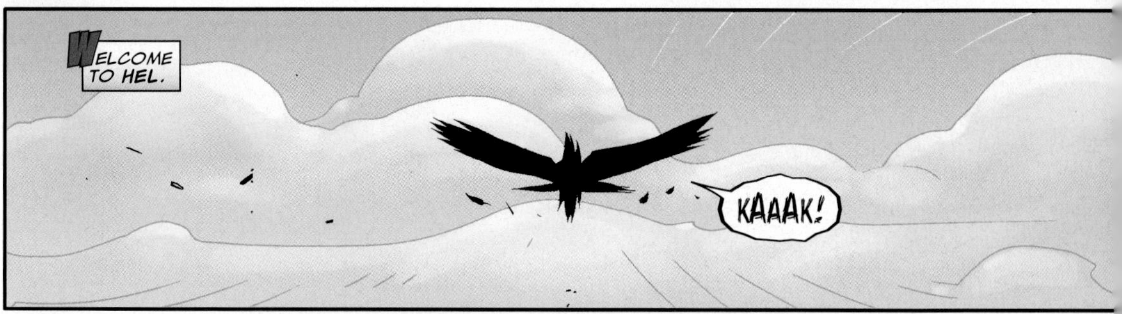
WELCOME TO HEL.
KAAAK!

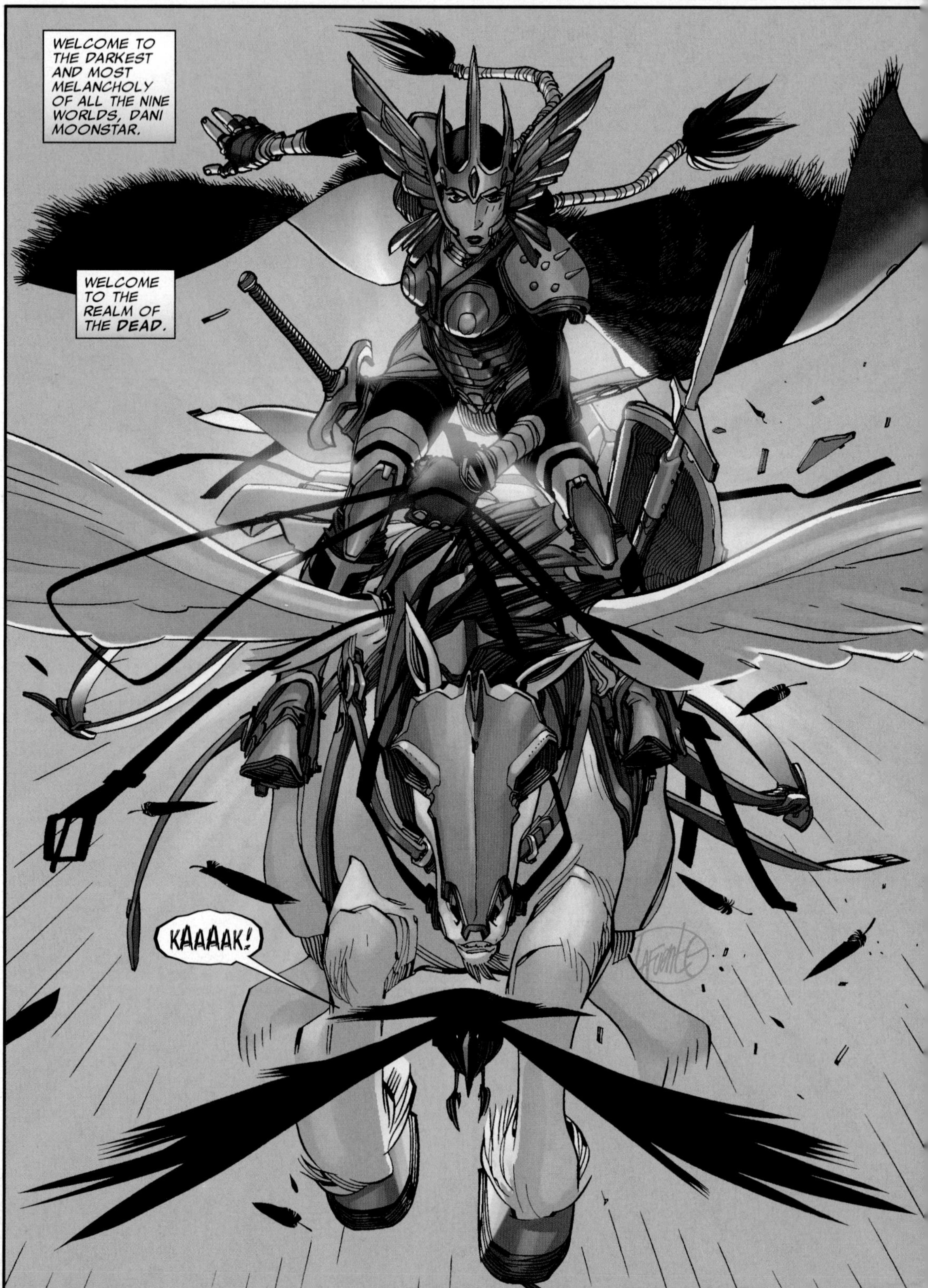
WELCOME TO THE DARKEST AND MOST MELANCHOLY OF ALL THE NINE WORLDS, DANI MOONSTAR.
WELCOME TO THE REALM OF THE DEAD.
KAAAAK!

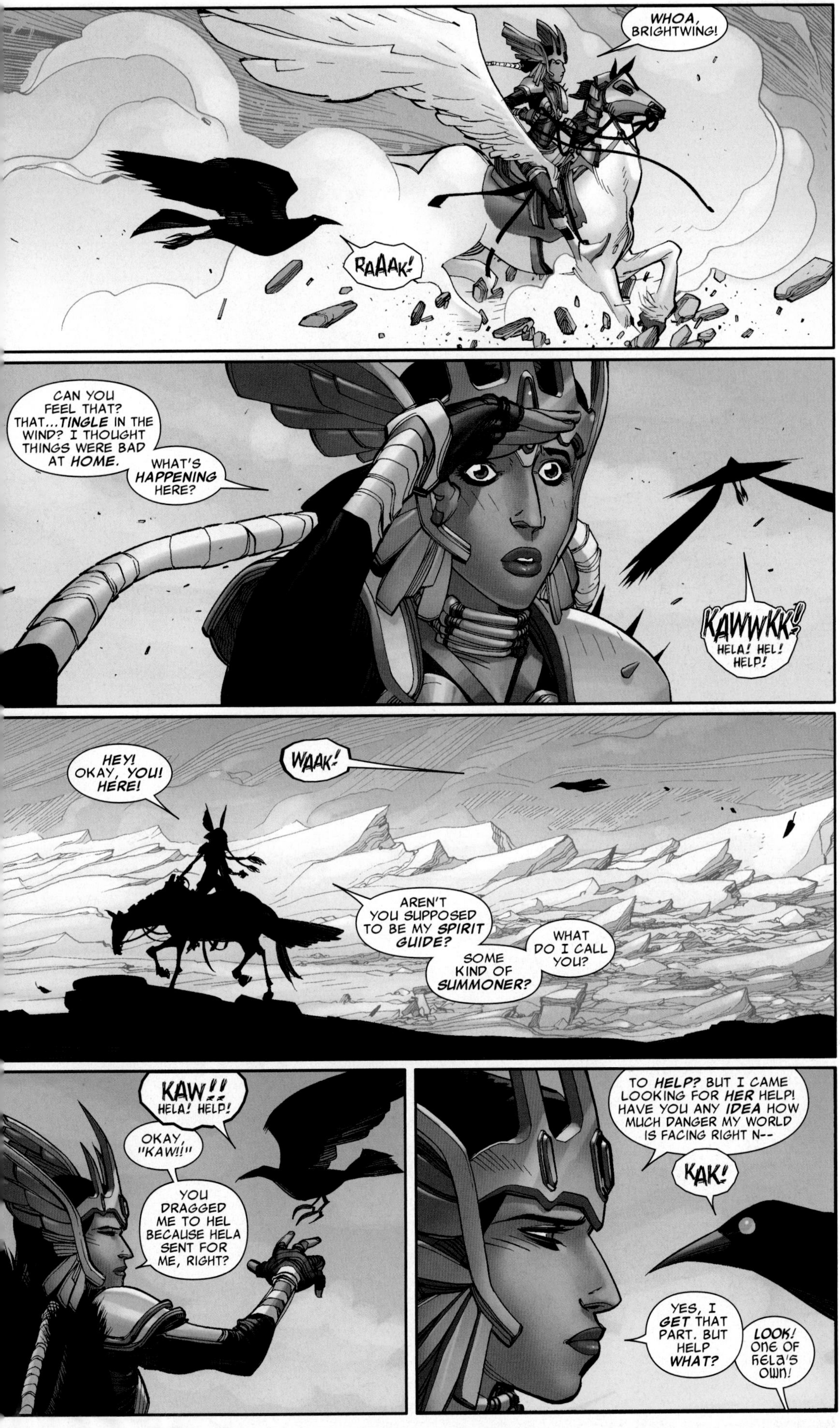
WHOA, BRIGHTWING!
RAAAK!
CAN YOU FEEL THAT? THAT...TINGLE IN THE WIND? I THOUGHT THINGS WERE BAD AT HOME.
WHAT'S HAPPENING HERE?
KAWWKK!
HELA! HEL! HELP!
HEY! OKAY, YOU! HERE!
WAAK!
AREN'T YOU SUPPOSED TO BE MY SPIRIT GUIDE?
SOME KIND OF SUMMONER?
WHAT DO I CALL YOU?
KAW!!
HELA! HELP!
OKAY, "KAW!!"
YOU DRAGGED ME TO HEL BECAUSE HELA SENT FOR ME, RIGHT?
TO HELP? BUT I CAME LOOKING FOR HER HELP! HAVE YOU ANY IDEA HOW MUCH DANGER MY WORLD IS FACING RIGHT N--
KAK!
YES, I GET THAT PART. BUT HELP WHAT?
LOOK! ONE OF HELA'S OWN!

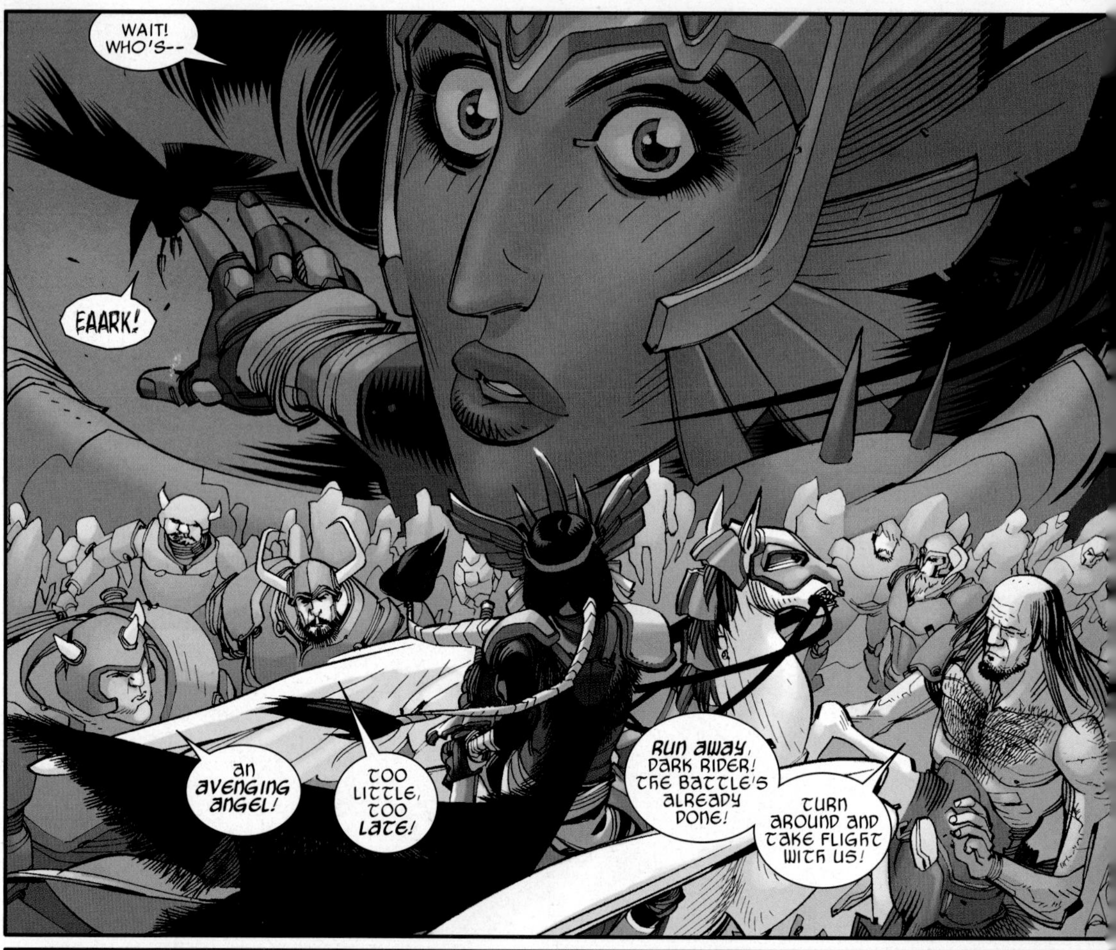
WAIT! WHO'S--
EAARK!
AN AVENGING ANGEL!
TOO LITTLE, TOO LATE!
RUN AWAY, DARK RIDER! THE BATTLE'S ALREADY DONE!
TURN AROUND AND TAKE FLIGHT WITH US!

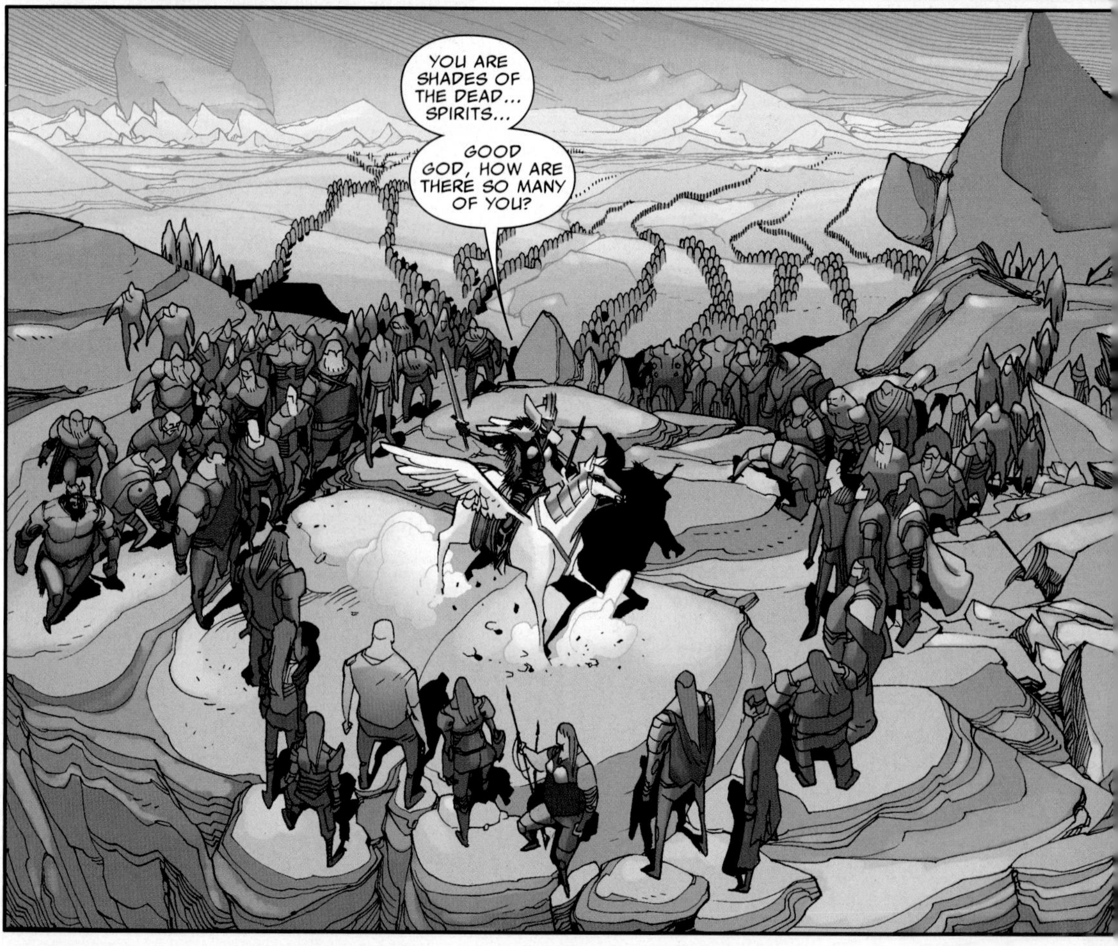
YOU ARE SHADES OF THE DEAD... SPIRITS...
GOOD GOD, HOW ARE THERE SO MANY OF YOU?

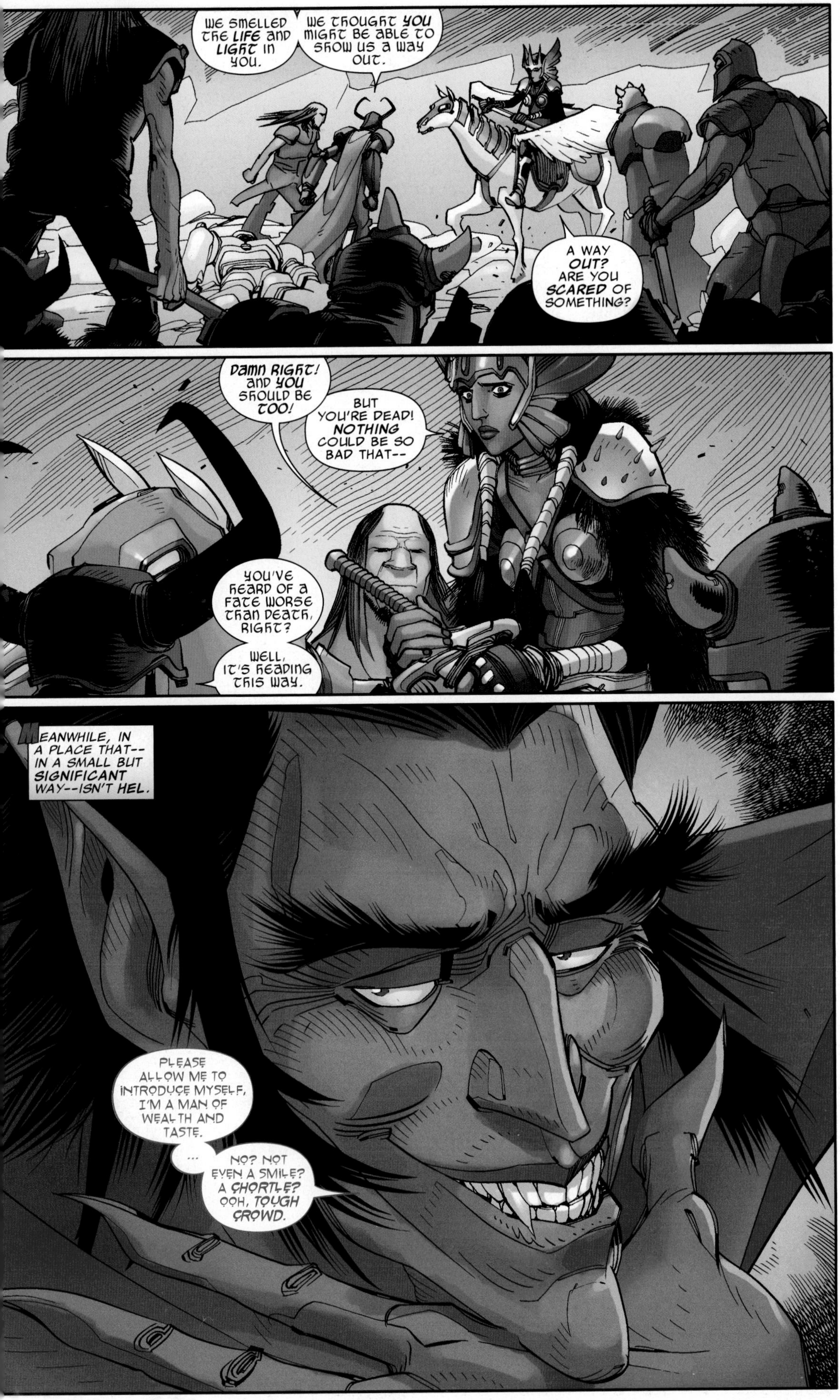
WE SMELLED THE LIFE AND LIGHT IN YOU.
WE THOUGHT YOU MIGHT BE ABLE TO SHOW US A WAY OUT.
A WAY OUT? ARE YOU SCARED OF SOMETHING?
DAMN RIGHT! AND YOU SHOULD BE TOO!
BUT YOU'RE DEAD! NOTHING COULD BE SO BAD THAT--
YOU'VE HEARD OF A FATE WORSE THAN DEATH, RIGHT?
WELL, IT'S HEADING THIS WAY.
MEANWHILE, IN A PLACE THAT-- IN A SMALL BUT SIGNIFICANT WAY--ISN'T HEL.
PLEASE ALLOW ME TO INTRODUCE MYSELF, I'M A MAN OF WEALTH AND TASTE.
...
NO? NOT EVEN A SMILE? A CHORTLE? OOH, TOUGH CROWD.

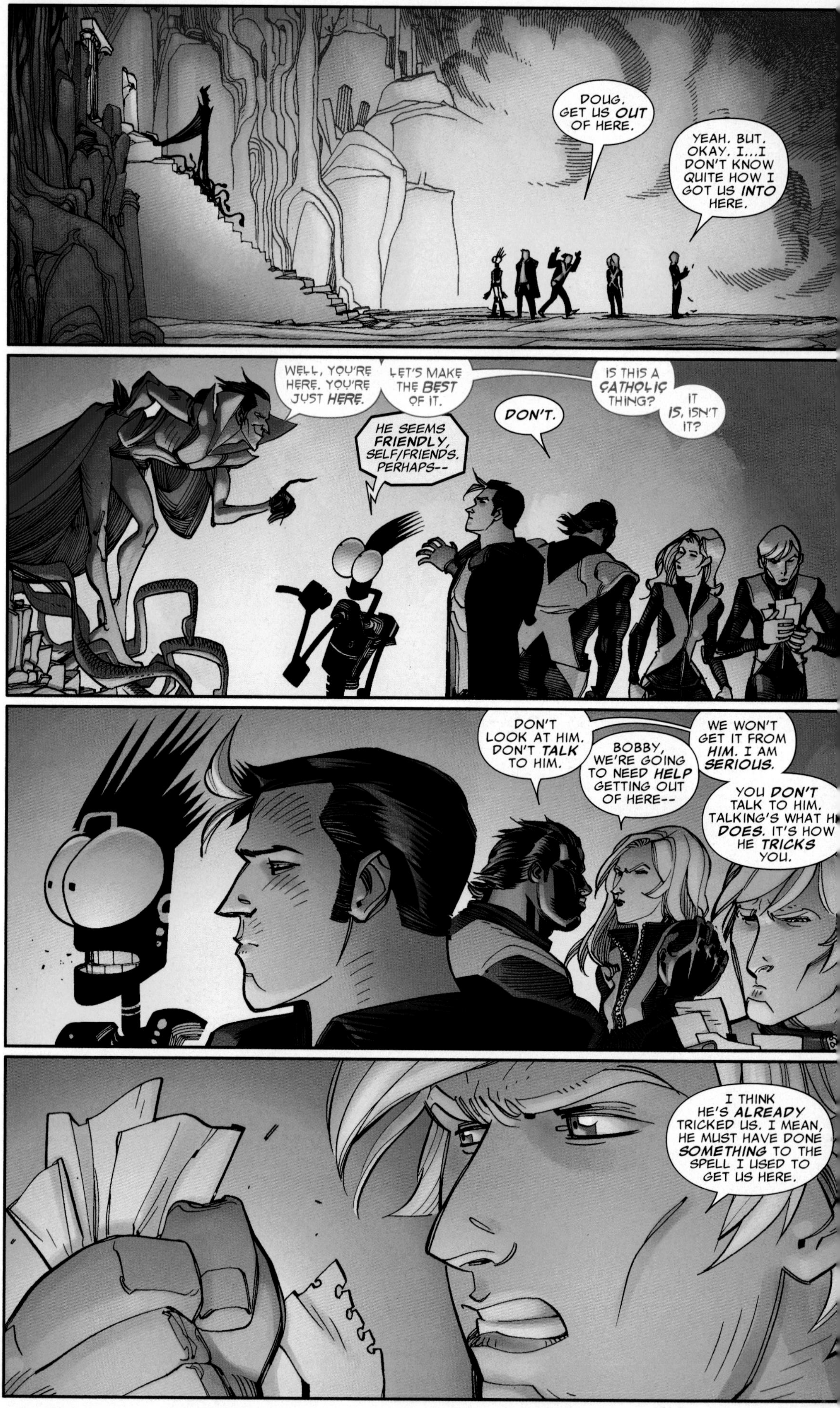
DOUG. GET US OUT OF HERE.
YEAH. BUT. OKAY. I...I DON'T KNOW QUITE HOW I GOT US INTO HERE.
WELL, YOU'RE HERE. YOU'RE JUST HERE.
LET'S MAKE THE BEST OF IT.
HE SEEMS FRIENDLY, SELF/FRIENDS. PERHAPS--
DON'T.
IS THIS A CATHOLIC THING?
IT IS, ISN'T IT?
DON'T LOOK AT HIM. DON'T TALK TO HIM.
BOBBY, WE'RE GOING TO NEED HELP GETTING OUT OF HERE--
WE WON'T GET IT FROM HIM. I AM SERIOUS.
YOU DON'T TALK TO HIM. TALKING'S WHAT H DOES. IT'S HOW HE TRICKS YOU.
I THINK HE'S ALREADY TRICKED US. I MEAN, HE MUST HAVE DONE SOMETHING TO THE SPELL I USED TO GET US HERE.

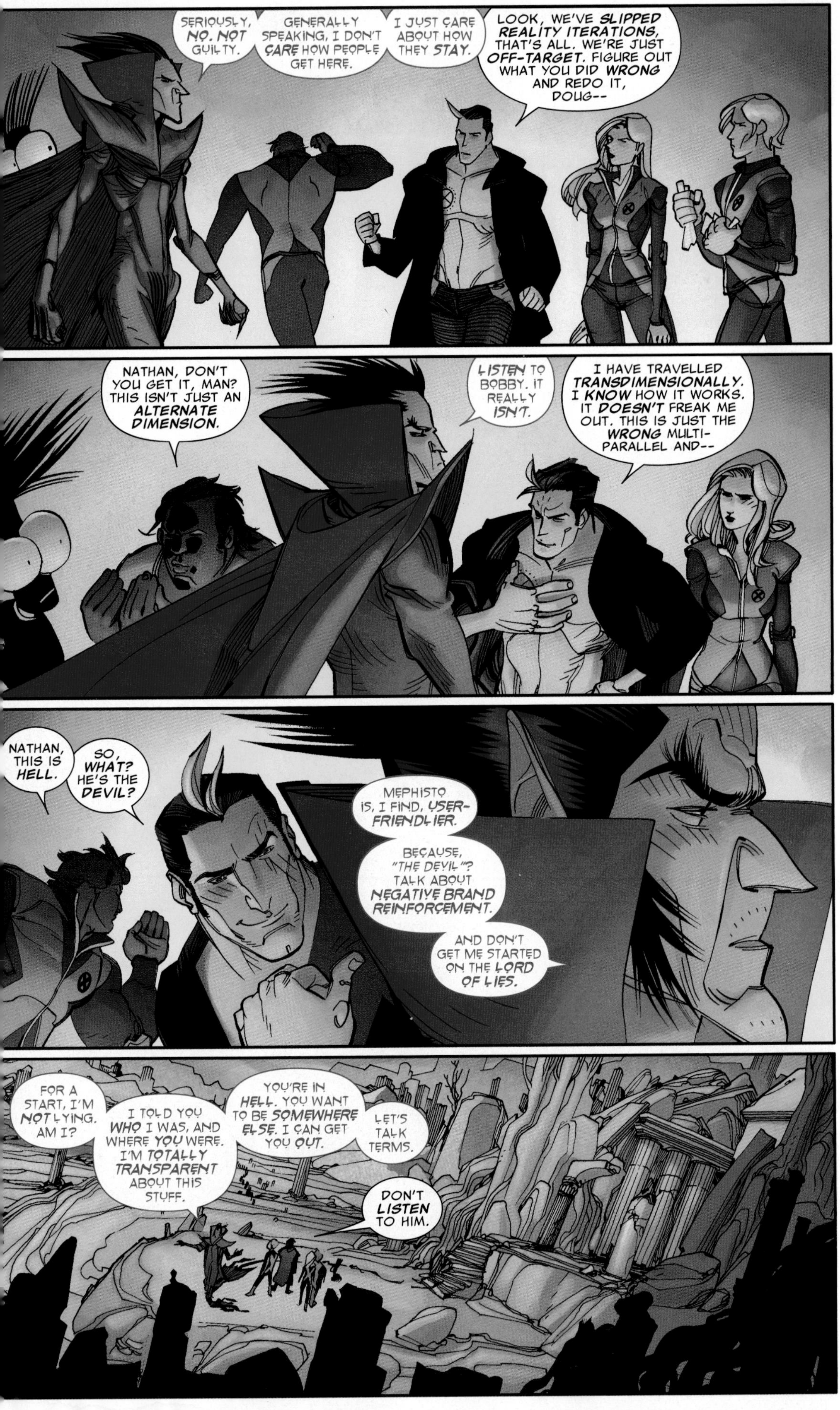

SERIOUSLY, NO. NOT GUILTY.
GENERALLY SPEAKING, I DON'T CARE HOW PEOPLE GET HERE.
I JUST CARE ABOUT HOW THEY STAY.
LOOK, WE'VE SLIPPED REALITY ITERATIONS, THAT'S ALL. WE'RE JUST OFF-TARGET. FIGURE OUT WHAT YOU DID WRONG AND REDO IT, DOUG--
NATHAN, DON'T YOU GET IT, MAN? THIS ISN'T JUST AN ALTERNATE DIMENSION.
LISTEN TO BOBBY. IT REALLY ISN'T.
I HAVE TRAVELLED TRANSDIMENSIONALLY. I KNOW HOW IT WORKS. IT DOESN'T FREAK ME OUT. THIS IS JUST THE WRONG MULTI-PARALLEL AND--
NATHAN, THIS IS HELL.
SO, WHAT? HE'S THE DEVIL?
MEPHISTO IS, I FIND, USER-FRIENDLIER.
BECAUSE, "THE DEVIL"? TALK ABOUT NEGATIVE BRAND REINFORCEMENT.
AND DON'T GET ME STARTED ON THE LORD OF LIES.
FOR A START, I'M NOT LYING. AM I?
I TOLD YOU WHO I WAS, AND WHERE YOU WERE. I'M TOTALLY TRANSPARENT ABOUT THIS STUFF.
YOU'RE IN HELL. YOU WANT TO BE SOMEWHERE ELSE. I CAN GET YOU OUT.
LET'S TALK TERMS.
DON'T LISTEN TO HIM.

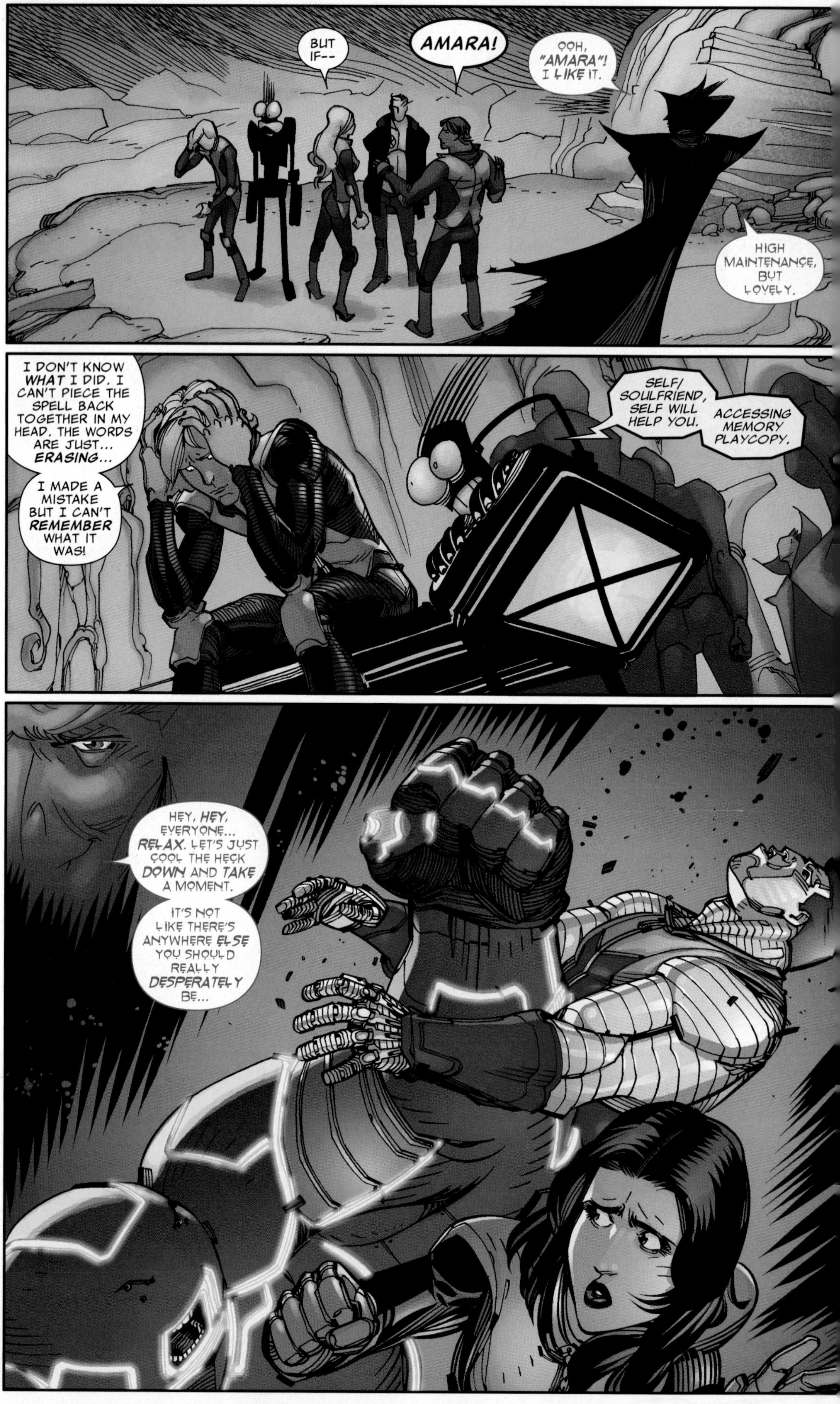
BUT IF--
AMARA!
OOH, "AMARA"! I LIKE IT.
HIGH MAINTENANCE, BUT LOVELY.
I DON'T KNOW WHAT I DID. I CAN'T PIECE THE SPELL BACK TOGETHER IN MY HEAD. THE WORDS ARE JUST... ERASING...
I MADE A MISTAKE BUT I CAN'T REMEMBER WHAT IT WAS!
SELF/ SOULFRIEND, SELF WILL HELP YOU.
ACCESSING MEMORY PLAYCOPY.
HEY, HEY, EVERYONE... RELAX. LET'S JUST COOL THE HECK DOWN AND TAKE A MOMENT.
IT'S NOT LIKE THERE'S ANYWHERE ELSE YOU SHOULD REALLY DESPERATELY BE...

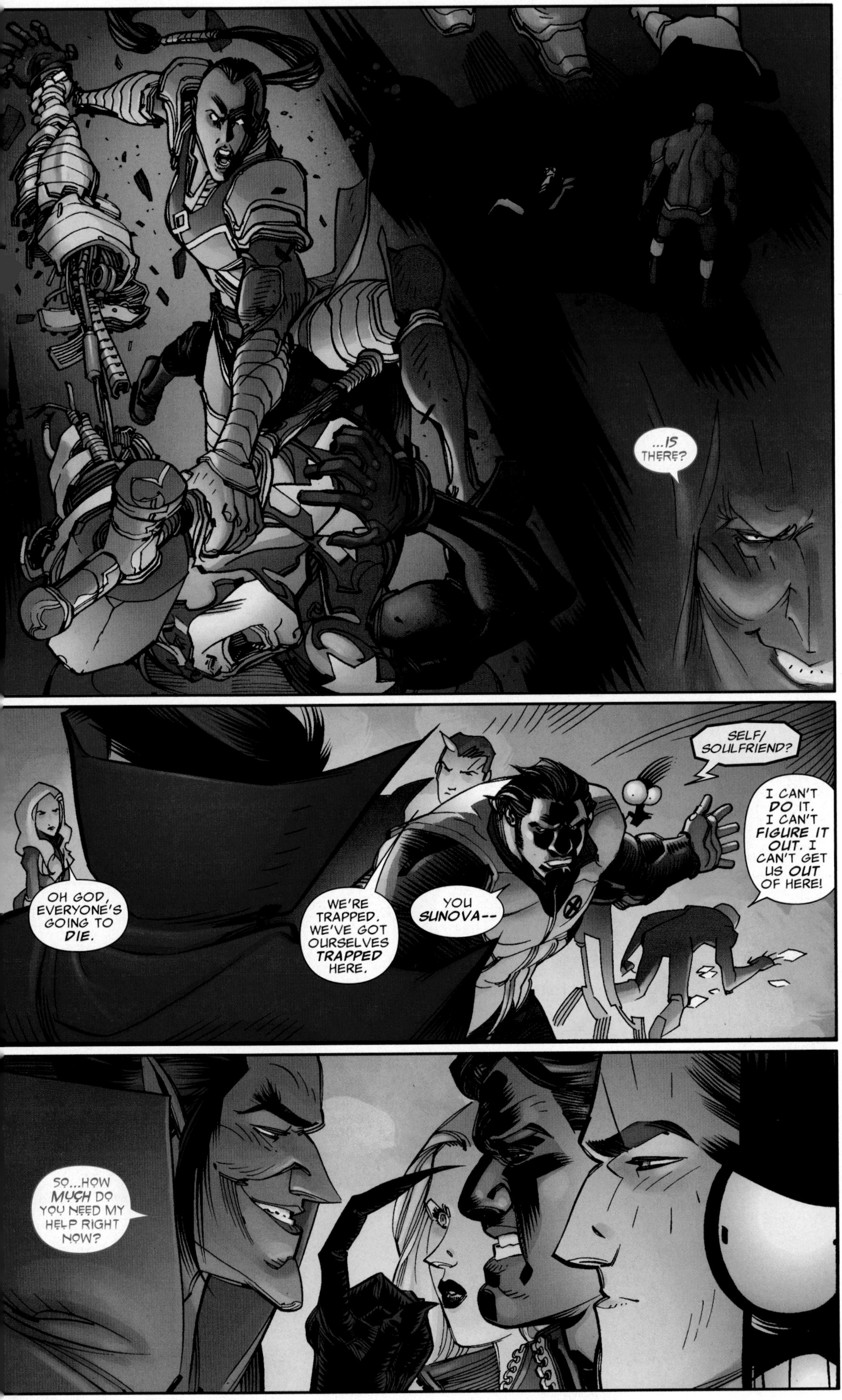
...IS THERE?
SELF/ SOULFRIEND?
I CAN'T DO IT. I CAN'T FIGURE IT OUT. I CAN'T GET US OUT OF HERE!
YOU SUNOVA--
WE'RE TRAPPED. WE'VE GOT OURSELVES TRAPPED HERE.
OH GOD, EVERYONE'S GOING TO DIE.
SO...HOW MUCH DO YOU NEED MY HELP RIGHT NOW?

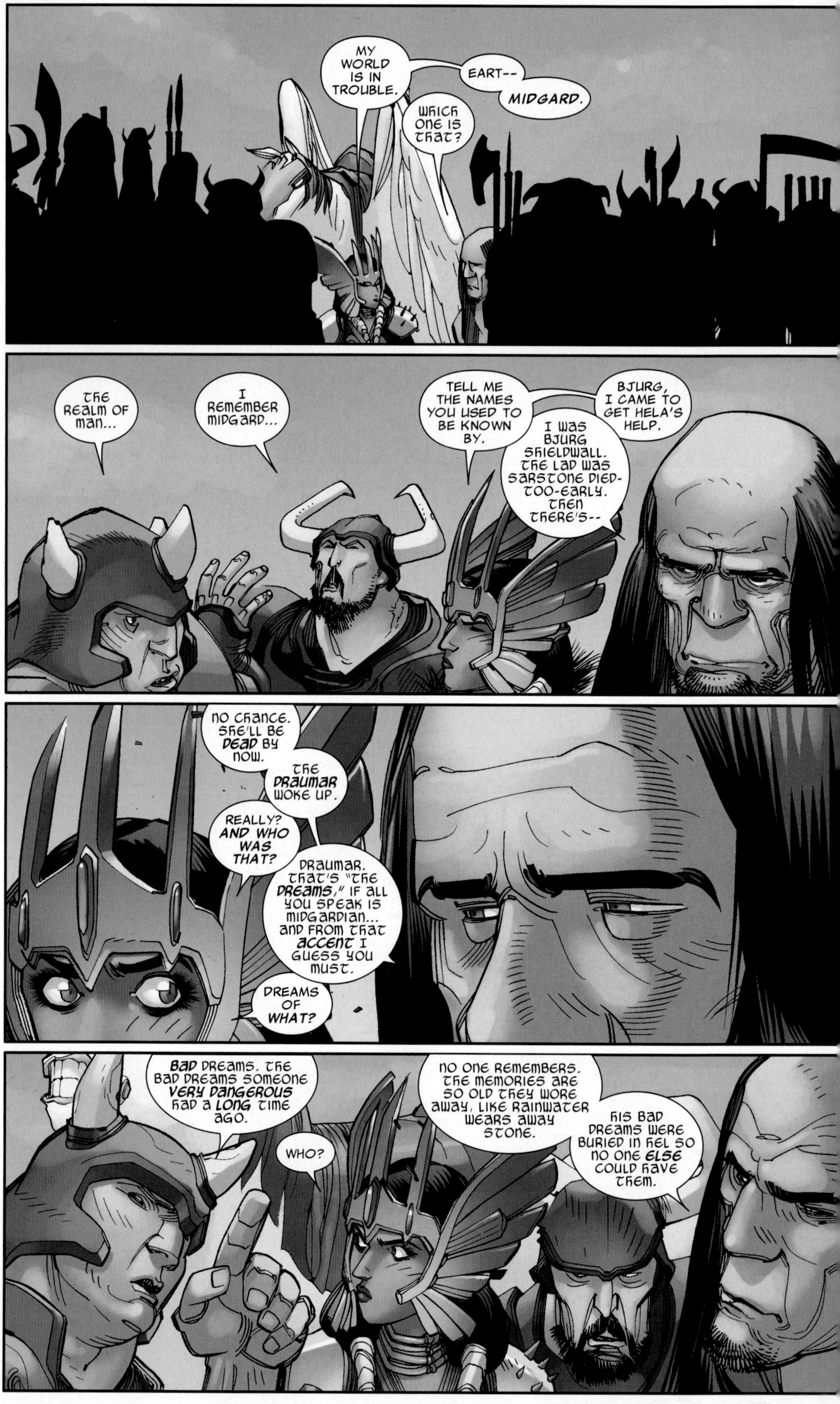
MY WORLD IS IN TROUBLE.
EART-- MIDGARD.
WHICH ONE IS THAT?
THE REALM OF MAN...
I REMEMBER MIDGARD...
TELL ME THE NAMES YOU USED TO BE KNOWN BY.
BJURG, I CAME TO GET HELA'S HELP.
I WAS BJURG SHIELDWALL. THE LAD WAS SARSTONE DIED-TOO-EARLY. THEN THERE'S--
NO CHANCE. SHE'LL BE DEAD BY NOW.
THE DRAUMAR WOKE UP.
REALLY? AND WHO WAS THAT?
DRAUMAR. THAT'S "THE DREAMS," IF ALL YOU SPEAK IS MIDGARDIAN... AND FROM THAT ACCENT I GUESS YOU MUST.
DREAMS OF WHAT?
BAD DREAMS. THE BAD DREAMS SOMEONE VERY DANGEROUS HAD A LONG TIME AGO.
WHO?
NO ONE REMEMBERS. THE MEMORIES ARE SO OLD THEY WORE AWAY, LIKE RAINWATER WEARS AWAY STONE.
HIS BAD DREAMS WERE BURIED IN HEL SO NO ONE ELSE COULD HAVE THEM.

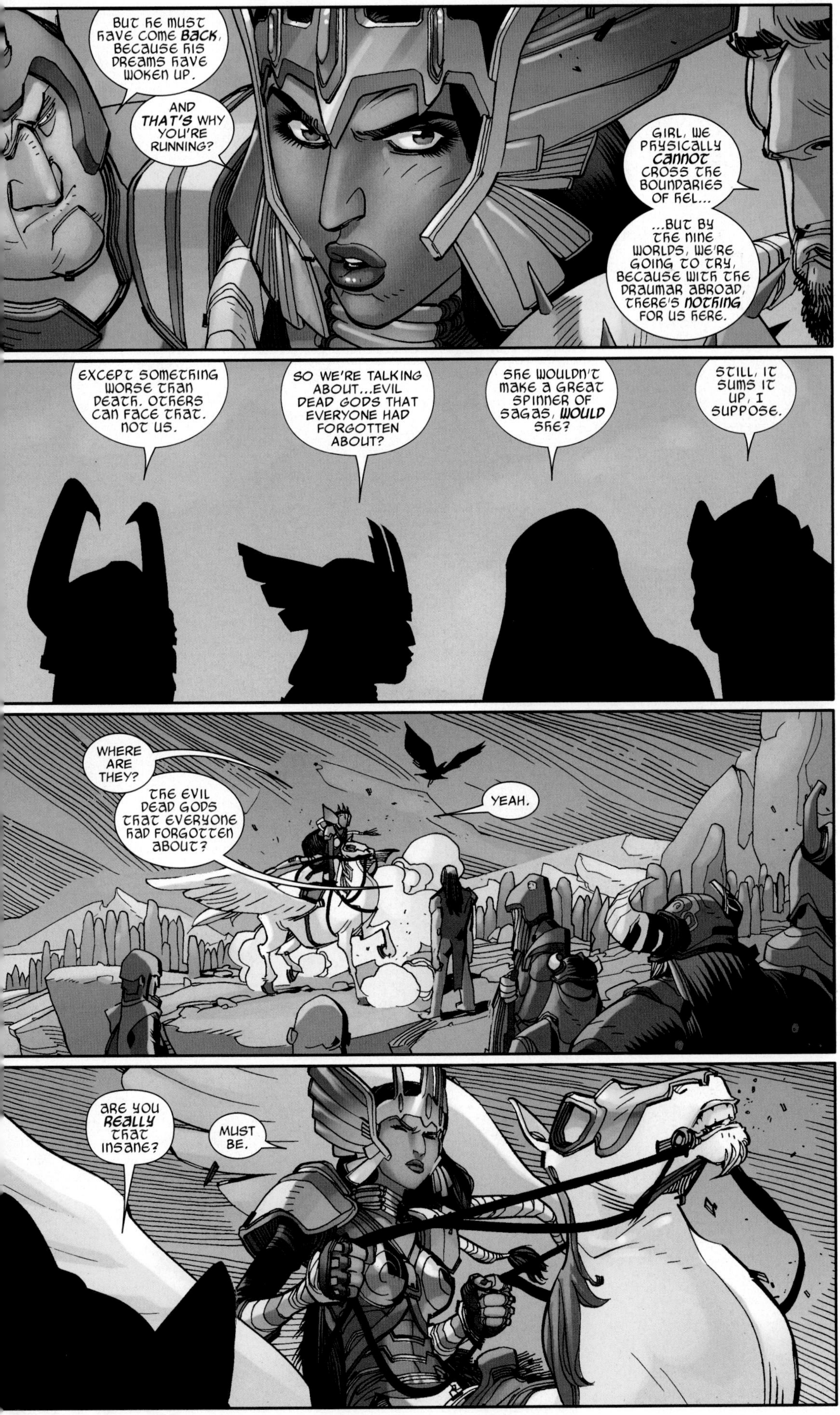
BUT HE MUST HAVE COME BACK, BECAUSE HIS DREAMS HAVE WOKEN UP.
AND THAT'S WHY YOU'RE RUNNING?
GIRL, WE PHYSICALLY CANNOT CROSS THE BOUNDARIES OF HEL...
...BUT BY THE NINE WORLDS, WE'RE GOING TO TRY, BECAUSE WITH THE DRAUMAR ABROAD, THERE'S NOTHING FOR US HERE.
EXCEPT SOMETHING WORSE THAN DEATH. OTHERS CAN FACE THAT. NOT US.
SO WE'RE TALKING ABOUT...EVIL DEAD GODS THAT EVERYONE HAD FORGOTTEN ABOUT?
SHE WOULDN'T MAKE A GREAT SPINNER OF SAGAS, WOULD SHE?
STILL, IT SUMS IT UP, I SUPPOSE.
WHERE ARE THEY?
THE EVIL DEAD GODS THAT EVERYONE HAD FORGOTTEN ABOUT?
YEAH.
ARE YOU REALLY THAT INSANE?
MUST BE.

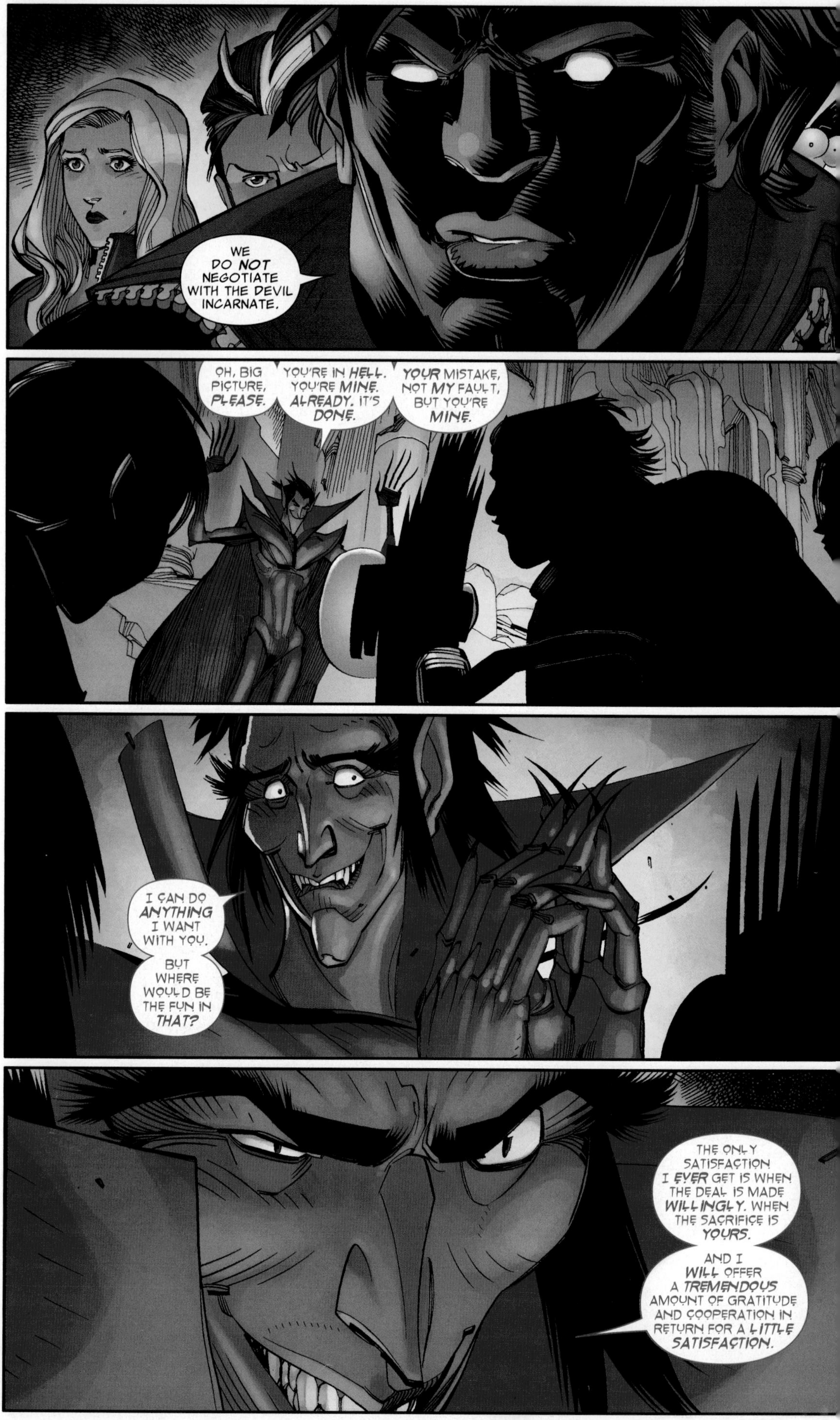
WE DO NOT NEGOTIATE WITH THE DEVIL INCARNATE.
OH, BIG PICTURE, PLEASE.
YOU'RE IN HELL. YOU'RE MINE. ALREADY. IT'S DONE.
YOUR MISTAKE, NOT MY FAULT, BUT YOU'RE MINE.
I CAN DO ANYTHING I WANT WITH YOU.
BUT WHERE WOULD BE THE FUN IN THAT?
THE ONLY SATISFACTION I EVER GET IS WHEN THE DEAL IS MADE WILLINGLY. WHEN THE SACRIFICE IS YOURS.
AND I WILL OFFER A TREMENDOUS AMOUNT OF GRATITUDE AND COOPERATION IN RETURN FOR A LITTLE SATISFACTION.

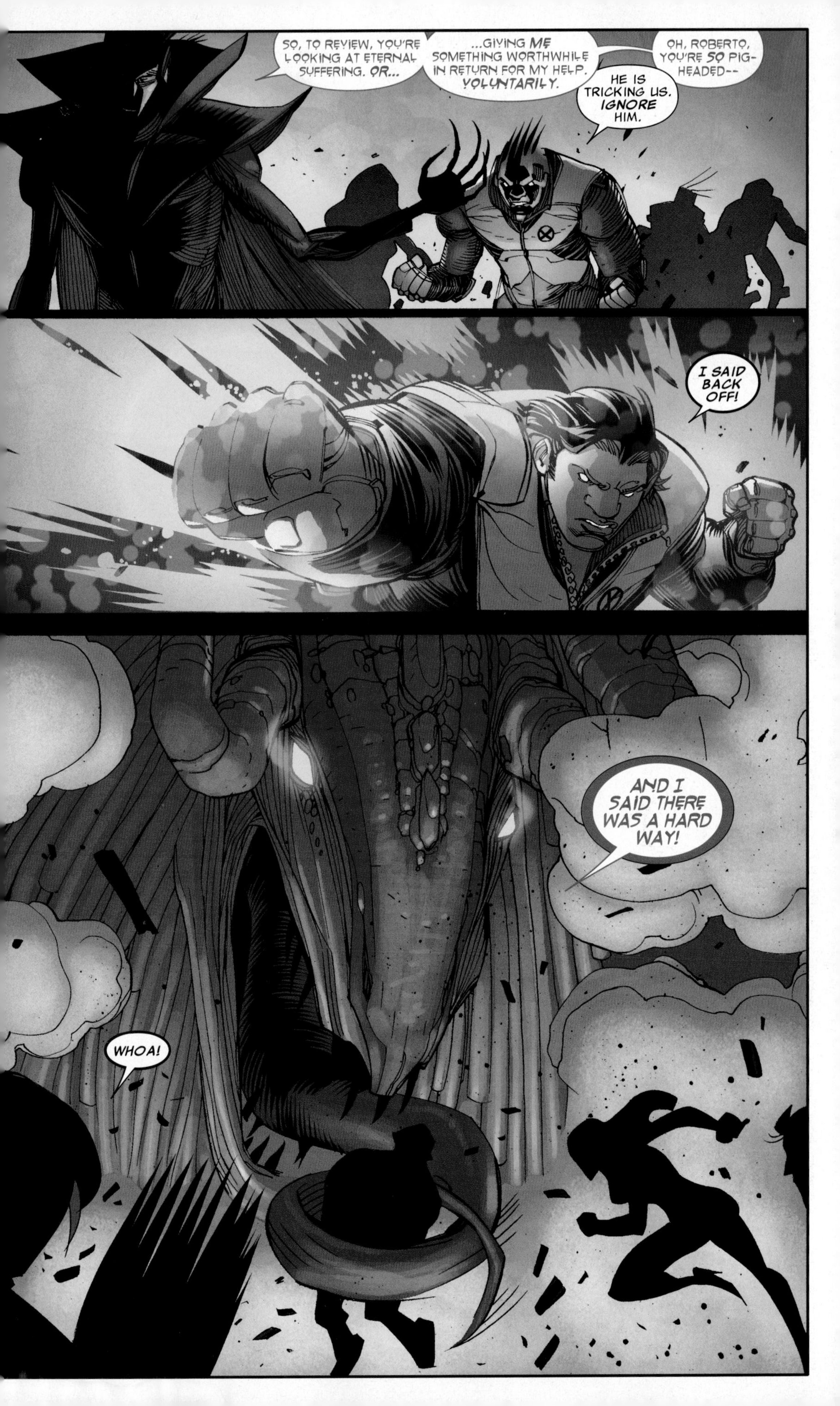
SO, TO REVIEW, YOU'RE LOOKING AT ETERNAL SUFFERING. OR...
...GIVING ME SOMETHING WORTHWHILE IN RETURN FOR MY HELP. VOLUNTARILY.
OH, ROBERTO, YOU'RE SO PIG-HEADED--
HE IS TRICKING US. IGNORE HIM.
I SAID BACK OFF!
AND I SAID THERE WAS A HARD WAY!
WHOA!

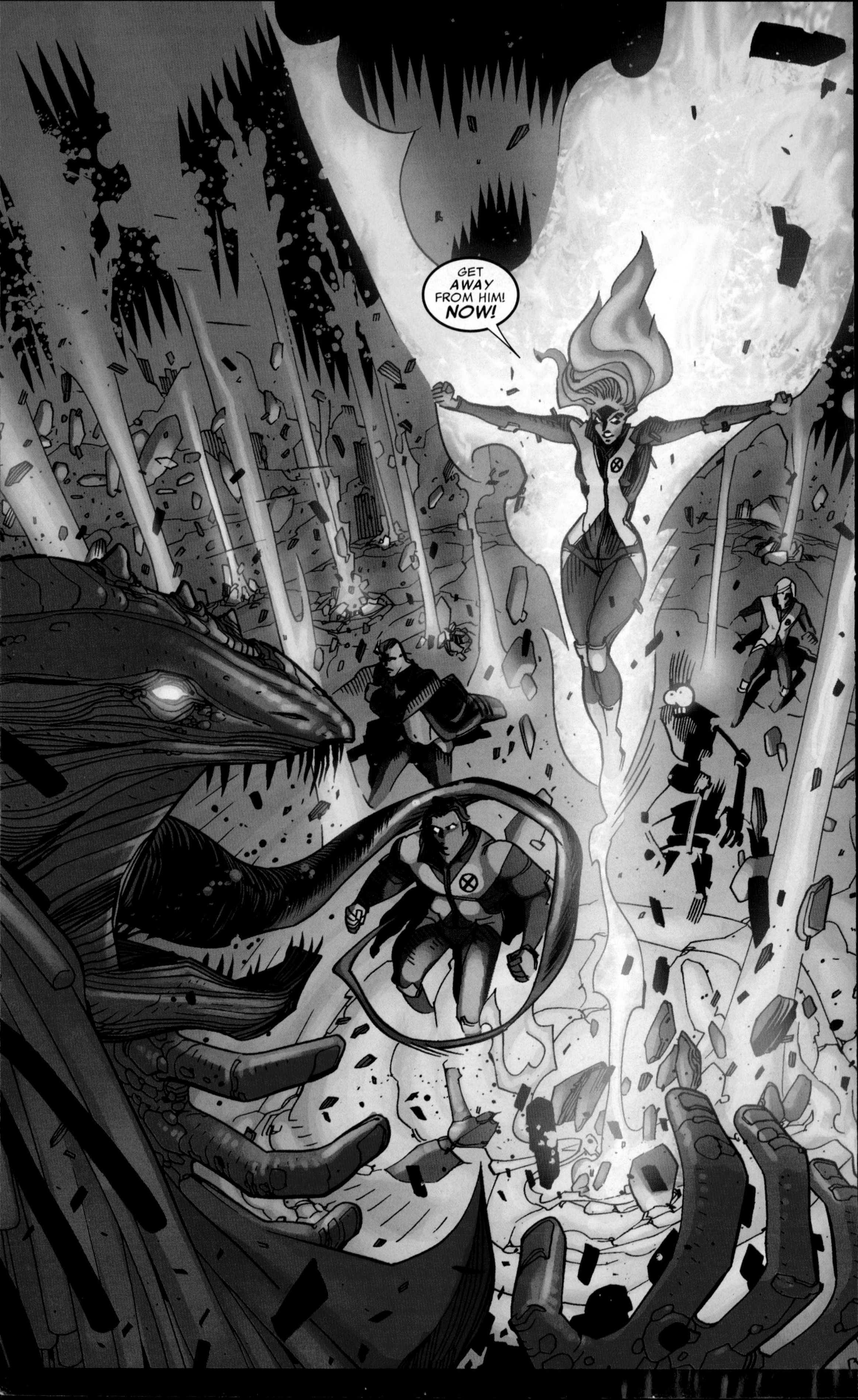
GET AWAY FROM HIM! NOW!

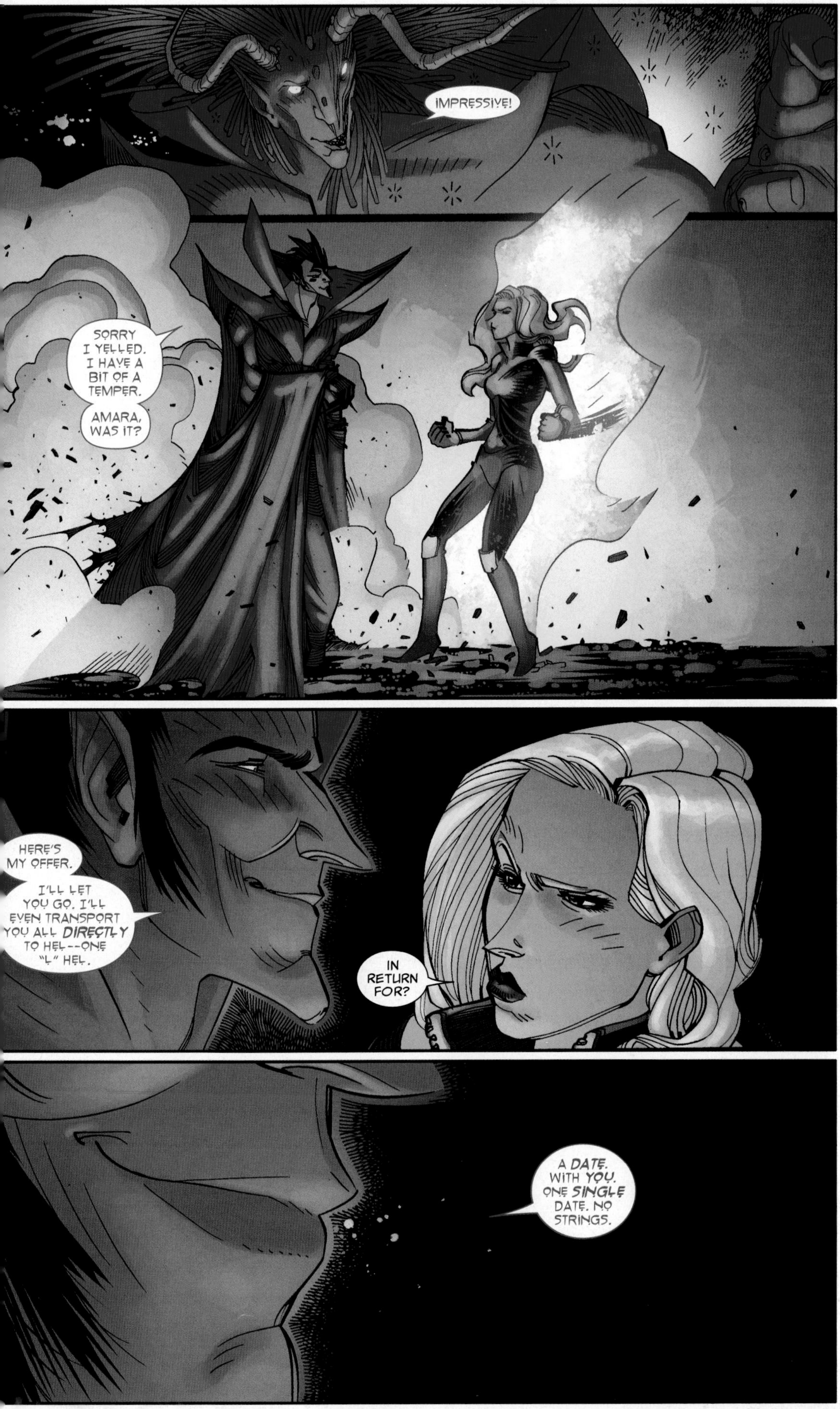

IMPRESSIVE!
SORRY I YELLED. I HAVE A BIT OF A TEMPER.
AMARA, WAS IT?
HERE'S MY OFFER.
I'LL LET YOU GO. I'LL EVEN TRANSPORT YOU ALL DIRECTLY TO HEL--ONE "L" HEL.
IN RETURN FOR?
A DATE. WITH YOU. ONE SINGLE DATE. NO STRINGS.

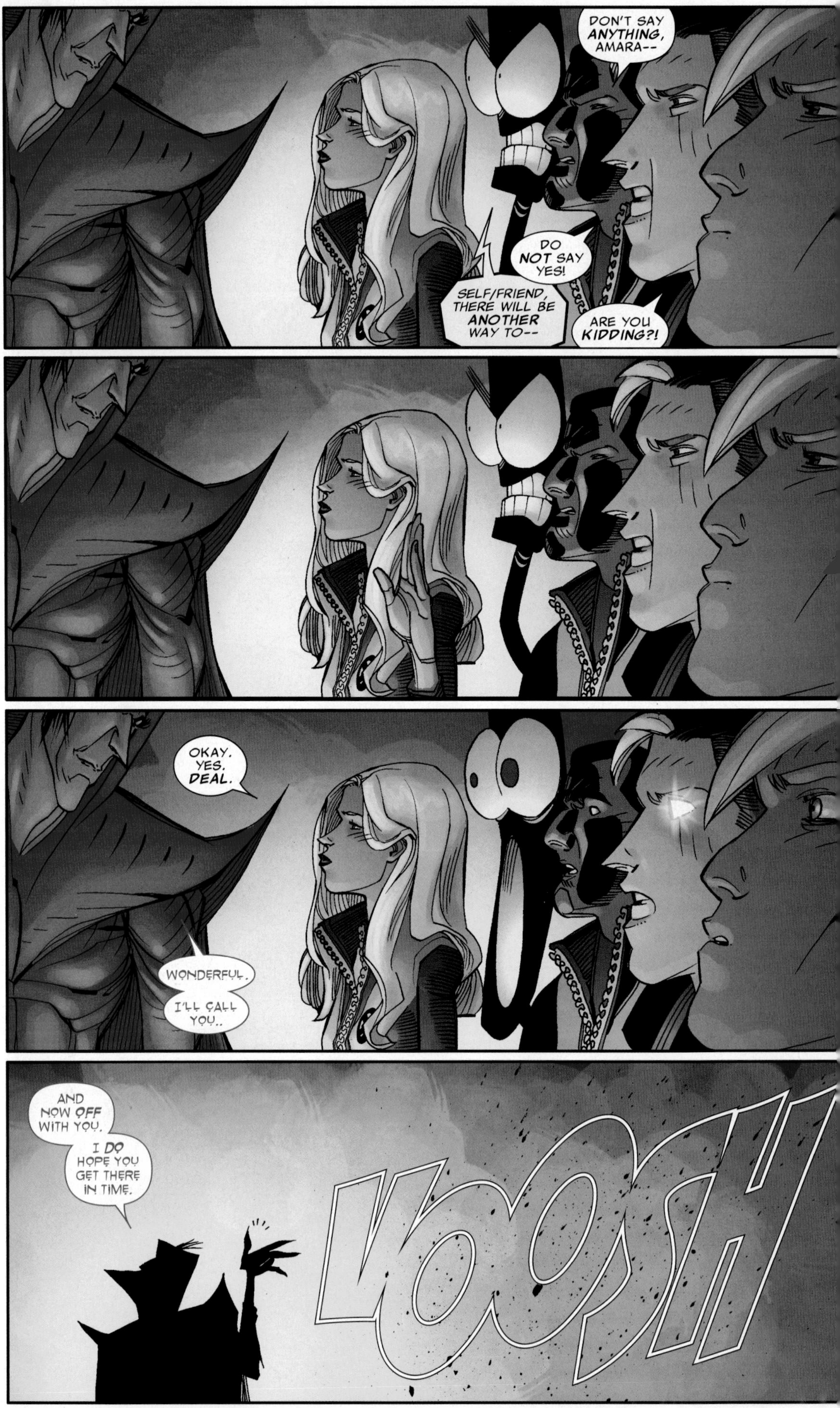
DON'T SAY ANYTHING, AMARA--
DO NOT SAY YES!
SELF/FRIEND, THERE WILL BE ANOTHER WAY TO--
ARE YOU KIDDING?!
OKAY. YES. DEAL.
WONDERFUL.
I'LL CALL YOU..
AND NOW OFF WITH YOU.
I DO HOPE YOU GET THERE IN TIME.
WOOSH

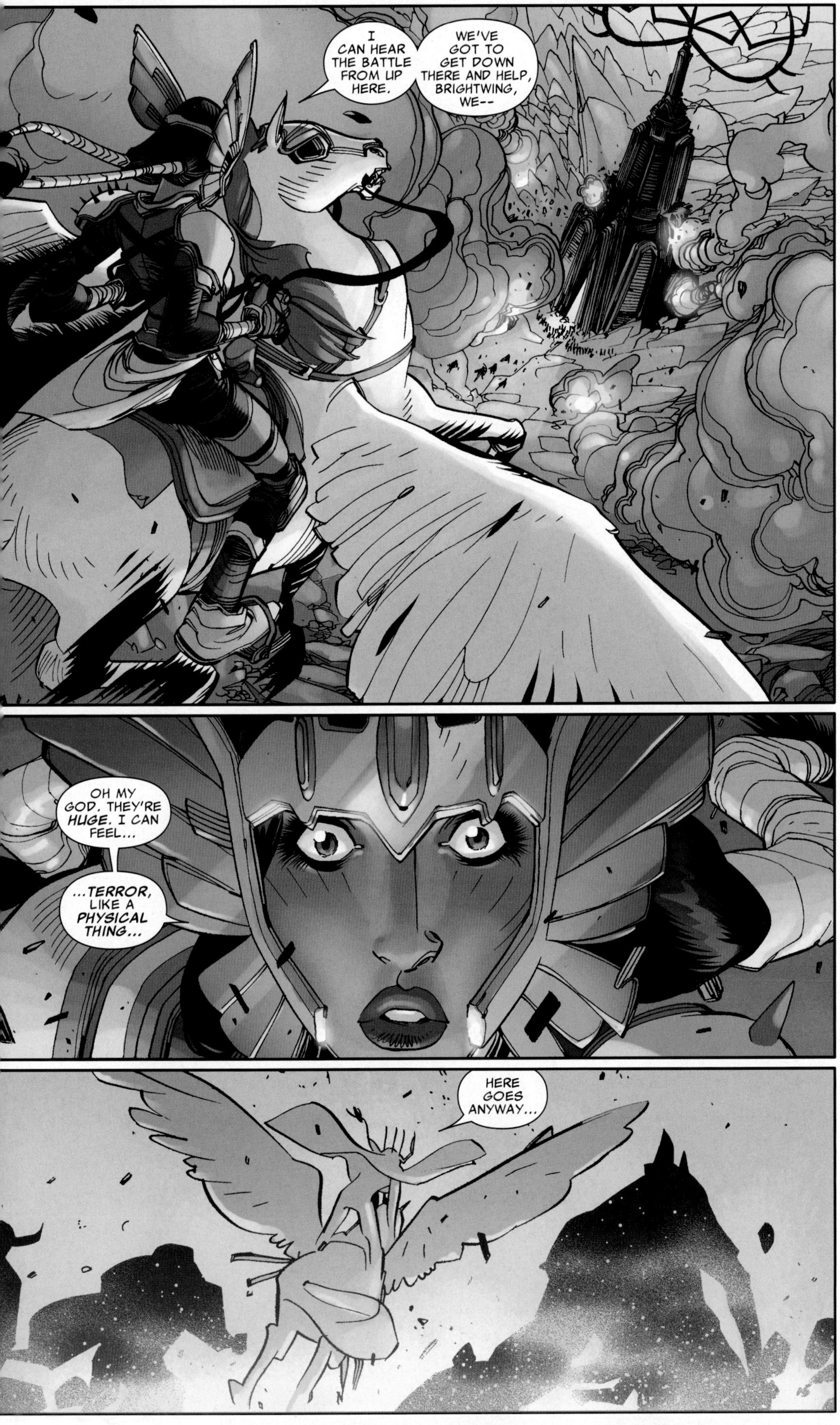
I CAN HEAR THE BATTLE FROM UP HERE.
WE'VE GOT TO GET DOWN THERE AND HELP, BRIGHTWING, WE--
OH MY GOD. THEY'RE HUGE. I CAN FEEL...
...TERROR, LIKE A PHYSICAL THING...
HERE GOES ANYWAY...

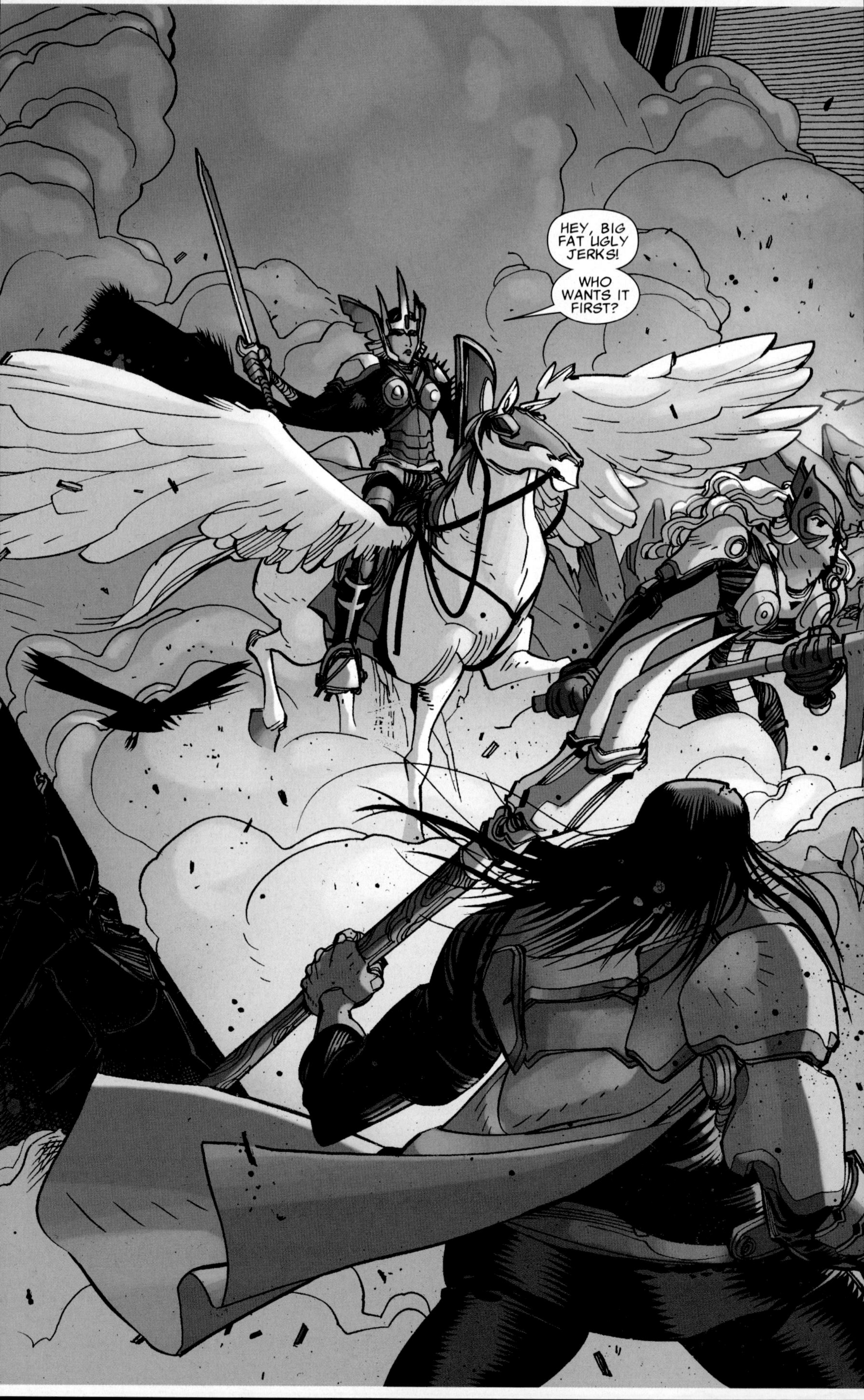
HEY, BIG FAT UGLY JERKS!
WHO WANTS IT FIRST?

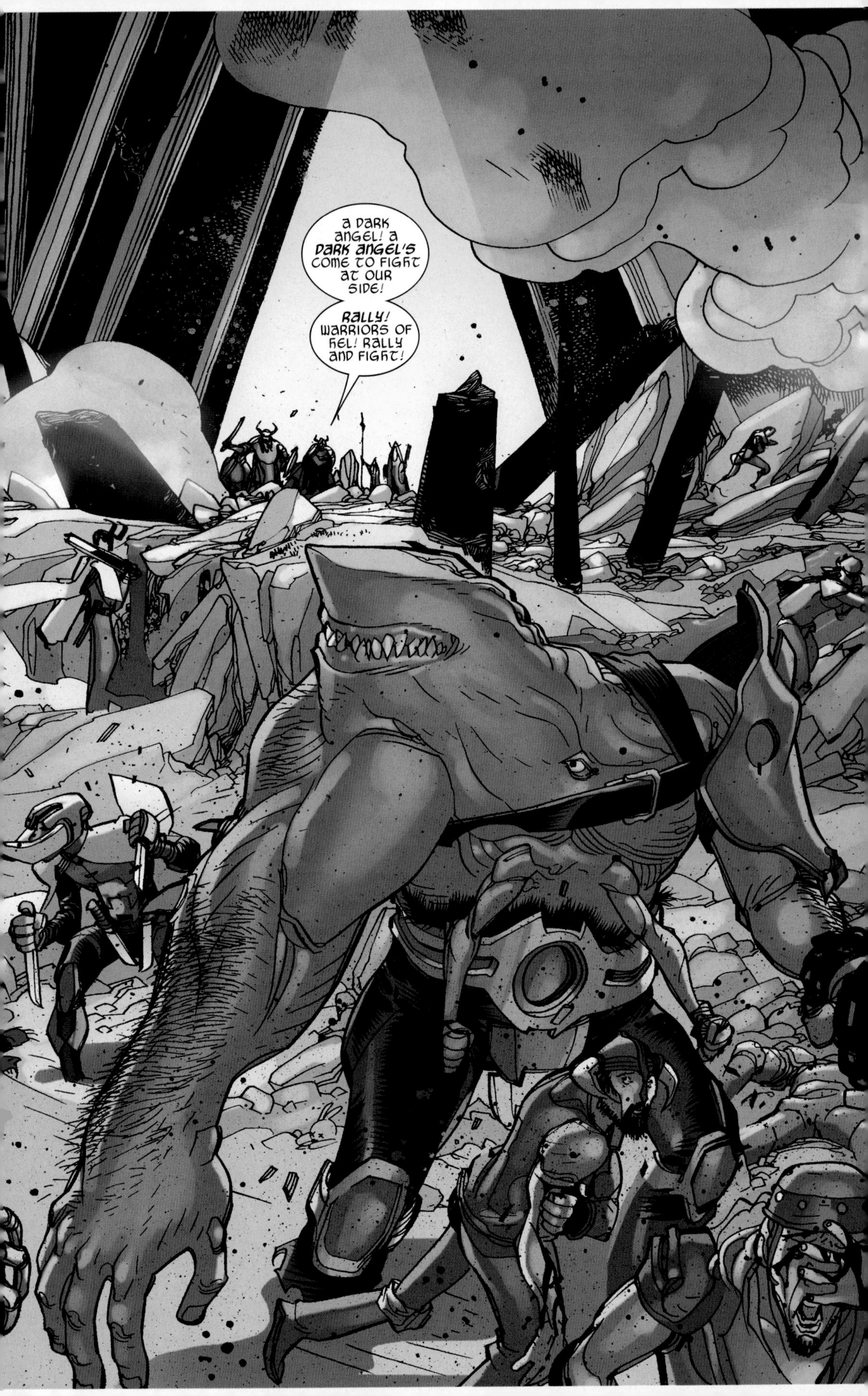
A DARK ANGEL! A DARK ANGEL'S COME TO FIGHT AT OUR SIDE!
RALLY! WARRIORS OF HEL! RALLY AND FIGHT!

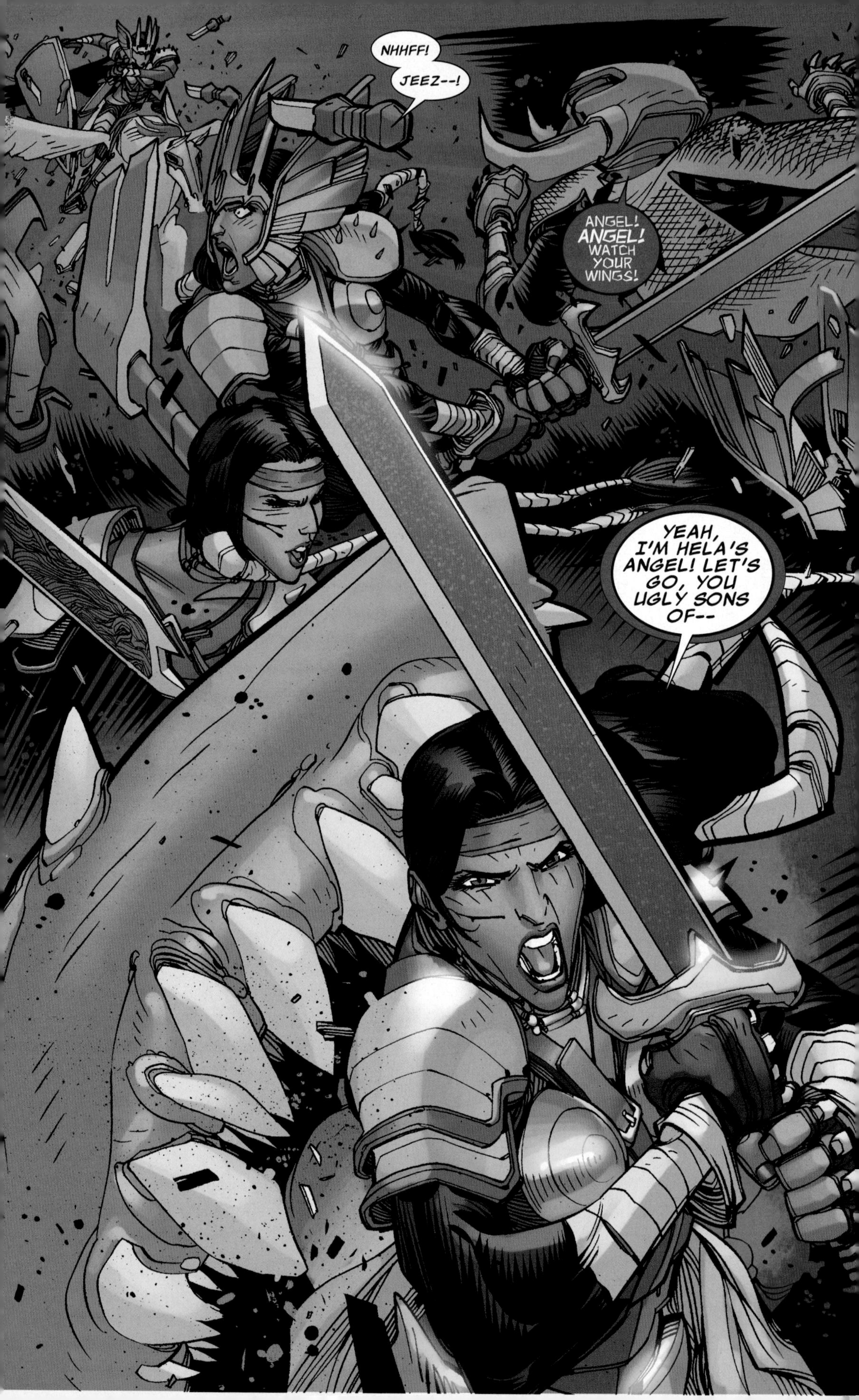
NHHFF!
JEEZ--!
ANGEL! ANGEL! WATCH YOUR WINGS!
YEAH, I'M HELA'S ANGEL! LET'S GO, YOU UGLY SONS OF--

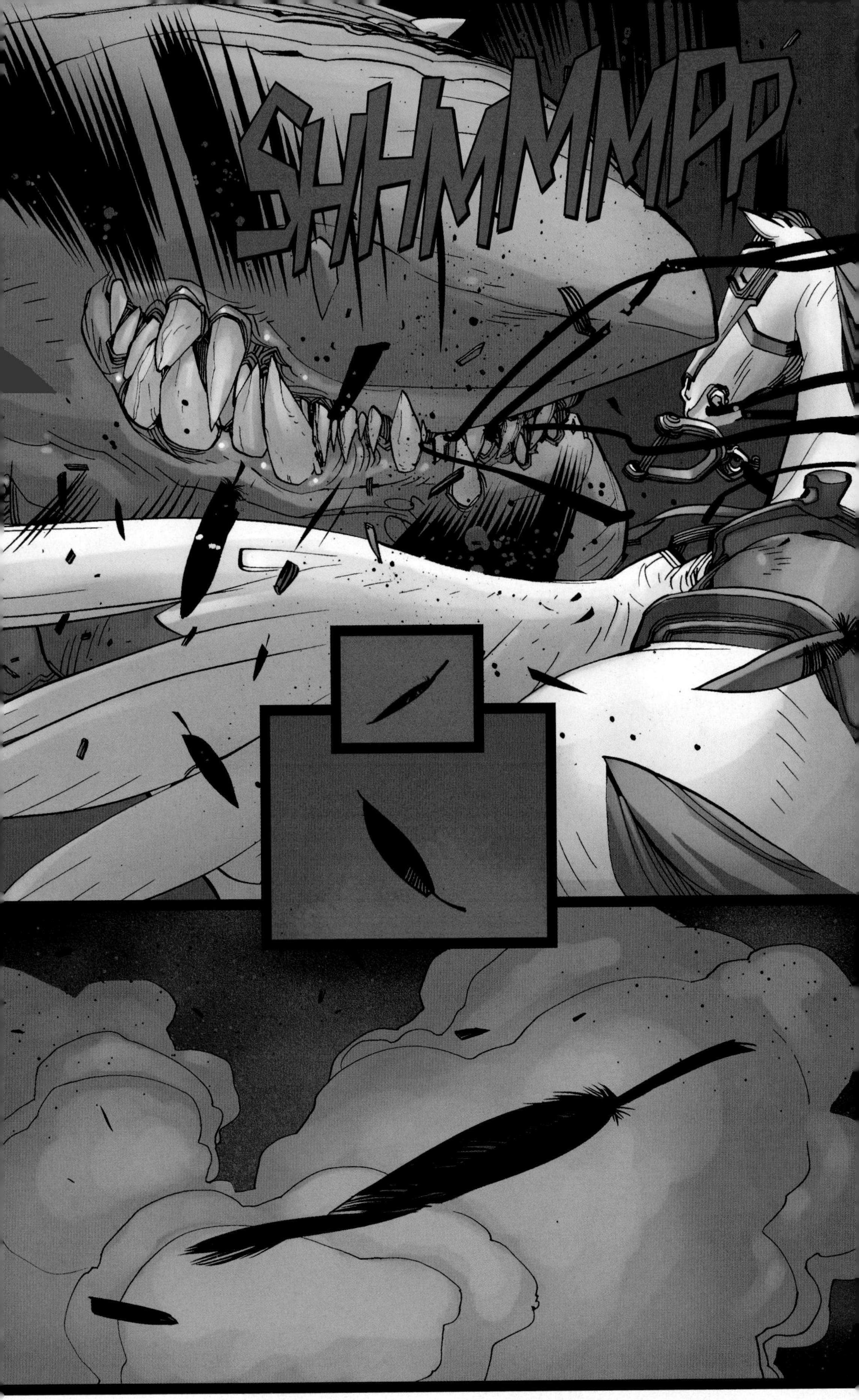
SHHMMMPP

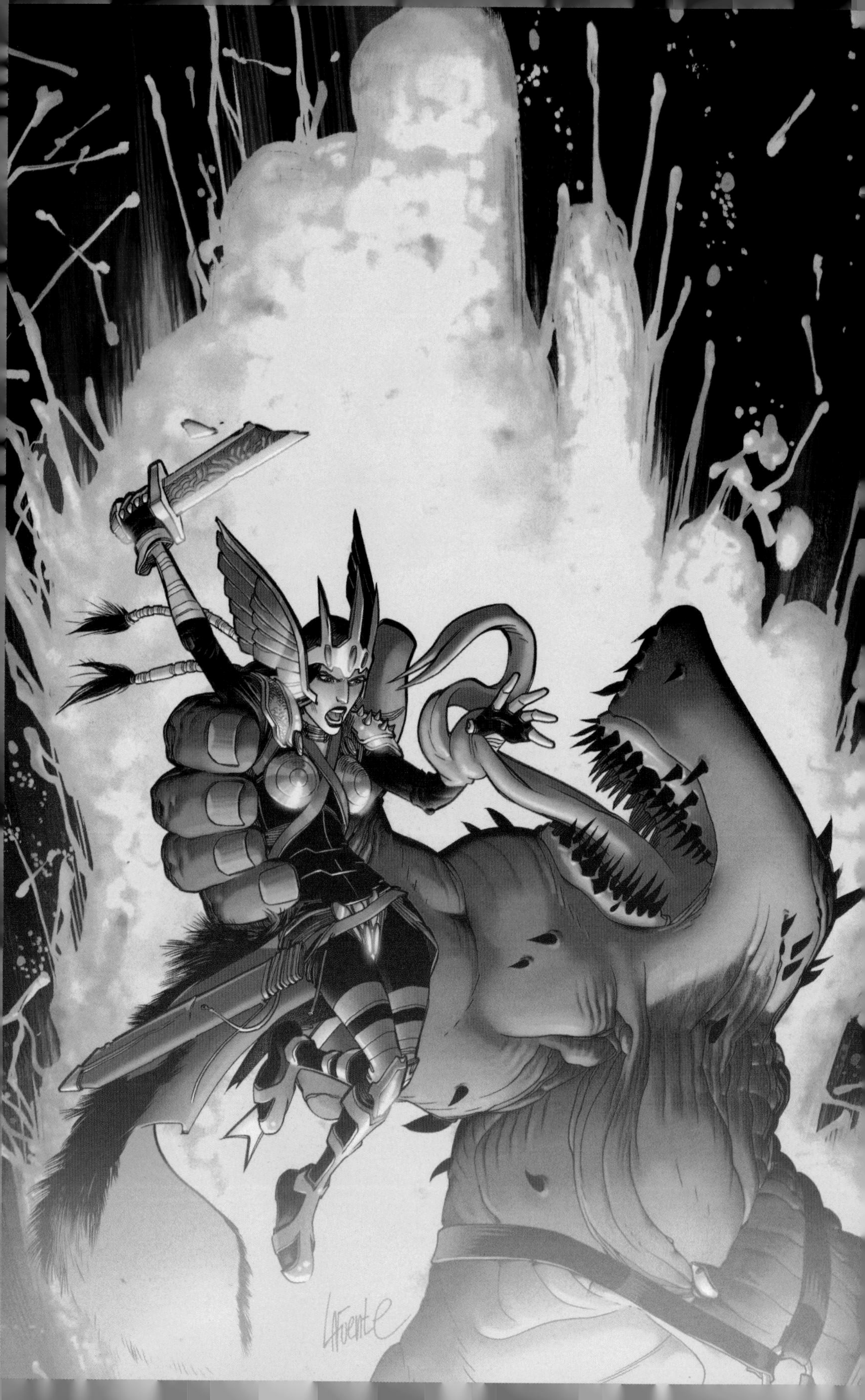
LaFuente

HEN YOU **DIE**, DANI MOONSTAR-- WHEN YOU DIE AND GO TO HEL...

WHEN DEATH **CLOSES ITS JAWS** AND SWALLOWS YOU WHOLE...

...IMAGINE HOW **ODD** IT WOULD BE IF IT WASN'T **YOUR** LIFE THAT FLASHED BEFORE YOUR EYES.

IMAGINE GETTING SOME **ELSE'S** LIFE STORY INSTEAD.

HIS NAME WAS **BONEGRINDER**.

WAS ONE OF E **DRALIMAR**, FOOTSOLDIERS THE **SERPENT**.

IN THE MEMORY, YOU SEE THEM AS THEY ARE **NOW**, TRANSMUTED BY **EONS** OF HATRED AND RAGE.

THEY WERE **WARRIORS** THEN, NOT **MONSTERS**. IT WAS A LONG TIME AGO BY **ANYONE'S** STANDARDS.

EVEN THE **MEMORY** STINKS OF AGE AND GRAVE-DIRT.

THE SERPENT HAD HIS CHAMPIONS, THE **WORTHY**, AND THE **DRALIMAR** WERE THE **HUSCARL COMPANY** WHO SERVED BOTH THE LORD AND HIS CHAMPIONS.

THAT DAY, THAT **LAST** DAY--

--GODS! SO LONG AGO!

THAT DAY, THE GREAT SERPENT WAS **ANGRY**, AND HE WAS **AFRAID**.

HE WAS IN HIS THRONE ROOM, ACCOMPANIED BY SKADI AND THE WORTHIES, SURROUNDED BY HIS LOYAL DRALIMAR, AND HE WAS **STILL** AFRAID...

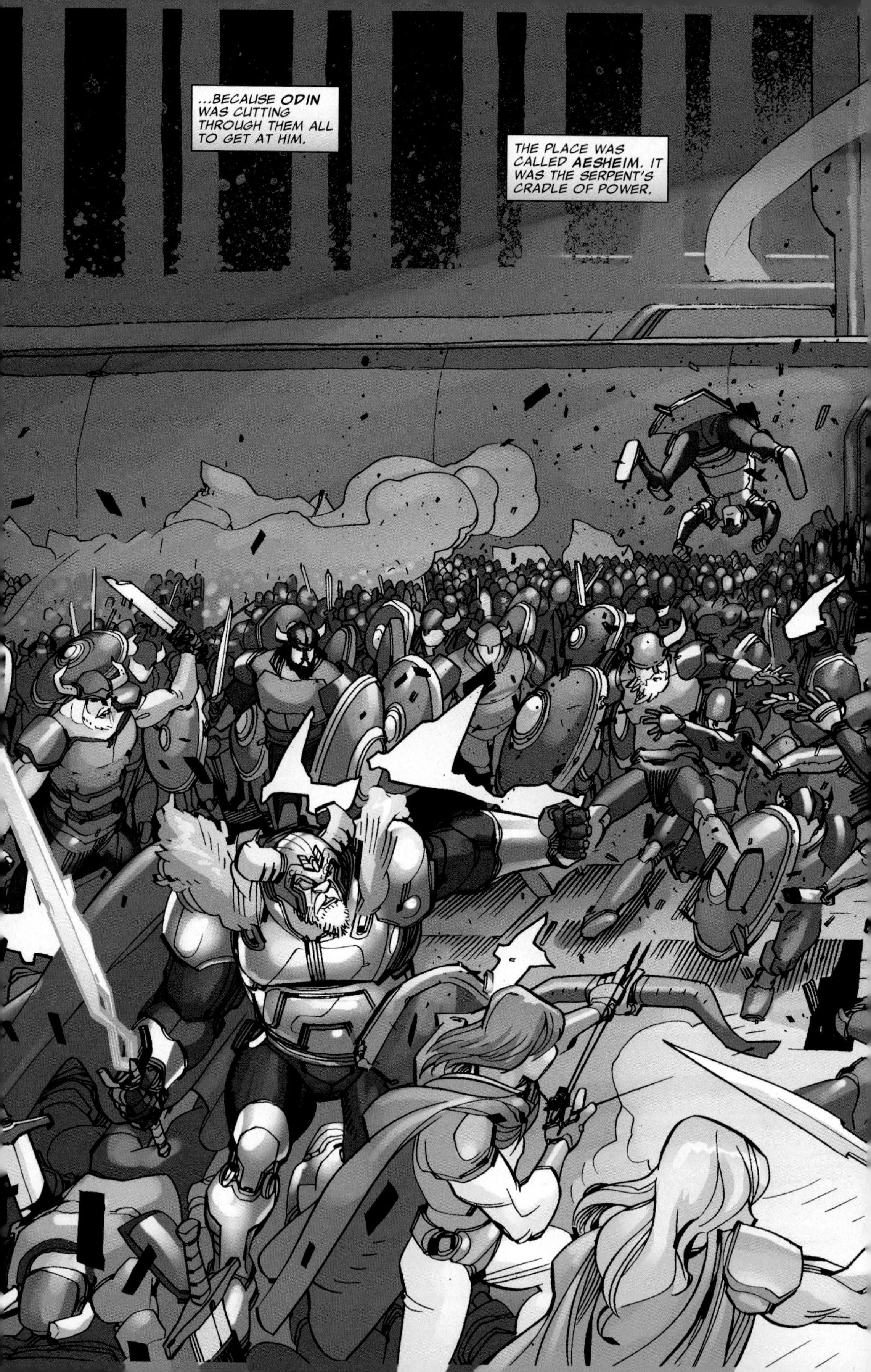
...BECAUSE ODIN WAS CUTTING THROUGH THEM ALL TO GET AT HIM.
THE PLACE WAS CALLED AESHEIM. IT WAS THE SERPENT'S CRADLE OF POWER.

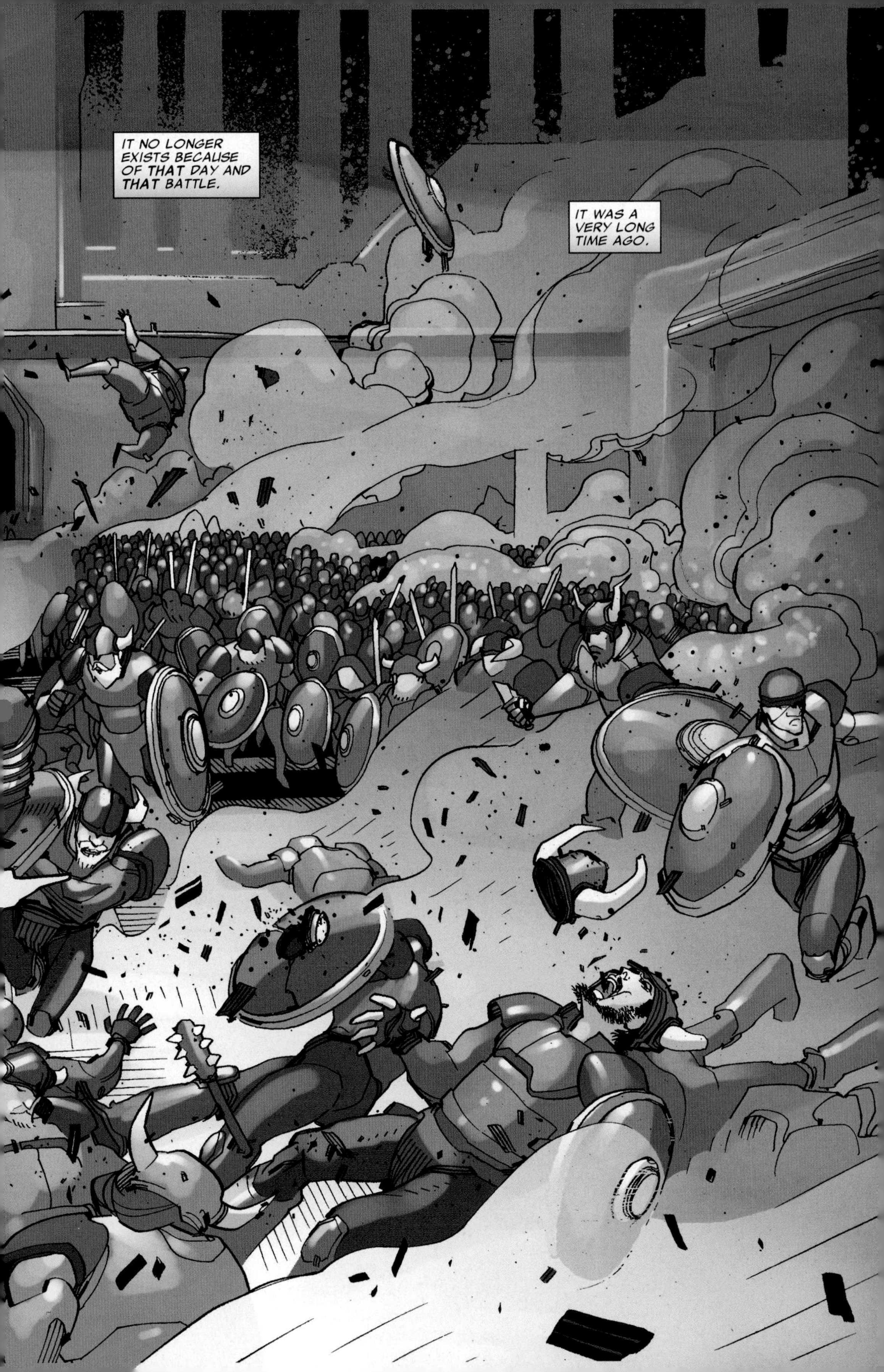
IT NO LONGER EXISTS BECAUSE OF THAT DAY AND THAT BATTLE.
IT WAS A VERY LONG TIME AGO.

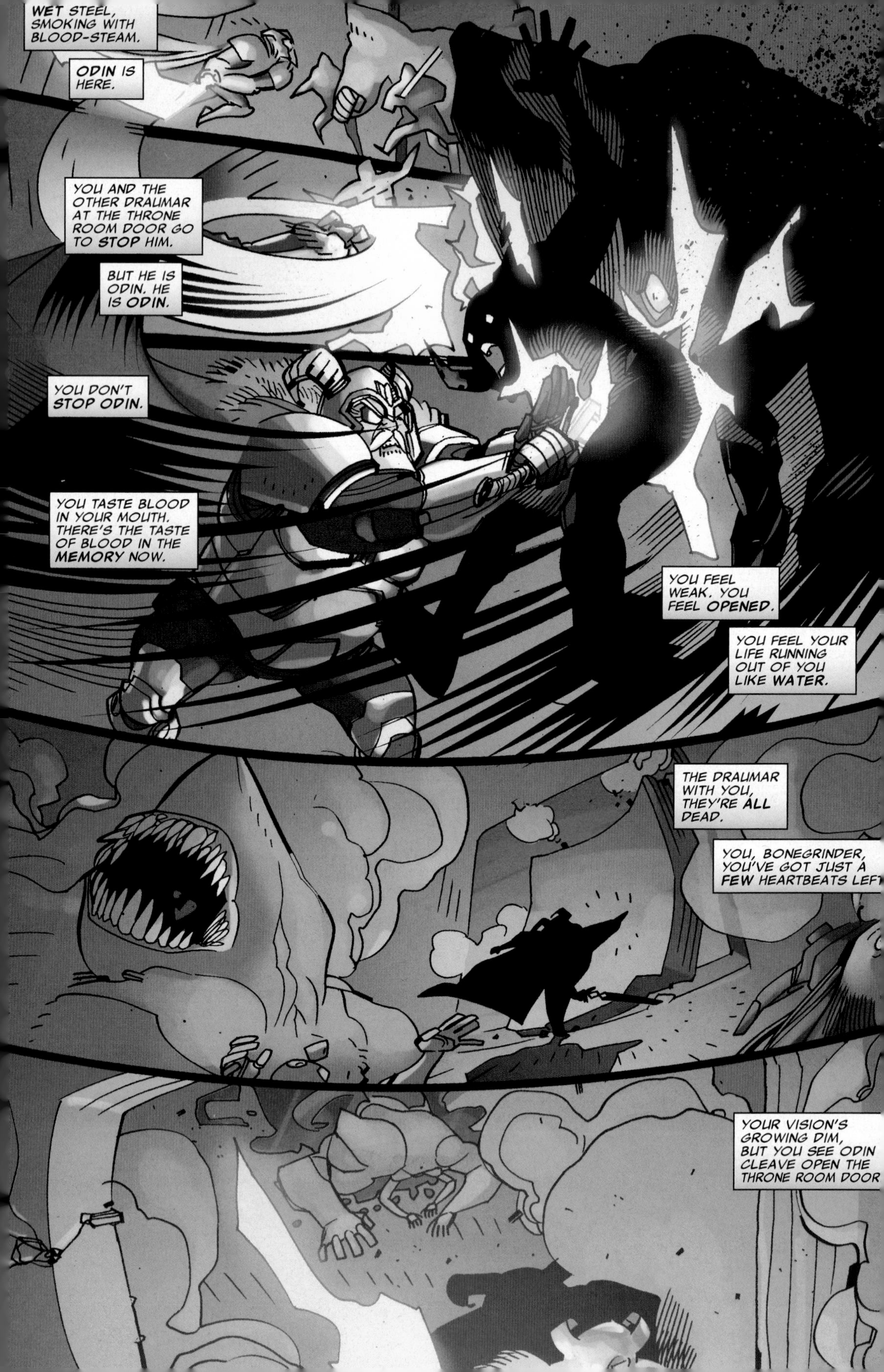
WET STEEL, SMOKING WITH BLOOD-STEAM.
ODIN IS HERE.
YOU AND THE OTHER DRAUMAR AT THE THRONE ROOM DOOR GO TO STOP HIM.
BUT HE IS ODIN. HE IS ODIN.
YOU DON'T STOP ODIN.
YOU TASTE BLOOD IN YOUR MOUTH. THERE'S THE TASTE OF BLOOD IN THE MEMORY NOW.
YOU FEEL WEAK. YOU FEEL OPENED.
YOU FEEL YOUR LIFE RUNNING OUT OF YOU LIKE WATER.
THE DRAUMAR WITH YOU, THEY'RE ALL DEAD.
YOU, BONEGRINDER, YOU'VE GOT JUST A FEW HEARTBEATS LEFT
YOUR VISION'S GROWING DIM, BUT YOU SEE ODIN CLEAVE OPEN THE THRONE ROOM DOOR

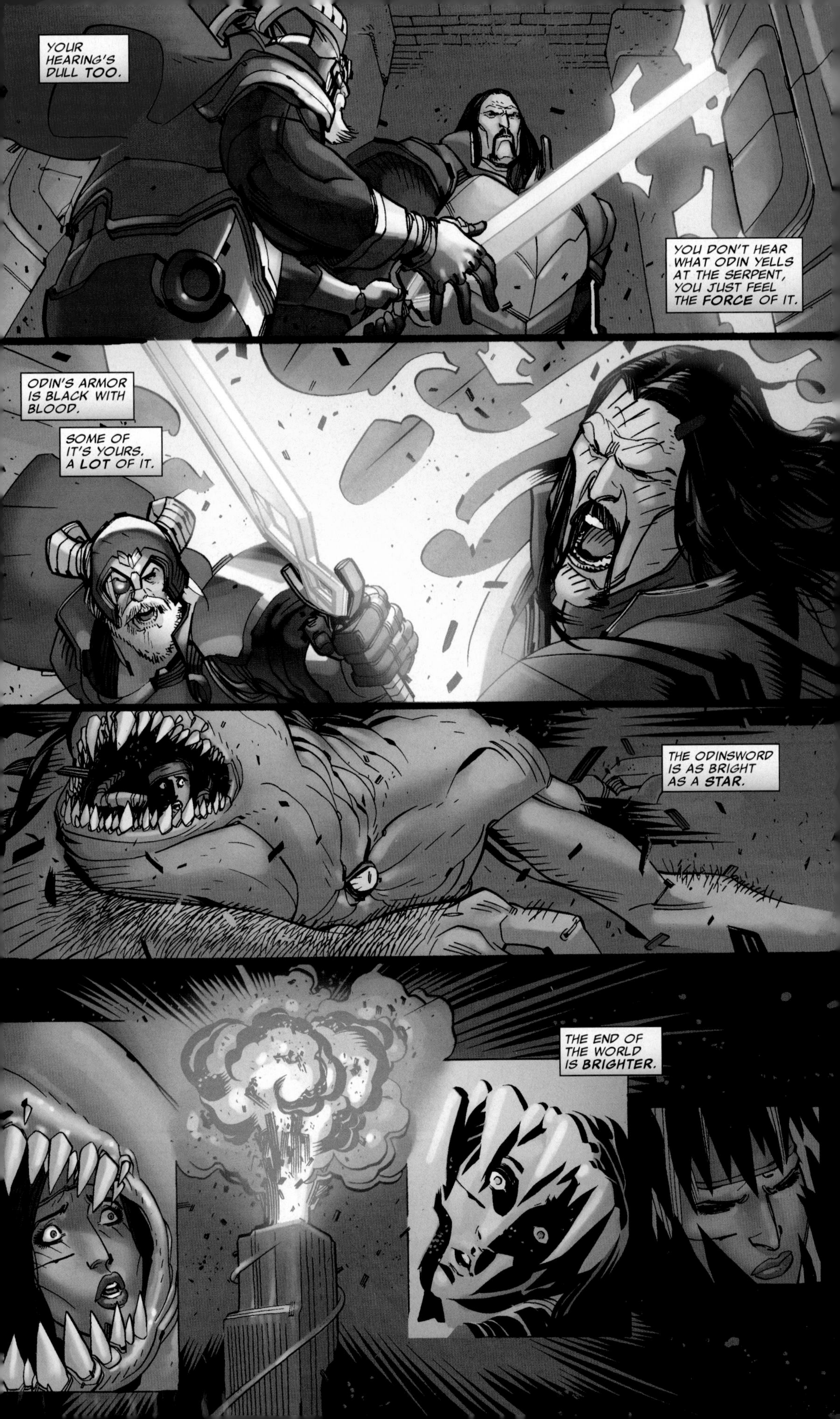
YOUR HEARING'S DULL TOO.
YOU DON'T HEAR WHAT ODIN YELLS AT THE SERPENT, YOU JUST FEEL THE **FORCE** OF IT.
ODIN'S ARMOR IS BLACK WITH BLOOD.
SOME OF IT'S YOURS. A **LOT** OF IT.
THE ODINSWORD IS AS BRIGHT AS A **STAR**.
THE END OF THE WORLD IS **BRIGHTER**.

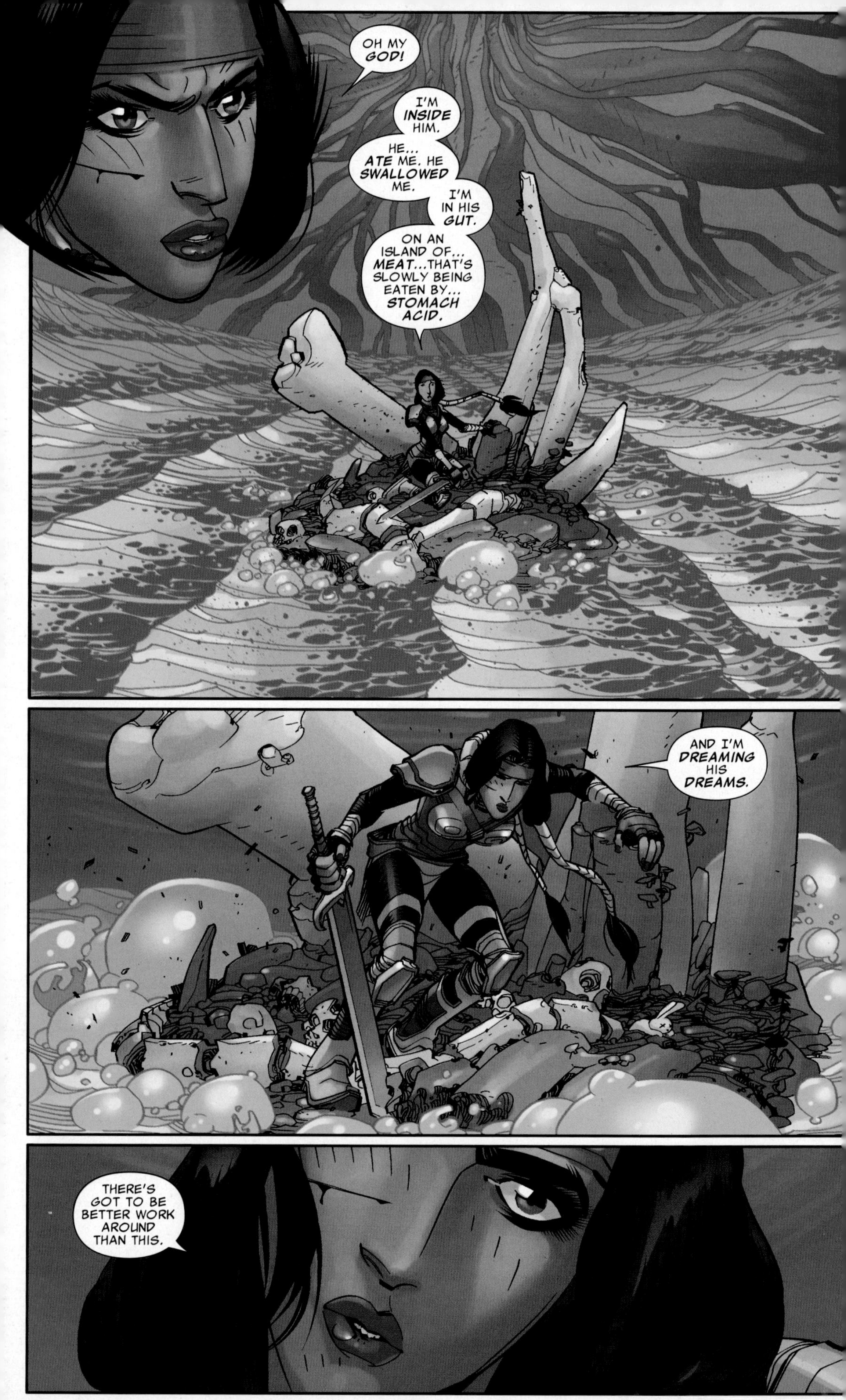
OH MY GOD!
I'M INSIDE HIM.
HE... ATE ME. HE SWALLOWED ME.
I'M IN HIS GUT.
ON AN ISLAND OF... MEAT...THAT'S SLOWLY BEING EATEN BY... STOMACH ACID.
AND I'M DREAMING HIS DREAMS.
THERE'S GOT TO BE BETTER WORK AROUND THAN THIS.

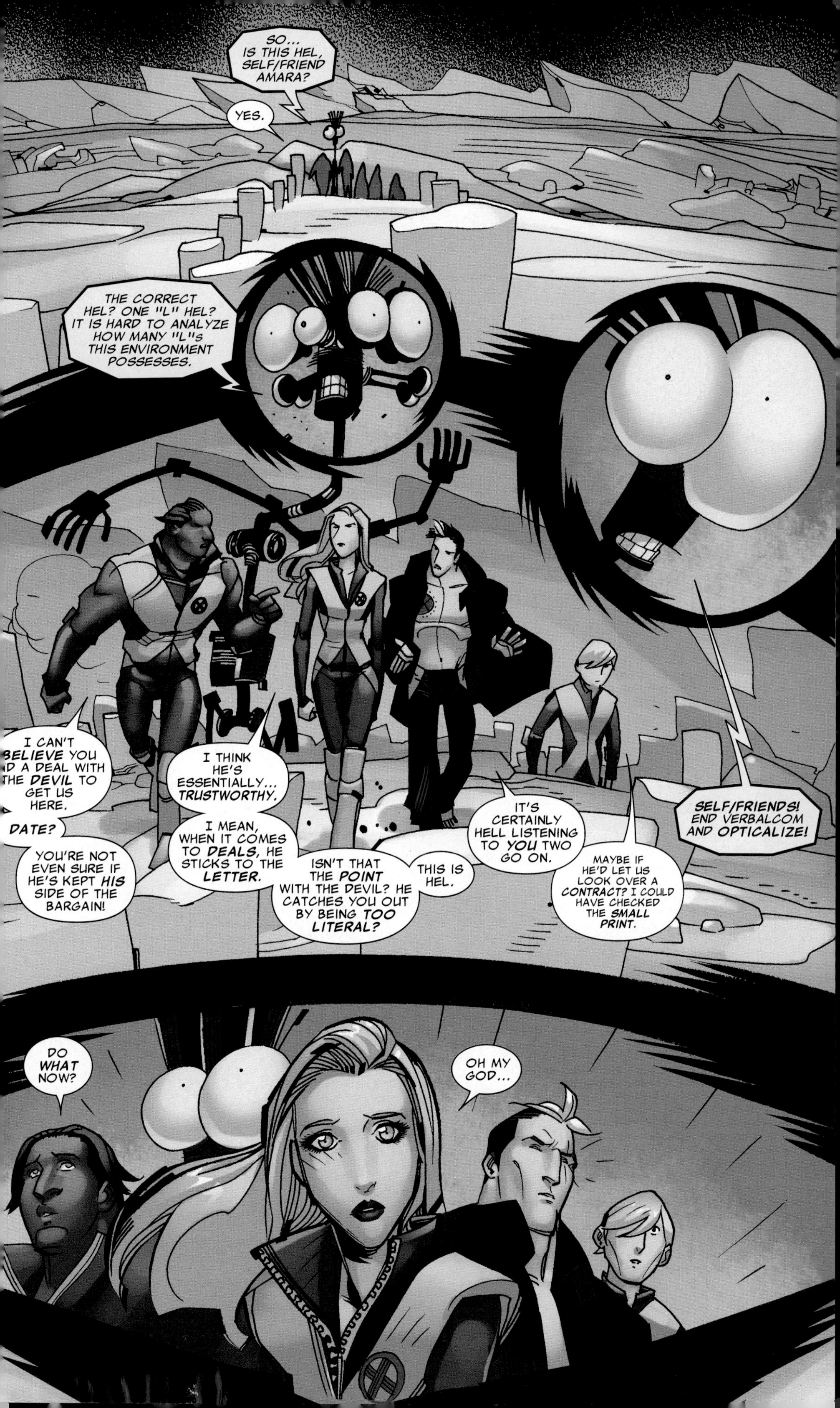
SO... IS THIS HEL, SELF/FRIEND AMARA?
YES.
THE CORRECT HEL? ONE "L" HEL? IT IS HARD TO ANALYZE HOW MANY "L"s THIS ENVIRONMENT POSSESSES.
I CAN'T BELIEVE YOU D A DEAL WITH THE DEVIL TO GET US HERE.
DATE?
YOU'RE NOT EVEN SURE IF HE'S KEPT HIS SIDE OF THE BARGAIN!
I THINK HE'S ESSENTIALLY... TRUSTWORTHY.
I MEAN, WHEN IT COMES TO DEALS, HE STICKS TO THE LETTER.
ISN'T THAT THE POINT WITH THE DEVIL? HE CATCHES YOU OUT BY BEING TOO LITERAL?
THIS IS HEL.
IT'S CERTAINLY HELL LISTENING TO YOU TWO GO ON.
MAYBE IF HE'D LET US LOOK OVER A CONTRACT? I COULD HAVE CHECKED THE SMALL PRINT.
SELF/FRIENDS! END VERBALCOM AND OPTICALIZE!
DO WHAT NOW?
OH MY GOD...

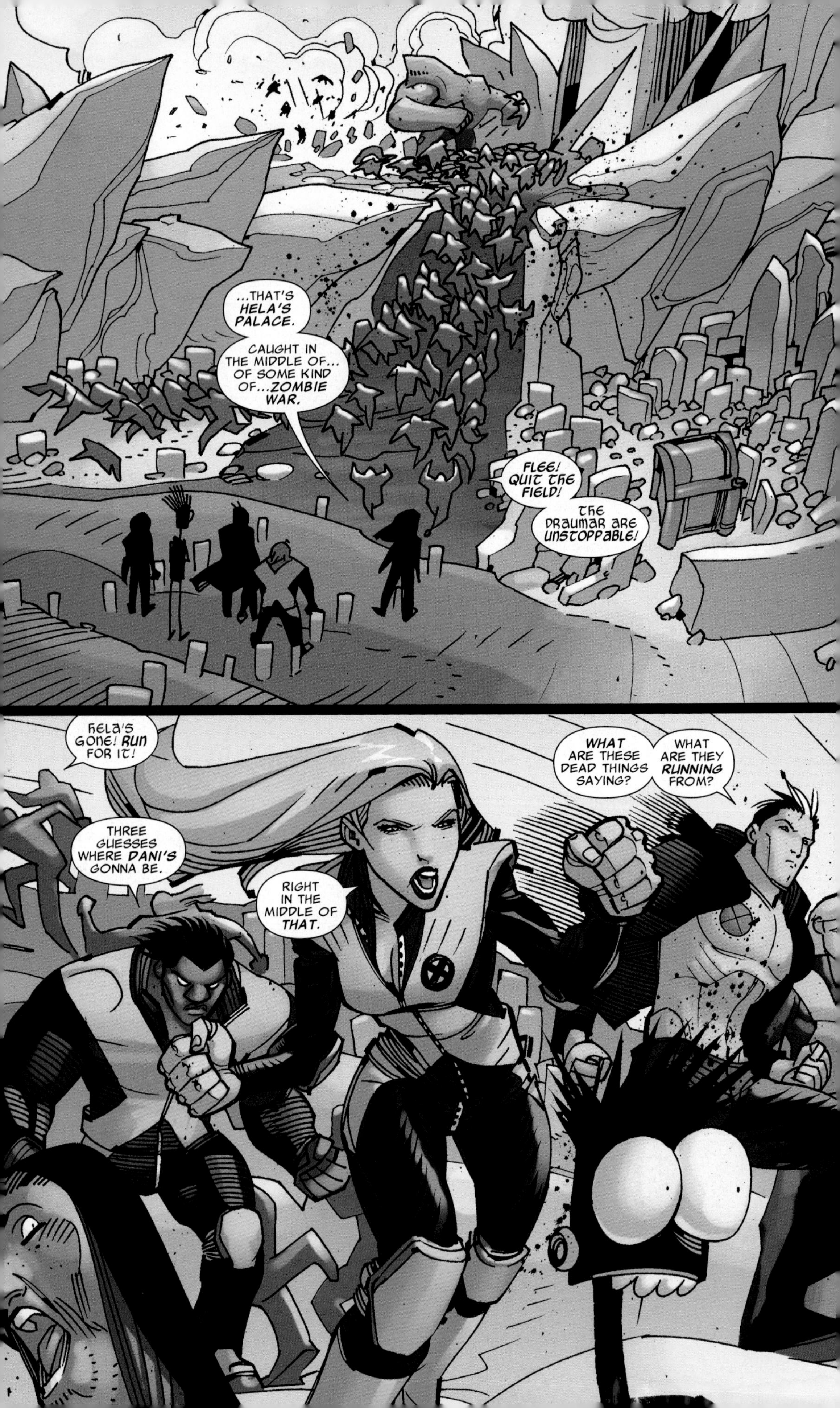
...THAT'S HELA'S PALACE.
CAUGHT IN THE MIDDLE OF... OF SOME KIND OF...ZOMBIE WAR.
FLEE! QUIT THE FIELD!
THE DRAUMAR ARE UNSTOPPABLE!
HELA'S GONE! RUN FOR IT!
WHAT ARE THESE DEAD THINGS SAYING?
WHAT ARE THEY RUNNING FROM?
THREE GUESSES WHERE DANI'S GONNA BE.
RIGHT IN THE MIDDLE OF THAT.

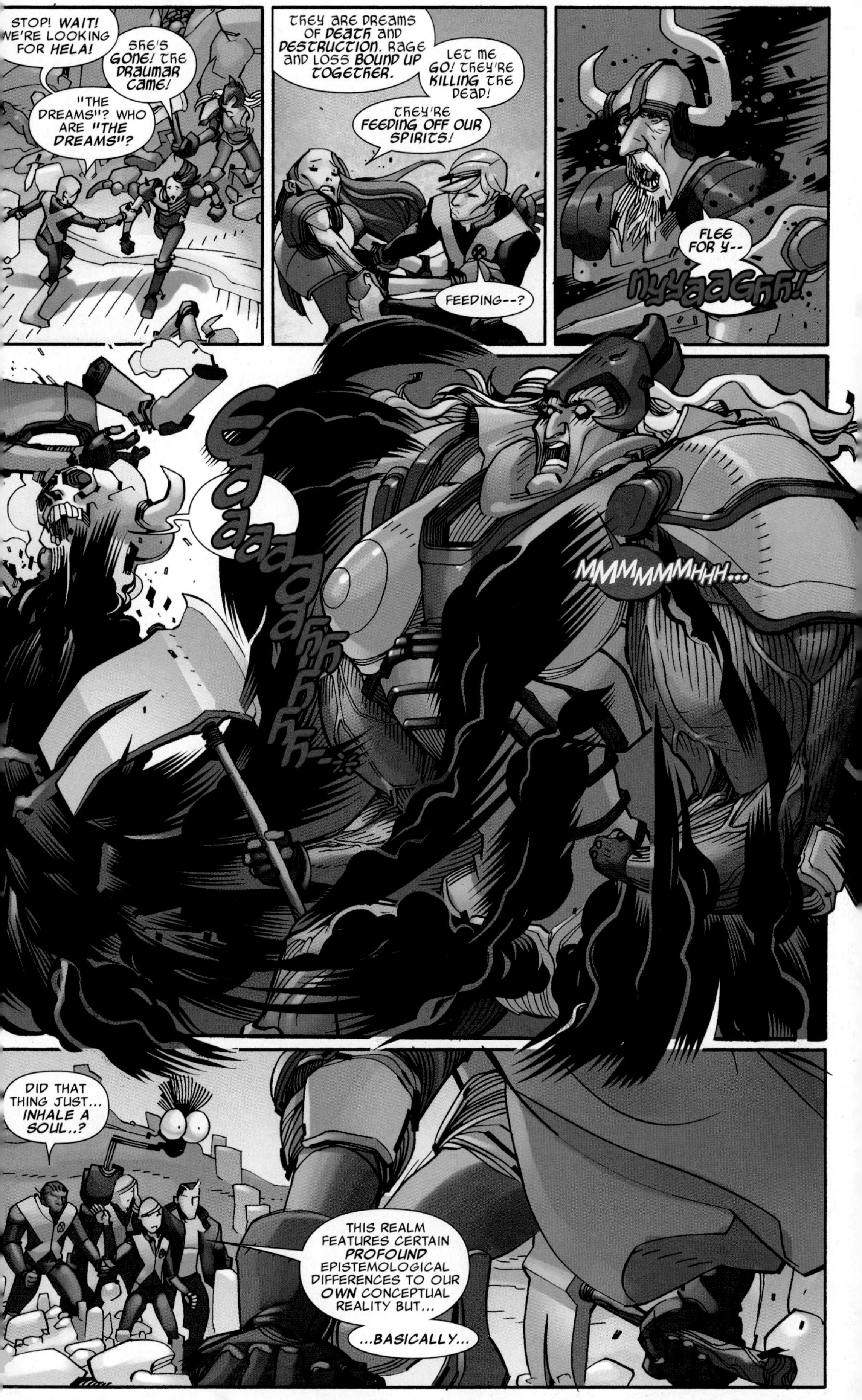
STOP! WAIT! WE'RE LOOKING FOR HELA!
SHE'S GONE! THE DRAUMAR CAME!
"THE DREAMS"? WHO ARE "THE DREAMS"?
THEY ARE DREAMS OF DEATH AND DESTRUCTION. RAGE AND LOSS BOUND UP TOGETHER.
LET ME GO! THEY'RE KILLING THE DEAD!
THEY'RE FEEDING OFF OUR SPIRITS!
FEEDING--?
FLEE FOR Y--
NYYAAGHH!
EAAAAAAHHHHHH--
MMMMMMHHH...
DID THAT THING JUST... INHALE A SOUL..?
THIS REALM FEATURES CERTAIN PROFOUND EPISTEMOLOGICAL DIFFERENCES TO OUR OWN CONCEPTUAL REALITY BUT...
...BASICALLY...

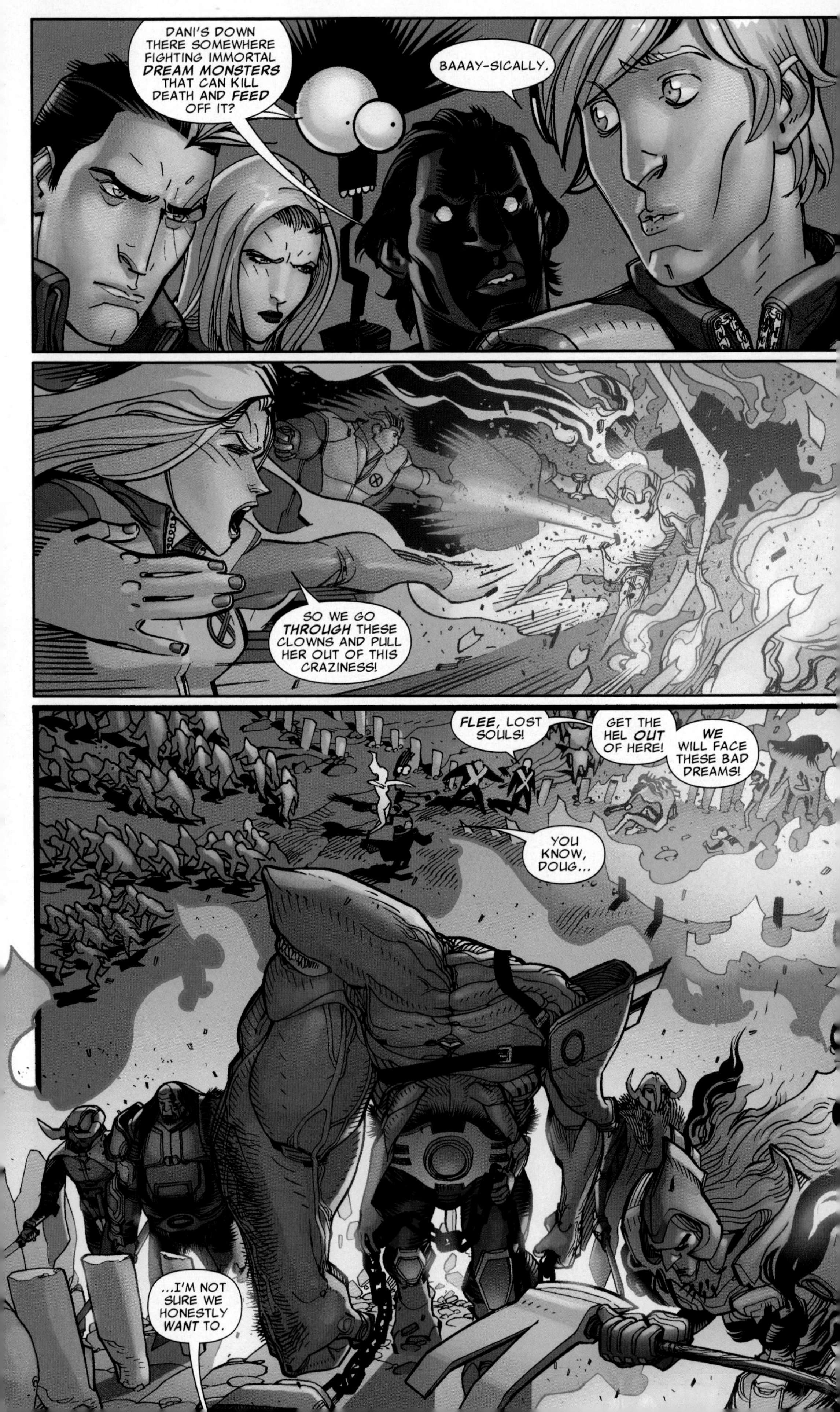
DANI'S DOWN THERE SOMEWHERE FIGHTING IMMORTAL DREAM MONSTERS THAT CAN KILL DEATH AND FEED OFF IT?
BAAAY-SICALLY.
SO WE GO THROUGH THESE CLOWNS AND PULL HER OUT OF THIS CRAZINESS!
FLEE, LOST SOULS!
GET THE HEL OUT OF HERE!
WE WILL FACE THESE BAD DREAMS!
YOU KNOW, DOUG...
...I'M NOT SURE WE HONESTLY WANT TO.

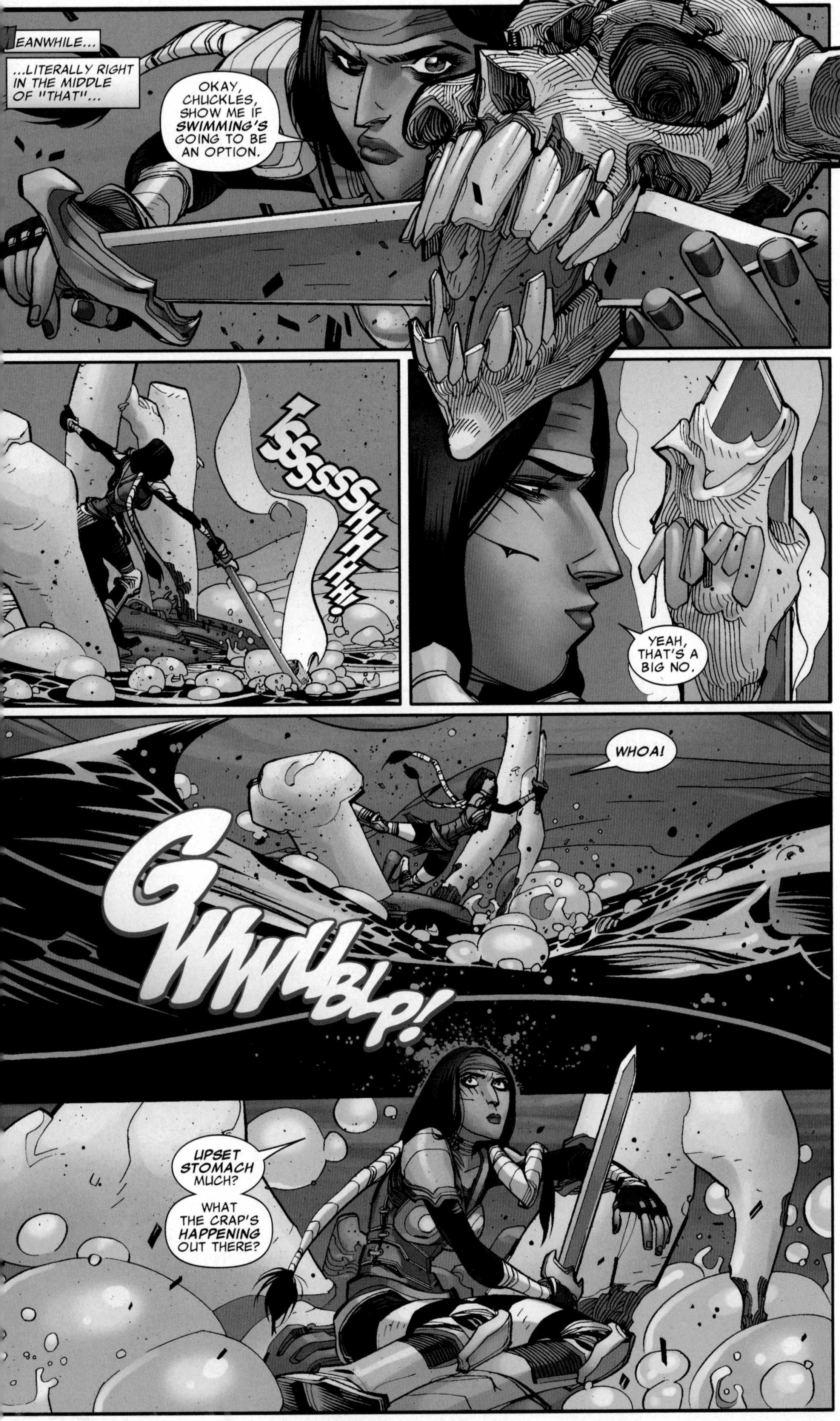
EANWHILE...
...LITERALLY RIGHT IN THE MIDDLE OF "THAT"...
OKAY, CHUCKLES, SHOW ME IF SWIMMING'S GOING TO BE AN OPTION.
ISSSSSHHHHH!
YEAH, THAT'S A BIG NO.
WHOA!
GWWUBLP!
UPSET STOMACH MUCH?
WHAT THE CRAP'S HAPPENING OUT THERE?

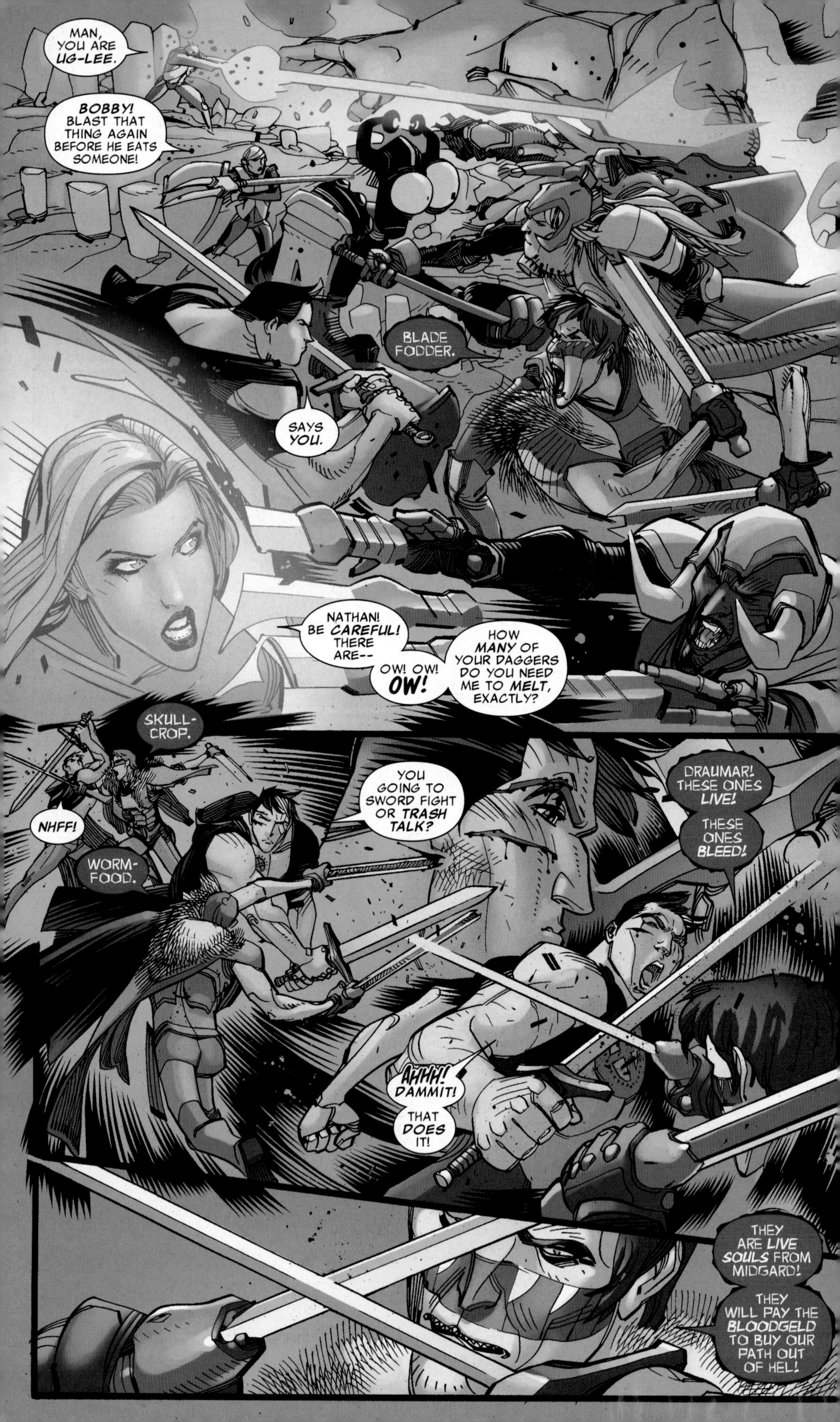
MAN, YOU ARE UG-LEE.
BOBBY! BLAST THAT THING AGAIN BEFORE HE EATS SOMEONE!
BLADE FODDER.
SAYS YOU.
NATHAN! BE CAREFUL! THERE ARE--
OW! OW! OW!
HOW MANY OF YOUR DAGGERS DO YOU NEED ME TO MELT, EXACTLY?
SKULL-CROP.
NHFF!
WORM-FOOD.
YOU GOING TO SWORD FIGHT OR TRASH TALK?
DRAUMAR! THESE ONES LIVE!
THESE ONES BLEED!
AHHH! DAMMIT!
THAT DOES IT!
THEY ARE LIVE SOULS FROM MIDGARD!
THEY WILL PAY THE BLOODGELD TO BUY OUR PATH OUT OF HEL!

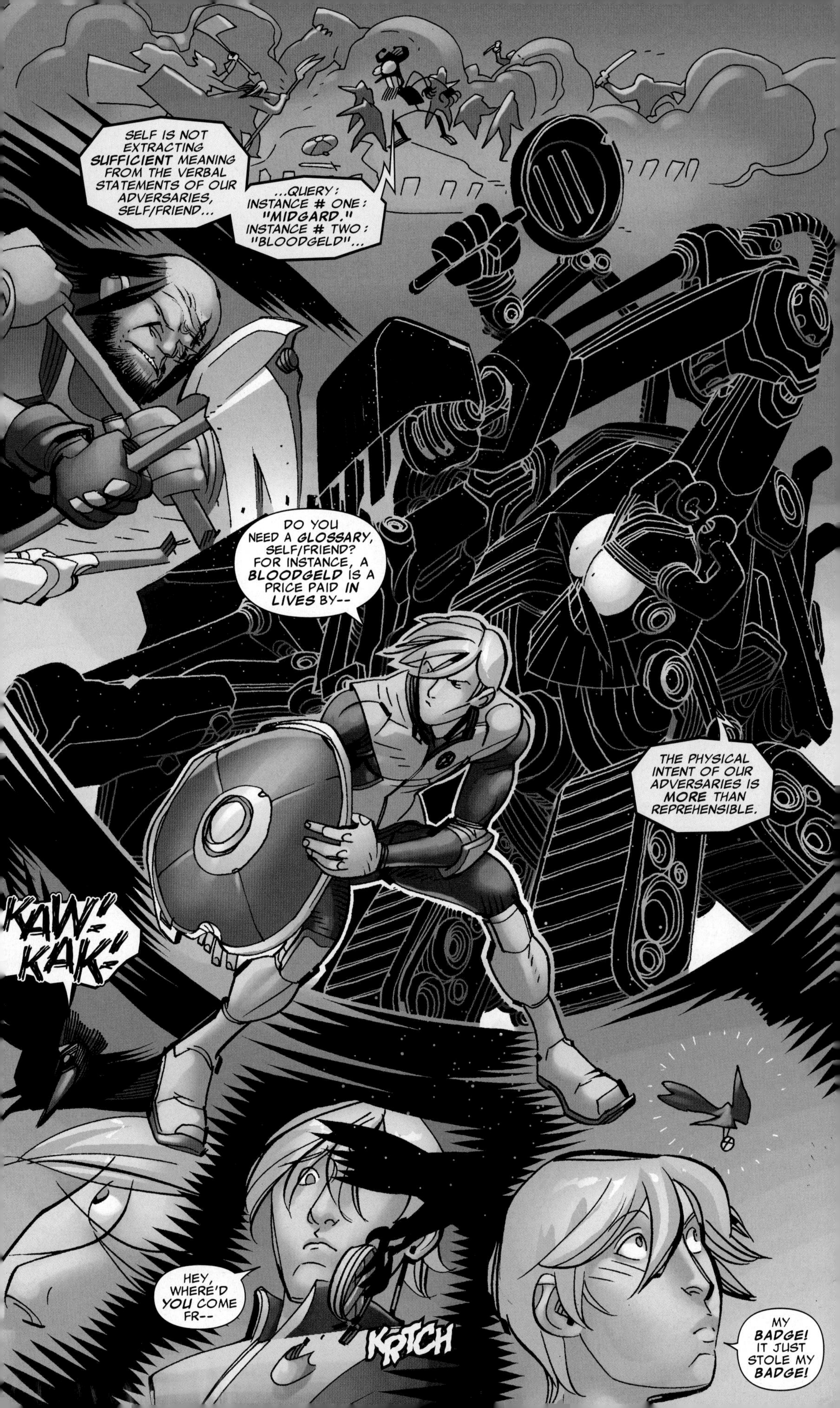

SELF IS NOT EXTRACTING SUFFICIENT MEANING FROM THE VERBAL STATEMENTS OF OUR ADVERSARIES, SELF/FRIEND...
...QUERY: INSTANCE # ONE: "MIDGARD." INSTANCE # TWO: "BLOODGELD"...
DO YOU NEED A GLOSSARY, SELF/FRIEND? FOR INSTANCE, A BLOODGELD IS A PRICE PAID IN LIVES BY--
THE PHYSICAL INTENT OF OUR ADVERSARIES IS MORE THAN REPREHENSIBLE.
KAW! KAK!
HEY, WHERE'D YOU COME FR--
KRTCH
MY BADGE! IT JUST STOLE MY BADGE!

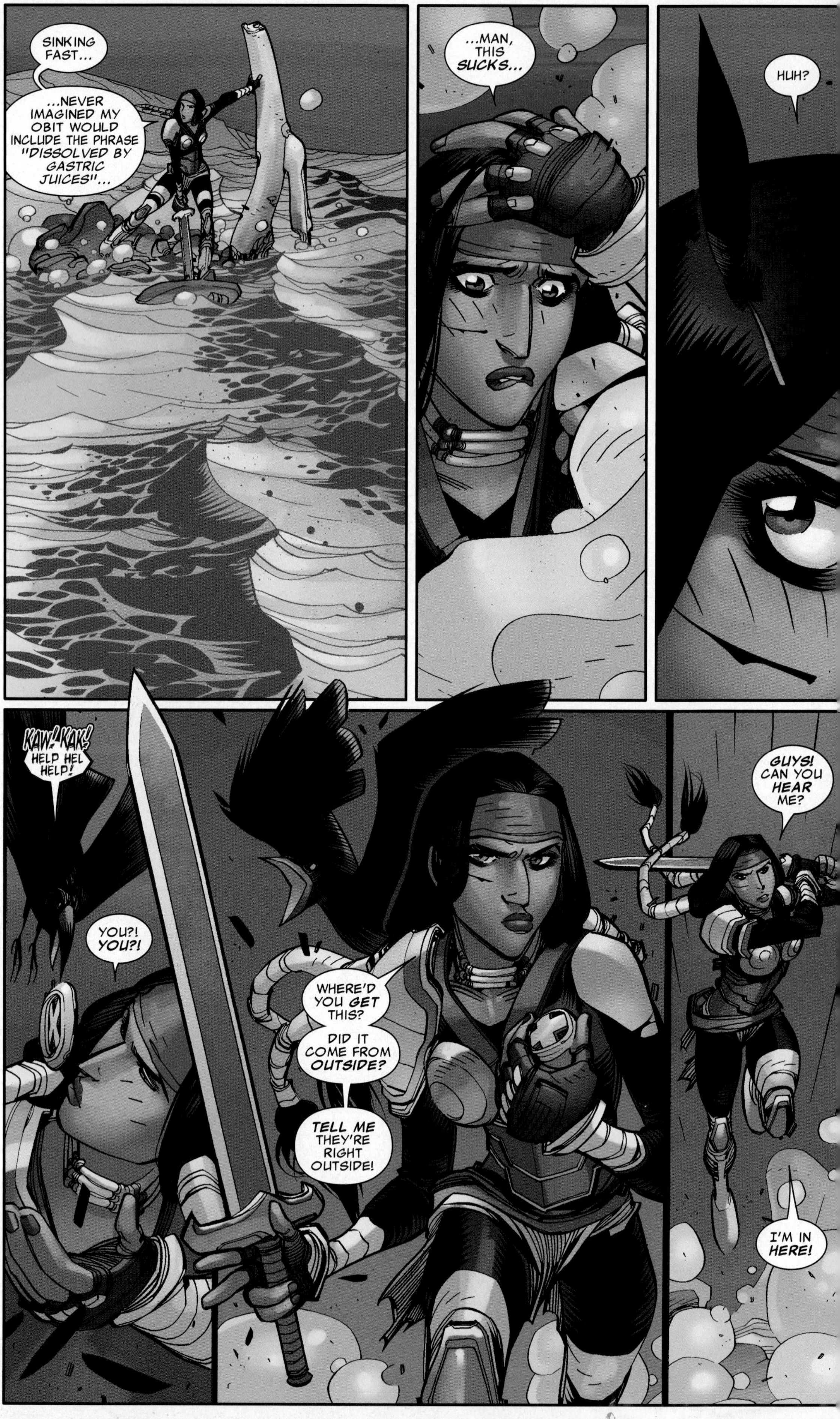

SINKING FAST...
...NEVER IMAGINED MY OBIT WOULD INCLUDE THE PHRASE "DISSOLVED BY GASTRIC JUICES"...
...MAN, THIS SUCKS...
HUH?
KAW! KAK!
HELP HEL HELP!
YOU?! YOU?!
WHERE'D YOU GET THIS?
DID IT COME FROM OUTSIDE?
TELL ME THEY'RE RIGHT OUTSIDE!
GUYS! CAN YOU HEAR ME?
I'M IN HERE!

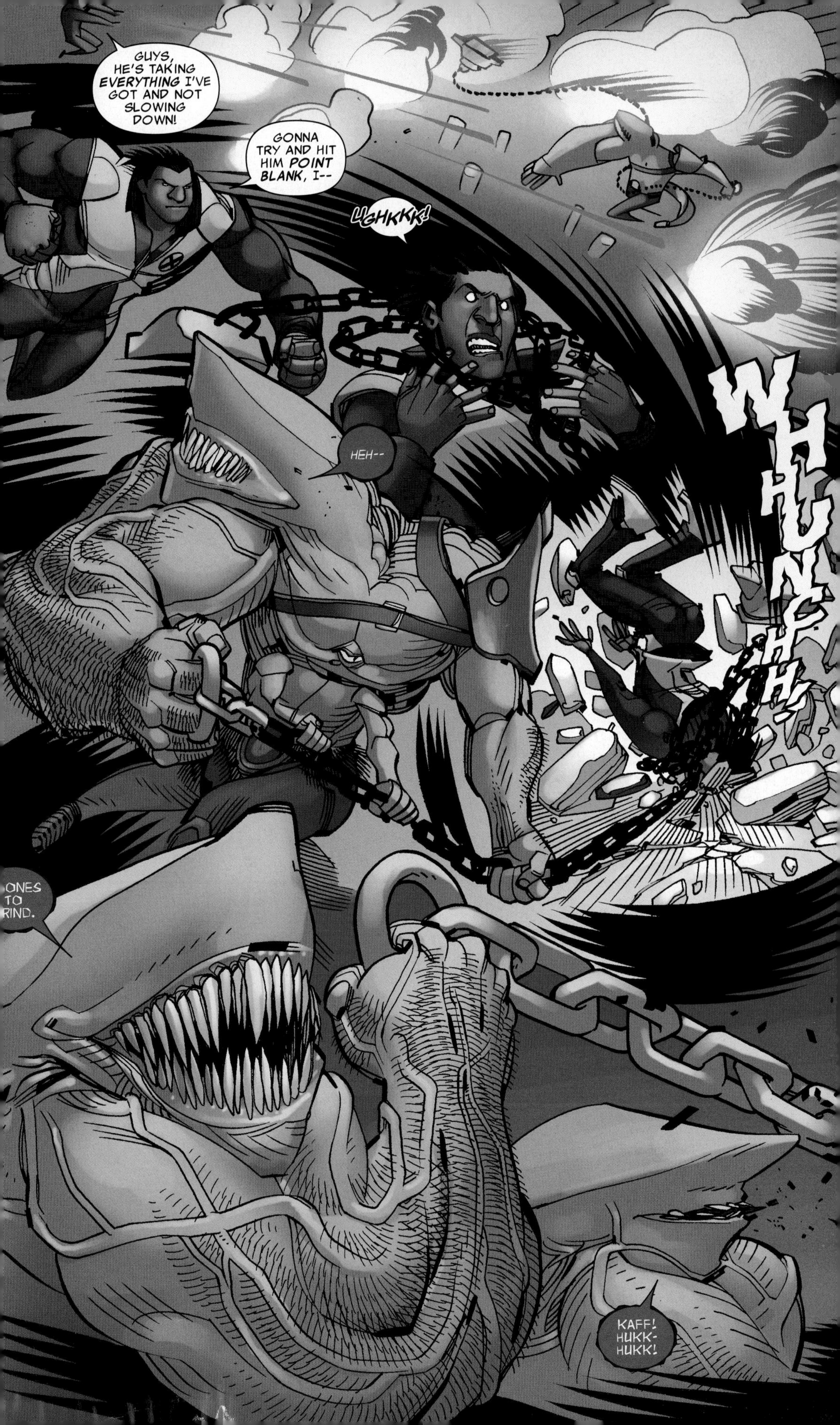
GUYS, HE'S TAKING EVERYTHING I'VE GOT AND NOT SLOWING DOWN!
GONNA TRY AND HIT HIM POINT BLANK, I--
UGHKKK!
WHHUNFHH!
HEH--
ONES TO RIND.
KAFF! HUKK-HUKK!

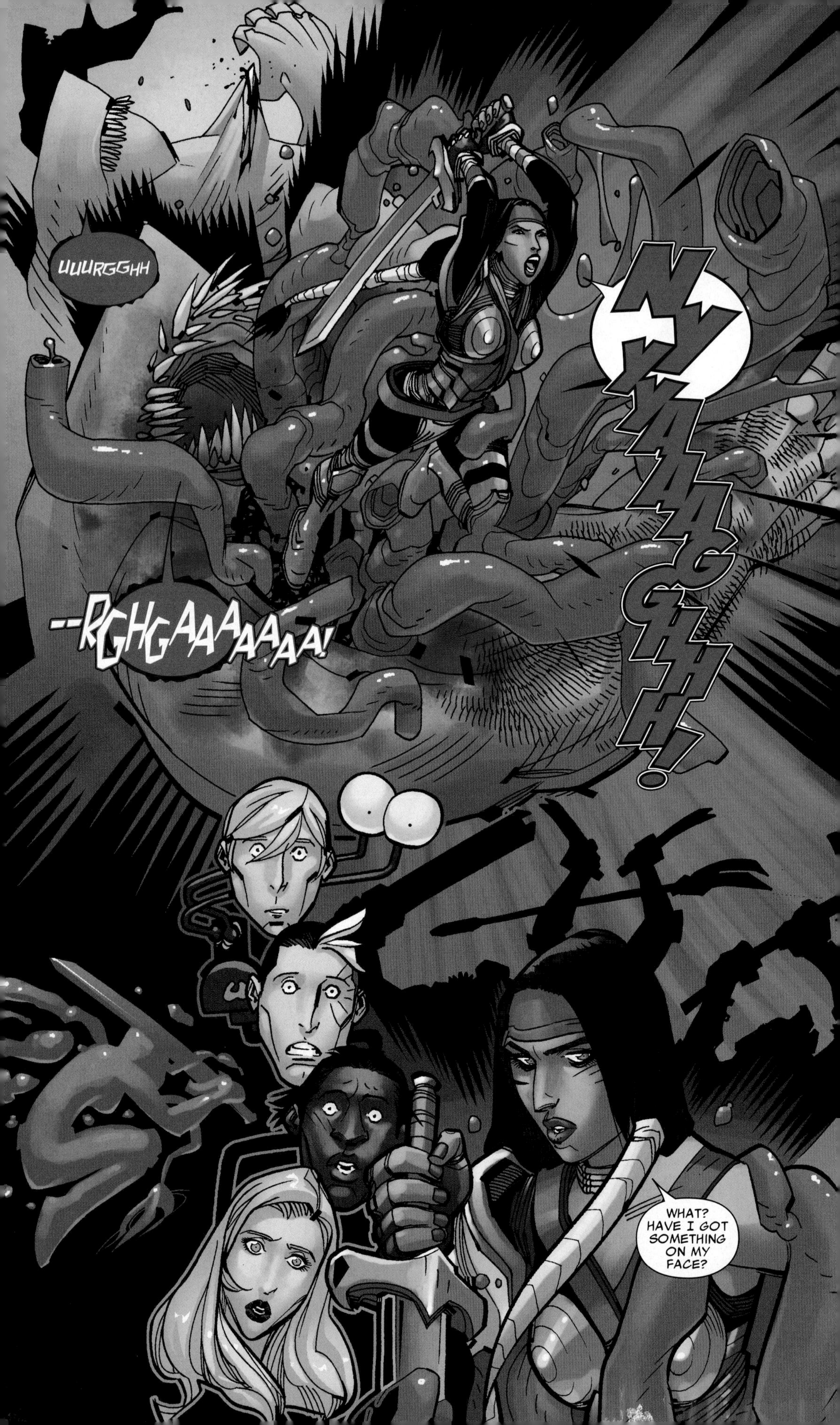
UUURGGHH
NYYAAAGGHHH!
--RGHGAAAAAAAA!
WHAT? HAVE I GOT SOMETHING ON MY FACE?

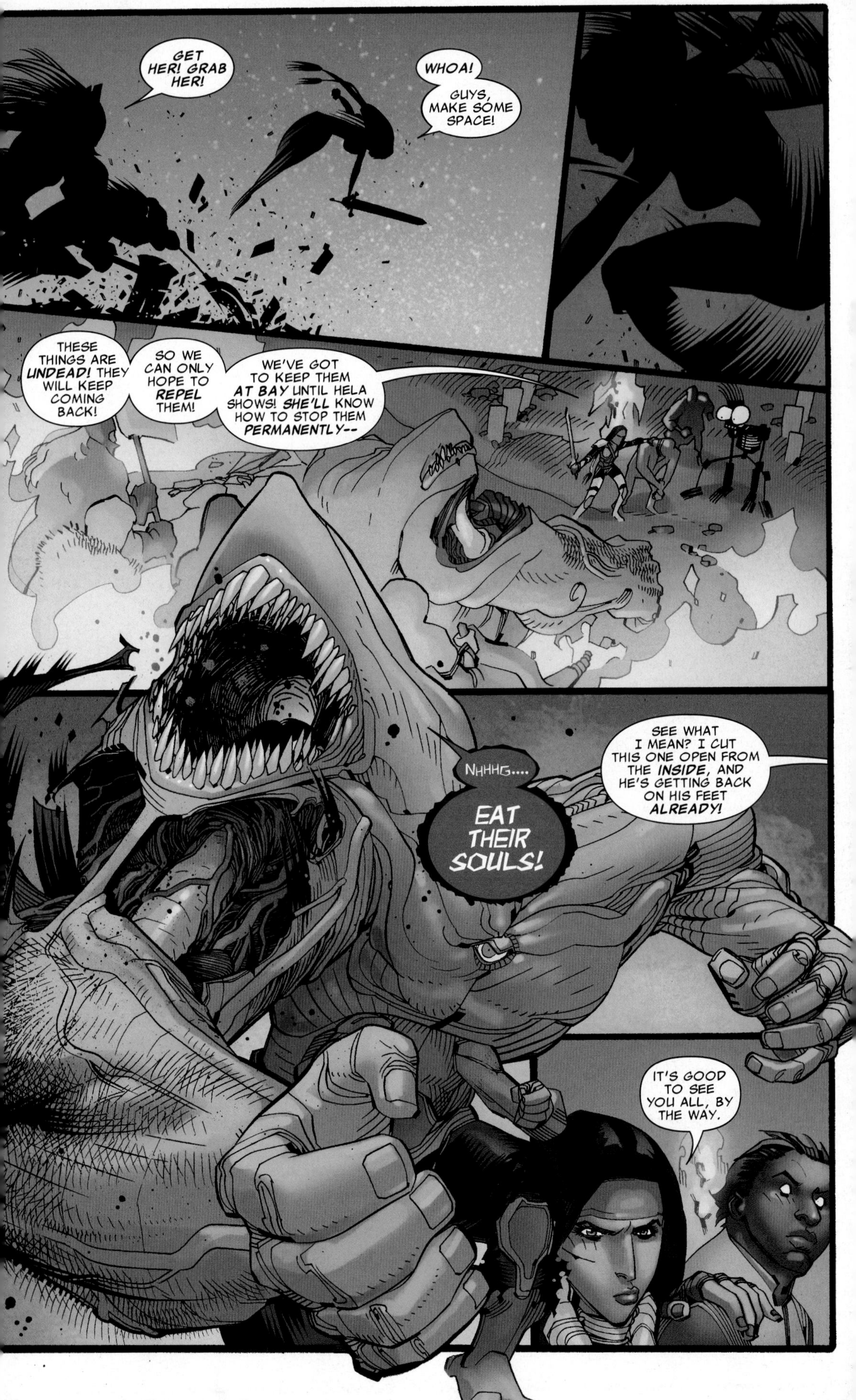
GET HER! GRAB HER!
WHOA!
GUYS, MAKE SOME SPACE!
THESE THINGS ARE UNDEAD! THEY WILL KEEP COMING BACK!
SO WE CAN ONLY HOPE TO REPEL THEM!
WE'VE GOT TO KEEP THEM AT BAY UNTIL HELA SHOWS! SHE'LL KNOW HOW TO STOP THEM PERMANENTLY--
NHHHG....
EAT THEIR SOULS!
SEE WHAT I MEAN? I CUT THIS ONE OPEN FROM THE INSIDE, AND HE'S GETTING BACK ON HIS FEET ALREADY!
IT'S GOOD TO SEE YOU ALL, BY THE WAY.

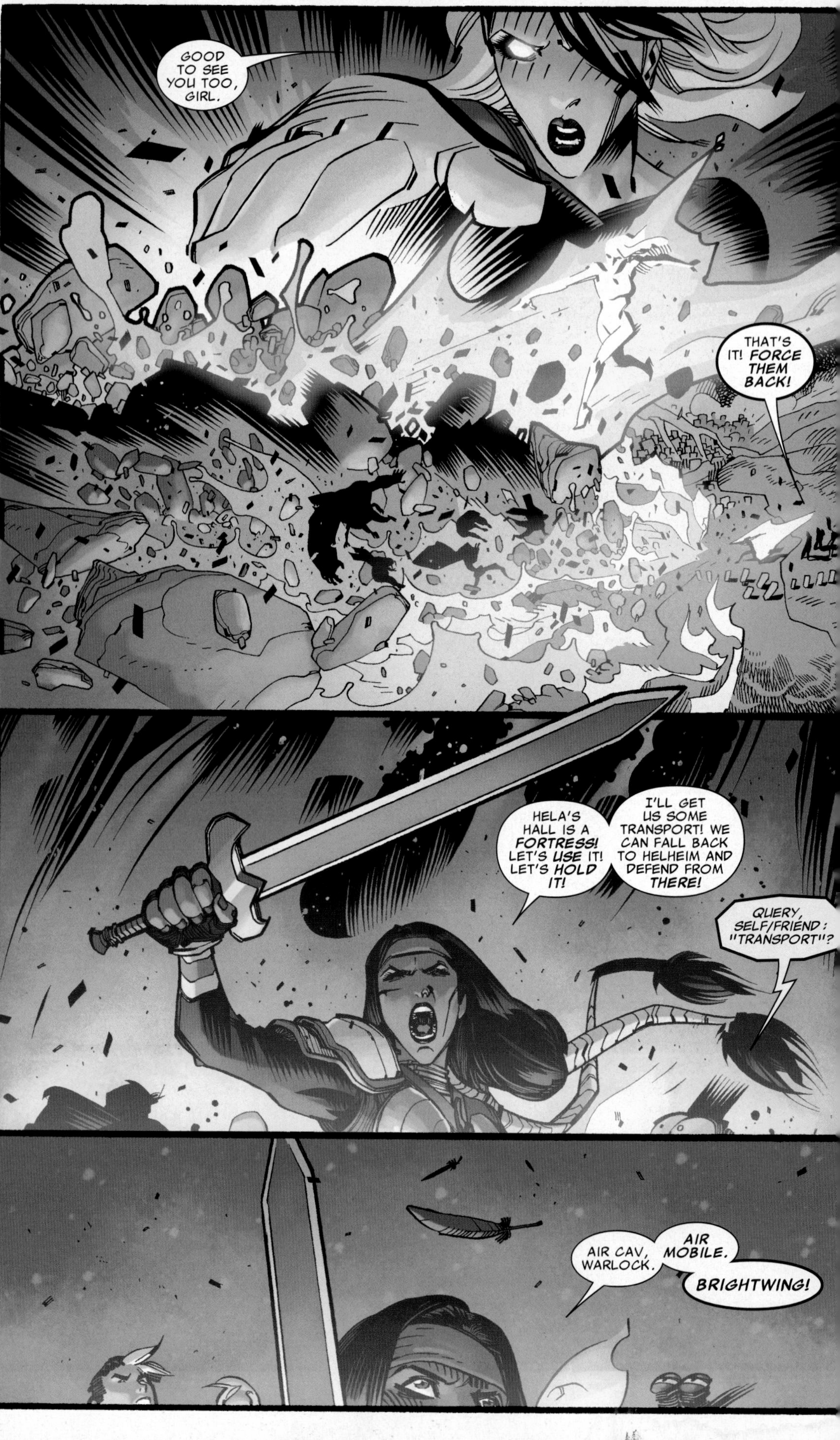
GOOD TO SEE YOU TOO, GIRL.
THAT'S IT! FORCE THEM BACK!
HELA'S HALL IS A FORTRESS! LET'S USE IT! LET'S HOLD IT!
I'LL GET US SOME TRANSPORT! WE CAN FALL BACK TO HELHEIM AND DEFEND FROM THERE!
QUERY, SELF/FRIEND: "TRANSPORT"?
AIR CAV, WARLOCK.
AIR MOBILE.
BRIGHTWING!

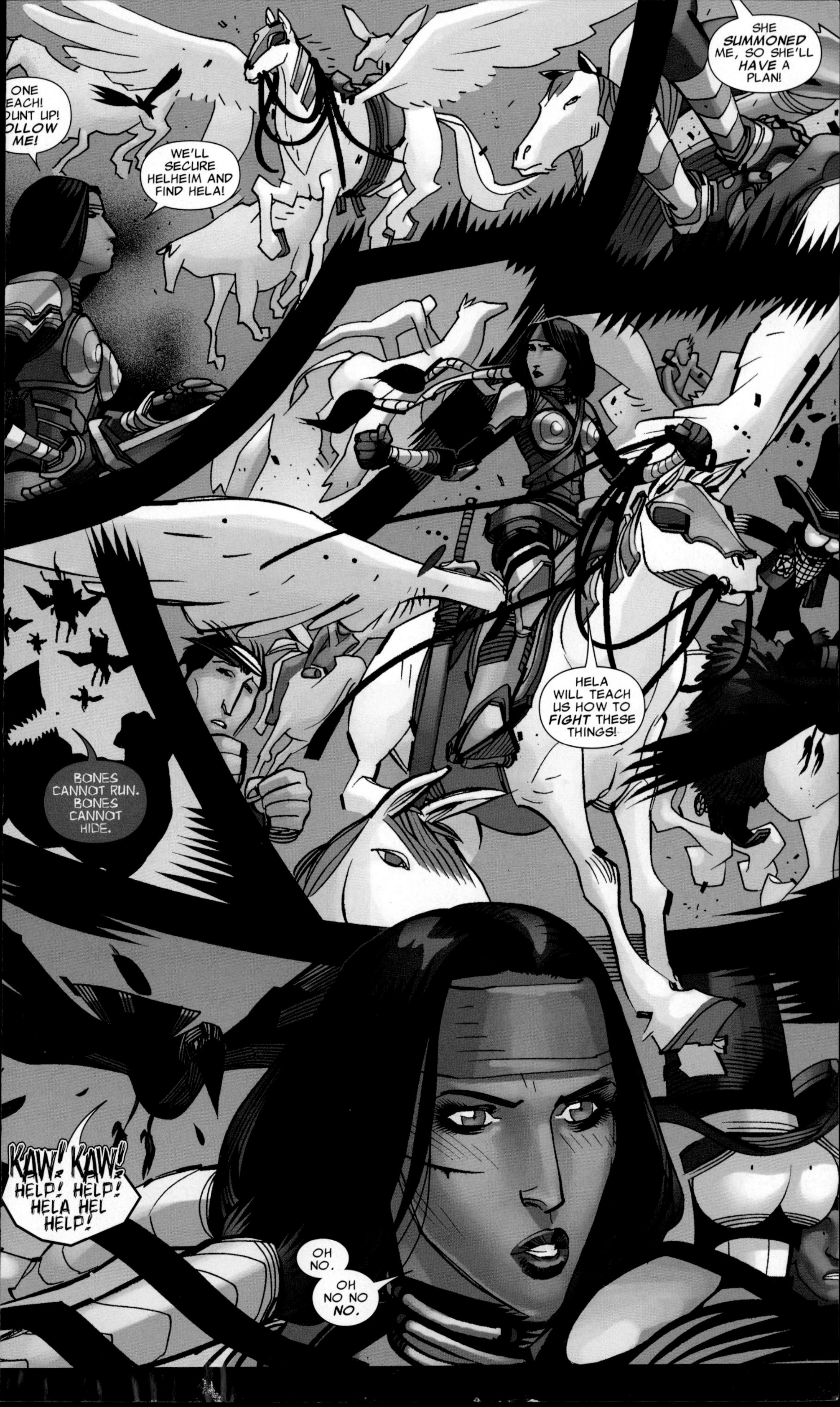
ONE EACH! MOUNT UP! FOLLOW ME!
WE'LL SECURE HELHEIM AND FIND HELA!
SHE SUMMONED ME, SO SHE'LL HAVE A PLAN!
HELA WILL TEACH US HOW TO FIGHT THESE THINGS!
BONES CANNOT RUN. BONES CANNOT HIDE.
KAW! KAW! HELP! HELP! HELA HEL HELP!
OH NO.
OH NO NO NO.

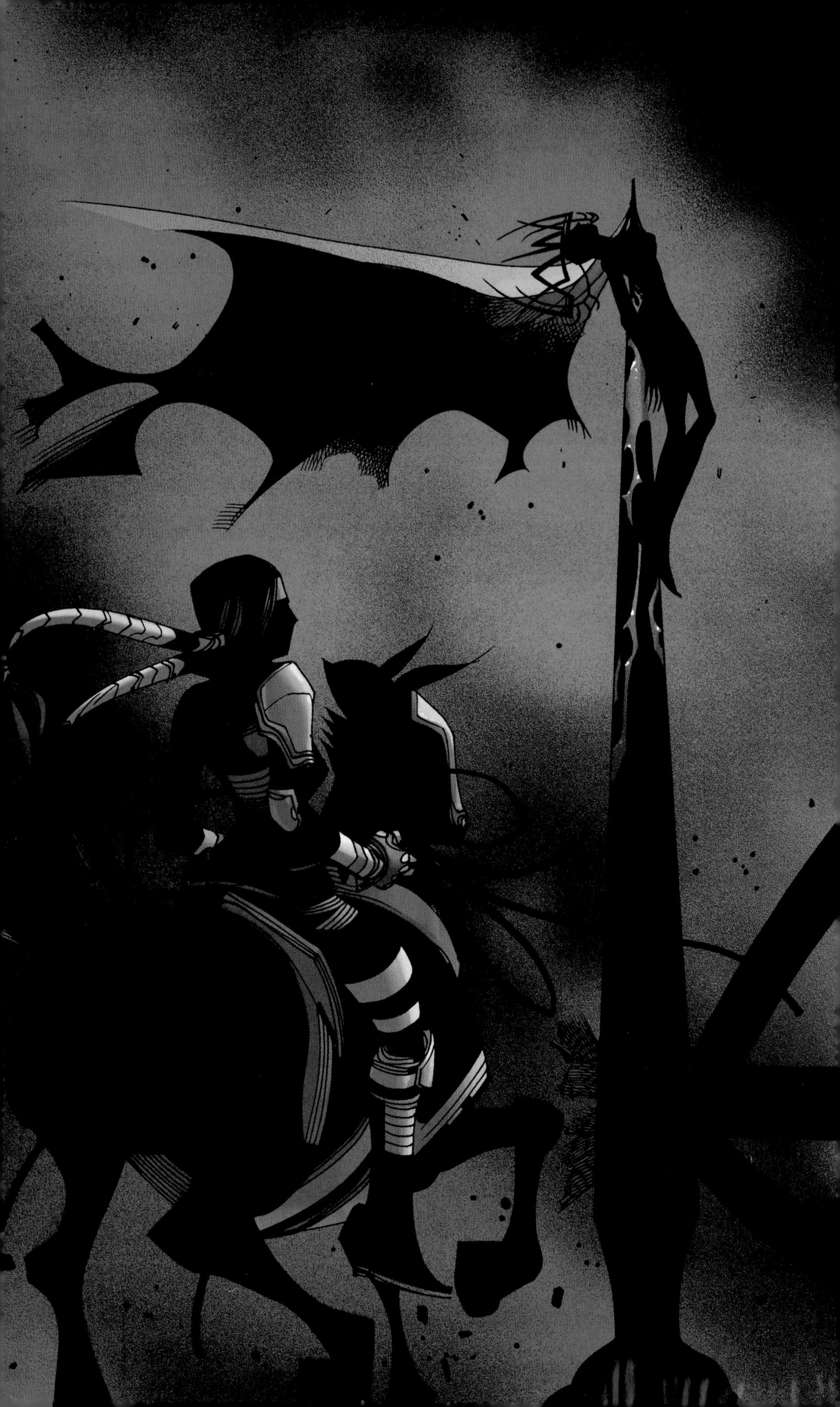

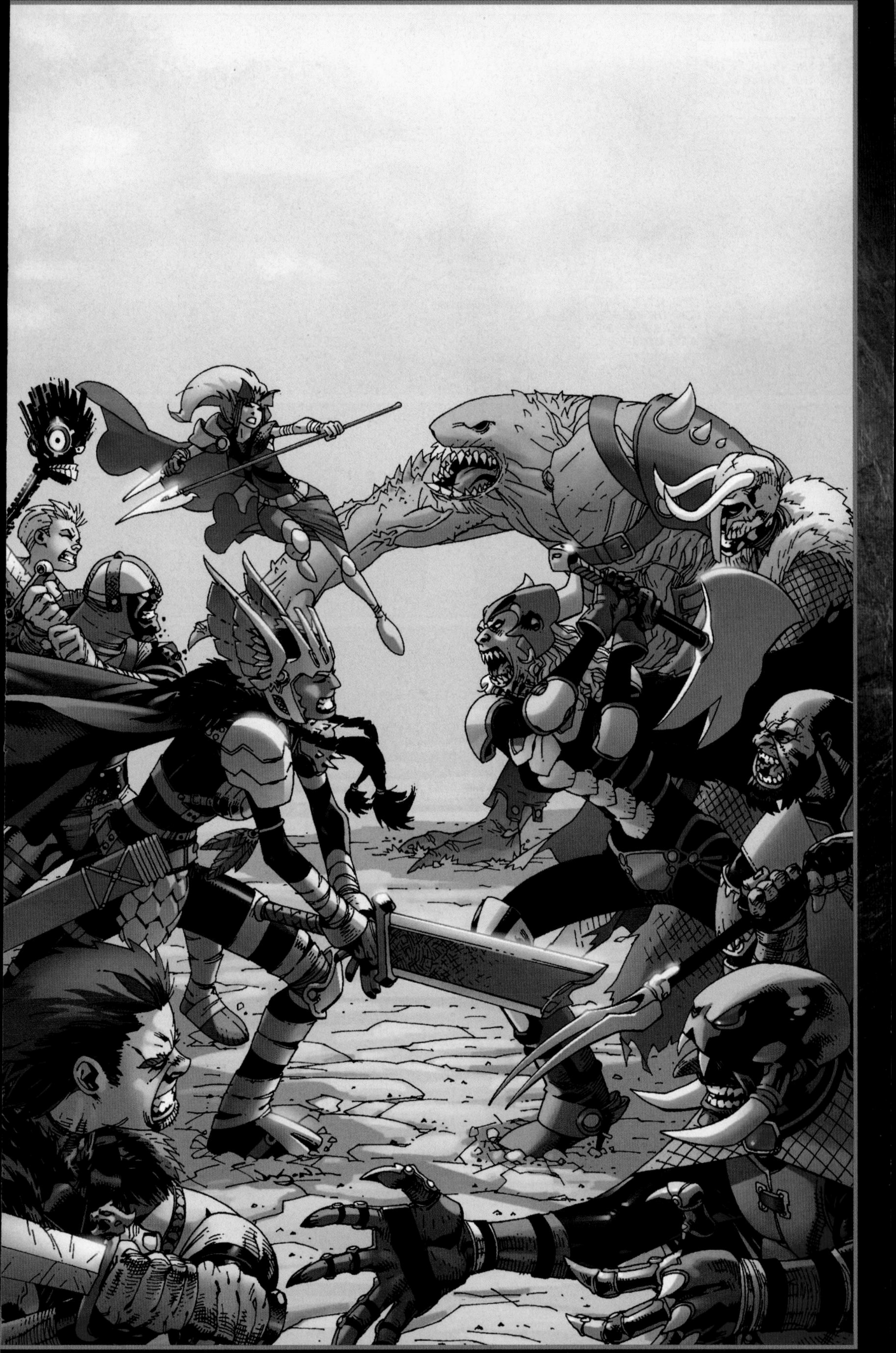

NEW MUTANTS #32

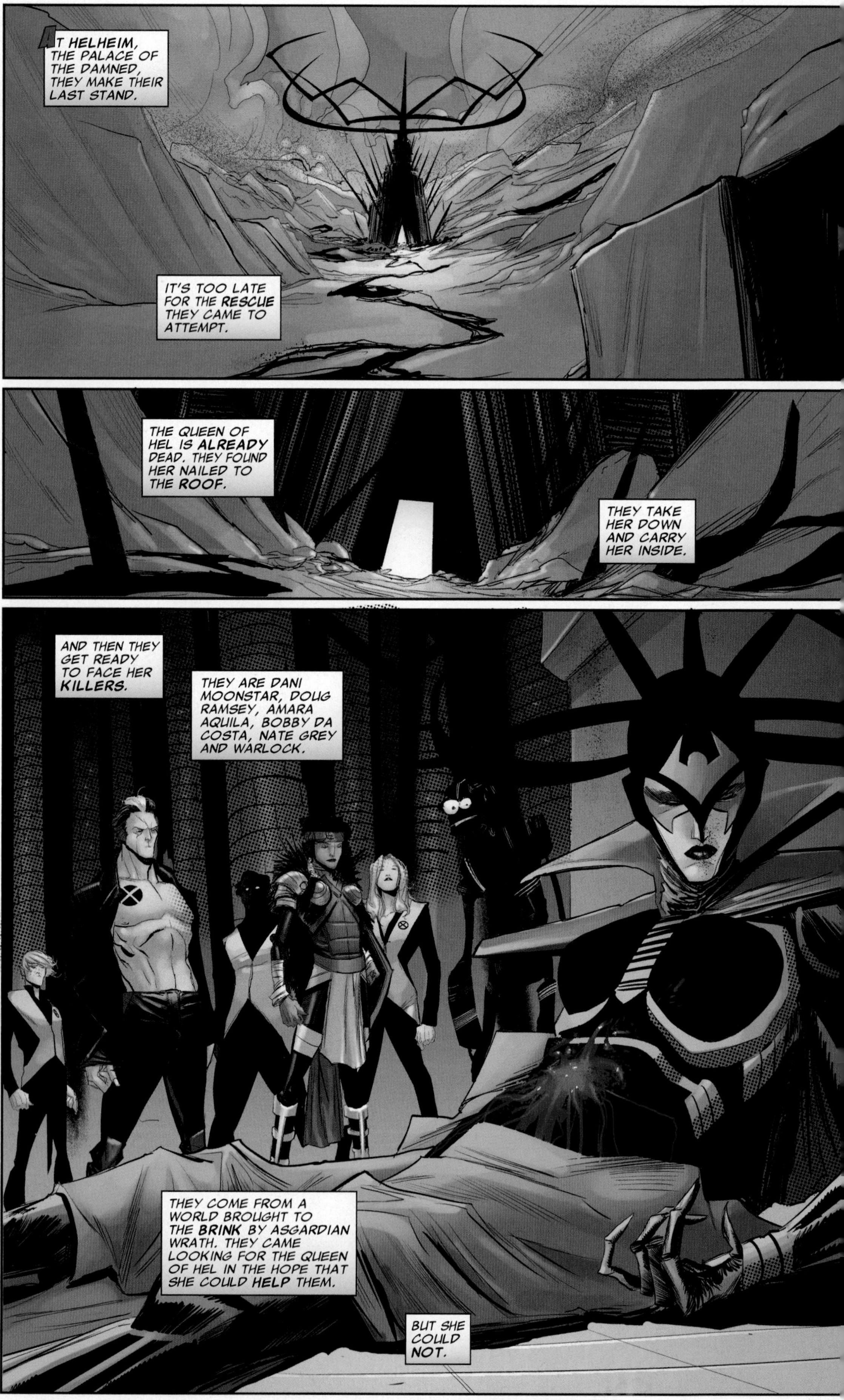
AT HELHEIM, THE PALACE OF THE DAMNED, THEY MAKE THEIR LAST STAND.
IT'S TOO LATE FOR THE RESCUE THEY CAME TO ATTEMPT.
THE QUEEN OF HEL IS ALREADY DEAD. THEY FOUND HER NAILED TO THE ROOF.
THEY TAKE HER DOWN AND CARRY HER INSIDE.
AND THEN THEY GET READY TO FACE HER KILLERS.
THEY ARE DANI MOONSTAR, DOUG RAMSEY, AMARA AQUILA, BOBBY DA COSTA, NATE GREY AND WARLOCK.
THEY COME FROM A WORLD BROUGHT TO THE BRINK BY ASGARDIAN WRATH. THEY CAME LOOKING FOR THE QUEEN OF HEL IN THE HOPE THAT SHE COULD HELP THEM.
BUT SHE COULD NOT.

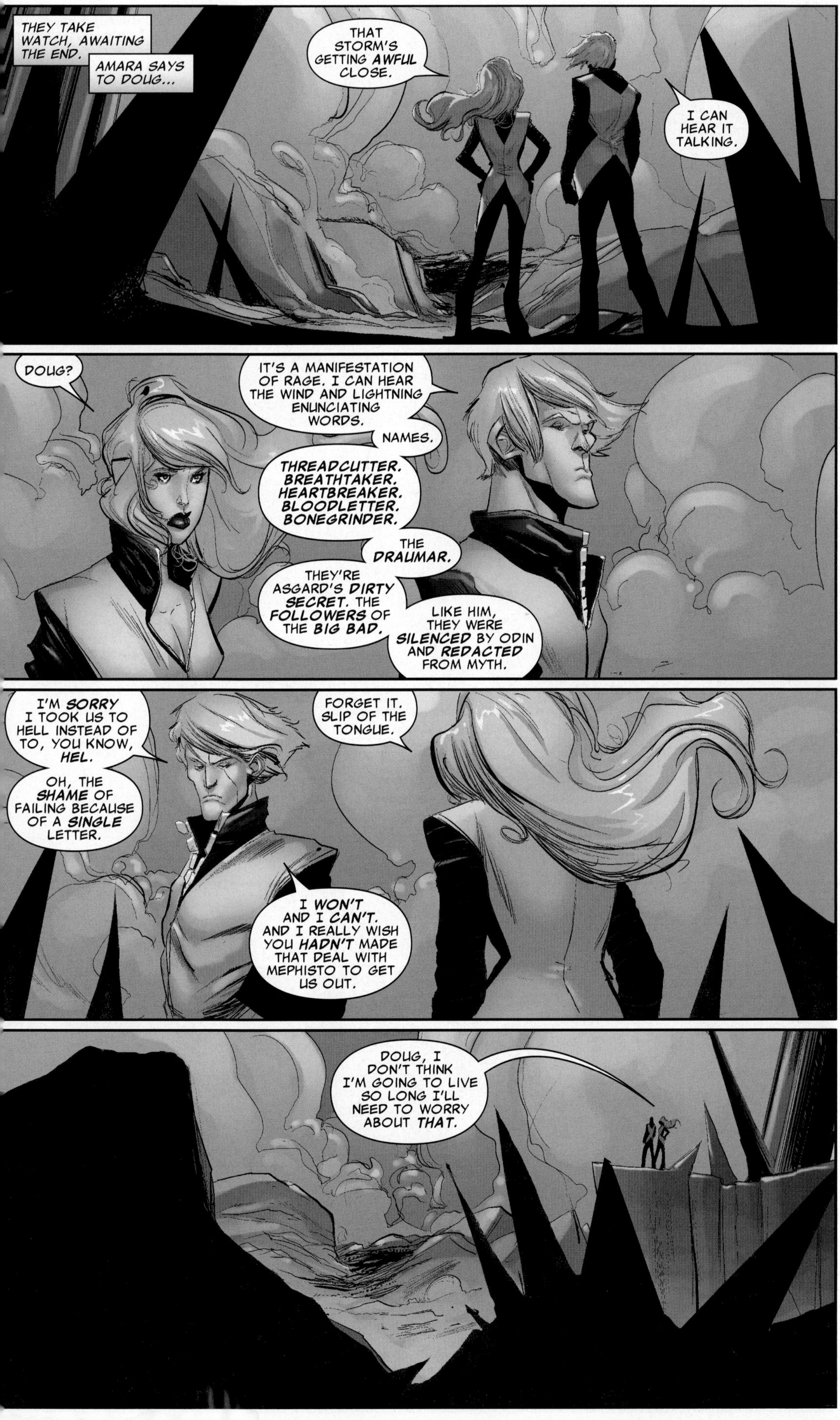

THEY TAKE WATCH, AWAITING THE END.
AMARA SAYS TO DOUG...
THAT STORM'S GETTING AWFUL CLOSE.
I CAN HEAR IT TALKING.
DOUG?
IT'S A MANIFESTATION OF RAGE. I CAN HEAR THE WIND AND LIGHTNING ENUNCIATING WORDS.
NAMES.
THREADCUTTER. BREATHTAKER. HEARTBREAKER. BLOODLETTER. BONEGRINDER.
THE DRAUMAR.
THEY'RE ASGARD'S DIRTY SECRET. THE FOLLOWERS OF THE BIG BAD.
LIKE HIM, THEY WERE SILENCED BY ODIN AND REDACTED FROM MYTH.
I'M SORRY I TOOK US TO HELL INSTEAD OF TO, YOU KNOW, HEL.
OH, THE SHAME OF FAILING BECAUSE OF A SINGLE LETTER.
FORGET IT. SLIP OF THE TONGUE.
I WON'T AND I CAN'T. AND I REALLY WISH YOU HADN'T MADE THAT DEAL WITH MEPHISTO TO GET US OUT.
DOUG, I DON'T THINK I'M GOING TO LIVE SO LONG I'LL NEED TO WORRY ABOUT THAT.

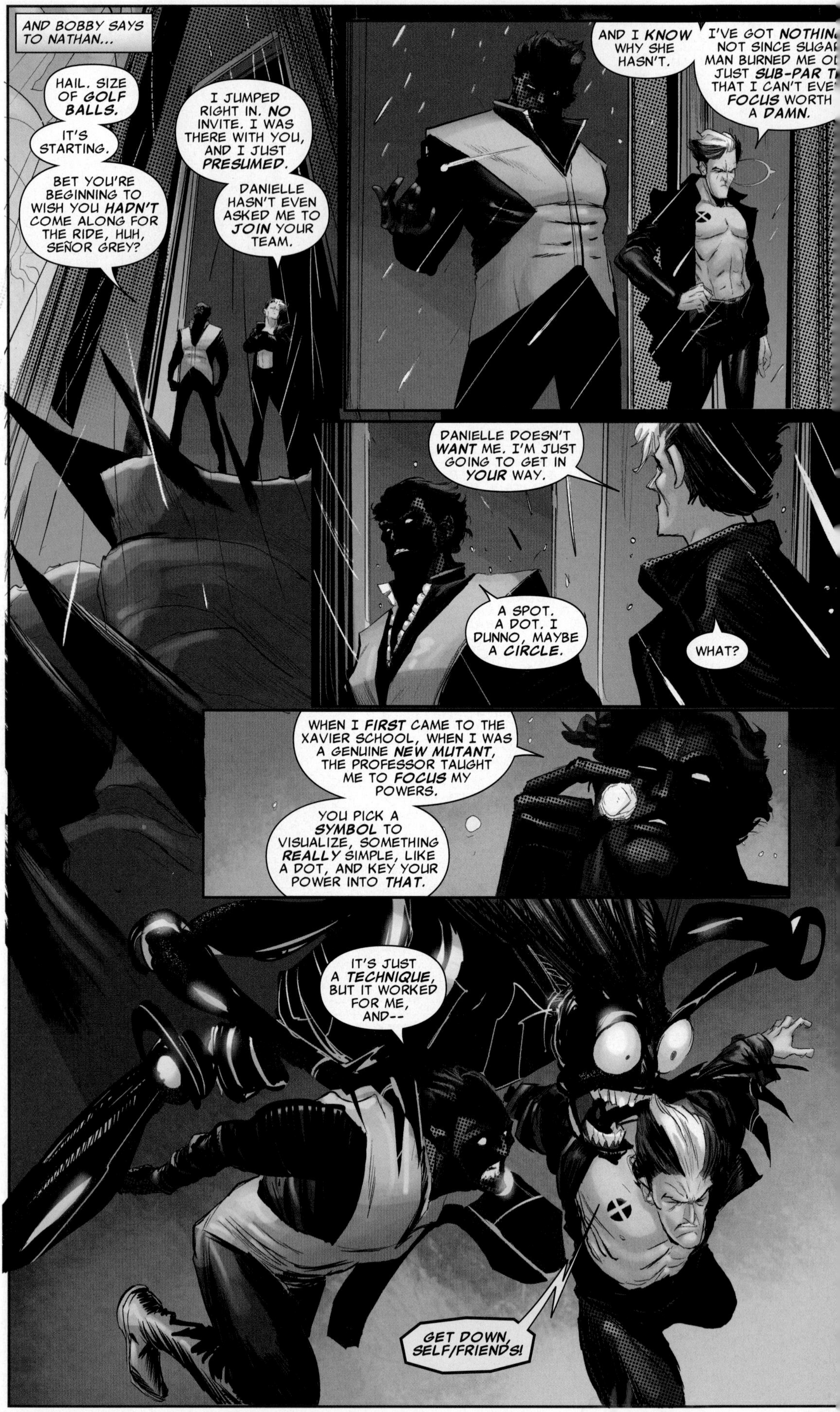
AND BOBBY SAYS TO NATHAN...
HAIL. SIZE OF GOLF BALLS.
IT'S STARTING.
BET YOU'RE BEGINNING TO WISH YOU HADN'T COME ALONG FOR THE RIDE, HUH, SEÑOR GREY?
I JUMPED RIGHT IN. NO INVITE. I WAS THERE WITH YOU, AND I JUST PRESUMED.
DANIELLE HASN'T EVEN ASKED ME TO JOIN YOUR TEAM.
AND I KNOW WHY SHE HASN'T.
I'VE GOT NOTHIN NOT SINCE SUGA MAN BURNED ME O JUST SUB-PAR T THAT I CAN'T EVE FOCUS WORTH A DAMN.
DANIELLE DOESN'T WANT ME. I'M JUST GOING TO GET IN YOUR WAY.
A SPOT. A DOT. I DUNNO, MAYBE A CIRCLE.
WHAT?
WHEN I FIRST CAME TO THE XAVIER SCHOOL, WHEN I WAS A GENUINE NEW MUTANT, THE PROFESSOR TAUGHT ME TO FOCUS MY POWERS.
YOU PICK A SYMBOL TO VISUALIZE, SOMETHING REALLY SIMPLE, LIKE A DOT, AND KEY YOUR POWER INTO THAT.
IT'S JUST A TECHNIQUE, BUT IT WORKED FOR ME, AND--
GET DOWN, SELF/FRIENDS!

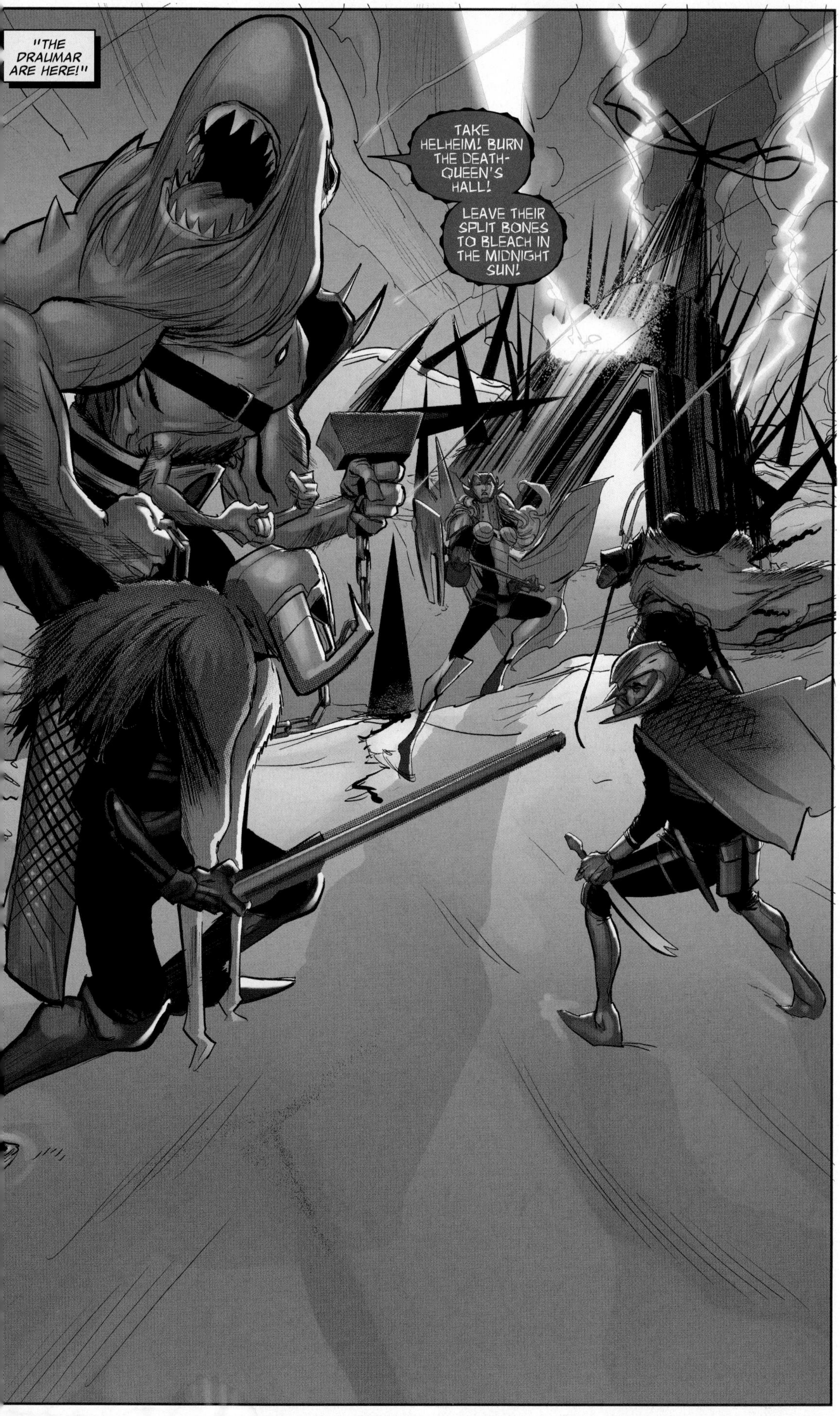
"THE DRAUMAR ARE HERE!"
TAKE HELHEIM! BURN THE DEATH-QUEEN'S HALL!
LEAVE THEIR SPLIT BONES TO BLEACH IN THE MIDNIGHT SUN!

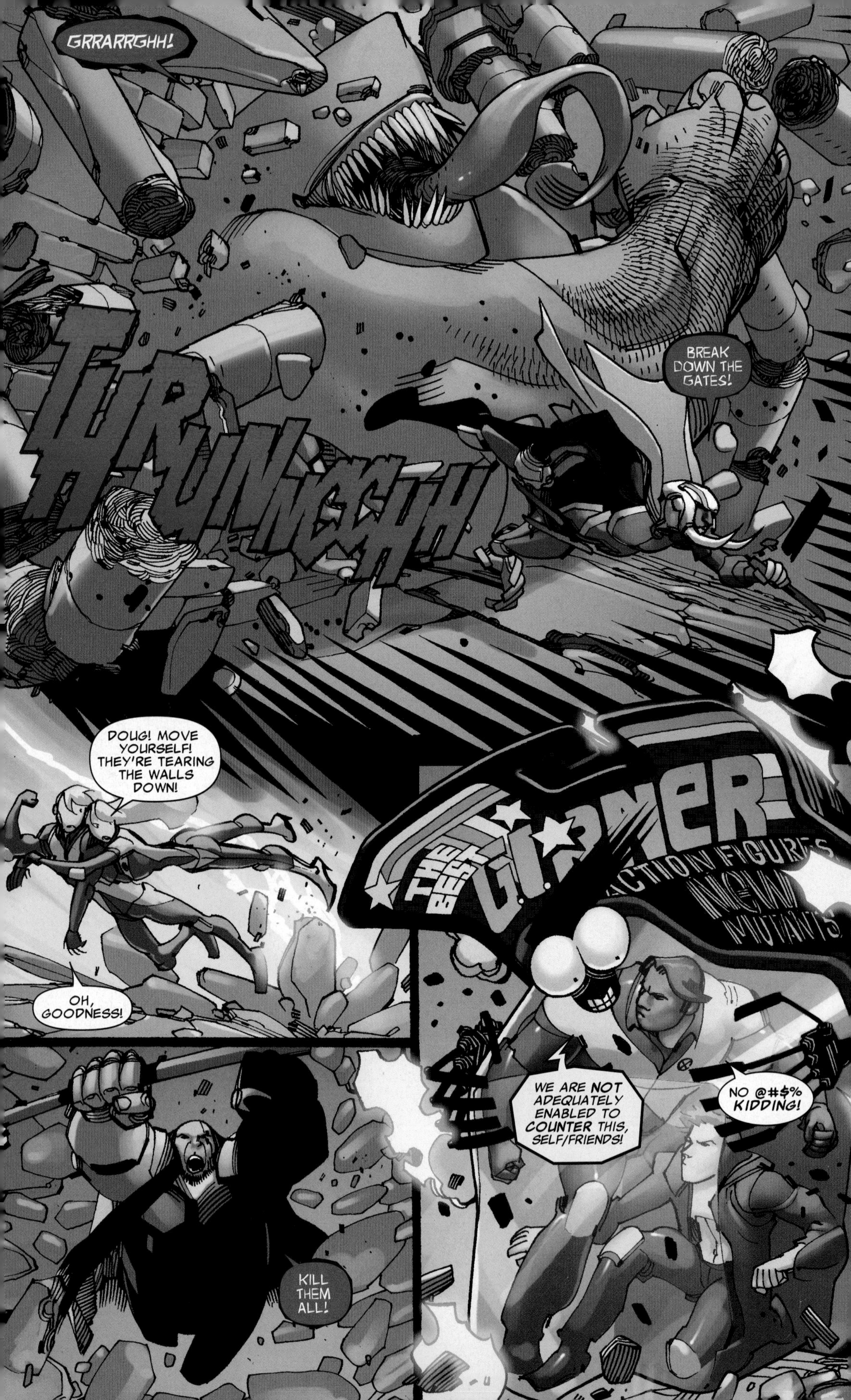
GRRARRGHH!
THRUNNCHH!
BREAK DOWN THE GATES!
DOUG! MOVE YOURSELF! THEY'RE TEARING THE WALLS DOWN!
OH, GOODNESS!
THE BEST G.I. GARNER ACTION FIGURES
NEW MUTANTS
KILL THEM ALL!
WE ARE NOT ADEQUATELY ENABLED TO COUNTER THIS, SELF/FRIENDS!
NO @#$% KIDDING!

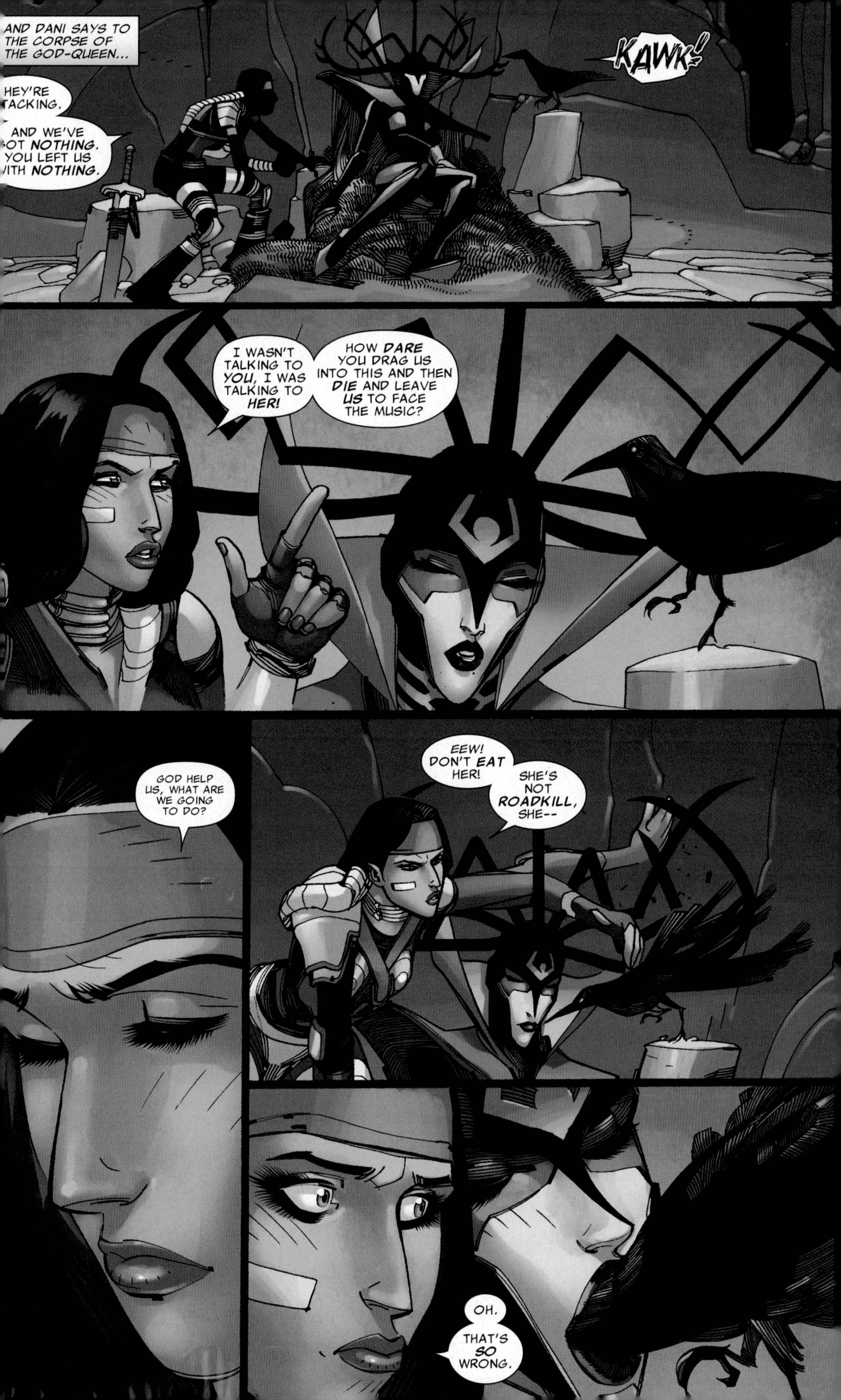
AND DANI SAYS TO THE CORPSE OF THE GOD-QUEEN...
KAWK!
HEY'RE TACKING.
AND WE'VE OT NOTHING. YOU LEFT US WITH NOTHING.
I WASN'T TALKING TO YOU, I WAS TALKING TO HER!
HOW DARE YOU DRAG US INTO THIS AND THEN DIE AND LEAVE US TO FACE THE MUSIC?
GOD HELP US, WHAT ARE WE GOING TO DO?
EEW! DON'T EAT HER!
SHE'S NOT ROADKILL, SHE--
OH.
THAT'S SO WRONG.

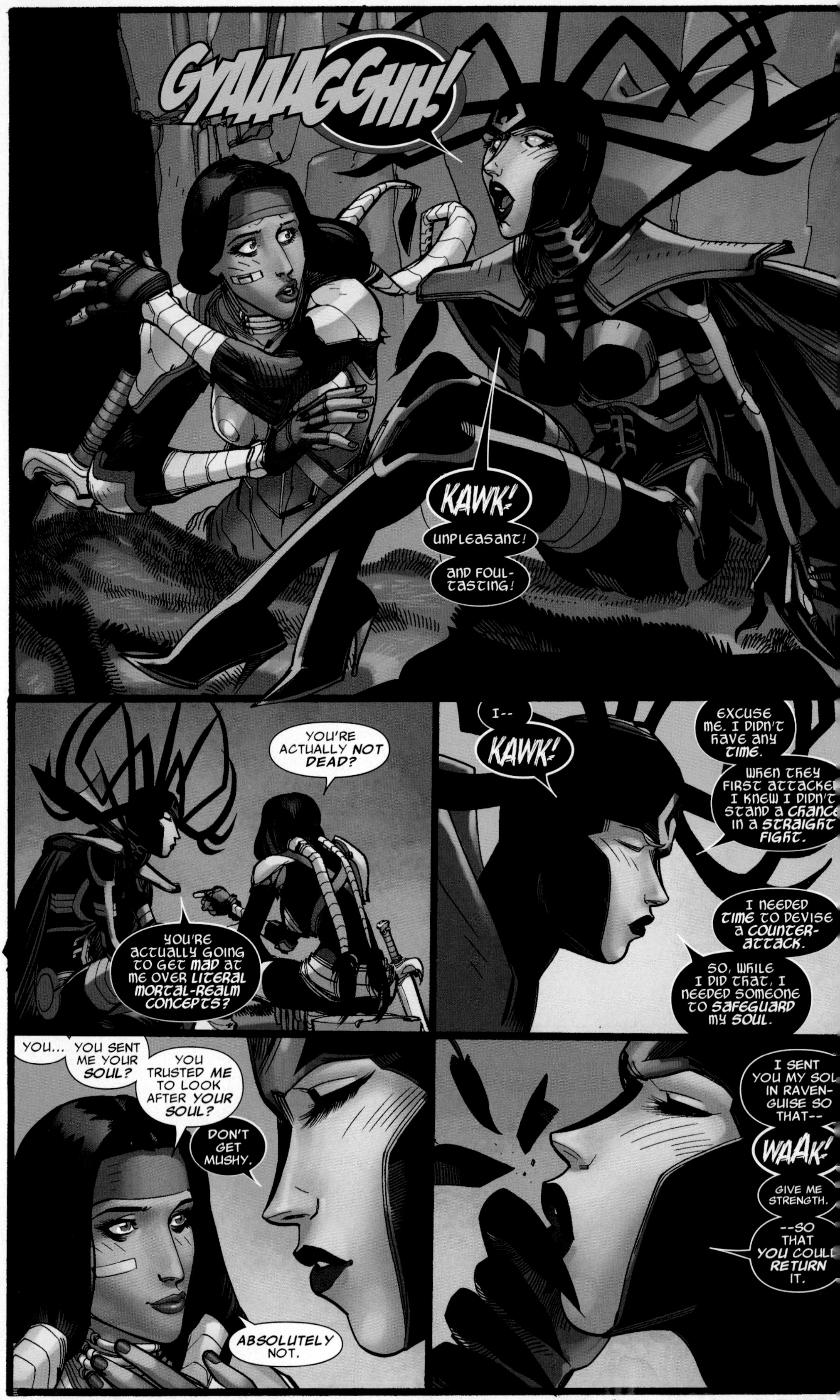
GYAAAGGHH!
KAWK!
UNPLEASANT!
AND FOUL-TASTING!
YOU'RE ACTUALLY NOT DEAD?
YOU'RE ACTUALLY GOING TO GET MAD AT ME OVER LITERAL MORTAL-REALM CONCEPTS?
I--
KAWK!
EXCUSE ME. I DIDN'T HAVE ANY TIME.
WHEN THEY FIRST ATTACKE I KNEW I DIDN'T STAND A CHANC IN A STRAIGHT FIGHT.
I NEEDED TIME TO DEVISE A COUNTER-ATTACK.
SO, WHILE I DID THAT, I NEEDED SOMEONE TO SAFEGUARD MY SOUL.
YOU... YOU SENT ME YOUR SOUL?
YOU TRUSTED ME TO LOOK AFTER YOUR SOUL?
DON'T GET MUSHY.
ABSOLUTELY NOT.
I SENT YOU MY SOU IN RAVEN-GUISE SO THAT--
WAAK!
GIVE ME STRENGTH.
--SO THAT YOU COUL RETURN IT.

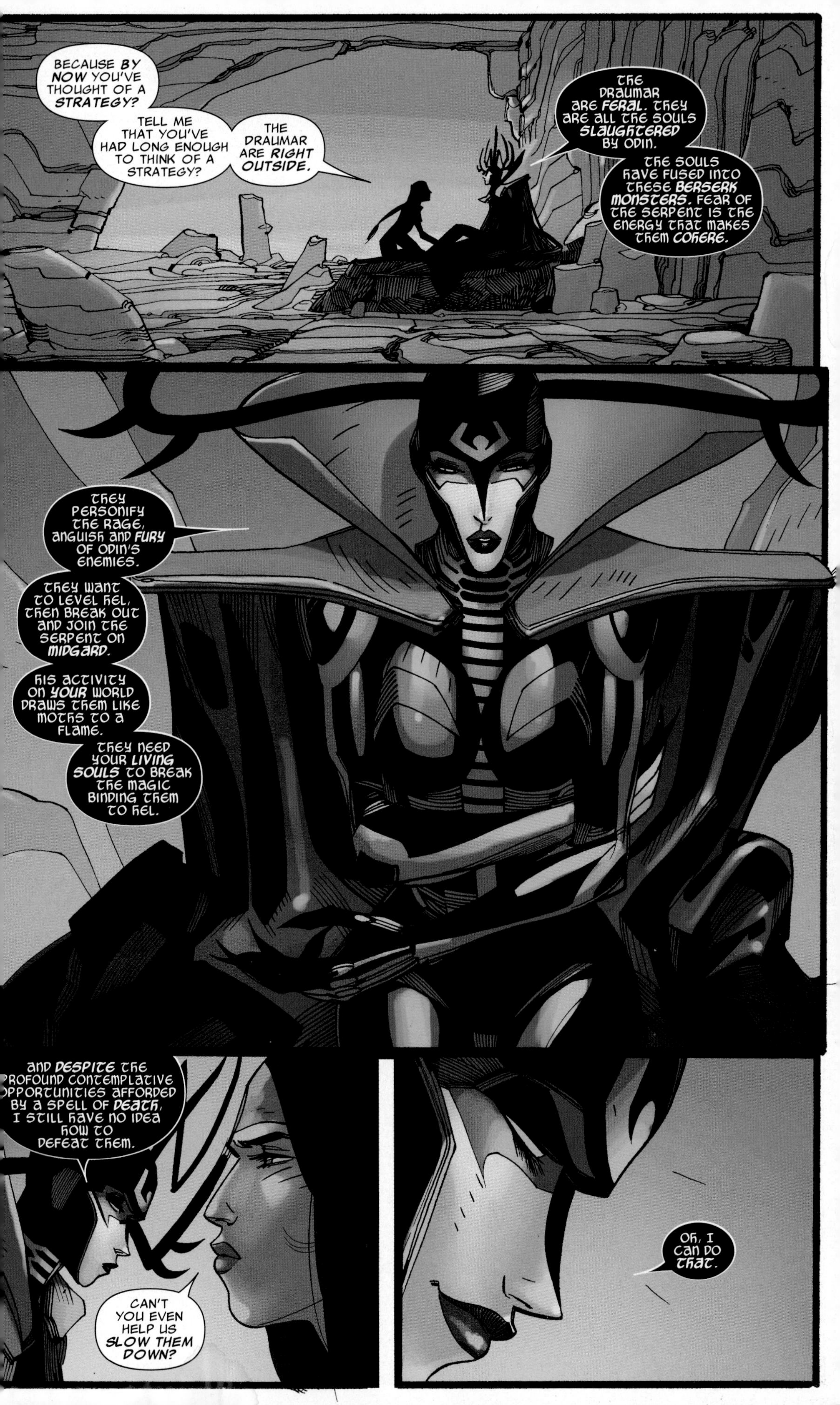
BECAUSE BY NOW YOU'VE THOUGHT OF A STRATEGY?
TELL ME THAT YOU'VE HAD LONG ENOUGH TO THINK OF A STRATEGY?
THE DRAUMAR ARE RIGHT OUTSIDE.
THE DRAUMAR ARE FERAL. THEY ARE ALL THE SOULS SLAUGHTERED BY ODIN.
THE SOULS HAVE FUSED INTO THESE BERSERK MONSTERS. FEAR OF THE SERPENT IS THE ENERGY THAT MAKES THEM COHERE.
THEY PERSONIFY THE RAGE, ANGUISH AND FURY OF ODIN'S ENEMIES.
THEY WANT TO LEVEL HEL, THEN BREAK OUT AND JOIN THE SERPENT ON MIDGARD.
HIS ACTIVITY ON YOUR WORLD DRAWS THEM LIKE MOTHS TO A FLAME.
THEY NEED YOUR LIVING SOULS TO BREAK THE MAGIC BINDING THEM TO HEL.
AND DESPITE THE PROFOUND CONTEMPLATIVE OPPORTUNITIES AFFORDED BY A SPELL OF DEATH, I STILL HAVE NO IDEA HOW TO DEFEAT THEM.
CAN'T YOU EVEN HELP US SLOW THEM DOWN?
OH, I CAN DO THAT.

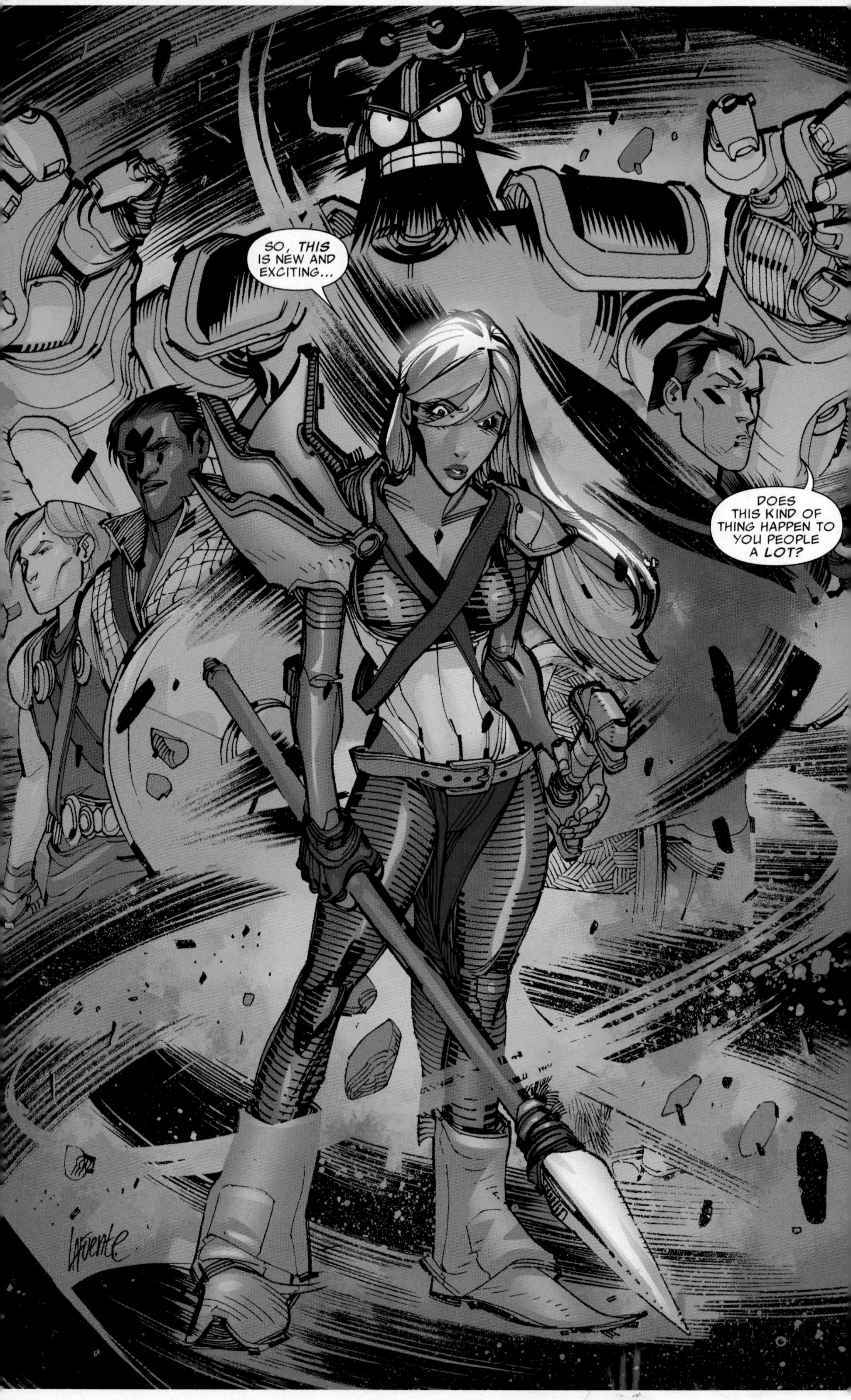
SO, THIS IS NEW AND EXCITING...
DOES THIS KIND OF THING HAPPEN TO YOU PEOPLE A LOT?

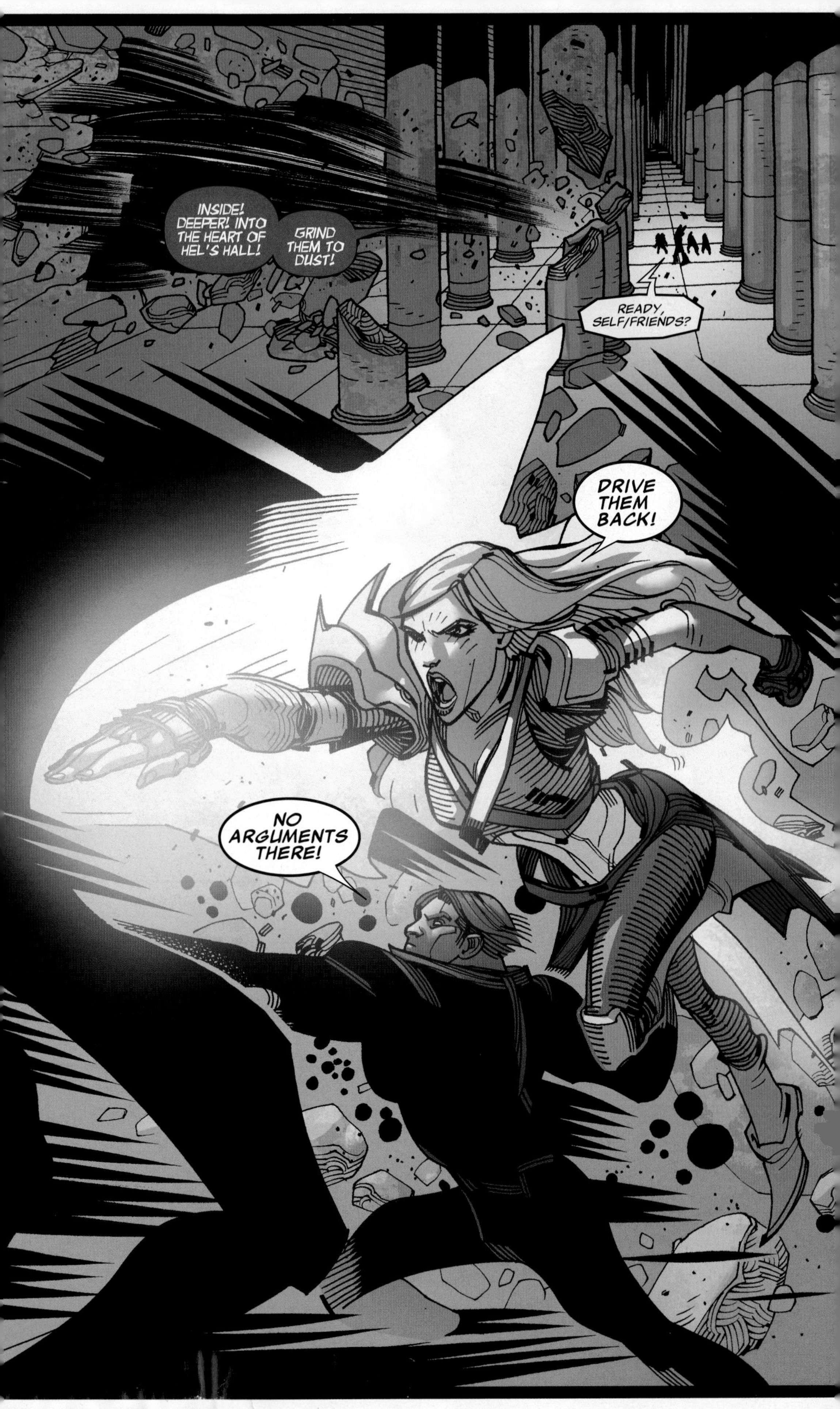
INSIDE! DEEPER! INTO THE HEART OF HEL'S HALL!
GRIND THEM TO DUST!
READY, SELF/FRIENDS?
DRIVE THEM BACK!
NO ARGUMENTS THERE!

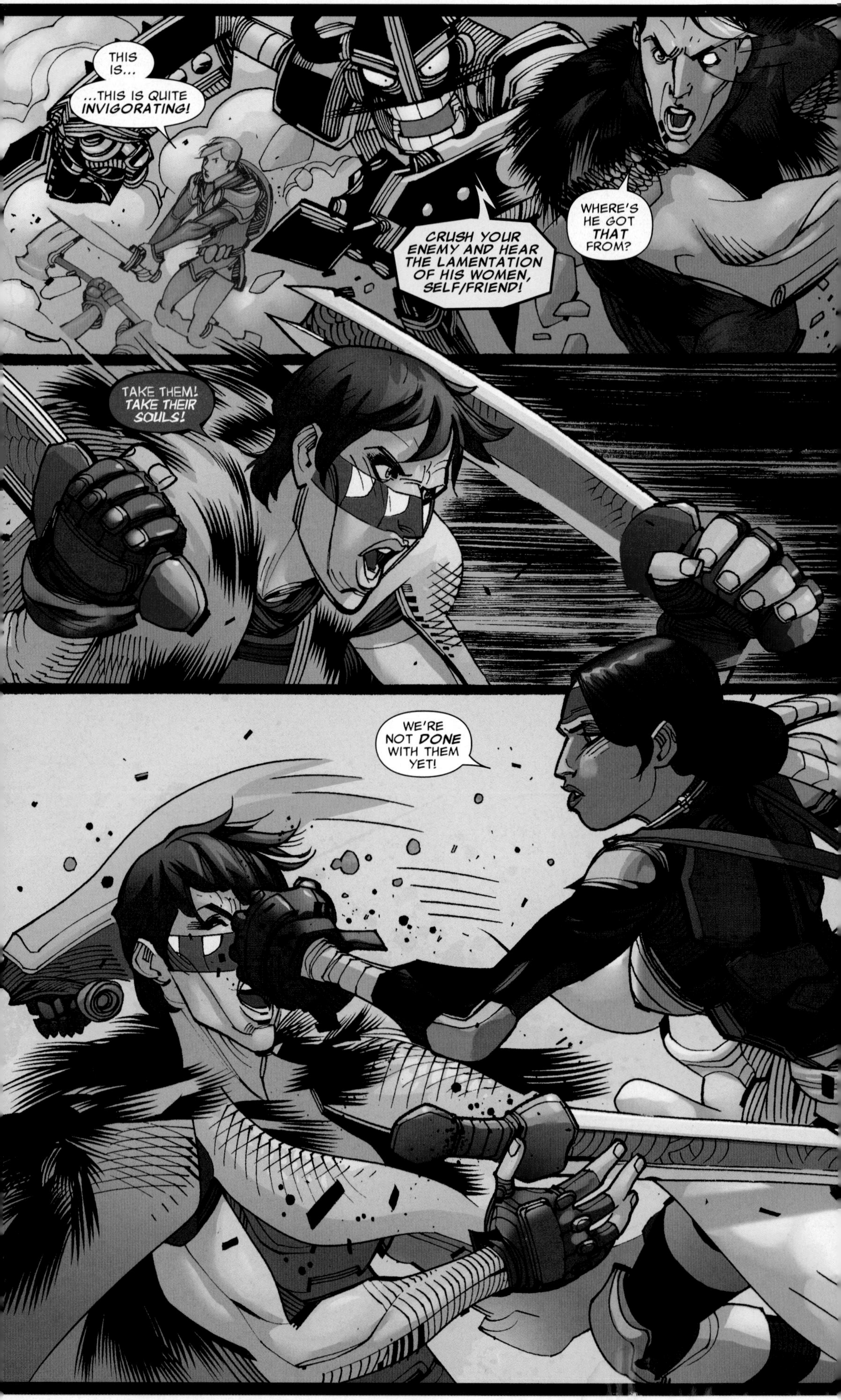
THIS IS...
...THIS IS QUITE INVIGORATING!
CRUSH YOUR ENEMY AND HEAR THE LAMENTATION OF HIS WOMEN, SELF/FRIEND!
WHERE'S HE GOT THAT FROM?
TAKE THEM! TAKE THEIR SOULS!
WE'RE NOT DONE WITH THEM YET!

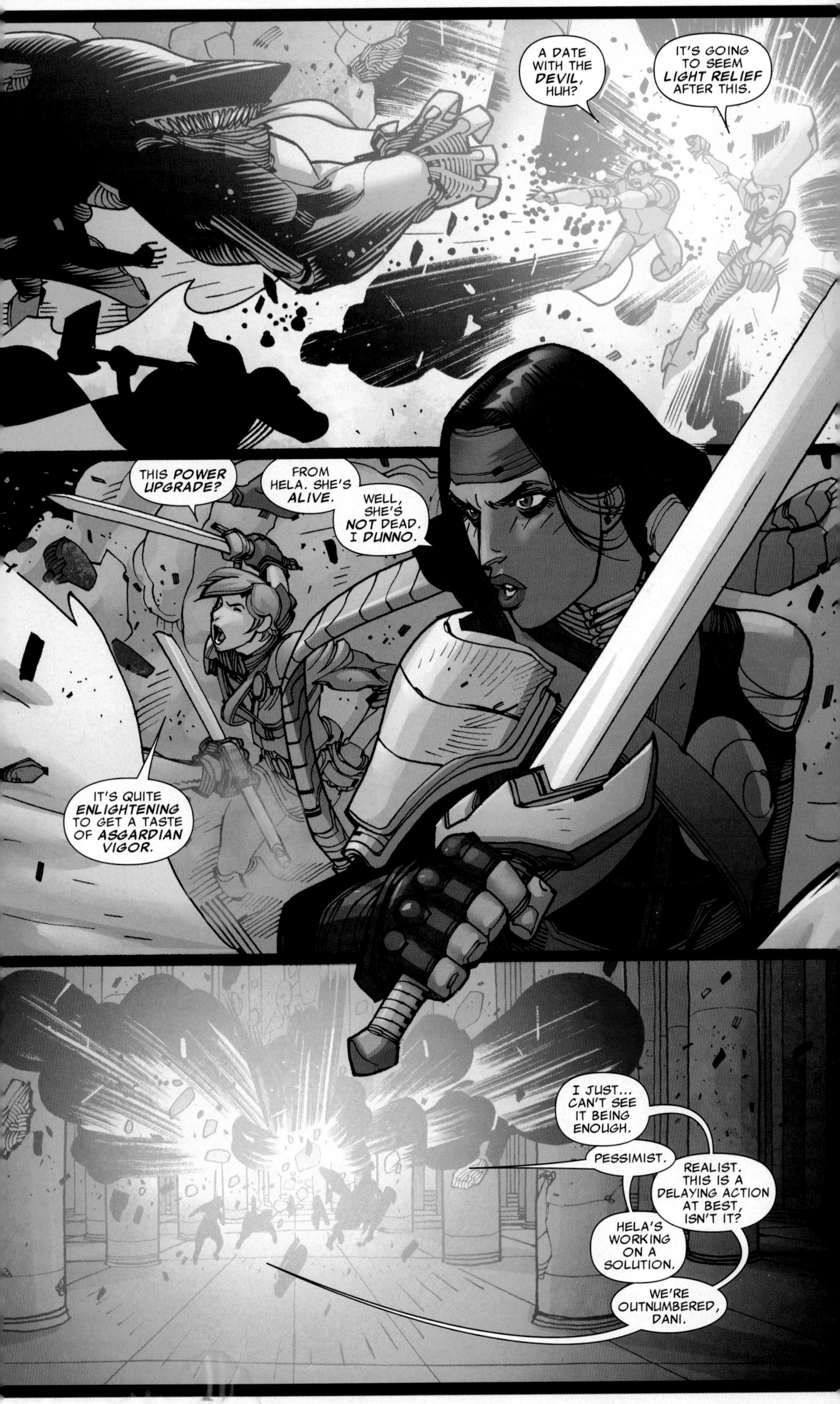
A DATE WITH THE DEVIL, HUH?
IT'S GOING TO SEEM LIGHT RELIEF AFTER THIS.
THIS POWER UPGRADE?
FROM HELA. SHE'S ALIVE.
WELL, SHE'S NOT DEAD. I DUNNO.
IT'S QUITE ENLIGHTENING TO GET A TASTE OF ASGARDIAN VIGOR.
I JUST... CAN'T SEE IT BEING ENOUGH.
PESSIMIST.
REALIST. THIS IS A DELAYING ACTION AT BEST, ISN'T IT?
HELA'S WORKING ON A SOLUTION.
WE'RE OUTNUMBERED, DANI.

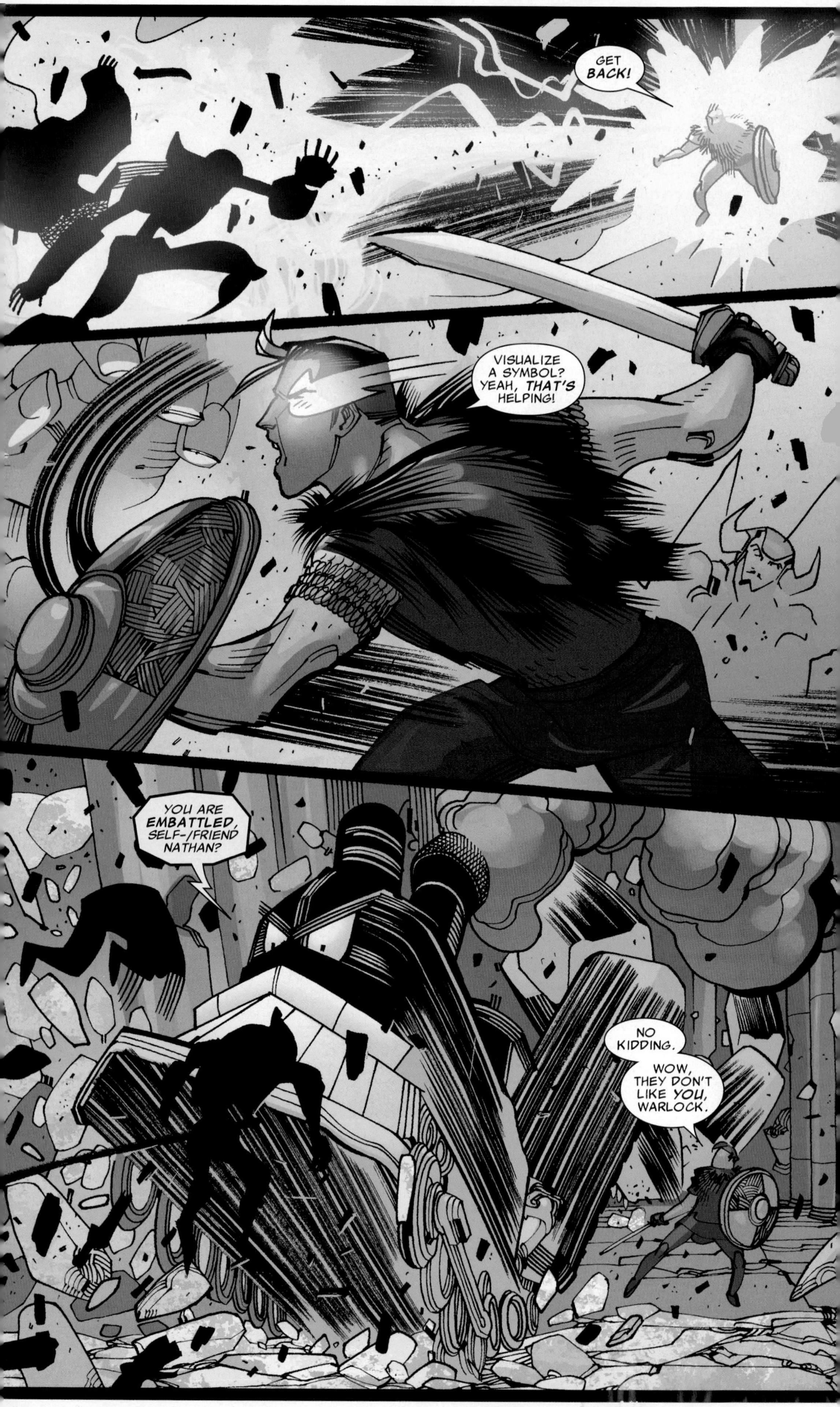
GET BACK!
VISUALIZE A SYMBOL? YEAH, THAT'S HELPING!
YOU ARE EMBATTLED, SELF-/FRIEND NATHAN?
NO KIDDING.
WOW, THEY DON'T LIKE YOU, WARLOCK.

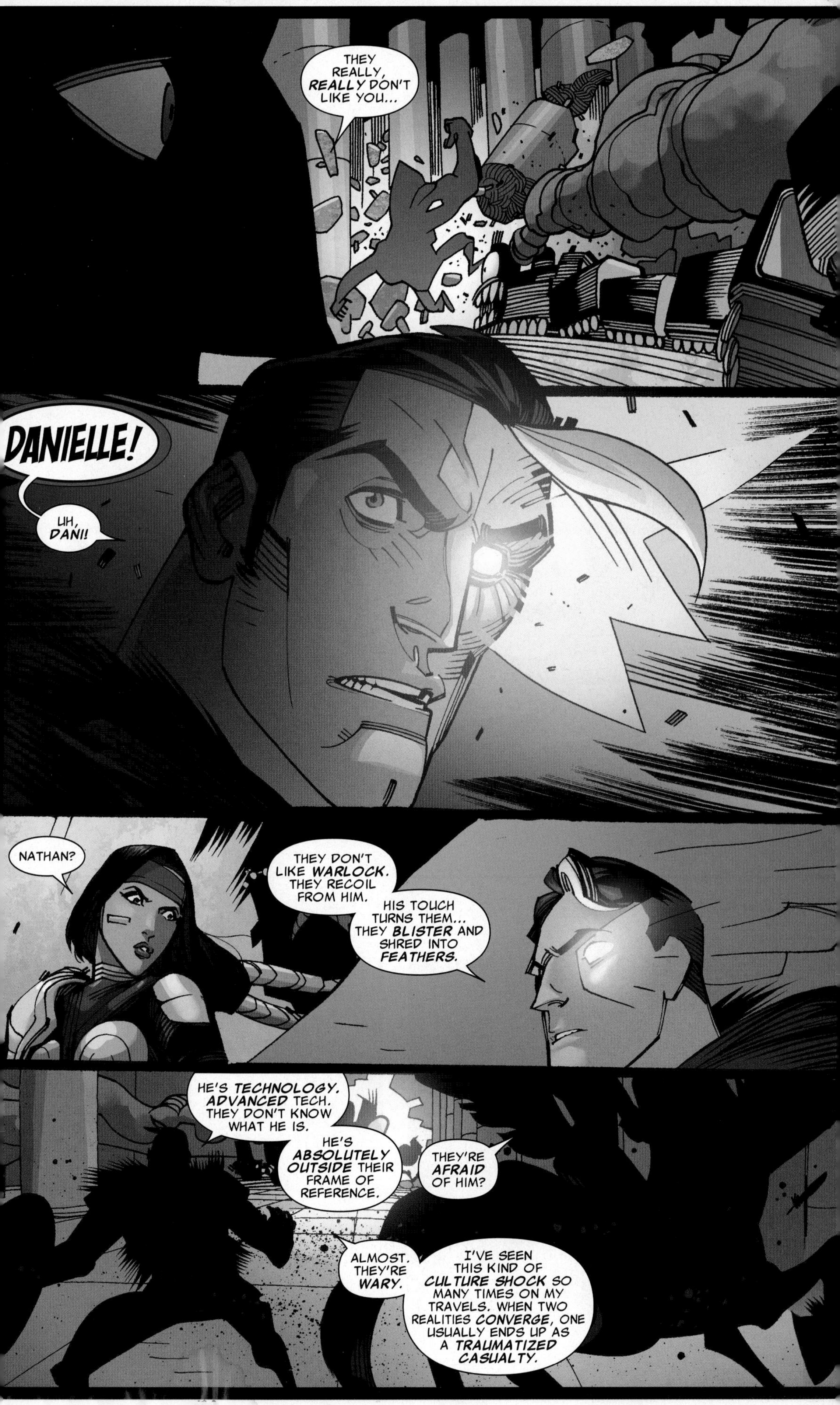
THEY REALLY, REALLY DON'T LIKE YOU...
DANIELLE!
UH, DANI!
NATHAN?
THEY DON'T LIKE WARLOCK. THEY RECOIL FROM HIM.
HIS TOUCH TURNS THEM... THEY BLISTER AND SHRED INTO FEATHERS.
HE'S TECHNOLOGY. ADVANCED TECH. THEY DON'T KNOW WHAT HE IS.
HE'S ABSOLUTELY OUTSIDE THEIR FRAME OF REFERENCE.
THEY'RE AFRAID OF HIM?
ALMOST. THEY'RE WARY.
I'VE SEEN THIS KIND OF CULTURE SHOCK SO MANY TIMES ON MY TRAVELS. WHEN TWO REALITIES CONVERGE, ONE USUALLY ENDS UP AS A TRAUMATIZED CASUALTY.

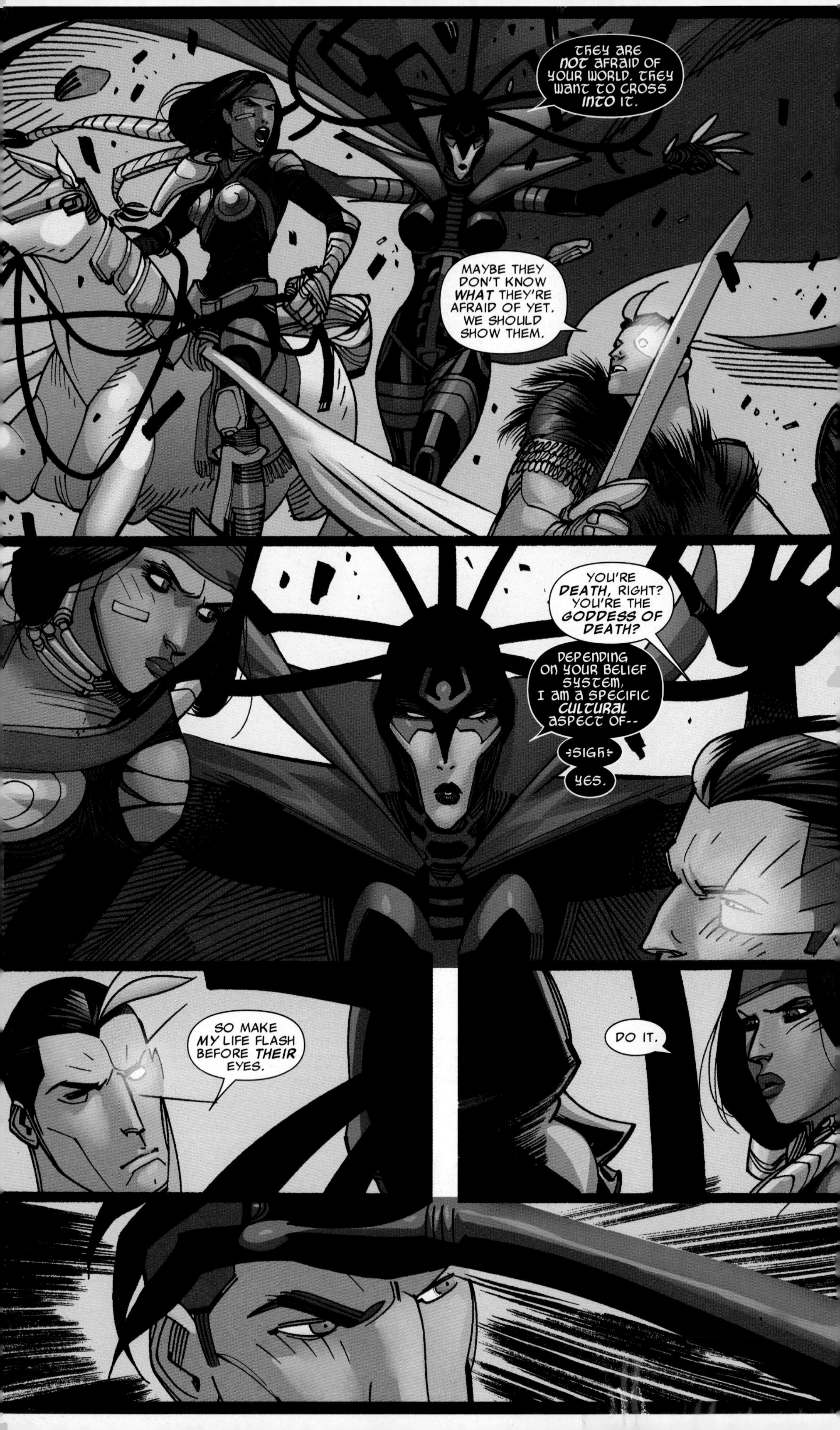
THEY ARE NOT AFRAID OF YOUR WORLD. THEY WANT TO CROSS INTO IT.
MAYBE THEY DON'T KNOW WHAT THEY'RE AFRAID OF YET. WE SHOULD SHOW THEM.
YOU'RE DEATH, RIGHT? YOU'RE THE GODDESS OF DEATH?
DEPENDING ON YOUR BELIEF SYSTEM, I AM A SPECIFIC CULTURAL ASPECT OF--
÷SIGH÷
YES.
SO MAKE MY LIFE FLASH BEFORE THEIR EYES.
DO IT.

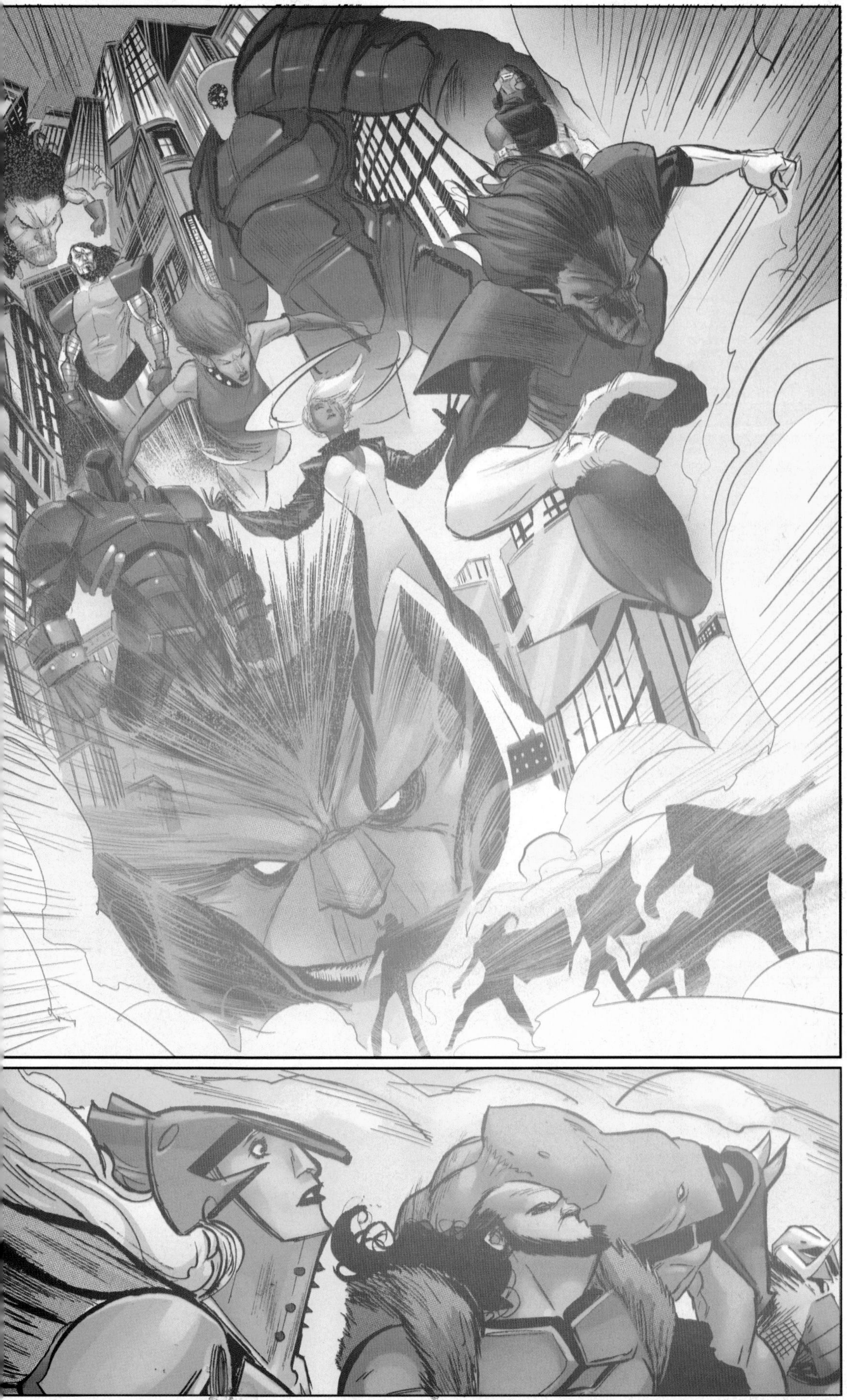

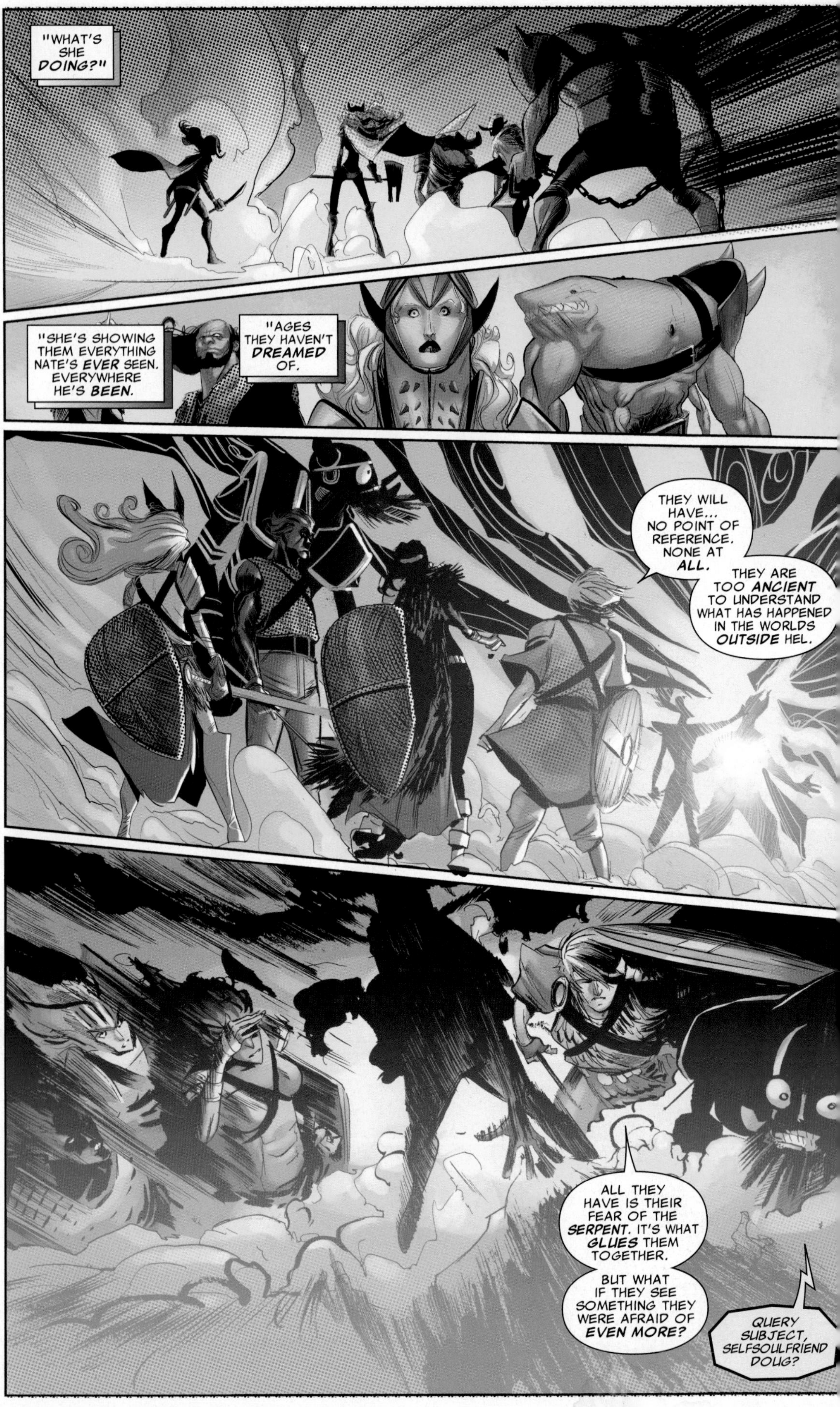
"WHAT'S SHE DOING?"
"SHE'S SHOWING THEM EVERYTHING NATE'S EVER SEEN. EVERYWHERE HE'S BEEN.
"AGES THEY HAVEN'T DREAMED OF.
THEY WILL HAVE... NO POINT OF REFERENCE. NONE AT ALL.
THEY ARE TOO ANCIENT TO UNDERSTAND WHAT HAS HAPPENED IN THE WORLDS OUTSIDE HEL.
ALL THEY HAVE IS THEIR FEAR OF THE SERPENT. IT'S WHAT GLUES THEM TOGETHER.
BUT WHAT IF THEY SEE SOMETHING THEY WERE AFRAID OF EVEN MORE?
QUERY SUBJECT, SELFSOULFRIEND DOUG?

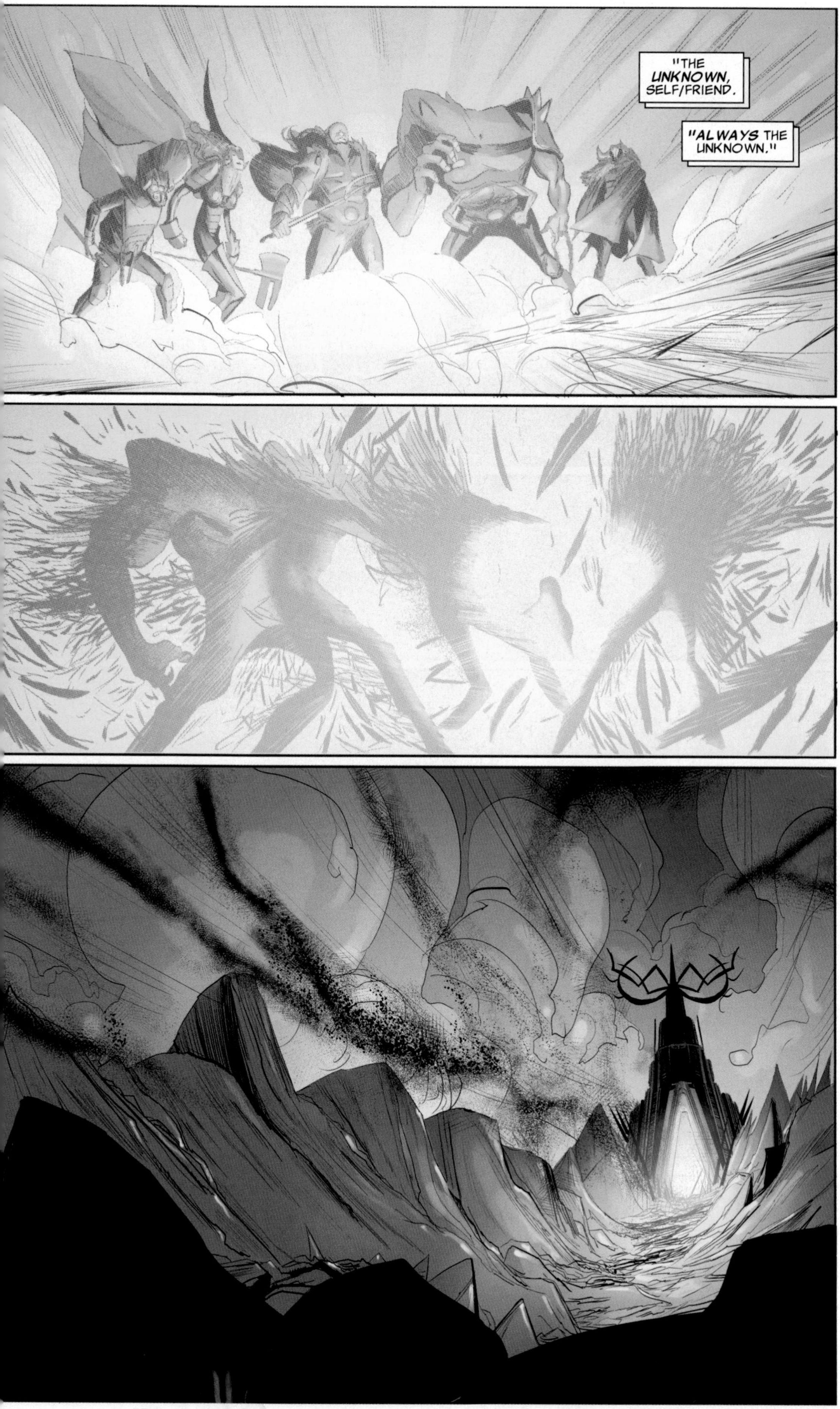
"THE UNKNOWN, SELF/FRIEND.
"ALWAYS THE UNKNOWN."

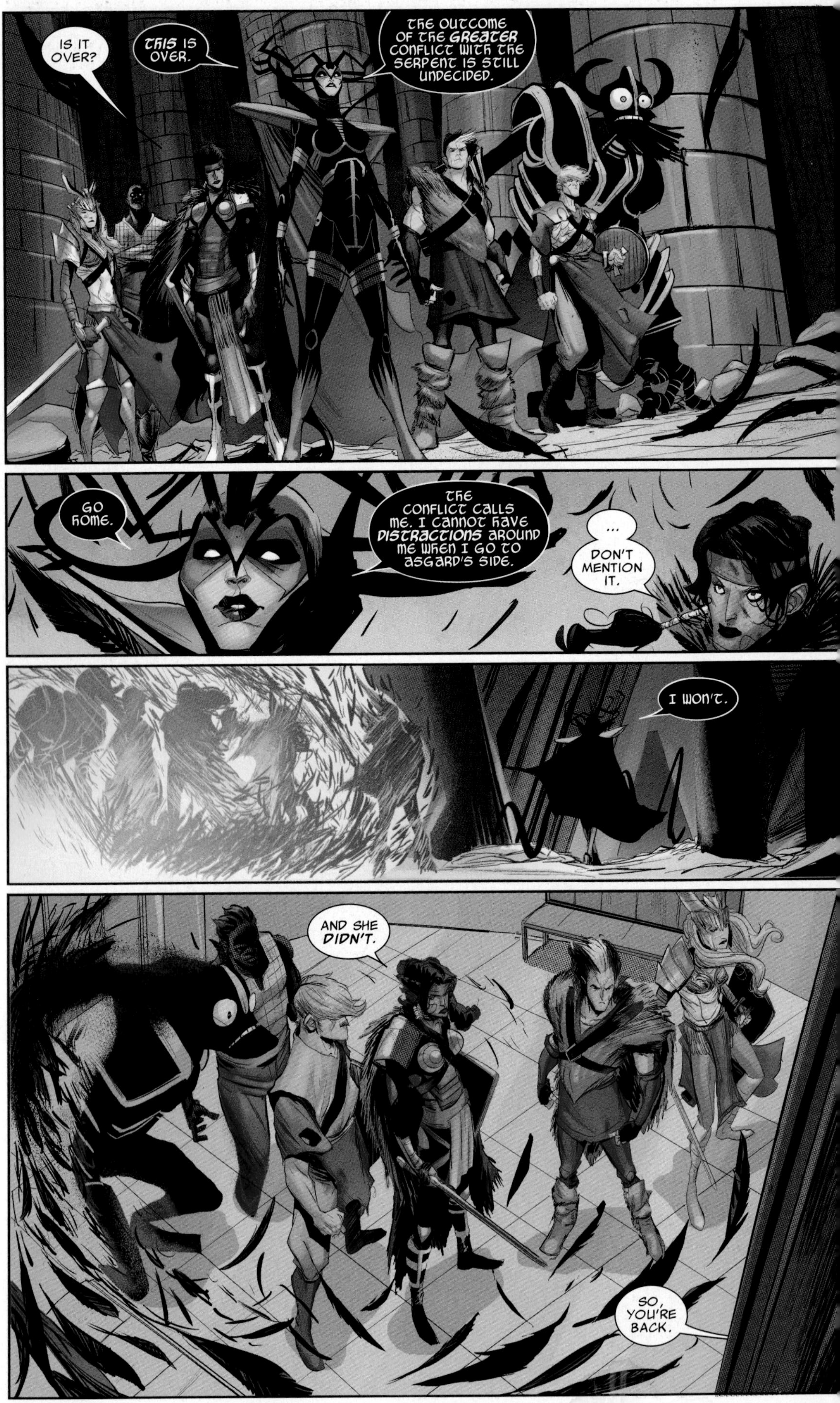
IS IT OVER?
THIS IS OVER.
THE OUTCOME OF THE GREATER CONFLICT WITH THE SERPENT IS STILL UNDECIDED.
GO HOME.
THE CONFLICT CALLS ME. I CANNOT HAVE DISTRACTIONS AROUND ME WHEN I GO TO ASGARD'S SIDE.
...
DON'T MENTION IT.
I WON'T.
AND SHE DIDN'T.
SO, YOU'RE BACK.

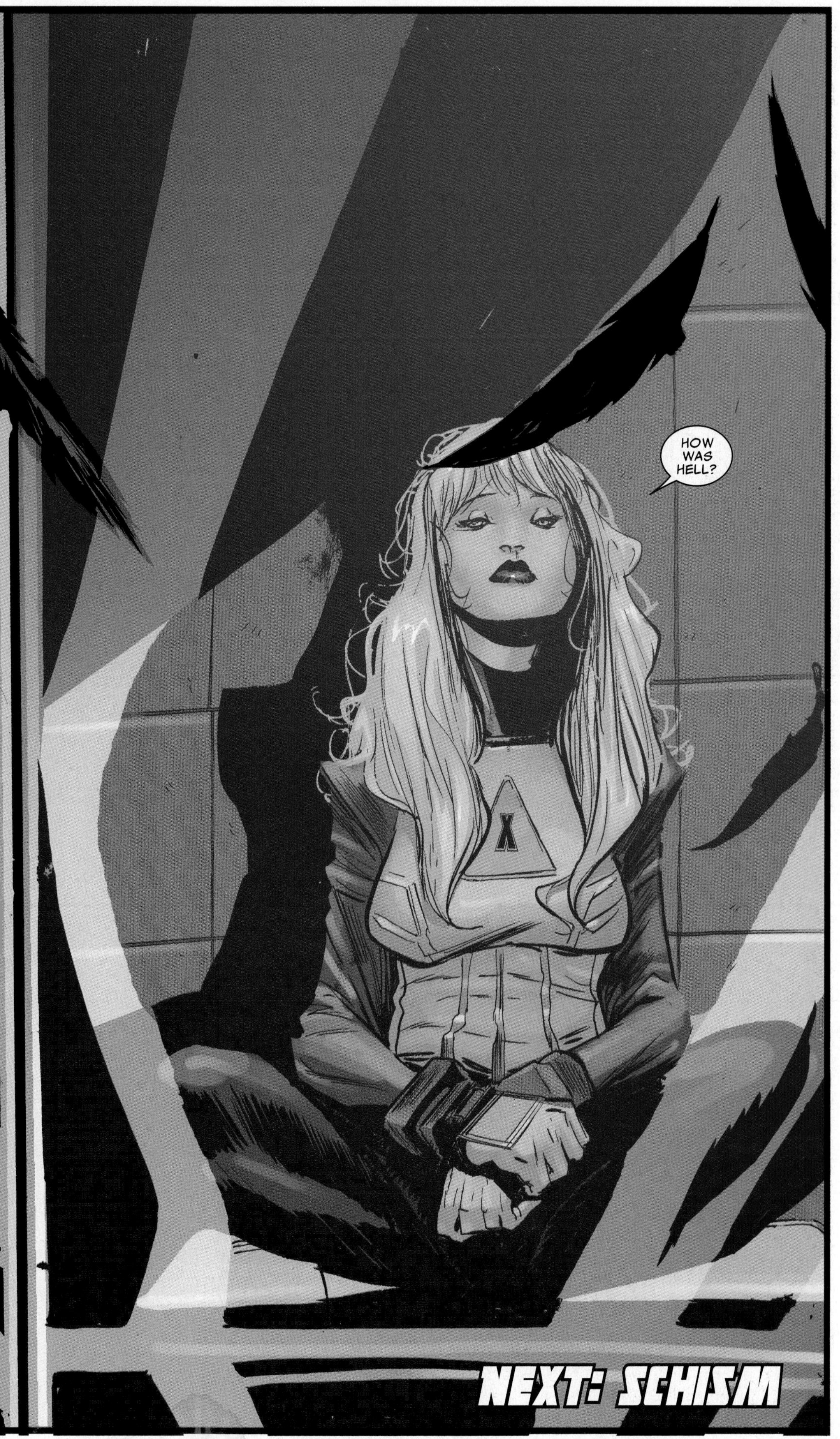
HOW WAS HELL?
NEXT: SCHISM

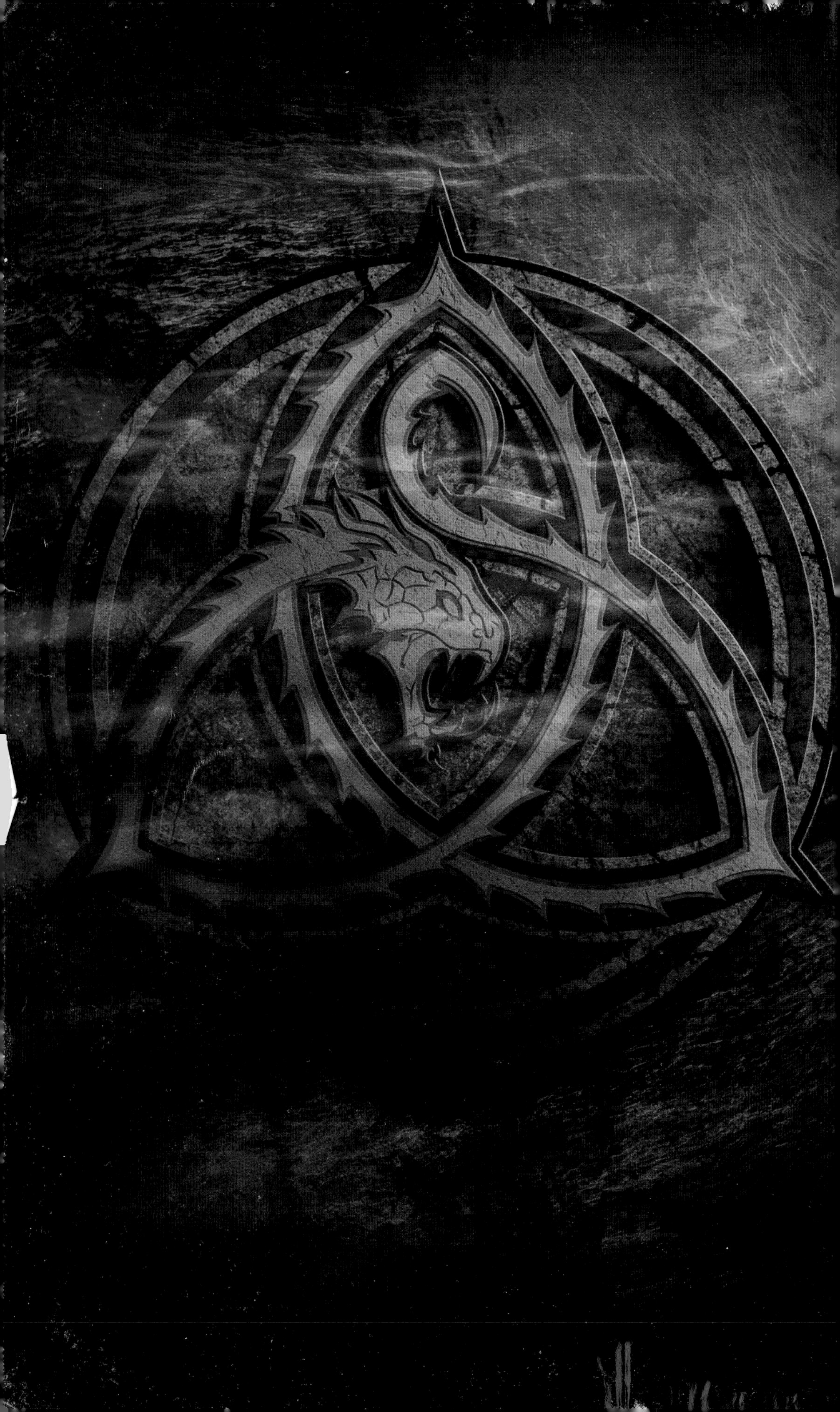